Learn CUDA Prog

A beginner's guide to GPU programming and parallel computing with CUDA 10.x and C/C++

Jaegeun Han
Bharatkumar Sharma

BIRMINGHAM - MUMBAI

Learn CUDA Programming

Copyright © 2019 Packt Publishing

Commissioning Editor: Richa Tripathi
Acquisition Editor: Alok Dhuri
Content Development Editor: Digvijay Bagul
Senior Editor: Afshaan Khan
Technical Editor: Romy Dias
Copy Editor: Safis Editing
Project Coordinator: Prajakta Naik
Proofreader: Safis Editing
Indexer: Priyanka Dhadke
Production Designer: Deepika Naik

First published: September 2019

Production reference: 1270919

Published by Packt Publishing Ltd.
Livery Place
35 Livery Street
Birmingham
B3 2PB, UK.

ISBN 978-1-78899-624-2

www.packt.com

`Packt.com`

Subscribe to our online digital library for full access to over 7,000 books and videos, as well as industry-leading tools to help you plan your personal development and advance your career. For more information, please visit our website.

Why subscribe?

- Spend less time learning and more time coding with practical eBooks and Videos from over 4,000 industry professionals

- Improve your learning with Skill Plans built especially for you

- Get a free eBook or video every month

- Fully searchable for easy access to vital information

- Copy and paste, print, and bookmark content

Did you know that Packt offers eBook versions of every book published, with PDF and ePub files available? You can upgrade to the eBook version at `www.packt.com` and as a print book customer, you are entitled to a discount on the eBook copy. Get in touch with us at `customercare@packtpub.com` for more details.

At `www.packt.com`, you can also read a collection of free technical articles, sign up for a range of free newsletters, and receive exclusive discounts and offers on Packt books and eBooks.

Contributors

About the authors

Jaegeun Han is currently working as a solutions architect at NVIDIA, Korea. He has around 9 years' experience and he supports consumer internet companies in deep learning. Before NVIDIA, he worked in system software and parallel computing developments, and application development in medical and surgical robotics fields. He obtained a master's degree in CSE from Seoul National University.

I would like to thank my wife, Kiyeon Kim, for supporting of book writing and taking care of our child. I also thank my son, Kyeol Han, for his joy and curiosity, and my parents and parents-in-law for their support. I also appreciate Simon See (NVIDIA) for supporting me in authoring this book and I'm thankful to my co-author, Bharat, for joining this challenge with me. Thanks to all NVIDIA GPU experts for sharing their knowledge and opening the new era of computing.

Bharatkumar Sharma obtained a master's degree in information technology from the Indian Institute of Information Technology, Bangalore. He has around 10 years of development and research experience in the domains of software architecture and distributed and parallel computing. He is currently working with NVIDIA as a senior solutions architect, South Asia.

I would like to acknowledge my mentors who helped me at different stages in my career: Jaya Panvalkar (NVIDIA), Simon See (NVIDIA), and the one and only accelerated computing rockstar, Jensen Huang (CEO NVIDIA).

About the reviewers

Christian Stehno studied computer science, receiving his diploma from Oldenburg University, Germany, in 2000. Since then, he's worked in different fields of computer science, first as a researcher in theoretical computer science at an academic institution, before subsequently switching to embedded system design at a research institute. In 2010, he started his own company, CoSynth, which develops embedded systems and intelligent cameras for industrial automation. In addition, he is a long-time member of the Irrlicht 3D engine developer team.

Minseok Lee is a developer technology engineer at NVIDIA. He works on parallelizing and optimizing scientific and AI applications for CPU-GPU heterogeneous systems. Before joining NVIDIA, he was a C++-based library designer/developer and received an M.Eng in computer science by working on utilizing GPU architectures more efficiently.

Aidan Temple is a software engineer and lead developer at Nanotek. He has recently graduated with honors from Glasgow Caledonian University, where he received a BSc in computer games software development.

While at university, Aidan also undertook a research degree outlining the benefits of implementing GUI-based game frameworks by means of parallel processing through the utilization of NVIDIA's CUDA architecture. He also received an IGDA scholarship.

Prior to his time at university, he studied computer games development at James Watt College of Further and Higher Education. Due to his excellent understanding and demonstration of game development and design methodologies, Aidan graduated from James Watt College with a distinction in his field.

Packt is searching for authors like you

If you're interested in becoming an author for Packt, please visit authors.packtpub.com and apply today. We have worked with thousands of developers and tech professionals, just like you, to help them share their insight with the global tech community. You can make a general application, apply for a specific hot topic that we are recruiting an author for, or submit your own idea.

Table of Contents

Preface

Don't take rest after your first victory. Because if you fail in second, more lips are waiting to say that your first victory was just luck.

- A. P. J. Abdul Kalam

Traditionally, computing requirements were associated with **Central Processing Units (CPUs)**, which have grown from having a single core to now having multiple cores. Every new generation of CPU has provided more performance, but the scientific and **High Performance Computing (HPC)** community has demanded more performance year on year, creating a compute gap between what applications have demanded and what hardware/software stacks could provide. At the same time, new architecture that was traditionally used for video graphics found its way into the scientific domain. **Graphics Processing Units (GPUs)**—essentially parallel computing processors used to accelerate computer graphics—made their mark on the HPC domain in 2007 when **Compute Unified Device Architecture (CUDA)** was launched. CUDA grew to become the de facto standard when it comes to using GPUs for general-purpose computation; that is, non-graphic applications.

There have been many releases of CUDA since its inception, and now CUDA stands at release 10.x. Each release provides new features that support the new hardware architecture. This book is designed to help you learn GPU parallel programming and guide you in its modern-day applications. With its help, you'll be able to discover CUDA programming approaches for modern GPU architectures. The book will not only guide you through GPU features, tools, and APIs, but also help you understand how to analyze performance with sample parallel programming algorithms. This book will ensure that you gain plenty of optimization experience and insights into CUDA programming platforms with various libraries, open accelerators (OpenACC), and other languages. As you progress, you'll discover how to generate additional computing power with multiple GPUs in a box, or multiple boxes. Finally, you'll explore how CUDA accelerates deep learning algorithms, including **convolutional neural networks (CNNs)** and **recurrent neural networks (RNNs)**.

This book is designed to be an entry point for any newcomer or novice developer. But by the end of it, you will be able to write optimized CUDA code for different domains, including artificial intelligence.

This book will be a useful resource if any of the following apply to you:

- You are new to HPC or parallel computing
- You have code and want to improve its performance by applying parallel computing to the GPU
- You are a deep learning expert and want to make use of the GPU to accelerate performance for deep learning algorithms such as CNNs and RNNs
- You want to learn tips and tricks to optimize code and analyze GPU application performance and discover optimization strategies
- You want to learn about the latest GPU features, along with efficient, distributed multi-GPU programming

If you feel you fall into any of those categories, please join us on this journey.

Who this book is for

This beginner-level book is for programmers who want to delve into parallel computing, become part of the high-performance computing community and build modern applications. Basic C and C++ programming experience is assumed. For deep learning enthusiasts, this book covers Python InterOps, DL libraries, and practical examples on performance estimation.

What this book covers

Chapter 1, *Introduction to CUDA Programming*, demystifies some of the myths around GPU and CUDA, and introduces the CUDA programming model with a Hello World CUDA program.

Chapter 2, *CUDA Memory Management*, introduces the GPU memory hierarchy and how to optimally utilize it with the CUDA APIs.

Chapter 3, *CUDA Thread Programming*, introduces how threads operate in the GPU, highlighting key metrics on which basis optimizations are performed.

Chapter 4, *Kernel Execution Model and Optimization Strategies*, describes optimization strategies for CUDA kernels.

Chapter 5, *CUDA Application Profiling and Debugging*, covers the basic usage of tools that help with profiling and debugging CUDA applications.

Chapter 6, *Scalable Multi-GPU Programming*, covers how to scale CUDA algorithms across multiple GPUs within and across different nodes.

Chapter 7, *Parallel Programming Patterns in CUDA*, covers parallel programming algorithms that are widely used in many applications.

Chapter 8, *Programming with Libraries and Other Languages*, introduces the CUDA ecosystem pre-existing libraries with sample code usage.

Chapter 9, *GPU Programming Using OpenACC*, introduces directive-based programming with a focus on more science and less programming.

Chapter 10, *Deep Learning Acceleration with CUDA*, briefly reviews neural network operations and discusses how these can be accelerated on GPUs.

Appendix, includes some subsidiary reference information to help engineers use GPUs.

To get the most out of this book

This book is designed for complete beginners and people who have just started to learn parallel computing. It does not require any specific knowledge besides the basics of computer architecture, and experience with C/C++ programming is assumed. For deep learning enthusiasts, in Chapter 10, *Deep Learning Acceleration with CUDA*, Python-based sample code is also provided, hence some Python knowledge is expected for that chapter specifically.

The code for this book is primarily developed and tested in a Linux environment. Hence, familiarity with the Linux environment is helpful. Any of the latest Linux flavors, such as CentOS or Ubuntu, are okay. The code can be compiled either using a makefile or the command line. The book primarily uses a free software stack, so there is no need to buy any software licenses. Two key pieces of software that will be used throughout are the CUDA Toolkit and PGI Community Edition.

Since the book primarily covers the latest GPU features making use of CUDA 10.x, in order to fully exploit all the training material, the latest GPU architecture (Pascal onward) will be beneficial. While not all chapters require the latest GPU, having the latest GPU will help you to reproduce the results achieved in the book. Each chapter has a section on the preferred or must-have GPU architecture in the *Technical requirements* section.

Download the example code files

You can download the example code files for this book from your account at
`www.packt.com`. If you purchased this book elsewhere, you can visit
`www.packtpub.com/support` and register to have the files emailed directly to you.

You can download the code files by following these steps:

1. Log in or register at `www.packt.com`.
2. Select the **Support** tab.
3. Click on **Code Downloads**.
4. Enter the name of the book in the **Search** box and follow the onscreen instructions.

Once the file is downloaded, please make sure that you unzip or extract the folder using the latest version of:

- WinRAR/7-Zip for Windows
- Zipeg/iZip/UnRarX for Mac
- 7-Zip/PeaZip for Linux

The code bundle for the book is also hosted on GitHub at
`https://github.com/PacktPublishing/Learn-CUDA-Programming`. In case there's an update to the code, it will be updated on the existing GitHub repository.

We also have other code bundles from our rich catalog of books and videos available at `https://github.com/PacktPublishing/`. Check them out!

Download the color images

We also provide a PDF file that has color images of the screenshots/diagrams used in this book. You can download it here: `https://static.packt-cdn.com/downloads/9781788996242_ColorImages.pdf`.

Conventions used

There are a number of text conventions used throughout this book.

`CodeInText`: Indicates code words in text, database table names, folder names, filenames, file extensions, pathnames, dummy URLs, user input, and Twitter handles. Here is an example: "Note that there is an asynchronous alternative to `cudaMemcpy`."

A block of code is set as follows:

```
#include<stdio.h>
#include<stdlib.h>

__global__ void print_from_gpu(void) {
    printf("Hello World! from thread [%d,%d] \
        From device\n", threadIdx.x,blockIdx.x);
}
```

When we wish to draw your attention to a particular part of a code block, the relevant lines or items are set in bold:

```
int main(void) {
    printf("Hello World from host!\n");
    print_from_gpu<<<1,1>>>();
    cudaDeviceSynchronize();
    return 0;
}
```

Any command-line input or output is written as follows:

```
$ nvcc -o hello_world hello_world.cu
```

Bold: Indicates a new term, an important word, or words that you see onscreen. For example, words in menus or dialog boxes appear in the text like this. Here is an example: "For Windows users, in the VS project properties dialog, you can specify your GPU's compute capability at **CUDA C/C++ | Device | Code Generation**."

 Warnings or important notes appear like this.

 Tips and tricks appear like this.

Get in touch

Feedback from our readers is always welcome.

General feedback: If you have questions about any aspect of this book, mention the book title in the subject of your message and email us at customercare@packtpub.com.

Errata: Although we have taken every care to ensure the accuracy of our content, mistakes do happen. If you have found a mistake in this book, we would be grateful if you would report this to us. Please visit www.packtpub.com/support/errata, selecting your book, clicking on the Errata Submission Form link, and entering the details.

Piracy: If you come across any illegal copies of our works in any form on the internet, we would be grateful if you would provide us with the location address or website name. Please contact us at copyright@packt.com with a link to the material.

If you are interested in becoming an author: If there is a topic that you have expertise in, and you are interested in either writing or contributing to a book, please visit authors.packtpub.com.

Reviews

Please leave a review. Once you have read and used this book, why not leave a review on the site that you purchased it from? Potential readers can then see and use your unbiased opinion to make purchase decisions, we at Packt can understand what you think about our products, and our authors can see your feedback on their book. Thank you!

For more information about Packt, please visit packt.com.

1
Introduction to CUDA Programming

Since its first release in 2007, **Compute Unified Device Architecture** (**CUDA**) has grown to become the de facto standard when it comes to using **Graphic Computing Units** (**GPUs**) for general-purpose computation, that is, non-graphics applications. So, what exactly is CUDA? Someone might ask the following:

- Is it a programming language?
- Is it a compiler?
- Is it a new computing paradigm?

In this chapter, we will demystify some of the myths around GPU and CUDA. This chapter lays the foundation for heterogeneous computing by providing a simplified view of **High-Performance Computing** (**HPC**) history and substantiating it with laws such as Moore's Law and Dennard Scaling, which were—and still are—driving the semiconductor industry and hence the processor architecture itself. You will also be introduced to the CUDA programming model and get to know the fundamental difference between CPU and GPU architecture. By the end of this chapter, you will be able to write and understand `Hello World!` programs using CUDA programming constructs in the C language.

While this chapter primarily uses C to demonstrate CUDA constructs, we will be covering other programming languages such as Python, Fortran, and OpenACC in other chapters.

The following topics will be covered in this chapter:

- The history of high-performance computing
- Hello World from CUDA
- Vector addition using CUDA
- Error reporting with CUDA
- Data type support in CUDA

The history of high-performance computing

HPC has always pushed the limits in order to deliver scientific discoveries. The fundamental shift in processor architecture and design has helped to cross FLOP barriers, starting from **Mega-Floating Point Operations (MFLOPs)** to now being able to do PetaFLOP calculation in a second.

Floating-Point Operations (FLOPs) per second is the fundamental unit for measuring the theoretical peak of any compute processor. MegaFLOP stands for 10 to the 6th power of FLOPS. PetaFLOP stands for 10 to the 15th power of FLOPS.

Instruction-Level Parallelism (ILP) is a concept wherein code-independent instructions can execute at the same time. For the instructions to execute in parallel, they need to be independent of each other. All modern CPU architecture (even GPU architecture) provides five to 15+ stages to allow for faster clock rates:

```
Instr 1: add = inp1 + inp2
Instr 2: mult = inp1 * inp2
Instr 3: final_result = mult / add
```

Operations for calculating the `mult` and `add` variables do not depend on each other, so they can be calculated simultaneously while calculating `final_result`, which depends on the results of the `Instr 1` and `Instr 2` operations. Therefore, it cannot be calculated until `add` and `mult` have been calculated.

When we look at the history of HPC in terms of technology changes, which resulted in a fundamental shift in designing new processors and its impact on the scientific community, there are three primary ones that stand out and can be referred to as epochs:

- **Epoch 1**: The history of the supercomputer goes back to CRAY-1, which was basically a single vector CPU architecture providing peak 160 MegaFLOP/MFLOP compute power.
- **Epoch 2**: The MegaFLOP barrier was crossed by moving from single-core design to multi-core design in CRAY-2, which was a 4 Core Vector CPU that gave 2 GigaFLOPs of peak performance.
- **Epoch 3**: Crossing GigaFLOP compute performance was a fundamental shift and required compute nodes to work with each other and communicate by a network to deliver higher performance. Cray T3D was one of the first machines that delivered 1 TeraFLOP of compute performance. The network was 3D Torus and provided a bandwidth of 300 MB/s. It was the first significant implementation of a rich *shell* around a standard microprocessor.

After this, for almost 20 years, there were no fundamental innovations. Technological innovations were primarily focused on three architectural innovations:

- Moving from an 8-bit to a 16-bit to a 32-bit and now a 64-bit instruction set
- Increasing ILP
- Increasing the number of cores

This was supported by increasing the clock rate, which currently stands at 4 GHz. It was possible to deliver this because of the fundamental laws that drove the semiconductor industry.

 Moore's Law: This law observes the number of transistors in a dense integrated circuit double every two years.

Moore's prediction proved accurate for several decades and still does. Moore's Law is an observation and projection of a historical trend.

Dennard scaling: This a scaling law that keeps Moore's Law alive. Dennard made an observation with respect to the relationship between transistor size and power density and summarized it in the following formula:

$$P = QfCV^2 + V\,I_{leakage}$$

In this equation, Q is the number of transistors, f is the operating frequency, C is the capacitance, V is the operating voltage, and $I_{leakage}$ is the leakage current.

Dennard scaling and Moore's Law are related to each other as it's inferred that reducing the size of transistors can lead to more and more transistors per chip in terms of cost-effectiveness.

With Dennard scaling rules, the total chip power for a given size stayed the same for many processor generations. Transistor count doubled while size kept shrinking (1/S rate) and increased in frequency by 40% every two years. This stopped after the feature size reached below 65 nm as these rules could no longer be sustained due to the leakage current growing exponentially. To reduce the effect of leakage current, new innovations were enforced on the switching process. However, these breakthroughs still were not sufficient to revive how voltage was scaled. The voltage remained constant at 1 V for many processor designs. It was no longer possible to keep the power envelope constant. This is also popularly known as Powerwall.

Dennard scaling held its own from 1977 until 1997 and then began to fade. Due to this, from 2007 to 2017, processors went from 45 nm to 16 nm but resulted in a threefold increase in energy/chip size.

At the same time, the pipeline stages went from five stages to 15+ in the latest architecture. To keep the instruction pipeline full, advance techniques such as speculation were used. The speculation unit involves predicting the program's behavior, such as predicting branches and memory addresses. If a prediction is accurate, it can proceed; otherwise, it undoes the work it did and restarts. Deep pipeline stages and the way legacy software is written resulted in unused transistors and wasted clock cycles, which means that there was no improvement in terms of performance for the application.

Then came GPU, which was primarily used for graphics processing. A researcher named Mark Harris made use of GPU for non-graphics tasks for the first time, and the new term **General Purpose Computation using GPU (GPGPU)** was coined. GPU was proven to be efficient when it came to certain tasks that fell into the category of data parallelism. Unsurprisingly, most of the compute-intensive tasks in many HPC applications are data-parallel in nature. They were mostly matrix to matrix multiplications, which is a routine in the **Basic Linear Algebra Specification (BLAS)** and used extensively.

The only problem for users when it came to adapting and using GPU was that they had to understand the graphics pipeline to make use of GPU. The only interface that was provided for any computation work on GPU centered around shader execution. There was a need to provide a more general interface that was known to developers who were working in the HPC community. This was solved by the introduction of CUDA in 2007.

While the GPU architecture is also bound by the same laws (Moore's Law and Dennard scaling), the design of processors takes a different approach and dedicates transistors for different usage and achieves higher performance than traditional homogeneous architectures.

The following diagram shows the evolution of computer architecture from sequential processing to distributed memory and its impact on programming models:

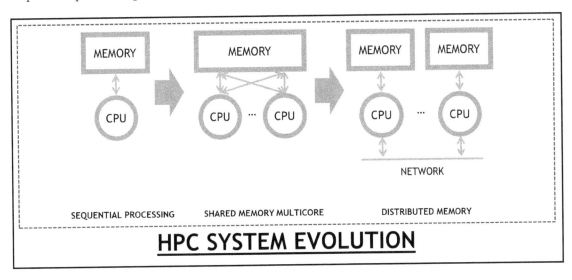

With GPU being added to existing servers, there are two types of processors (CPU and GPU) on which the application runs, which brings in a notion of heterogeneity. This is what we will introduce in the next section.

Heterogeneous computing

The common misconception around GPU is that it is an alternative to CPU. GPUs are used to accelerate the parts of the code that are parallel in nature. **Accelerator** is a common term that's used for GPUs because they accelerate an application by running the parallel part of the code faster, while CPUs run the other part of the code, which is latency bound. Hence, a highly efficient CPU coupled with a high throughput GPU results in improved performance for the application.

The following diagram represents an application running on multiple processor types:

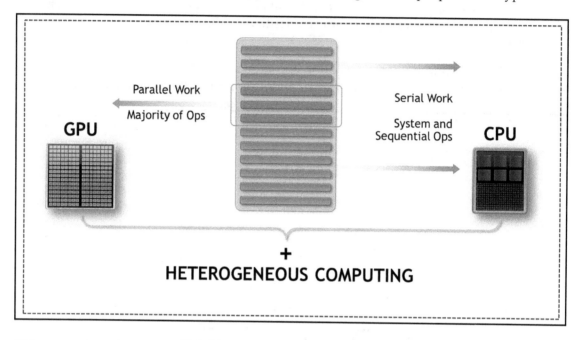

This concept can be very well defined with the help of Amdahl's law. Amdahl's law is used to define the maximum speedup that can be achieved when only a fraction of the application is parallelized. To demonstrate this, the preceding diagram shows two parts of the code. One part is latency bound, while the other is throughput bound. We will cover what these two terms mean in the next section, which differentiates between the CPU and GPU architecture.

The key point is that CPU is good for a certain fraction of code that is latency bound, while GPU is good at running the **Single Instruction Multiple Data (SIMD)** part of the code in parallel. If only one of them, that is, CPU code or GPU code, runs faster after optimization, this won't necessarily result in good speedup for the overall application. It is required that both of the processors, when used optimally, give maximum benefit in terms of performance. This approach of essentially *offloading* certain types of operations from the processor onto a GPU is called **heterogeneous computing**.

The following diagram depicts the two types of sections that all applications have, that is, latency bound and throughput bound:

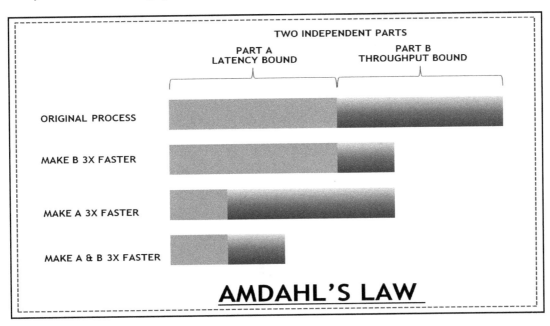

Here, the importance of improving both sections is demonstrated using Amdahl's law.

Programming paradigm

The classification of computer architecture was done using Flynn's taxonomy, which describes four classes of architecture. One of Flynn's classification SIMDs is used to describe GPU architecture. However, there is a subtle difference between the two. SIMD is used to describe an architecture where the same instruction is applied in parallel to multiple data points. This description is suitable for processors that have the capability of doing vectorization. In contrast, in **Single Instruction Multiple Threads** (**SIMTs**), rather than a single thread issuing the instructions, multiple threads issue the same instruction to different data. The GPU architecture is more suitable in terms of the SIMT category compared to SIMD.

Let's look at an example of adding two arrays and storing data in a third array. The dataset for this operation consists of the arrays *A*, *B*, and *C*. The same operations that are used for addition are used on each element of the array:

$$Cx = Ax + Bx$$

It is obvious that each task is independent of each other, but the same operation is being applied by all of the threads.

The following screenshot shows vector addition, depicting an example of this paradigm:

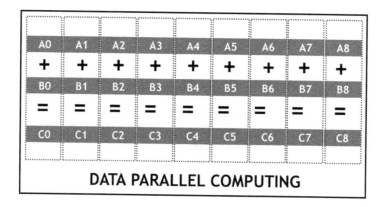

DATA PARALLEL COMPUTING

Low latency versus higher throughput

As we mentioned in the previous section, CPU architecture is optimized for low latency access while GPU architecture is optimized for data parallel throughput computation. As shown in the following screenshot, the CPU architecture has a large amount of cache compared to GPU and has many types. The higher we go, that is, L3 to L1, the lower the amount of cache is present, but less latency. The CPU architecture is designed for low latency access to cached datasets. A large number of transistors are used to implement the speculative execution and out of order execution. Since CPUs run at a very high clock speed, it becomes necessary to hide the latency of fetching the data by frequently storing used data in caches and predicting the next instruction to execute. Applications that can explore this temporal locality can optimally make use of a CPU cache. Also, applications where it is easy to fill the instruction pipeline, for example, an application with no `if` and `else` statements in its code, can benefit from this by hiding the latency of fetching the instruction. Hence, the CPU architecture is a latency reducing architecture.

The following screenshot shows how the **CPU** and **GPU** architecture dedicate the chip die area for different memory and compute units. While **GPU** uses a lot of transistors for computing **ALUs**, **CPU** uses it to reduce latency:

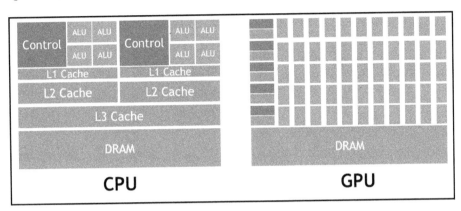

The GPU architecture, on the other hand, is called a **latency reducing** or **high throughput architecture**. The GPU architecture hides latency with computations from other threads. When one thread is waiting for the data to be available for computation, the other threads can start execution and hence not waste any clock cycles. If you are familiar with CUDA, then you might know about the concept of warps. We will cover the concept of warps in the upcoming chapters. (In CUDA, the execution unit is a warp and not a thread. Due to this, context switching happens between warps and not threads).

Some of you might be already wondering why we can't create these threads in the CPU and do the same thing to hide latency. The reason for this is that GPUs have lots of registers, and all of the thread context switching information is already present in them. This is the fastest memory that's available. However, in CPU, there are limited sets of registers and hence thread-related information is usually stored in a lower memory hierarchy such as a cache. For example, Volta contains 20 MB of register storage. Due to this, the context switching time between threads in CPU, compared to GPU, is much higher.

Now, let's take a look at the different approaches when it comes to programming on GPU.

Programming approaches to GPU

Let's go back to our original question, that is, what is CUDA? CUDA is a parallel computing platform and programming model architecture developed by NVIDIA that exposes general-purpose computations on GPU as first-class capabilities. Like any other processor, the GPU architecture can be coded using various methods. The easiest method, which provides drop-in acceleration, is making use of existing libraries. Alternatively, developers can choose to make use of **OpenACC** directives for quick acceleration results and portability. Another option is to choose to dive into CUDA by making use of language constructs in C, C++, Fortran, Python, and more for the highest performance and flexibility. We will be covering all of these methods in detail in the subsequent chapters.

The following screenshot represents the various ways we can perform GPU programming:

Applications		
Libraries	Compiler Directives	Programming Languages
Easy to use	Easy to Start	Most Performance
Most Performance	Portable Code	Most Flexibility
	OpenACC	CUDA

In this section, we provided you with a perspective of how processors and high-performance computing have evolved over time. We provided you with an overview of why the heterogeneous programming model is key to getting the best performance from an application, followed by approaches to GPU programming. In the next section, we will start writing a Hello World program on a GPU.

Technical requirements

A Linux/Windows PC with a modern NVIDIA GPU (Pascal architecture onwards) is required for this chapter, along with all of the necessary GPU drivers and the CUDA Toolkit (10.0 onward) installed. If you're unsure of your GPU's architecture, please visit NVIDIA's GPU site (https://developer.nvidia.com/cuda-gpus) and confirm your GPU's architecture. This chapter's code is also available on GitHub at https://github.com/PacktPublishing/Learn-CUDA-Programming.

The code examples in this chapter have been developed and tested with version 10.1 of CUDA Toolkit, but it is recommended to use the latest CUDA version, if possible.

Hello World from CUDA

CUDA is a heterogeneous programming model that includes provisions for both CPU and GPU. The CUDA C/C++ programming interface consists of C language extensions so that you can target portions of source code for parallel execution on the device (GPU). It is based on industry-standard C/C++ and provides a library of C functions that can be executed on the host (CPU) so that it can interact with the device.

In CUDA, there are two processors that work with each other. The host is usually referred to as the CPU, while the device is usually referred to as the GPU. The host is responsible for calling the device functions. As we've already mentioned, part of the code that runs on the GPU is called **device code**, while the serial code that runs on the CPU is called **host code**.

Let's start by writing our first CUDA code in C. The intention is to take a systematic step-wise approach, start with some sequential code, and convert it into CUDA-aware code by adding some additional keywords. As we mentioned earlier, there is no necessity to learn a new language—all we need to do is add some keywords to the existing language so that we can run it in a heterogeneous environment with CPU and GPU.

Let's take a look at our first piece of code. All this code does is print Hello World! from both the host and device:

```
#include<stdio.h>
#include<stdlib.h>

__global__ void print_from_gpu(void) {
    printf("Hello World! from thread [%d,%d] \
        From device\n", threadIdx.x,blockIdx.x);
}
```

```
int main(void) {
    printf("Hello World from host!\n");
    print_from_gpu<<<1,1>>>();
    cudaDeviceSynchronize();
    return 0;
}
```

Let's try to compile and run the preceding snippet:

1. **Compile the code**: Place the preceding code into a file called `hello_world.cu` and compile it using the **NVIDIA C Compiler** (**nvcc**). Note that the extension of the file is `.cu`, which tells the compiler that this file has GPU code inside it:

   ```
   $ nvcc -o hello_world hello_world.cu
   ```

2. **Execute the GPU code**: We should receive the following output after executing the GPU code:

   ```
   [bharatk@hsw215 ~]$ ./hello_world
   Hello World from host!
   Hello World from thread [0,0]!          From device
   ```

By now, you might have already observed that the CUDA C code isn't used very differently and only requires that we learn some additional constructs to tell the compiler which function is GPU code and how to call a GPU function. It isn't like we need to learn a new language altogether.

In the preceding code, we added a few constructs and keywords, as follows:

- __global__: This keyword, when added before the function, tells the compiler that this is a function that will run on the device and not on the host. However, note that it is called by the host. Another important thing to note here is that the return type of the device function is always "void". Data-parallel portions of an algorithm are executed on the device as kernels.
- <<<, >>>: This keyword tells the compiler that this is a call to the device function and not the host function. Additionally, the 1, 1 parameter basically dictates the number of threads to launch in the kernel. We will cover the parameters inside angle brackets later. For now, the 1, 1 parameter basically means we are launching the kernel with only one thread, that is, sequential code with a thread since we are not doing anything important in the code apart from printing.
- threadIdx.x, blockIdx.x: This is a unique ID that's given to all threads. We will cover this topic more in the next section.

- `cudaDeviceSynchronize()`: All of the kernel calls in CUDA are asynchronous in nature. The host becomes free after calling the kernel and starts executing the next instruction afterward. This should come as no big surprise since this is a heterogeneous environment and hence both the host and device can run in parallel to make use of the types of processors that are available. In case the host needs to wait for the device to finish, APIs have been provided as part of CUDA programming that make the host code wait for the device function to finish. One such API is `cudaDeviceSynchronize`, which waits until all of the previous calls to the device have finished.

Try removing the `cudaDeviceSynchronize()` call and see whether the device output is visible or not. Alternatively, try putting this call before printing it on the host code.

Thread hierarchy

Now, let's start playing around with the two parameters, that is, `threadIdx.x` and `blockIdx.x`.

Experiment 1: First, change the parameter from `<<<1,1>>>` to `<<<2,1>>` and view the output. The output of running multiple thread-single blocks of Hello World code should be as follows:

```
[bharatk@hsw215 ~]$ ./hello_world
Hello World from host!
Hello World! from thread [0,0]        From device
Hello World! from thread [0,1]        From device
```

As we can see, instead of one thread, we now have two threads printing the value. Note that their unique IDs are different.

Experiment 2: Now, instead of changing the first parameter, let's change the second, that is, change `<<<1,1>>>` to `<<<1,2>>>` and observe the output of running multiple single-thread blocks of Hello World code, as follows:

```
[bharatk@hsw215 ~]$ ./hello_world
Hello World from host!
Hello World! from thread [0,0]        From device
Hello World! from thread [1,0]        From device
```

As you can see, the total number of threads that were launched into the kernel is two, just like before—the only difference is that their IDs are different. So, what are these thread and block concepts? To combat this, let's dive into the GPU architecture some more.

GPU architecture

One of the key reasons why CUDA became so popular is because the hardware and software have been designed and tightly bound to get the best performance out of the application. Due to this, it becomes necessary to show the relationship between the software CUDA programming concepts and the hardware design itself.

The following screenshot shows the two sides of CUDA:

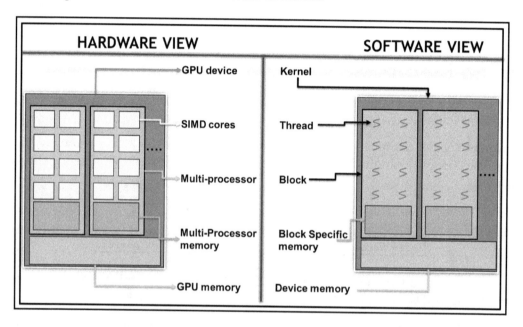

We can see that the CUDA software has been mapped to the GPU hardware.

The following table, in accordance with the preceding screenshot, explains software and hardware mapping in terms of the CUDA programming model:

Software	Executes on/as	Hardware
CUDA thread		CUDA Core/SIMD code
CUDA block		Streaming multiprocessor
GRID/kernel		GPU device

Let's take a look at the preceding table's components in detail:

- **CUDA Threads**: CUDA threads execute on a CUDA core. CUDA threads are different from CPU threads. CUDA threads are extremely lightweight and provide fast context switching. The reason for fast context switching is due to the availability of a large register size in a GPU and hardware-based scheduler. The thread context is present in registers compared to CPU, where the thread handle resides in a lower memory hierarchy such as a cache. Hence, when one thread is idle/waiting, another thread that is ready can start executing with almost no delay. Each CUDA thread must execute the same kernel and work independently on different data (SIMT).
- **CUDA blocks**: CUDA threads are grouped together into a logical entity called a CUDA block. CUDA blocks execute on a single **Streaming Multiprocessor (SM)**. One block runs on a single SM, that is, all of the threads within one block can only execute on cores in one SM and do not execute on the cores of other SMs. Each GPU may have one or more SM and hence to effectively make use of the whole GPU; the user needs to divide the parallel computation into blocks and threads.
- **GRID/kernel**: CUDA blocks are grouped together into a logical entity called a CUDA GRID. A CUDA GRID is then executed on the device.

This may sound somewhat complicated at first glance. In this next section, we'll take a look at an example of vector addition to explain this. Hopefully, things will become much clearer.

Vector addition using CUDA

The problem that we are trying to solve is vector addition. As we are aware, **vector** addition is a data parallel operation. Our dataset consists of three arrays: A, B, and C. The same operation is performed on each element:

$$Cx = Ax + Bx$$

Each addition is independent of each other, but the same operation is applied by all CUDA threads. To get started, configure your environment according to the following steps:

1. Prepare your GPU application. This code will be placed in
   `01_cuda_introduction/01_vector_addition`.
2. Compile your application with the nvcc compiler with the following command:

   $nvcc -o vector_addition vector_addition.cu

The preceding code is sequential code. We will convert this code so that it can run on a GPU using a step-by-step approach, as follows:

```
#include<stdio.h>
#include<stdlib.h>

#define N 512

void host_add(int *a, int *b, int *c) {
    for(int idx=0;idx<N;idx++)
        c[idx] = a[idx] + b[idx];
}

//basically just fills the array with index.
void fill_array(int *data) {
    for(int idx=0;idx<N;idx++)
        data[idx] = idx;
}

void print_output(int *a, int *b, int*c) {
    for(int idx=0;idx<N;idx++)
        printf("\n %d + %d = %d", a[idx] , b[idx], c[idx]);
}

int main(void) {
    int *a, *b, *c;
    int size = N * sizeof(int);
    // Alloc space for host copies of a, b, c and setup input values
    a = (int *)malloc(size); fill_array(a);
    b = (int *)malloc(size); fill_array(b);
    c = (int *)malloc(size);
    host_add(a,b,c);
    print_output(a,b,c);
    free(a); free(b); free(c);
    return 0;
}
```

Before converting the sequential code, let's take a look at the fundamental changes or steps that are taken between the CUDA and sequential code:

Sequential code		CUDA code	
Step 1	Allocate memory on the CPU, that is, `malloc new`.	Step 1	Allocate memory on the CPU, that is, `malloc new`.
Step 2	Populate/initialize the CPU data.	Step 2	Allocate memory on the GPU, that is, `cudaMalloc`.
Step 3	Call the CPU function that has the crunching of data. The actual algorithm is vector addition in this case.	Step 3	Populate/initialize the CPU data.
Step 4	Consume the crunched data, which is printed in this case.	Step 4	Transfer the data from the host to the device with `cudaMemcpy`.
		Step 5	Call the GPU function with <<<, >>> brackets.
		Step 6	Synchronize the device and host with `cudaDeviceSynchronize`.
		Step 7	Transfer data from the device to the host with `cudaMemcpy`.
		Step 8	Consume the crunched data, which is printed in this case.

 This book is not a replacement for the CUDA API guide and does not cover all CUDA APIs. For extensive use of the API, please refer to the CUDA API guide.

As we can see, the CUDA processing flow has some additional steps that need to be added to the sequential code. These are as follows:

1. **Memory allocation on GPU:** CPU memory and GPU memory are physically separate memory. `malloc` allocates memory on the CPU's RAM. The GPU kernel/device function can only access memory that's allocated/pointing to the device memory. To allocate memory on the GPU, we need to use the `cudaMalloc` API. Unlike the `malloc` command, `cudaMalloc` does not return a pointer to allocated memory; instead, it takes a pointer reference as a parameter and updates the same with the allocated memory.

2. **Transfer data from host memory to device memory:** The host data is then copied to the device's memory, which was allocated using the cudaMalloc command used in the previous step. The API that's used to copy the data between the host and device and vice versa is cudaMemcpy. Like other memcopy commands, this API requires the destination pointer, source pointer, and size. One additional parameter it takes is the direction of copy, that is, whether we are copying from the host to the device or from the device to the host. In the latest version of CUDA, this is optional since the driver is capable of understanding whether the pointer points to the host memory or device memory. Note that there is an asynchronous alternative to cudaMemcpy. This will be covered in more detail in other chapters.

3. **Call and execute a CUDA function:** As shown in the Hello World CUDA program, we call a kernel by using <<<, >>> brackets, which provide parameters for the block and thread size, respectively. We will cover this in more detail after all of the steps are complete.

4. **Synchronize:** As we mentioned in the Hello World program, kernel calls are asynchronous in nature. In order for the host to make sure that kernel execution has finished, the host calls the cudaDeviceSynchronize function. This makes sure that all of the previously launched device calls have finished.

5. **Transfer data from host memory to device memory:** Use the same cudaMemcpy API to copy the data back from the device to the host for post-processing or validation duties such as printing. The only change here, compared to the first step, is that we reverse the direction of the copy, that is, the destination pointer points to the host while the source pointer points to the device allocated in memory.

6. **Free the allocated GPU memory:** Finally, free the allocated GPU memory using the cudaFree API.

Change the sequential vector addition code's main function to reflect these new steps. The main function will look like this:

```
int main(void) {
    int *a, *b, *c;
    int *d_a, *d_b, *d_c; // device copies of a, b, c
    int size = N * sizeof(int);

    // Alloc space for host copies of a, b, c and setup input values
    a = (int *)malloc(size); fill_array(a);
    b = (int *)malloc(size); fill_array(b);
    c = (int *)malloc(size);

    // Alloc space for device copies of vector (a, b, c)
```

```
cudaMalloc((void *)&d_a, N * sizeof(int));
cudaMalloc((void *)&d_b, N *sizeof(int));
cudaMalloc((void *)&d_c, N * sizeof(int));

// Copy from host to device
cudaMemcpy(d_a, a, N * sizeof(int), cudaMemcpyHostToDevice);
cudaMemcpy(d_b, b, N* sizeof(int), cudaMemcpyHostToDevice);

device_add<<<1,1>>>(d_a,d_b,d_c);

// Copy result back to host
cudaMemcpy(c, d_c, N * sizeof(int), cudaMemcpyDeviceToHost);

print_output(a,b,c);
free(a); free(b); free(c);

//free gpu memory
cudaFree(d_a); cudaFree(d_b); cudaFree(d_c);
return 0;
}
```

Now, let's look at how kernel code is written and manage the thread and block sizes. For this, we will be conducting multiple experiments.

Experiment 1 – creating multiple blocks

In this section, we will make use of CUDA blocks to run the vector addition code in parallel on the GPU. Additional keywords will be exposed that are related to how we can index CUDA blocks. Change the call to the device_add function, as follows:

```
//changing from device_add<<<1,1>>> to
device_add<<<N,1>>>
```

This will execute the device_add function N times in parallel instead of once. Each parallel invocation of the device_add function is referred to as a block. Now, let's add a __global__ device function, as follows:

```
__global__ void device_add(int *a, int *b, int *c) {
 c[blockIdx.x] = a[blockIdx.x] + b[blockIdx.x];
}
```

By using `blockIdx.x` to index the array, each block handles a different element of the array. On the device, each block can execute in parallel. Let's take a look at the following screenshot:

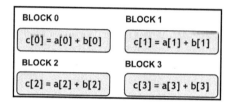

The preceding screenshot represents the vector addition GPU code in which every block shows indexing for multiple single-thread blocks.

Experiment 2 – creating multiple threads

In this section, we will make use of CUDA threads to run the vector addition code in parallel on GPU. Additional keywords will be exposed that are related to how we can index CUDA threads.

A block can be split into multiple threads. Change the call to the `device_add` function, as follows:

```
//changing from device_add<<<1,1>>> to
device_add<<<1,N>>>
```

This will execute the `device_add` function N times in parallel instead of once. Each parallel invocation of the `device_add` function is referred to as a thread. Change the device routine to reflect the kernel, as follows:

```
__global__ void device_add(int *a, int *b, int *c) {
    c[threadIdx.x] = a[threadIdx.x] + b[threadIdx.x];
}
```

One notable difference is that, instead of `blockIdx.x`, we make use of `threadIdx.x`, as shown in the following screenshot:

THREAD 0	THREAD 1
c[0] = a[0] + b[0]	c[1] = a[1] + b[1]
THREAD 2	THREAD 3
c[2] = a[2] + b[2]	c[3] = a[3] + b[3]

The preceding screenshot represents vector addition GPU code in which every block shows indexing for a single block-multiple threads.

Experiment 3 – combining blocks and threads

So far, we've looked at parallel vector addition through the use of several blocks with one thread in the *Experiment 1 – creating multiple blocks* section and one block with several threads in the *Experiment 2 – creating multiple threads* section. In this experiment, we'll use multiple blocks as well as separate blocks containing multiple threads. This becomes more challenging in terms of how to find the index because we need to combine both `threadIdx` and `blockIdx` to generate a unique ID.

Let's take a look at two scenarios that depict different combinations that the developer can choose from:

- **Scenario 1:** Let's consider that the total number of vector elements is 32. Each block contains eight threads and a total of four blocks.
- **Scenario 2:** Let's consider that the total number of vector elements is 32. Each block contains four threads and a total of eight blocks.

In both scenarios, the number of parallel executions is 32, where all 32 elements get populated in parallel. The developer makes the choice between the threads within a block and the number of blocks based on the problem's size and restriction by each piece of hardware. We will be covering details about the right choice of sizing based on the architecture in another chapter.

The following screenshot shows the vector addition GPU indexing code for different block and thread configurations:

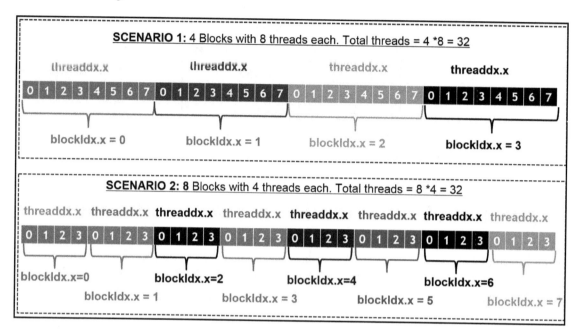

Now, let's look at how the kernel code can be changed to combine both threads and blocks to calculate a global index:

```
__global__ void device_add(int *a, int *b, int *c) {
    int index = threadIdx.x + blockIdx.x * blockDim.x;
    c[index] = a[index] + b[index];
}
```

While calling the kernel from the `main()` function, the developer chooses the block and thread configuration, as depicted in the following code, for the two scenarios we mentioned previously:

- **Scenario 1:** Following is the code for vector addition GPU grid and block size calculation for eight threads per block:

```
threads_per_block = 8;
no_of_blocks = N/threads_per_block;
device_add<<<no_of_blocks,threads_per_block>>>(d_a,d_b,d_c);
```

- **Scenario 2:** Following is the code for vector addition GPU grid and block size calculation for four threads per block:

```
threads_per_block = 4;
no_of_blocks = N/threads_per_block;
device_add<<<no_of_blocks,threads_per_block>>>(d_a,d_b,d_c);
```

With a combination of threads and blocks, the unique ID of a thread can be calculated. As shown in the preceding code, another variable is given to all threads. This is called `blockDim`. This variable consists of the block's dimensions, that is, the number of threads per block. Let's take a look at the following screenshot:

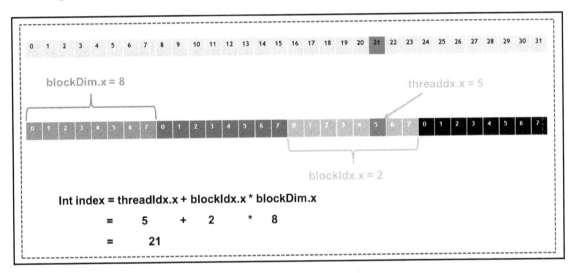

Here, we can see a vector addition GPU indexing calculation for scenario 1.

Why bother with threads and blocks?

It might not be obvious why we need this additional hierarchy of threads and blocks. They add a level of complexity where the developer needs to find out the right block and grid size. Also, global indexing becomes a challenge. The reason for this is because of the restrictions that the CUDA programming model put it place.

Unlike parallel blocks, threads have mechanisms to communicate and synchronize efficiently. Real-world applications require threads to communicate with each other and may want to wait for certain data to be interchanged before proceeding further. This kind of operation requires threads to communicate, and the CUDA programming model allows this communication for threads within the same block. Threads belonging to different blocks cannot communicate/synchronize with each other during the execution of the kernel. This restriction allows the scheduler to schedule the blocks on the SM independently of each other. The result of this is that, if new hardware is released with more SMs and if the code has enough parallelism, the code can be scaled linearly. In other words, this allows the hardware to scale the number of blocks running in parallel based on the GPU's capability.

The threads communicate with each other using a special memory known as shared memory. We will cover shared memory extensively in Chapter 2, *CUDA Memory Management*, where we will expose other memory hierarchies in the GPU and their optimal usage. The following screenshot demonstrates scaling blocks across different GPUs consisting of different amounts of SMs:

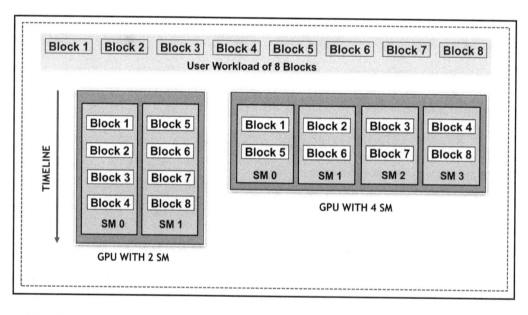

Now, let's find out more about launching kernels in multiple dimensions.

Launching kernels in multiple dimensions

So far, we have been launching threads and blocks in one dimension. This means we have only using indexes for one dimension; for example, we've been using `threadIdx.x`, where x represents that we are using only an x dimension thread index. Similarly, we've been using `blockIdx.x`, where x represents that we are using only an x dimension block index. We can launch threads and blocks in one, two, or three dimensions. One example of launching threads and blocks in two dimensions is when we use parallel operations on an image, for example, to blur the image using a filter. The developer has the choice of launching threads and blocks in two dimensions, which is a more natural choice given that images are two-dimensional in nature.

It is important to understand that every GPU architecture also puts a restriction on the dimensions of threads and blocks. For example, the NVIDIA Pascal card allows a maximum of 1,024 threads per thread block in the x and y dimensions, while in the z dimension, you can only launch 64 threads. Similarly, the maximum blocks in a grid are restricted to 65,535 in the y and z dimensions in the Pascal architecture and $2\textasciicircum31\ -1$ in the x dimension. If the developer launches a kernel with an unsupported dimension, the application throws a runtime error.

So far, we have been assuming that the code we have written is error-free. But in the real world, every programmer writes code that has bugs in it, and it is necessary to catch those errors. In this next section, we'll take a look at how error reporting in CUDA works.

Error reporting in CUDA

In CUDA, the host code manages errors. Most CUDA functions call `cudaError_t`, which is basically an enumeration type. `cudaSuccess` (value 0) indicates a 0 error. The user can also make use of the `cudaGetErrorString()` function, which returns a string describing the error condition, as follows:

```
cudaError_t e;
e = cudaMemcpy(...);
if(e)
    printf("Error: %sn", cudaGetErrorString(err));
```

Kernel launches have no return value. We can make use of a function such as `cudaGetLastError()` here, which returns the error code for the last CUDA function (including kernel launches). In the case of multiple errors, only the last one is reported:

```
MyKernel<<< ... >>> (...);
cudaDeviceSynchronize();
e = cudaGetLastError();
```

When it comes to production code, it is advised to make use of error checking code at logical checkpoints as the CPU code will continue with normal execution even if the GPU kernel has crashed, resulting in incorrect results.

In the next section, we will introduce you to the data types that are supported in the CUDA programming model.

Data type support in CUDA

Like any processor architecture, a GPU also has different types of memories, each meant for a different purpose. We will cover them in more detail in Chapter 2, *CUDA Memory Management*. However, it is important to understand the different data types that are supported and their implications on performance and accuracy. CUDA programming supports all of the standard data types that developers are familiar with in terms of their respective languages. Along with standard data types with different sizes (`char` is 1 byte, `float` is 4 bytes, `double` is 8 bytes, and so on), it also supports vector types such as `float2` and `float4`.

It is recommended that the data types are naturally aligned since aligned data access for data types that are 1, 2, 4, 8, or 16 bytes in size ensure that the GPU calls a single memory instruction. If they are not aligned, the compiler generates multiple instructions, which are interleaved, resulting in inefficient utilization of the memory and instruction bus. Due to this, the recommendation is to use types that are naturally aligned for data residing in GPU memory. The alignment requirement is automatically fulfilled for the built-in types of `char`, `short`, `int`, `long`, `long long`, `float`, and `double` such as `float2` and `float4`.

Also, CUDA programming supports complex data structures such as structures and classes (in the context of C and C++). For complex data structures, the developer can make use of alignment specifiers to the compiler to enforce the alignment requirements, as shown in the following code:

```
struct __align__(16) {
    float r;
    float g;
```

```
    float b;
};
```

Every GPU has a limited set of cores and so the FLOPS are different. For example, a Tesla V100 card with the Volta architecture has 2,560 FP64 cores (double precision), while it has double the number of 32-bit single precision cores. It is quite evident that using the right data types based on the precision requirements of the algorithm is essential. Mixed precision algorithms are now being developed to make use of different types of cores where some part of the algorithm runs with higher precision while some parts run with lower precision. We will cover more on this topic in the upcoming chapters as well. For now, it is important to understand that the GPU memory hierarchy is different and, hence, using the right data type matters.

 While this was a general introduction to the data types that are supported in GPU, more details about all of the supported data types can be found at https://docs.nvidia.com/cuda/cuda-c-programming-guide/index. html#built-in-vector-types.

Summary

In this chapter, we provided you with a perspective on heterogeneous computing with the help of history and high-performance computing. We went into detail about how the two processors, that is, CPU and GPU, are different. We also wrote a Hello World and vector addition CUDA program on a GPU. Finally, we looked at how to detect errors in CUDA since the majority of calls that are made to a CUDA API are asynchronous in nature.

In the next chapter, we will look at the different types of GPU memory that are available and how to utilize them optimally.

CUDA Memory Management

2

As we described in `Chapter 1`, *Introduction to CUDA Programming*, the CPU and GPU architectures are fundamentally different and so is their memory hierarchy. They not only differ in terms of sizes and types but also in terms of their purpose and design. So far, we have studied how each thread accesses its own data with the help of indexing (`blockIdx` and `threadIdx`). We also made use of APIs such as `cudaMalloc` to allocate memory on the device. Many memory paths are available in a GPU, each with different performance characteristics. Launching the CUDA kernel can help us to achieve maximum performance, but only when the right type of memory hierarchy is used in an optimal way. It is the developer's responsibility to map datasets to the right memory type.

Empirically, if we were to plot a graph that outlines the top application performance constraints on the GPU, it would look something like the following diagram:

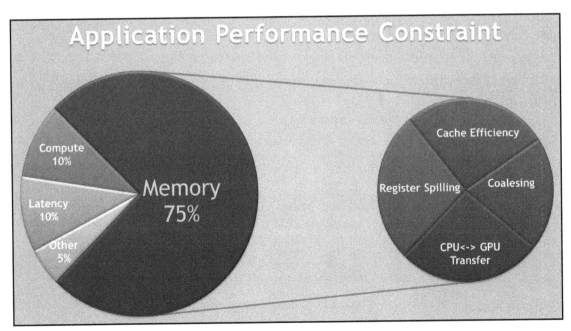

The preceding pie charts represent a rough breakdown of the performance problems that are seen in the majority of CUDA-based applications. It is clearly visible that, most of the time, the application's performance will be bottlenecked by memory-related constraints. Based on the application and which memory path is taken, the memory-related constraints are divided further.

Let's take a different view of this approach and understand the importance of using the right memory type efficiently. The latest NVIDIA GPU with Volta Architecture provides 7,000 GFLOP of peak performance and its device memory bandwidth is 900 GB/s. The first observation you will have will be regarding the ratio of FLOP to memory bandwidth, which is approximately 7:1. This is assuming that all of the threads are accessing 4 bytes (float) of data for performing an operation. The total required bandwidth that's required to perform this operation in one go is *4*7,000 = 28,000* GB/s, that is, to achieve peak performance. 900 GB/s limits the execution to 225 GFLOP. This bounds the execution rate to 3.2% (225 GFLOP is 3.2% of the peak, which is 7,000 GFLOP) of the peak floating-point execution rate of the device. As you are aware by now, GPU is a latency hiding architecture that has many threads available for execution, which means it can, theoretically, tolerate long memory access latencies. Still, surplus calls to memory can prevent very few threads from stalling or waiting and will result in some of the SMs being idle. The CUDA architecture provides several other methods that we can use to access memory to solve this problem of memory bottlenecks.

The path of data traversing from CPU memory until being utilized by the SM for processing is demonstrated in the following diagram. Here, we can see the journey of the data element before it reaches the SM core for computation. Each memory bandwidth is orders of magnitude different, and so is the latency to access them:

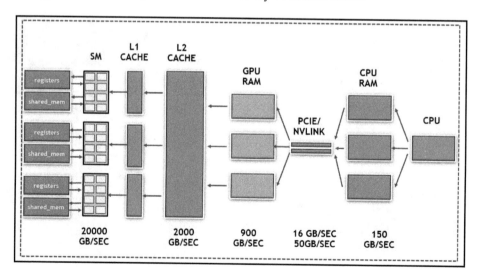

In the preceding diagram, we can see the data path from the CPU until it reaches the registers where the final calculation is done by the ALU/cores.

The following diagram shows the different types of memory hierarchies that are present in the latest GPU architecture. Each memory may have a different size, latency, throughput, and visibility for the application developer:

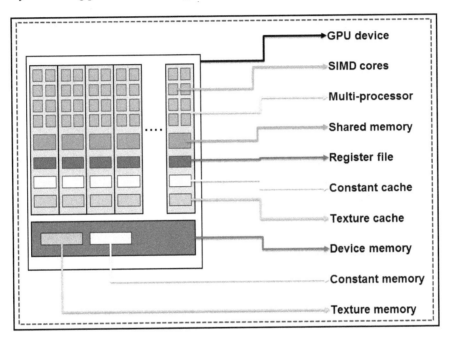

The preceding diagram shows different types of memory that are present in the latest GPU architecture and their placement in the hardware.

In this chapter, you will learn how to optimally utilize different types of GPU memories. We will also be looking at the latest features of GPU-like unified memory, which makes the life of a programmer much simpler. The following memory topics will be covered in detail in this chapter:

- Global memory/device memory
- Shared memory
- Read-only data/cache
- Pinned memory
- Unified memory

But before we look at the memory hierarchy, we will follow the cycle of optimization, which is as follows:

- Step 1: Analyze
- Step 2: Parallelize
- Step 3: Optimize

Analysis of the application requires us to not only understand the characteristics of our application but how effectively it runs on the GPU. For this purpose, we will introduce you to Visual Profiler first, before going into the GPU memory. Since we have used some of the latest features of CUDA here, please read the following section before proceeding with this chapter.

Technical requirements

A Linux PC with a modern NVIDIA GPU (Pascal architecture onward) is required for this chapter, along with all of the necessary GPU drivers and the CUDA Toolkit (10.0 onward) installed. If you are unsure of your GPU's architecture, please visit the NVIDIA GPU's site at `https://developer.nvidia.com/cuda-gpus` and confirm it. This chapter's code is also available on GitHub at `https://github.com/PacktPublishing/Learn-CUDA-Programming`.

The sample code examples for this chapter have been developed and tested with version 10.1 of CUDA Toolkit. However, it is recommended to use the latest CUDA version or higher.

In the next section, we will introduce you to the Visual Profiler, which will help us to analyze our applications. We will also look at how well it runs on the GPU.

NVIDIA Visual Profiler

To understand the effective utilization of different memory hierarchies, it is important to analyze the characteristics of applications at runtime. Profilers are very handy tools that measure and show different metrics that help us to analyze the way memory, SM, cores, and other resources are used. NVIDIA made a decision to provide an API that developers of profiler tools can use to hook into a CUDA application, and a number of profiling tools have evolved over time, such as TAU Performance systems, Vampir Trace, and the HPC Toolkit. These all make use of the **CUDA Profiler Tools Interface** (**CUPTI**) to provide profiling information for CUDA applications.

NVIDIA itself develops and maintains profiling tools that are given as part of the CUDA Toolkit. This chapter makes use of these two profiling tools (NVPROF and NVVP) to demonstrate the efficient use of different memory types and is not a guide to profiling tools.

We will be demonstrating the characteristics of CUDA applications using either NVPROF or NVVP. NVPROF is a command-line tool, while nvvp has a visual interface. nvvp comes in two formats, one being a standalone version and another being an integrated version inside Nsight Eclipse.

The NVVP Profiler window that we will be using extensively looks as follows:

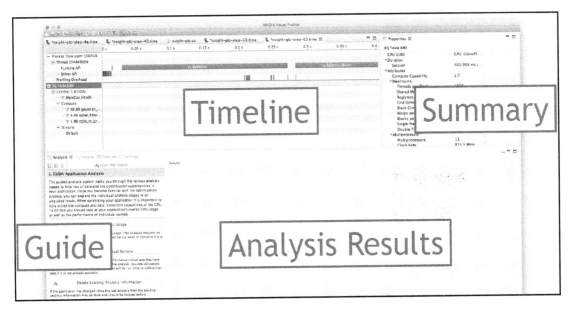

This is an NVVP version 9.0 window snapshot that was taken on macOS.

There are four views available in the window: Timeline, Guide, Analysis Results, and Summary. The Timeline view, as the name denotes, shows the CPU and GPU activity that occurred across time. The Visual Profiler shows a summary view of the memory hierarchy of the CUDA programming model. The Analysis view shows the analysis result. The Visual Profiler provides two modes of analysis:

- **Guided analysis:** As the name suggests, it guides the developer by taking a step-by-step approach to understanding the key performance limiters. We would suggest this mode for beginners before moving on to the unguided mode once they become experts in understanding different metrics.
- **Unguided analysis:** The developer has to manually look at the results in this mode to understand the performance limiter.

The CUDA Toolkit provides two GPU application profile tools, the **NVIDIA Profiler** (**NVPROF**) and the **NVIDIA Visual Profiler** (**NVVP**). To obtain performance limiter information, we need to have to types of profiling: timeline analysis and metric analysis. This code can be accessed at `02_memory_overview/04_sgemm`. The profiling command can be executed as follows:

```
$ nvcc -o sgemm sgemm.cu
$ nvprof -o sgemm.nvvp ./sgemm
$ nvprof --analysis-metrics -o sgemm-analysis.nvvp ./sgemm
```

Let's open the Visual Profiler. If you are using Linux or OSX, you can execute `nvvp` in Terminal. Or, you can find the `nvvp` binary from the CUDA Toolkit installed binary. If you are using Windows, you can execute this tool using the Windows search box with the `nvvp` command.

To open two-profiled data, we will use the **File | Import...** menu, as follows:

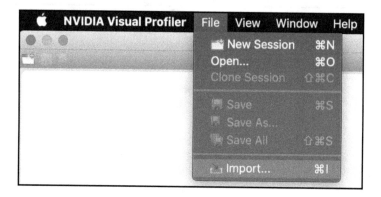

Then, we'll continue by clicking the **Next** button at the bottom:

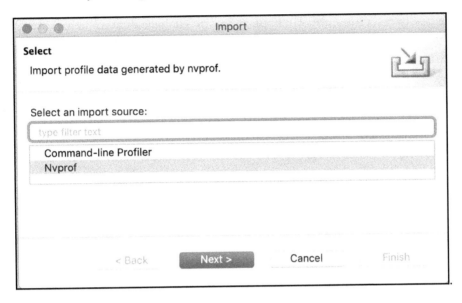

Our CUDA application uses one process. So, let's continue by clicking the **Next** button at the bottom:

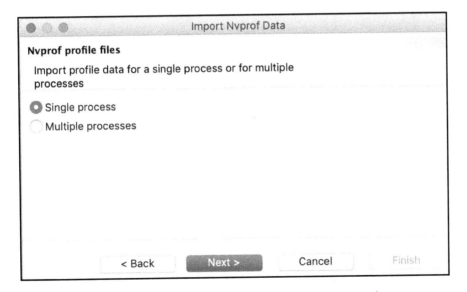

Now, let's put the collected profiled data into the Visual Profiler. The following screenshot shows an example. Put the timeline data in the second textbox by using the **Browse...** button on the right. Then, place metric analysis data in the next textbox in the same way:

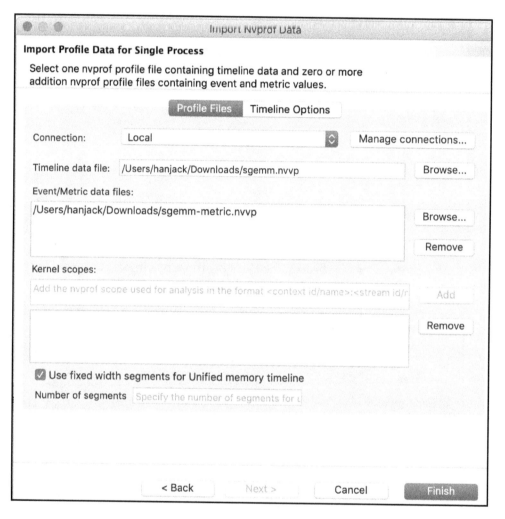

For detailed usage of profiling tools, please refer to the CUDA Profiling guide, which comes as part of the CUDA Toolkit (the respective web link is `https://docs.nvidia.com/cuda/profiler-users-guide/index.html`).

In Windows-based systems, after the CUDA Toolkit's installation, you can launch the Visual Profiler from the Start menu. On a Linux system with X11 forwarding, you can launch Visual Profiler by running the `nvvp` command, which stands for NVIDIA Visual Profiler:

```
$ ./nvvp
```

Since we now have a fair understanding of the analysis tool that we will use, let's jump into the first and definitely most critical GPU memory—global memory/device memory.

Global memory/device memory

This section will provide details on how to make use of global memory, also referred to as device memory. In this section, we will also talk about how efficiently we can load/store data from global memory into the cache. Since global memory is a staging area where all of the data gets copied from CPU memory, the best utilization of this memory is essential. Global memory or device memory is visible to all of the threads in the kernel. This memory is also visible to the CPU.

The programmer explicitly manages allocation and deallocation with `cudaMalloc` and `cudaFree`, respectively. Data is allocated with `cudaMalloc` and declared as `__device__`. Global memory is the default staging area for all of the memory that's transferred from the CPU using the `cudaMemcpy` API.

Vector addition on global memory

The Vector addition example we used in the first chapter demonstrates the use of global memory. Let's look at the code snippet again and try to understand how global memory is used:

```
__global__ void device_add(int *a, int *b, int *c) {
    int index = threadIdx.x + blockIdx.x * blockDim.x;
    c[index] = a[index] + b[index];
}
int main (void) {
...
```

```
    // Alloc space for device copies of a, b, c
    cudaMalloc((void **)&d_a, size);
    cudaMalloc((void **)&d_b, size);
    cudaMalloc((void **)&d_c, size);
...

    // Free space allocated for device copies
    cudaFree(d_a); cudaFree(d_b); cudaFree(d_c);
...

}
```

cudaMalloc allocates the data on the device memory. The pointers in the arguments in the kernel (a, b, and c) point to this device memory. We free this memory using the cudaFree API. As you can see, all of the threads in the blocks have access to this memory inside the kernel.

This code can be accessed at 02_memory_overview/01_vector_addition. In order to compile this code, you can use the following command:

$ **nvcc -o vec_addition ./vector_addition_gpu_thread_block.cu**

This is a simple example of making use of global memory. In the next section, we will look at how to access the data optimally.

Coalesced versus uncoalesced global memory access

To effectively use global memory, it is important to understand the concept of warp in the CUDA programming model, which we have ignored so far. The warp is a unit of thread scheduling/execution in SMs. Once a block has been assigned to an SM, it is divided into a 32 -thread unit known as a **warp**. This is the basic execution unit in CUDA programming.

To demonstrate the concept of a warp, let's look at an example. If two blocks get assigned to an SM and each block has 128 threads, then the number of warps within a block is *128/32 = 4 warps* and the total number of warps on the SM is *4 * 2 = 8 warps*. The following diagram shows how a CUDA block gets divided and scheduled on a GPU SM:

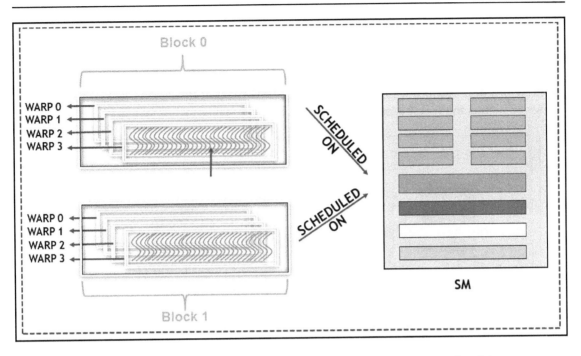

How the block and warps are scheduled on the SM and its core is more of architecture-specific and will be different for generations such as Kepler, Pascal, and the latest architecture, Volta. For now, we can ignore the integrities of scheduling. Among all of the available warps, the ones with operands that are ready for the next instruction become eligible for execution. Based on the scheduling policy of the GPU where the CUDA program is running, the warps are selected for execution. All of the threads in a warp execute the same instruction when selected. CUDA follows the **Single Instruction, Multiple Thread** (**SIMT**) model, that is, all threads in a warp fetch and execute the same instruction at one instance in time. To optimally utilize access from global memory, the access should coalesce. The difference between coalesced and uncoalesced is as follows:

- **Coalesced global memory access:** Sequential memory access is adjacent.
- **Uncoalesced global memory access:** Sequential memory access is not adjacent.

The following diagram shows an example of this access pattern in more detail. The left-hand side of the diagram shows coalesced access where threads from the warp access adjacent data and hence resulting in one 32-wide operation and 1 cache miss. The right-hand side of the diagram shows a scenario where access from threads within a warp is random and may result in calling 32 one wide operation and hence may have 32 cache misses, which is the worst-case scenario:

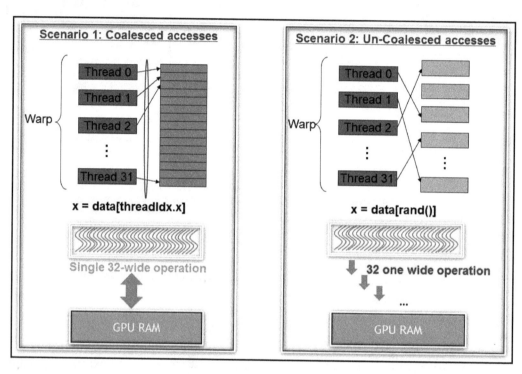

To understand this concept further, we need to understand how data reaches from global memory via cache lines.

Scenario 1: Warp request 32 aligned, 4 consecutive bytes

The address falls within 1 cache line and one 32-wide operation. The bus utilization is 100%, that is, we are utilizing all of the data being fetched from the global memory into a cache and not wasting any bandwidth at all. This is shown in the following diagram:

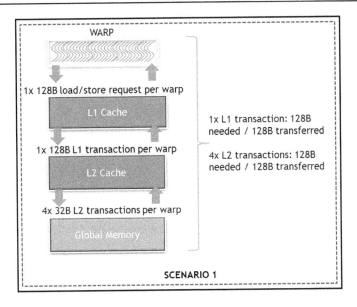

The preceding diagram shows coalesced access, resulting in optimal utilization of the bus.

Scenario 2: Warp request 32 scattered 4-byte words

While the warp needs 128 bytes, there are 32 one wide fetches being executed, resulting in *32 * 128* bytes moving across the bus on a miss. Bus utilization is effectively less than 1%, as shown in the following diagram:

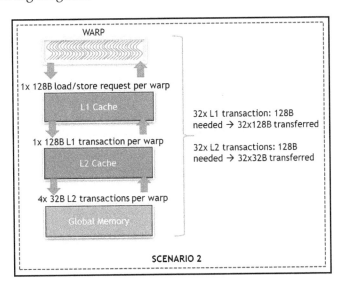

The preceding diagram shows uncoalesced access, resulting in a waste of bus bandwidth.

As we can see in the preceding diagram, it is important how threads within the warp access the data from global memory. To optimally utilize global memory, it is important to improve coalescing. There are multiple strategies that can be used. One such strategy is to change the data layout to improve locality. Let's look at an example. Computer vision algorithms that apply filters onto an image or apply masks onto an image requires the image to be stored onto a data structure. The developer has two choices when it comes to declaring an image type.

The following code snippet makes use of the `Coefficients_SOA` data structure to store data in an array format. The `Coefficients_SOA` structure stores image-related data such as RGB, hue, and saturation values:

```
//Data structure representing an image stored in Structure of Array Format
struct Coefficients_SOA {
  int r;
  int b;
  int g;
  int hue;
  int saturation;
  int maxVal;
  int minVal;
  int finalVal;
};
```

The following diagram shows the data layout regarding how data is stored for `Coefficients_SOA` and accessed by different threads in a kernel:

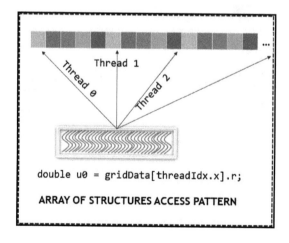

```
double u0 = gridData[threadIdx.x].r;
```

ARRAY OF STRUCTURES ACCESS PATTERN

By doing this, we can see how the use of the AOS data structure resulted in uncoalesced global memory access.

The same image can be stored in an array structure format, as shown in the following code snippet:

```
//Data structure representing an image stored in Array of Structure Format
struct Coefficients_AOS {
  int* r;
  int* b;
  int* g;
  int* hue;
  int* saturation;
  int* maxVal;
  int* minVal;
  int* finalVal;
};
```

The following diagram shows the data layout regarding how data is stored for `Coefficients_AOS` and accessed by different threads in a kernel:

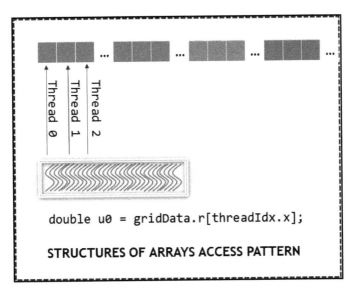

```
double u0 = gridData.r[threadIdx.x];
```

STRUCTURES OF ARRAYS ACCESS PATTERN

By doing this, we can see how using the SOA data structure results in uncoalesced global memory access.

While sequential code on CPU prefers AOS for cache efficiency, SOA is preferred in **Single Instruction Multiple Thread (SIMT)** models such as CUDA for execution and memory efficiency.

Let's try to analyze this aspect by making use of a profiler. Configure your environment according to the following steps:

1. Prepare your GPU application. As an example, we will use two pieces of code to demonstrate the efficient use of global memory. While the `aos_soa.cu` file contains the naive implementation that uses the AOS data structure, `aos_soa_solved.cu` makes use of the SOA data structure, which utilizes global memory efficiently. This code can be found in `02_memory_overview/02_aos_soa`.

2. Compile your application with the `nvcc` compiler and then profile it using the `nvprof` compiler. The following commands are an example of the `nvcc` command for this. We then use the `nvprof` command to profile the application. The `--analysis-metrics` flag is also passed so that we can get metrics for the kernels.

3. The generated profiles, that is, `aos_soa.prof` and `aos_soa_solved.prof`, are then loaded into the NVIDIA Visual Profiler. The user needs to load the profiling output from the **File | Open** menu. Also, don't forget to choose **All Files** as part of the file name options:

```
$ nvcc -o aos_soa ./aos_soa.cu
$ nvcc -o aos_soa_solved ./aos_soa_solved.cu
$ nvprof --analysis-metrics --export-profile aos_soa.prof ./aos_soa
$ nvprof --analysis-metrics --export-profile aos_soa_solved.prof
./aos_soa_solved
```

The profile output is shown in the following screenshot. It is a naive implementation that uses the AOS data structure:

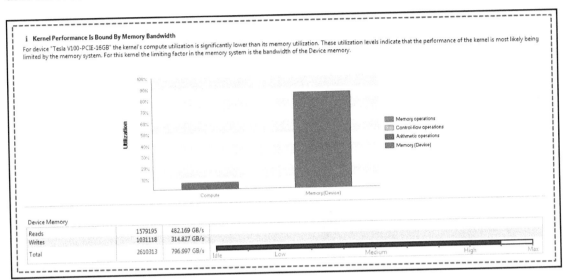

The preceding diagram shows the output of the profiler in guided analysis mode.

The first thing you will see is that the profiler clearly states that the application is memory bound. As you can see, the profilers don't just show metrics but also the analysis of what those metrics mean. In this example, since we are using AOS, the profiler clearly states that the access pattern is not efficient. But how did the compiler come to this conclusion? Let's take a look at the following screenshot, which gives more details about it:

As we can see, it clearly states that the ideal number transaction for accessing data is four, while the run is doing 32 transactions/accesses.

When we change the data structure from AOS to SOA, the bottlenecks are solved. When you run the `aos_soa_solved` executable, you will see that the kernel time reduces, which is an improvement for our timings. On a V100 16 GB card, the time reduces from 104 μs to 47 μs, which is a speedup factor of 2.2x. The profiler output, `aos_soa_solved.prof`, will show that the kernel is still memory-bound, which is quite obvious since we are reading and writing more memory data compared to doing the computation.

Memory throughput analysis

It becomes important for an application developer to understand the memory throughput of an application. This can be defined in two ways:

- **From an app point of view:** Counts the bytes that were requested by the application
- **From a hardware point of view:** Count the bytes that were moved by the hardware

The two numbers are completely different. There are many reasons for this, including uncoalesced access resulting in not all of the transaction bytes being utilized, shared memory bank conflicts, and so on. The two aspects we should use to analyze the application from a memory point of view are as follows:

- **Address pattern:** Determining the access pattern in real code is quite difficult and hence the use of tools such as profilers becomes really important. The metrics that are shown by the profiler, such as global memory efficiency and L1/L2 transactions per access need to be carefully looked at.
- **The number of concurrent accesses in flight:** As a GPU is a latency-hiding architecture, it becomes important to saturate the memory bandwidth. But determining the number of concurrent accesses is generally insufficient. Also, the throughput from an HW point of view is much more different than the theoretical value.

The following diagram demonstrates that ~6 KB of data in flight per SM can reach 90% of peak bandwidth for the Volta architecture. The same experiment, when done on a previous generation architecture, will yield a different graph. In general, it is recommended to understand the GPU memory characteristic for a particular architecture in order to get the best performance from that hardware:

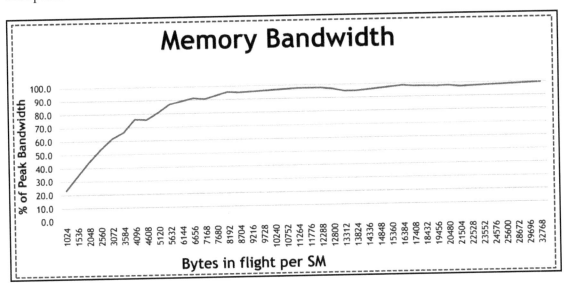

This section provided us with sample uses of global memory and how we can utilize it in an optimal fashion. Sometimes, coalesced data access from global memory is difficult (for example, in CFD domains, in the case of unstructured grids, the data of neighboring cells may not reside next to each other in memory). To solve a problem like this or to reduce the impact on performance, we need to make use of another form of memory, known as shared memory.

Shared memory

Shared memory has always had a vital role to play in the CUDA memory hierarchy known as the **User-Managed Cache**. This provides a mechanism for users so that they can read/write data in a coalesced fashion from global memory and store it in memory, which acts like a cache but can be controlled by the user. In this section, we will not only go through the steps we can take to make use of shared memory but also talk about how we can efficiently load/store data from shared memory and how it is internally arranged in banks. Shared memory is only visible to threads in the same block. All of the threads in a block see the same version of a shared variable.

Shared memory has similar benefits to a CPU cache; however, while a CPU cache cannot be explicitly managed, shared memory can. Shared memory has an order of magnitude lower latency than global memory and an order of magnitude higher bandwidth than global memory. But the key usage of shared memory comes from the fact that threads within a block can share memory access. CUDA programmers can use shared variables to hold the data that was reused many times during the execution phase of the kernel. Also, since threads within the same block can share results, this helps to avoid redundant calculations. The CUDA Toolkit, up until version 9.0, did not provide a reliable communication mechanism between threads in different blocks. We will be covering the CUDA 9.0 communication mechanism in more detail in subsequent chapters. For now, we will assume that communication between threads is only possible in CUDA by making use of shared memory.

Matrix transpose on shared memory

One of the most primitive examples that's used for demonstrating shared memory is that of the matrix transpose. Matrix transpose is a memory-bound operation. The following code snippet, which uses the `matrix_transpose_naive` kernel, shows a sample implementation of the matrix transpose kernel:

```
__global__ void matrix_transpose_naive(int *input, int *output) {
    int indexX = threadIdx.x + blockIdx.x * blockDim.x;
    int indexY = threadIdx.y + blockIdx.y * blockDim.y;
    int index = indexY * N + indexX;
    int transposedIndex = indexX * N + indexY;
    output[index] = input[transposedIndex];
}
```

The preceding code shows the naive implementation of matrix transpose using global memory. If this is implemented in a naive way, this will result in uncoalesced access either while reading the matrix or writing the matrix. The execution time of the kernel on a V100 PCIe 16 GB card is ~60 μs.

Configure your environment according to the following steps:

1. Prepare your GPU application. This code can be found in `02_memory_overview/02_matrix_transpose`.
2. Compile your application with the `nvcc` compiler and then profile it using the `nvprof` compiler. The following commands are an example of the `nvcc` command for this. Then, we use the `nvprof` command to profile the application. The `--analysis-metrics` flag is also passed to get metrics for the kernels.

3. The generated profile, that is, `matrix_transpose.prof`, is then loaded in the NVIDIA Visual Profiler. The user needs to load the profiling output from the **File | Open** menu. Also, don't forget to choose **All Files** as part of the filename options:

```
$ nvcc -o matrix_transpose ./matrix_transpose.cu
$ nvcc -o conflict_solved ./conflict_solved.cu
$ nvprof --analysis-metrics --export-profile matrix_transpose.prof
./matrix_transpose
$ nvprof --analysis-metrics --export-profile conflict_solved.prof
./conflict_solved
```

The following screenshot shows the output of profiling. The output clearly states that there is uncoalesced access to global memory, which is a key indicator that needs to be worked on so that we can improve performance:

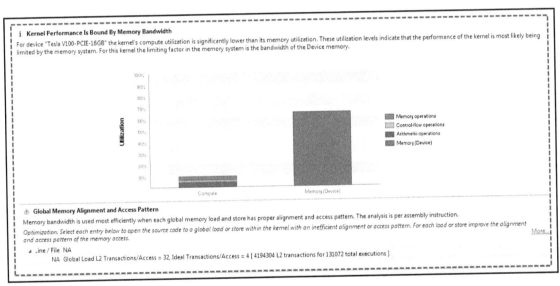

One way to solve this problem is to make use of high bandwidth and low latency memory, such as shared memory. The trick here is to read and write from global memory in a coalesced fashion. Here, the read or write to shared memory can be an uncoalesced pattern. The use of shared memory results in better performance and the time is reduced to 21 microseconds, which is a factor of 3x time speedup:

```
__global__ void matrix_transpose_shared(int *input, int *output) {

    __shared__ int sharedMemory [BLOCK_SIZE] [BLOCK_SIZE];

    //global index
```

```
int indexX = threadIdx.x + blockIdx.x * blockDim.x;
int indexY = threadIdx.y + blockIdx.y * blockDim.y;

//transposed global memory index
int tindexX = threadIdx.x + blockIdx.y * blockDim.x;
int tindexY = threadIdx.y + blockIdx.x * blockDim.y;

//local index
int localIndexX = threadIdx.x;
int localIndexY = threadIdx.y;
int index = indexY * N + indexX;
int transposedIndex = tindexY * N + tindexX;

//transposed the matrix in shared memory.
// Global memory is read in coalesced fashion
sharedMemory[localIndexX][localIndexY] = input[index];
__syncthreads();
//output written in global memory in coalesed fashion.
output[transposedIndex] = sharedMemory[localIndexY][localIndexX];
}
```

The preceding code snippet shows the implementation of matrix transpose using shared memory. Global memory reads/writes coalesce, while the transpose happens in the shared memory.

Bank conflicts and its effect on shared memory

Good speedup compared to using global memory does not necessarily imply that we are using shared memory effectively. This becomes clearer if we look at the profiler metrics. If we shift from guided analysis to unguided analysis for the profiler output, that is, `matrix_transpose.prof`, we will see that the shared memory access pattern shows alignment problems, as shown in the following screenshot:

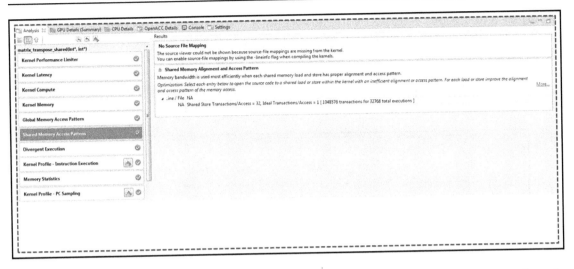

We can see how the profiler shows nonoptimal usage of shared memory, which is a sign of a bank conflict.

To effectively understand this alignment problem, it is important to understand the concept of *banks*. Shared memory is organized into banks to achieve higher bandwidth. Each bank can service one address per cycle. Memory can serve as many simultaneous accesses as it has banks. The Volta GPU has 32 banks, each 4 bytes wide. When an array is stored in shared memory, the adjacent 4-byte words go to successive banks, as demonstrated in the following diagram:

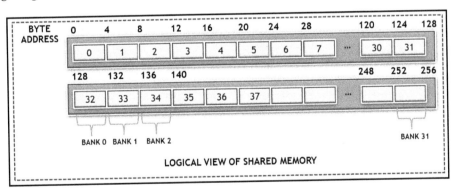

LOGICAL VIEW OF SHARED MEMORY

The logical view in the preceding diagram shows how data is stored in shared memory.

Multiple simultaneous accesses by threads within a warp to a bank results in a bank conflict. In other words, a bank conflict occurs when, inside a warp, two or more threads access different 4-byte words in the same bank. Logically, this is when two or more threads access different *rows* in the same bank. The following diagrams show examples of different *n*-way bank conflicts. The worst case is a 32-way conflict | 31 replays – each replay adds a few cycles of latency:

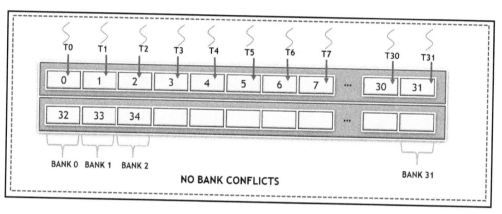

The preceding scenario shows threads from the same warp accessing the adjacent 4-byte elements that reside in different banks, resulting in no bank conflict. Take a look at the following diagram:

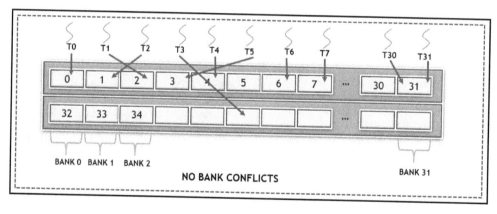

This is another no bank conflict scenario where threads from the same warp access random 4-byte elements that reside in different banks, resulting in no bank conflict. Sequential access due to a 2-way bank conflict in shared memory is shown in the following diagram:

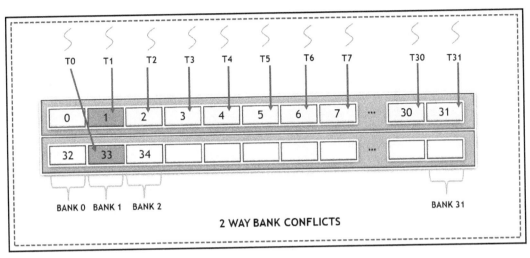

The preceding diagram shows a scenario where threads **T0** and **T1** from the same warp access 4-byte elements residing in the same bank and hence resulting in a 2-way bank conflict.

In the preceding example of the matrix transpose, we made use of shared memory to get better performance. However, we can see a 32-way bank conflict. To resolve this, a simple technique known as padding can be used. All this does is pad the shared memory with a dummy, that is, one additional column, which results in threads accessing different banks and hence resulting in better performance:

```
__global__ void matrix_transpose_shared(int *input, int *output) {

    __shared__ int sharedMemory [BLOCK_SIZE] [BLOCK_SIZE + 1];

  //global index
    int indexX = threadIdx.x + blockIdx.x * blockDim.x;
    int indexY = threadIdx.y + blockIdx.y * blockDim.y;

  //transposed index
    int tindexX = threadIdx.x + blockIdx.y * blockDim.x;
    int tindexY = threadIdx.y + blockIdx.x * blockDim.y;
    int localIndexX = threadIdx.x;
    int localIndexY = threadIdx.y;
    int index = indexY * N + indexX;
```

```
    int transposedIndex = tindexY * N + tindexX;

    //reading from global memory in coalesed manner
    // and performing tanspose in shared memory
    sharedMemory[localIndexX][localIndexY] = input[index];

    __syncthreads();

    //writing into global memory in coalesed fashion
    // via transposed data in shared memory
    output[transposedIndex] = sharedMemory[localIndexY][localIndexX];
}
```

The preceding code snippet, where we used the `matrix_transpose_shared` kernel, shows this concept of padding, which results in removing bank conflicts and hence better utilization of shared memory bandwidth. As usual, run the code and verify this behavior with the help of the Visual Profiler. With these changes, you should see the time of the kernel reduce to 13 microseconds, which is a further speedup of 60%.

In this section, we saw how to optimally utilize shared memory, which provides both read and write access as a scratchpad. But sometimes, the data is just read-only input and does not require write access. In this scenario, GPU provides an optimal memory known as **texture** memory. We will take a look at this in the next chapter, along with other advantages that it provides to developers. We will cover read-only data in the following section.

Read-only data/cache

As you may have already guessed based on the memory name, a read-only cache is suitable for storing data that is read-only and does not change during the course of kernel execution. The cache is optimized for this purpose and, based on the GPU architecture, frees up and reduces the load on the other cache, resulting in better performance. In this section, we will provide details on how to make use of a read-only cache with the help of an image processing code sample that does image resizing.

Read-only data is visible to all of the threads in the grid in a GPU. The data is marked as read-only for the GPU, which means any changes to this data will result in unspecified behavior in the kernel. CPU, on the other hand, has both read and write access to this data.

Traditionally, this cache is also referred to as the texture cache. While the user can explicitly call the texture API to make use of the read-only cache, with the latest GPU architecture, developers can take advantage of this cache without making use of the CUDA texture API explicitly. With the latest CUDA version and GPUs such as Volta, kernel pointer arguments marked as `const __restrict__` are qualified to be read-only data that traverses through the read-only cache data path. A developer can also force loading through this cache with the `__ldg` intrinsic.

Read-only data is ideally used when an algorithm demands the entire warp to read the same address/data, which primarily results in a broadcast to all of the threads requesting the data per clock cycle. The texture cache is optimized for 2D and 3D locality. With threads being part of the same warp, read data from texture addresses that have 2D and 3D locality tend to achieve better performance. Textures have proven useful in applications that demand random memory access, especially prior to Volta architecture cards.

Texture provides support for bilinear and trilinear interpolation, which is particularly useful for image process algorithms such as scaling an image.

The following diagram shows an example of threads within a warp accessing elements spatially located in a 2D space. The texture is suitable for these kinds of workloads:

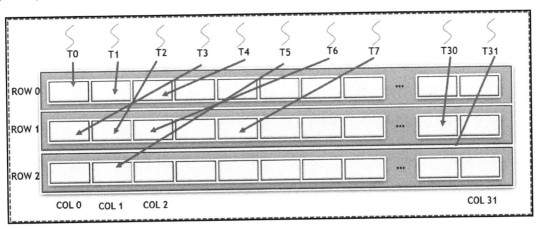

Now, let's take a look at a small real-world algorithm about scaling to demonstrate the use of texture memory.

Computer vision – image scaling using texture memory

We will be using image scaling as an example to demonstrate the use of texture memory. An example of image scaling is shown in the following screenshot:

Image scaling requires interpolation of an image pixel in 2 dimensions. Texture provides both of these functionalities (interpolation and efficient access to 2D locality) which, if accessed by global memory directly, would result in unconcealed memory access.

Configure your environment according to the following steps:

1. Prepare your GPU application. This code can be found at `02_memory_overview/03_image_scaling`.

2. Compile your application with the `nvcc` compiler with the following command:

```
$nvcc -c scrImagePgmPpmPackage.cpp
$nvcc -c image_scaling.cu
$nvcc -o image_scaling image_scaling.o scrImagePgmPpmPackage.o
```

The `scrImagePgmPpmPackage.cpp` file contains the source code for reading and writing images with `.pgm` extensions. The texture code is present in `image_scaling.cu`.

 For viewing the `pgm` files users can make use of viewers like IrfanView (`https://www.irfanview.com/main_download_engl.htm`) which are free to use.

Primarily, there are four steps that are required so that we can make use of texture memory:

1. Declare the texture memory.
2. Bind the texture memory to a texture reference.
3. Read the texture memory using a texture reference in the CUDA kernel.
4. Unbind the texture memory from your texture reference.

The following code snippet shows the four steps we can use to make use of texture memory. From the Kepler GPU architecture and CUDA 5.0 onward, a new feature called bindless textures was introduced. This exposes texture objects, which is basically a C++ object that can be passed to the CUDA kernel. They are referred to as bindless as they don't require manual binding/unbinding, which was the case for earlier GPU and CUDA versions. Texture objects are declared using the `cudaTextureObject_t` class API. Let's go through these steps now:

1. First, declare the texture memory:

   ```
   texture<unsigned char, 2, cudaReadModeElementType> tex;
   ```

   Create a channel description, which will be used while we link to the texture:

   ```
   cudaArray* cu_array;
   cudaChannelFormatKind kind = cudaChannelFormatKindUnsigned;
   cudaChannelFormatDesc channelDesc = cudaCreateChannelDesc(8, 0, 0,
   0, kind);
   ```

2. Then, specify the texture object parameters:

   ```
   struct cudaTextureDesc texDesc;
   memset(&texDesc, 0, sizeof(texDesc));
   //set the memory to zero
   texDesc.addressMode[0] = cudaAddressModeClamp;
   // setting the x dimension addressmode to Clamp
   texDesc.addressMode[1] = cudaAddressModeClamp;
   //Setting y dimension addressmode to Clamp
   texDesc.filterMode = cudaFilterModePoint;
   // Filter mode set to Point
   texDesc.readMode = cudaReadModeElementType;
   // Reading element type and not interpolated
   texDesc.normalizedCoords = 0;
   ```

3. Next, read the texture memory from your texture reference in the CUDA kernel:

```
imageScaledData[index] = tex2D<unsigned
char>(texObj,(float)(tidX*scale_factor),(float)(tidY*scale_factor))
;
```

4. Finally, destroy the texture object:

```
cudaDestroyTextureObject(texObj);
```

The important aspects of texture memory, which act like configurations and are set by the developer, are as follows:

- **Texture dimension:** This defines whether the texture is addressed as a 1D, 2D, or 3D array. Elements within a texture are also referred to as texels. The depth, width, and height are also set to define each dimension. Note that each GPU architecture defines the maximum size for each dimension that is acceptable.
- **Texture type:** This defines the size in terms of whether it is a basic integer or floating-point texel.
- **Texture read mode:** Read mode for texture defines how the elements are read. They can be either read in `NormalizedFloat` or `ModeElement` format. Normalized float mode expects the index within a range of [0.0 1.0] and [-1.0 1.0] for unsigned integer and signed integer types.
- **Texture addressing mode:** One of the unique features of texture is how it can address access that is out of range. This might sound unusual but, in fact, is pretty common in many imaging algorithms. As an example, if you are applying interpolation by averaging the neighboring pixels, what should be the behavior for the boundary pixels? Texture provides this as an option to the developer so that they can choose whether to treat out of range as clamped, wrapped, or mirrored. In the resizing example, we have set it to clamp mode, which basically means that out of range access is clamped to the boundary.
- **Texture filtering mode:** Setting the mode defines how the return value is computed when fetching the texture. Two types of filtering modes are supported: `cudaFilterModePoint` and `cudaFilterModeLinear`. When set to linear mode, interpolation is possible (simple linear for 1D, bilinear for 2D, and trilinear for 3D). Linear mode only works when the return type is of the float type. `ModePoint`, on the other hand, does not perform interpolation but returns a texel of the nearest coordinate.

The key intention of introducing texture memory in this section is to provide you with an example of its usage and to show you where texture memory is useful. It provides a good overview of the different configuration parameters. Please refer to the CUDA API guide (`https://docs.nvidia.com/cuda/cuda-runtime-api/index.html`) for more information.

In this section, we described the purpose of using texture memory by the use of an example. In the next section, we will look at the fastest (lowest latency) available GPU memory (registers). This is present in abundance in GPU compared to CPU.

Registers in GPU

One of the fundamental differences between the CPU and GPU architectures is the abundance of registers in GPU compared to CPU. This helps the threads to keep most of their data in registers and hence reducing the latency of context switching. Hence, it is also important to make this memory optimally.

Registers have a scope of a single thread. A private copy of the variable is created for all of the launched threads in the GRID. Each thread has access to its private copy of the variable, while other thread's private variables cannot be accessed. For example, if a kernel is launched with 1,000 threads, then a variable whose scope is a thread gets its own copy of the variable.

Local variables that are declared as part of the kernel are stored in the registers. Intermediate values are also stored in registers. Every SM has a fixed set of registers. During compilation, a compiler (`nvcc`) tries to find the best number of registers per thread. In case the number of registers falls short, which generally happens when the CUDA kernel is large and has a lot of local variables and intermediate calculations, the data gets pushed to local memory, which may reside either in an L1/L2 cache or even lower in the memory hierarchy, such as global memory. This is also referred to as register spills. The number of registers per thread plays an important role in how many blocks and threads can be active on an SM. This concept is covered in detail in the next chapter, which has a section dedicated to occupancy. In general, it is recommended to not declare lots of unnecessary local variables. If the registers are restricting the number of threads that can be scheduled on an SM, then the developer should look at restructuring the code by splitting the kernel into two—or more, if possible.

A variable that's declared as part of the vecAdd kernel is stored in register memory. The arguments that are passed to the kernel, that is, A, B, and C, point to global memory, but the variable themselves are stored either in the shared memory of registers based on the GPU architecture. The following diagram shows the UDA memory hierarchy and the default locations of the different variable types:

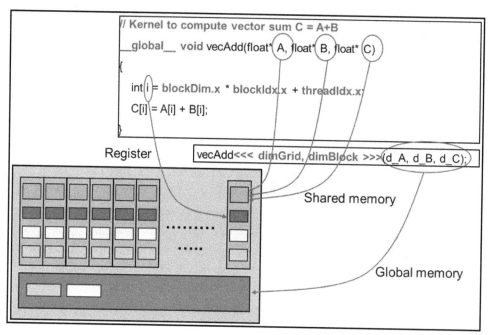

So far, we have seen the purpose and optimal usage of the key memory hierarchy (global, texture, shared, and registers). In the next section, we will look at some of the optimizations and features of GPU memory that can improve the performance of the application and increase the productivity of developers while they are writing CUDA programs.

Pinned memory

It is time to recall the path that's taken by data, that is, from CPU memory to the GPU registers, which are finally consumed by the GPU cores for computation. Even though GPU has more compute performance and higher memory bandwidth, the overall benefit of the speedup gained by the application can become normalized due to the transfer between CPU memory and GPU memory. This transfer of data happens via bus/links/protocols such as PCIe (in the case of CPU architectures from Intel and AMD) or NVLink (for CPU architectures such as power from OpenPower Foundation).

In order to overcome these bottlenecks, the following tricks/guidelines are recommended:

- First, it is recommended to minimize the amount of data that's transferred between the host and device when possible. This may even mean to run a portion of sequential code as a kernel on the GPU, thereby giving little or no speedup compared to running them sequentially on the host CPU.
- Second, it is important to achieve higher bandwidth between the host and the device by making use of pinned memory.
- It is advised to batch small transfers into one large transfer. This helps to reduce the latency involved in calling the data transfer CUDA API, which may range from a few microseconds to a few milliseconds based on the system's configuration.
- Lastly, applications can make use of asynchronous data transfers to overlap the kernel execution with data transfers.

We will be covering pinned memory transfer in more detail in this section. Asynchronous transfers will be covered in more detail in Chapter 4, *Kernel Execution Model and Optimization Strategies*, where we will make use of a concept called CUDA streams.

Bandwidth test – pinned versus pageable

By default, the memory allocation API known as `malloc()` allocates a memory type that's pageable. What this means is that, if needed, the memory that is mapped as pages can be swapped out by other applications or the OS itself. Hence, most devices, including GPUs and others such as InfiniBand, which also sit on the PCIe bus, expect the memory to be pinned before the transfer. By default, the GPU will not access the pageable memory. Hence, when a transfer of memory is invoked, the CUDA driver allocates the temporary pinned memory, copies the data from the default pageable memory to this temporary pinned memory, and then transfers it to the device via a **Device Memory Controller (DMA)**.

This additional step not only adds latency but also has a chance to get the page that was requested transferred to the GPU memory, which has been swapped and needs to be brought back to GPU memory.

To understand the impact of making use of pinned memory, let's try to compile and run a piece of sample code. This has been provided as part of the CUDA samples. Configure your environment according to the following steps:

1. Prepare your GPU application. This code is present in<CUDA_SAMPLES DIR>/1 Utilities/bandwidthTest

2. Compile your application with the `make` command.

3. Run the executable in two modes, that is, `pageable` and `pinned`, as follows:

```
$make
$./bandwidthTest --mode=shmoo --csv --memory=pageable >
pageable.csv
$./bandwidthTest --mode=shmoo --csv --memory=pinned > pinned.csv
```

 Note that `CUDA_SAMPLES_DIR` is the path to the directory where the CUDA installation has been placed.

As we can see, the key change, compared to the previous pieces of code, is that we have written so far is a data allocation API. The following code snippet shows the allocation of memory using the `cudaMallocHost` API instead of `malloc`:

```
cudaError_t status = cudaMallocHost((void**)&h_aPinned, bytes);
if (status != cudaSuccess)
 printf("Error allocating pinned host memory\n");
```

The `cudaMallocHost` API makes the memory pinned memory instead of pageable memory. While the allocation API has changed, we can still use the same data transfers API, that is, `cudaMemcpy()`. Now, the important question is, *what is this pinned memory and why does it provide better bandwidth?* We will cover this in the next section.

The impact on performance can be seen from the output of the bandwidth test. We have plotted the results in a graph so that you can easily understand the impact. The *x* axis shows that data that was transferred in KB, while the *y* axis shows the achieved bandwidth in MB/sec.

The first graph is for **Host to Device** transfer, while the second graph is for **Device to Host** transfers. The first thing you will see is that the maximum bandwidth that can be achieved is ~12 GB/sec. PCIe Gen3's theoretical bandwidth is 16 GB/sec, but what's achievable is in the range of 12 GB/sec. Achievable bandwidth highly depends on the system (motherboard, CPU, PCIe topology, and so on):

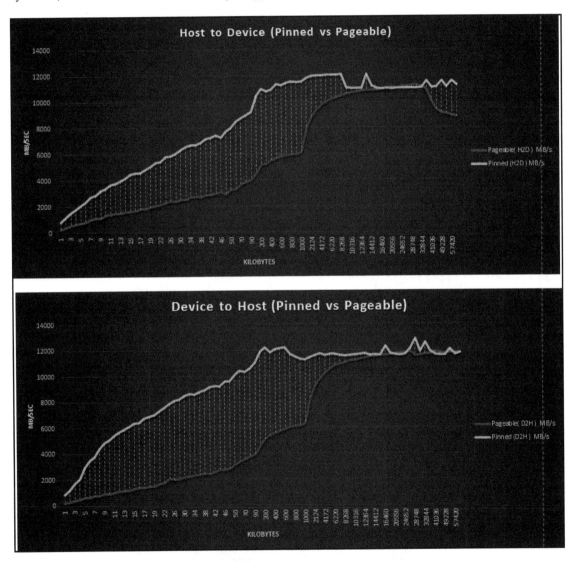

As you can see, for pinned memory, bandwidth is always higher for the lower transfer sizes while pageable memory bandwidth becomes equal at higher data size transfers since the driver and DMA engine start optimizing the transfers by applying concepts such as overlapping. As much as it is advised to make use of pinned memory, there is a downside to overdoing it as well. Allocating the whole system memory as pinned for the application(s) can reduce overall system performance. This happens because it takes away the pages that are available for other application and operating system tasks. The right size that should be pinned is very application and system-dependent and there is no-off-the-shelf formula available for this. The best thing we can do is test the application on the available system and choose the optimal performance parameters.

Also, it is important to understand that new interconnects such as NVLink provide higher bandwidth and lower latency for applications that are bound by these data transfers. Currently, NVLink between CPU and GPU is only provided with the Power CPU.

In this section, we looked at how to improve the data transfer speed between CPU and GPU. We will now move on to making use of one of the new features of CUDA, called unified memory, which has helped to improve the productivity of developers writing CUDA programs.

Unified memory

With every new CUDA and GPU architecture release, new features are added. These new features provide more performance and ease of programming or allow developers to implement new algorithms that otherwise weren't possible to port on GPUs using CUDA. One such important feature that was released from CUDA 6.0 onward and finds its implementation from the Kepler GPU architecture is unified memory. We will refer to unified memory as UM in this chapter.

In simpler words, UM provides the user with a view of single memory space that's accessible by all GPUs and CPUs in the system. This is illustrated in the following diagram:

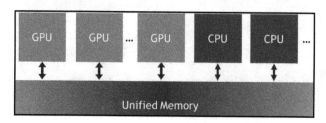

In this section, we will cover how to make use of UM, optimize it, and highlight the key advantages of making use of it. Like global memory access, if done in an uncoalesced fashion, results in bad performance, the UM feature, if not used in the right manner, will result in degradation in terms of the application's overall performance. We will take a step-wise approach, starting with a simple program, and build over it so that we can understand UM and its implication on performance.

Let's try to compile and run some sample pieces of code. Configure your environment according to the following steps:

1. Prepare your GPU application. This code can be found in
    `02_memory_overview/unified_memory`.

2. Compile your application with the following `nvcc` command:

    ```
    $nvcc -o unified_simple.out unified_memory.cu
    $nvcc -o unified_initialized.out unified_memory_initialized.cu
    $nvcc -o unified_prefetch.out unified_memory_prefetch.cu
    $nvcc -o unified_64align.out unified_memory_64align.cu
    ```

Please note that the results that are shown in this section are for the Tesla P100 card. The same code, when run on other architectures such as Kepler, is expected to give different results. The concentration of this section is on the latest architectures, such as Pascal and Volta.

Understanding unified memory page allocation and transfer

Let's start with the naive implementation of UM. The first piece of code, `unified_memory.cu`, demonstrates the basic usage of this concept. The key change in the code is the usage of the `cudaMallocManaged()` API instead of allocating the memory using `malloc`, as shown in the following code snippet:

```
float *x, *y;
int size = N * sizeof(float);
...
cudaMallocManaged(&x, size);
cudaMallocManaged(&y, size);
...

  for (int ix = 0; ix < N; ix++) {
     x[ix] = rand()%10;
     y[ix] = rand()%20;
  }
```

. . .

```
add<<<numBlocks, blockSize>>>(x, y, N);
```

If we look at the source code carefully, we will see that the x and y variables are allocated only once and point to unified memory. The same pointer is being sent to both the GPU add<<<>>>() kernel and used for initialization in the CPU using the for loop. This makes things really simple for programmers as they don't need to keep track of whether the pointer is pointing to CPU memory or GPU memory. But does it necessarily mean that we get good performance or transfer speeds out of it? Not necessarily, so let's try to dig deeper by profiling this code, as shown in the following screenshot:

```
[bharatk@hsw224 unified_memory]$ nvprof ./unified_simple.out
==36853== NVPROF is profiling process 36853, command: ./unified_simple.out
Max error: 0
==36853== Profiling application: ./unified_simple.out
==36853== Profiling result:
            Type  Time(%)      Time     Calls       Avg       Min       Max  Name
 GPU activities:  100.00%   2.6205ms         1   2.6205ms   2.6205ms   2.6205ms  add(int, float*, float*)
      API calls:   95.58%   245.06ms         2   122.53ms   57.390us   245.00ms  cudaMallocManaged
                    1.89%   4.8428ms         4   1.2107ms   1.1380ms   1.3143ms  cuDeviceTotalMem
                    1.10%   2.8126ms       384   7.3240us     113ns   317.24us  cuDeviceGetAttribute
                    1.02%   2.6247ms         1   2.6247ms   2.6247ms   2.6247ms  cudaDeviceSynchronize
                    0.30%   758.70us         2   379.35us   341.52us   417.19us  cudaFree
                    0.09%   228.41us         4   57.103us   53.321us   59.556us  cuDeviceGetName
                    0.02%   48.725us         1   48.725us   48.725us   48.725us  cudaLaunchKernel
                    0.00%   7.3320us         4   1.8330us     801ns   3.0330us  cuDeviceGetPCIBusId
                    0.00%   3.9480us         8     493ns     184ns   2.1290us  cuDeviceGet
                    0.00%   1.1400us         3     380ns     157ns     511ns  cuDeviceGetCount

==36853== Unified Memory profiling result:
Device "Tesla V100-PCIE-32GB (0)"
   Count   Avg Size   Min Size   Max Size   Total Size   Total Time  Name
     173   47.353KB   4.0000KB   976.00KB   8.000000MB   1.091584ms  Host To Device
      24   170.67KB   4.0000KB   0.9961MB   4.000000MB   359.9040us  Device To Host
       8          -          -          -            -   2.606944ms  Gpu page fault groups
Total CPU Page faults: 36
```

We used the following command to get the profiling output:

```
$ nvprof ./unified_simple.out
```

As expected, most of the time is spent in the add<<<>>> kernel. Let's try to theoretically calculate the bandwidth. We will use the following formula to calculate the bandwidth:

Bandwidth = Bytes / Seconds = (3 * 4,194,304 bytes * 1e-9 bytes/GB) / 2.6205e-3s = 5 GB/s

As you can see, P100 provides a theoretical bandwidth of 720 GB/s, while we are able to achieve only 5 GB/s, which is really poor. You may be wondering why were are only calculating the memory bandwidth. The reason for this is that the application is memory-bound as it completes three memory operations and only one addition. Therefore, it makes sense to concentrate on this aspect only.

From Pascal cards onward, `cudaMallocManaged()` does not allocate physical memory but allocates memory based on a first-touch basis. If the GPU first touches the variable, the page will be allocated and mapped in the GPU page table; otherwise, if the CPU first touches the variable, it will be allocated and mapped to the CPU. In our code, the x and y variables get used in the CPU for initialization. Hence, the page is allocated to the CPU. In the `add<<<>>>` kernel, when these variables are accessed, there is a page fault which occurs and the time of page migration gets added to the kernel time. This is the fundamental reason why kernel time is high. Now, let's dive deep into the steps for page migration.

The sequence of operations that are completed in a page migration are as follows:

1. First, we need to allocate new pages on the GPU and CPU (first-touch basis). If the page is not present and mapped to another, a device page table page fault occurs. When ***x**, which resides in **page 2**, is accessed in the GPU that is currently mapped to CPU memory, it gets a page fault. Take a look at the following diagram:

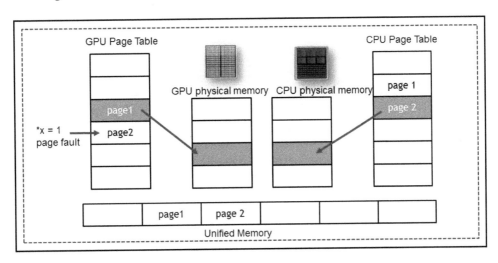

2. In the next step, the old page on the CPU is unmapped, as shown in the following diagram:

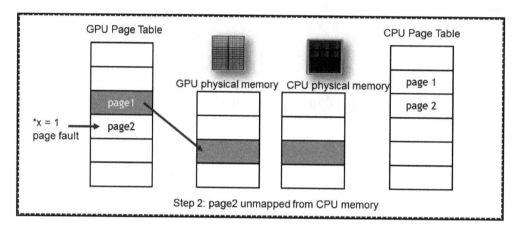

Step 2: page2 unmapped from CPU memory

3. Next, the data is copied from the CPU to the GPU, as shown in the following diagram:

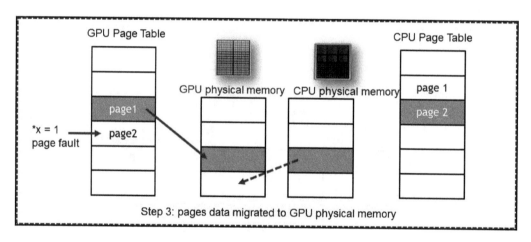

Step 3: pages data migrated to GPU physical memory

4. Finally, the new pages are mapped on the GPU, while the old pages are freed on the CPU, as shown in the following diagram:

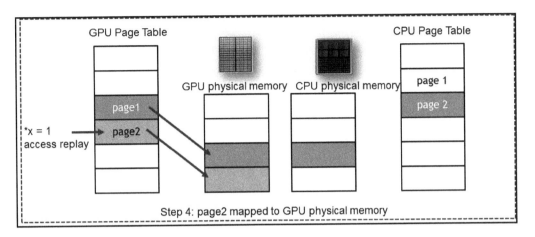

Step 4: page2 mapped to GPU physical memory

The **Translation Lookaside Buffer** (**TLB**) in GPU, much like in the CPU, performs address translation from the physical address to the virtual address. When a page fault occurs, the TLB for the respective SM is locked. This basically means that the new instructions will be stalled until the time the preceding steps are performed and finally unlock the TLB. This is necessary to maintain coherency and maintain a consistent state of memory view within an SM. The driver is responsible for removing these duplicates, updating the mapping, and transferring page data. All of this time, as we mentioned earlier, is added to the overall kernel time.

So, we know the problem now. What is the solution, though? To solve this problem, we are going to make use of two approaches:

- First, we will create an initialization kernel on the GPU so that there are no page faults during the add<<<>>> kernel run. Then, we will optimize the page faults by making use of the warp per page concept.
- We will prefetch the data.

We will cover these methods in the next sections.

Optimizing unified memory with warp per page

Let's start with the first approach, which is the initialization kernel. If you take a look at the source code in the `unified_memory_initialized.cu` file, we added a new kernel there named `init<<<>>>`, as shown in the following code:

```
__global__ void init(int n, float *x, float *y) {
  int index = threadIdx.x + blockIdx.x * blockDim.x;
  int stride = blockDim.x * gridDim.x;
  for (int i = index; i < n; i += stride) {
    x[i] = 1.0f;
    y[i] = 2.0f;
  }
}
```

By adding a kernel to initialize the array in the GPU itself, the pages are allocated and mapped to the GPU memory as they are touched first in the `init<<<>>>` kernel. Let's look at the output of the profiling results for this code, where profiling the output with the initialization kernel is shown:

```
[bharatk@hsw224 unified_memory]$ nvprof ./unified_initialized.out
==36952== NVPROF is profiling process 36952, command: ./unified_initialized.out
Max error: 0
==36952== Profiling application: ./unified_initialized.out
==36952== Profiling result:
            Type  Time(%)      Time   Calls      Avg      Min       Max  Name
 GPU activities:   98.33%  1.1078ms       1  1.1078ms  1.1078ms  1.1078ms  init(int, float*, float*)
                    1.67%  18.848us       1  18.848us  18.848us  18.848us  add(int, float*, float*)
      API calls:   96.23%  252.05ms       2  126.03ms  59.410us  251.99ms  cudaMallocManaged
                    1.80%  4.7206ms       4  1.1802ms  1.1484ms  1.2327ms  cuDeviceTotalMem
                    1.21%  3.1814ms     384  8.2850us    117ns  711.17us  cuDeviceGetAttribute
                    0.43%  1.1224ms       1  1.1224ms  1.1224ms  1.1224ms  cudaDeviceSynchronize
                    0.20%  522.49us       2  261.24us  92.656us  429.83us  cudaFree
                    0.09%  233.63us       4  58.406us  55.197us  61.184us  cuDeviceGetName
                    0.03%  91.098us       2  45.549us  8.4680us  82.630us  cudaLaunchKernel
                    0.00%  7.4340us       4  1.8580us    833ns  3.0820us  cuDeviceGetPCIBusId
                    0.00%  4.5400us       8    567ns    160ns  2.4620us  cuDeviceGet
                    0.00%  1.1090us       3    369ns    135ns    497ns  cuDeviceGetCount

==36952== Unified Memory profiling result:
Device "Tesla V100-PCIE-32GB (0)"
   Count  Avg Size  Min Size  Max Size  Total Size  Total Time  Name
      24  170.67KB  4.0000KB  0.9961MB  4.000000MB  354.4960us  Device To Host
      10         -         -         -           -  1.094880ms  Gpu page fault groups
Total CPU Page faults: 12
```

We used the following command to get the profiling output

```
nvprof ./unified_initialized.out
```

As you can see, the time of the add<<<>>> kernel was reduced to 18 μs. This effectively gives us the following kernel bandwidth:

Bandwidth = Bytes / Seconds = (3 * 4,194,304 bytes * 1e-9 bytes/GB) / 18.84e-6s = 670 GB/s

This bandwidth is what you would expect in a non-unified memory scenario. As we can see from the naive implementation in the preceding screenshot, there is no host to device row in the profiling output. However, you might have seen that even though the add<<<>>> kernel time has reduced, the init<<<>>> kernel has not become the hotspot taking maximum time. This is because we touch the memory for the first time in the init<<<>>> kernel. Also, you might be wondering what these GPU fault groups are. As we discussed earlier, individual page faults may be grouped together in groups to improve bandwidth based on heuristics, as well as the access pattern. To dive further into this, let's reprofile the code with --print-gpu-trace so that we can see individual page faults. As you can see the following screenshot, the GPU trace shows the overall trace of faults and virtual addresses on which this fault happened:

```
[bharatk@hsw224 unified_memory]$ nvprof --print-gpu-trace ./unified_initialized.out
==38016== NVPROF is profiling process 38016, command: ./unified_initialized.out
Max error: 0
==38016== Profiling application: ./unified_initialized.out
==38016== Profiling result:
   Start   Duration   Grid Size   Block Size   Regs*   SSMem*   DSMem*        Device   Context   Stream   Unified Memory   Virtual Address   Name
435.51ms   1.2463ms   (4096 1 1)   (256 1 1)      16      0B       0B   Tesla V100-PCIE      1        7           -               -          init(int, float*, float*) [410]
435.51ms   357.92ns       -           -           -       -        -   Tesla V100-PCIE      -        -          11         0x2abb56000000    [Unified Memory GPU page faults]
435.87ms   77.888us       -           -           -       -        -   Tesla V100-PCIE      -        -           7         0x2abb56020000    [Unified Memory GPU page faults]
435.95ms   55.136ns       -           -           -       -        -   Tesla V100-PCIE      -        -           4         0x2abb56040000    [Unified Memory GPU page faults]
436.00ms   49.504ns       -           -           -       -        -   Tesla V100-PCIE      -        -           1         0x2abb56080000    [Unified Memory GPU page faults]
436.05ms   71.232ns       -           -           -       -        -   Tesla V100-PCIE      -        -           4         0x2abb56480000    [Unified Memory GPU page faults]
436.13ms   183.87ns       -           -           -       -        -   Tesla V100-PCIE      -        -          14         0x2abb56100000    [Unified Memory GPU page faults]
436.31ms   112.74ns       -           -           -       -        -   Tesla V100-PCIE      -        -           5         0x2abb56200000    [Unified Memory GPU page faults]
436.43ms   63.360ns       -           -           -       -        -   Tesla V100-PCIE      -        -           1         0x2abb56248000    [Unified Memory GPU page faults]
436.49ms   60.736ns       -           -           -       -        -   Tesla V100-PCIE      -        -           3         0x2abb56640000    [Unified Memory GPU page faults]
436.55ms   69.312ns       -           -           -       -        -   Tesla V100-PCIE      -        -           4         0x2abb56280000    [Unified Memory GPU page faults]
436.62ms   129.54ns       -           -           -       -        -   Tesla V100-PCIE      -        -          10         0x2abb56300000    [Unified Memory GPU page faults]
436.75ms   18.304ns   (4096 1 1)   (256 1 1)      16      0B       0B   Tesla V100-PCIE      1        7           -               -          add(int, float*, float*) [411]
436.78ms       -           -           -           -       -        -                        -        -   PC 0x4035d8   0x2abb56400000    [Unified Memory CPU page faults]
436.82ms   1.8880ms       -           -           -       -        -   Tesla V100-PCIE      -        -   4.000000KB   0x2abb56400000    [Unified Memory Memcpy DtoH]
436.92ms   5.7600us       -           -           -       -        -   Tesla V100-PCIE      -        -   60.000000KB  0x2abb56401000    [Unified Memory Memcpy DtoH]
```

We used the following command to get the profiling output:

```
$ nvprof --print-gpu-trace ./unified_initialized.out
```

The second row shows **11** page faults for the same page. As we discussed earlier, the role of the driver is to filter these duplicate faults and transfer each page just once. In a complicated access pattern, generally, the driver doesn't have enough information about what data can be migrated to the GPU. To improve this scenario, we will further implement the warp per page concept, which basically means that each warp will access elements that are in the same pages. This requires additional effort from the developer. Let's reimplement the init<<<>>> kernel. You can see this implementation in the unified_memory_64align.cu file, which we compiled earlier. The snapshot of the kernel is shown in the following code snippet:

```
#define STRIDE_64K 65536
__global__ void init(int n, float *x, float *y) {
```

```
int lane_id = threadIdx.x & 31;
size_t warp_id = (threadIdx.x + blockIdx.x * blockDim.x) >> 5;
size_t warps_per_grid = (blockDim.x * gridDim.x) >> 5;
size_t warp_total = ((sizeof(float)*n) + STRIDE_64K-1) / STRIDE_64K;
for(; warp_id < warp_total; warp_id += warps_per_grid) {
    #pragma unroll
    for(int rep = 0; rep < STRIDE_64K/sizeof(float)/32, rep++) {
        size_t ind = warp_id * STRIDE_64K/sizeof(float) + rep * 32 + lane_id;
        if (ind < n) {
            x[ind] = 1.0f;
            y[ind] = 2.0f;
        }
    }
}
```

The kernel shows that the indexing is based on `warp_id`. The warp size in the GPU is 32 and is responsible for populating the x and y variables within an index that has a range of 64 KB, that is, warp 1 is responsible for the first 64 KB, while warp 2 is responsible for the elements in the next 64 KB. Each thread in a warp loops (the innermost `for` loop) to populate the index within the same 64 KB. Let's look at the profiling results of this code. As we can see from the profiling output in the following screenshot, the time for the `init<<<>>>` kernel has reduced, and the GPU fault group has also considerably reduced:

```
[bharatk@hsw224 unified_memory]$ nvprof ./unified_64align.out
==37476== NVPROF is profiling process 37476, command: ./unified_64align.out
Max error: 0
==37476== Profiling application: ./unified_64align.out
==37476== Profiling result:
            Type  Time(%)      Time     Calls       Avg       Min       Max  Name
 GPU activities:   97.63%   557.12us         1   557.12us   557.12us   557.12us  init(int, float*, float*)
                    2.37%   13.536us         1   13.536us   13.536us   13.536us  add(int, float*, float*)
      API calls:   98.53%   633.19ms         2   316.59ms   23.749us   633.16ms  cudaMallocManaged
                    0.75%   4.7915ms         4   1.1979ms   1.1408ms   1.2397ms  cuDeviceTotalMem
                    0.51%   3.2467ms       384   8.4540us      113ns   702.88us  cuDeviceGetAttribute
                    0.09%   569.63us         1   569.63us   569.63us   569.63us  cudaDeviceSynchronize
                    0.08%   495.83us         2   247.92us   87.785us   408.05us  cudaFree
                    0.04%   261.40us         4   65.350us   55.349us   75.675us  cuDeviceGetName
                    0.01%   53.867us         2   26.933us   7.7190us   46.148us  cudaLaunchKernel
                    0.00%   7.5120us         4   1.8780us      813ns   3.0180us  cuDeviceGetPCIBusId
                    0.00%   4.4300us         8      553ns      179ns   2.1480us  cuDeviceGet
                    0.00%   1.1900us         3      396ns      275ns      541ns  cuDeviceGetCount

==37476== Unified Memory profiling result:
Device "Tesla V100-PCIE-32GB (0)"
   Count  Avg Size  Min Size  Max Size  Total Size  Total Time  Name
      24  170.67KB  4.0000KB  0.9961MB  4.000000MB  344.3520us  Device To Host
       2         -         -         -           -  516.7360us  Gpu page fault groups
Total CPU Page faults: 12
```

We can reconfirm this by running the profiler with `--print-gpu-trace`:

```
$ nvprof --print-gpu-trace ./unified_64align.out
```

The following screenshot clearly shows that the GPU page faults per page have decreased:

```
[bharath@hsw224 unified_memory]$ nvprof --print-gpu-trace ./unified_64align.out
==38276== NVPROF is profiling process 38276, command: ./unified_64align.out
Max error: 0
==38276== Profiling application: ./unified_64align.out
==38276== Profiling result:
   Start  Duration   Grid Size    Block Size  Regs*  SSMem*  DSMem*     Device   Context  Stream    Unified Memory  Virtual Address  Name
814.02ms  467.87us   (8 1 1)      (256 1 1)     32     0B      0B   Tesla V100-PCIE     1       7           -              -          init(int, float*, float*) [410]
814.02ms  354.21us      -            -           -     -       -    Tesla V100-PCIE     -       -           2         0x2b376e000000   [Unified Memory GPU page faults]
814.38ms   72.576us     -            -           -     -       -    Tesla V100-PCIE     -       -           1         0x2b376e440000   [Unified Memory GPU page faults]
814.49ms   14.431us  (4096 1 1)   (256 1 1)     16     0B      0B   Tesla V100-PCIE     1       7           -              -          add(int, float*, float*) [411]
814.51ms      -          -            -           -     -       -          -           -       -       PC 0x40360a    0x2b376e400000   [Unified Memory CPU page faults]
814.55ms   1.8560us     -            -           -     -       -    Tesla V100-PCIE     -       -      4.000000KB    0x2b376e400000   [Unified Memory Memcpy DtoH]
814.55ms   5.9520us     -            -           -     -       -    Tesla V100-PCIE     -       -     60.000000KB    0x2b376e401000   [Unified Memory Memcpy DtoH]
```

Optimizing unified memory using data prefetching

Now, let's look at an easier method, called data prefetching. One key thing about CUDA is that it provides different methods to the developer, starting from the easiest ones to the ones that require ninja programming skills. **Data prefetching** are basically hints to the driver to prefetch the data that we believe will be used in the device prior to its use. CUDA provides a prefetching API called `cudaMemPrefetchAsync()` for this purpose. To see its implementation, let's look at the `unified_memory_prefetch.cu` file, which we compiled earlier. A snapshot of this code is shown in the following code snippet:

```
// Allocate Unified Memory -- accessible from CPU or GPU
 cudaMallocManaged(&x, N*sizeof(float));  cudaMallocManaged(&y,
N*sizeof(float));
// initialize x and y arrays on the host
 for (int i = 0; i < N; i++) {  x[i] = 1.0f;  y[i] = 2.0f;  }
//prefetch the memory to GPU
cudaGetDevice(&device);
cudaMemPrefetchAsync(x, N*sizeof(float), device, NULL);
cudaMemPrefetchAsync(y, N*sizeof(float), device, NULL);

 ...

 add<<<numBlocks, blockSize>>>(N, x, y);
//prefetch the memory to CPU
 cudaMemPrefetchAsync(y, N*sizeof(float), cudaCpuDeviceId, NULL);
 // Wait for GPU to finish before accessing on host
 cudaDeviceSynchronize();

 ...

for (int i = 0; i < N; i++)
 maxError = fmax(maxError, fabs(y[i]-3.0f));
```

The code is quite simple and explains itself. The concept is fairly simple: in the case where it is known what memory will be used on a particular device, the memory can be prefetched. Let's take a look at the profiling result, which is shown in the following screenshot.

As we can see, the `add<<<>>>` kernel provides the bandwidth that we expect it to provide:

```
[bharatk@hsw224 unified_memory]$ nvprof ./unified_prefetch.out
==37058== NVPROF is profiling process 37058, command: ./unified_prefetch.out
Max error: 0
==37058== Profiling application: ./unified_prefetch.out
==37058== Profiling result:
            Type  Time(%)      Time   Calls       Avg       Min       Max  Name
 GPU activities:  100.00%  17.696us       1  17.696us  17.696us  17.696us  add(int, float*, float*)
      API calls:   96.00%  249.72ms       2  124.86ms  24.730us  249.70ms  cudaMallocManaged
                    1.77%  4.5919ms       4  1.1480ms  1.1137ms  1.1861ms  cuDeviceTotalMem
                    1.05%  2.7235ms     384  7.0920us     112ns  309.97us  cuDeviceGetAttribute
                    0.51%  1.3269ms       1  1.3269ms  1.3269ms  1.3269ms  cudaDeviceSynchronize
                    0.32%  830.56us       2  415.28us  305.64us  524.92us  cudaFree
                    0.24%  629.54us       3  209.85us  7.7910us  490.67us  cudaMemPrefetchAsync
                    0.09%  242.68us       4  60.668us  53.750us  75.485us  cuDeviceGetName
                    0.02%  43.850us       1  43.850us  43.850us  43.850us  cudaLaunchKernel
                    0.00%  7.9190us       4  1.9790us     823ns  2.9600us  cuDeviceGetPCIBusId
                    0.00%  4.6770us       8     584ns     187ns  2.2770us  cuDeviceGet
                    0.00%  3.0310us       1  3.0310us  3.0310us  3.0310us  cudaGetDevice
                    0.00%  1.2720us       3     424ns     126ns     717ns  cuDeviceGetCount

==37058== Unified Memory profiling result:
Device "Tesla V100-PCIE-32GB (0)"
   Count  Avg Size  Min Size  Max Size  Total Size  Total Time  Name
       4  2.0000MB  2.0000MB  2.0000MB  8.000000MB  739.9040us  Host To Device
       2  2.0000MB  2.0000MB  2.0000MB  4.000000MB  325.3120us  Device To Host
Total CPU Page faults: 24
```

Unified memory is an evolving feature and changes with every CUDA version and GPU architecture release. It is expected that you keep yourself informed by accessing the latest CUDA programming guide (`https://docs.nvidia.com/cuda/cuda-c-programming-guide/index.html#um-unified-memory-programming-hd`).

So far, we have seen the usefulness of the UM concept, which not only provides ease of programming (not explicitly managing memory using the CUDA API) but is much more powerful and helpful when it comes to porting applications that were otherwise either not possible to be ported on GPU or were too difficult to port. One of the key advantages of using UM is over-subscription. GPU memory is quite limited compared to CPU memory. The latest GPU (Volta card V100) provides 32 GB max per GPU. With the help of UM, multiple pieces of GPU memory, along with CPU memory, can be seen as one big memory. For example, the NVIDIA DGX2 machine, which has a 16 Volta GPU of 323 GB, can be seen as a collection of GPU memory with a maximum size of 512 GB. The advantages of these are enormous for applications such as **Computational Fluid Dynamics** (**CFD**) and analytics. Previously, where it was difficult to fit the problem size in GPU memory, it is now possible. Moving pieces by hand is error-prone and requires tuning the memory size.

Also, the advent of high speed interconnects such as NVLink and NVSwitch allow for fast transfer between GPU with high bandwidth and low latency. You can actually get high performance with unified memory!

Data prefetching, combined with hints specifying where the data will actually reside, is helpful for multiple processors that need to simultaneously access the same data. The API name that's used in this case is `cudaMemAdvice()`. Hence, by knowing your application inside out, you can optimize the access by making use of these hints. These are also useful if you wish to override some of the driver heuristics. Some of the advice that's currently being taken by the API is as follows:

- `cudaMemAdviseSetReadMostly`: As the name suggests, this implies that the data is mostly read-only. The driver creates a read-only copy of the data, resulting in a reduction of the page fault. It is important to note that the data can still be written to. In that case, the page copies become invalidated, except for the device that wrote the memory:

```
// Sets the data readonly for the GPU
cudaMemAdvise(data, N, ..SetReadMostly, processorId);
mykernel<<<..., s>>>(data, N);
```

- `cudaMemAdviseSetPreferredLocation`: This advice sets the preferred location for the data to be the memory belonging to the device. Setting the preferred location does not cause data to migrate to that location immediately. Like in the following code, `mykernel<<<>>>` will page fault and generate direct mapping to data on the CPU. The driver tries to *resist* migrating data away from the set preferred location using `cudaMemAdvise`:

```
cudaMemAdvise(input, N, ..PreferredLocation, processorId);
mykernel<<<..., s>>>(input, N);
```

- `cudaMemAdviseSetAccessedBy`: This advice implies that the data will be accessed by the device. The device will create a direct mapping of input in the CPU memory and no page faults will be generated:

```
cudaMemAdvise(input, N, ..SetAccessedBy, processorId);
mykernel<<<..., s>>>(input, N);
```

In the next section, we will use a holistic view to see how different memories in GPU have evolved with the newer architecture.

GPU memory evolution

GPU architectures have evolved over time and memory architectures have changed considerably. If we take a look at the last four generations, there are some common patterns which emerge, some of which are as follows:

- The memory capacity, in general, has increased in levels.
- The memory bandwidth and capacity have increased with new generation architectures.

The following table shows the properties for the last four generations:

Memory type	Properties	Volta V100	Pascal P100	Maxwell M60	Kepler K80
Register	Size per SM	256 KB	256 KB	256 KB	256 KB
L1	Size	32...128 KiB	24 KiB	24 KiB	16...48 KiB
	Line size	32	32 B	32 B	128 B
L2	Size	6144 KiB	4,096 KiB	2,048 KiB	1,536 Kib
	Line size	64 B	32B	32B	32B
Shared memory	Size per SMX	Up to 96 KiB	64 KiB	64 KiB	48 KiB
	Size per GPU	up to 7,689 KiB	3,584 KiB	1,536 KiB	624 KiB
	Theoretical bandwidth	13,800 GiB/s	9,519 GiB/s	2,410 GiB/s	2,912 GiB/s
Global memory	Memory bus	HBM2	HBM2	GDDR5	GDDR5
	Size	32,152 MiB	16,276 MiB	8,155 MiB	12,237 MiB
	Theoretical bandwidth	900 GiB/s	732 GiB/s	160 GiB/s	240 GiB/s

In general, the preceding observations have helped CUDA applications to run faster with the newer architectures. But in parallel, some fundamental changes were also brought to the CUDA programming model, as well as the memory architecture, to make life easy for CUDA programmers. One such change we observed was for texture memory where, prior to CUDA 5.0, the developer had to manually bind and unbind the textures and had to be declared globally. With CUDA 5.0, it was not necessary to do so. It also removed the restrictions on the number of texture references a developer could have in an application.

We also looked at the Volta architecture and some of the fundamental changes that were made to simplify programming for developers. The total capacity in Volta is 128 KB/SM, which is seven times more than its previous generation card, Pascal P100, which makes larger caches available for developers. Also, since the L1 cache in the Volta architecture has much less latency due to unification, this makes it a high-bandwidth and low-latency access to frequently reused data. The key reason to do this is to allow L1 cache operations to attain the benefits of shared memory performance. The key problem with shared memory is that it needs to be explicitly controlled by developers. This becomes less necessary when working with newer architectures such as Volta. This does not mean that shared memory becomes redundant, however. Ninja programmers who want to extract every inch of performance still prefer to use shared memory, but many other applications do not require this expertise anymore. The difference between the Pascal and Volta L1 cache and shared memory is shown in the following diagram:

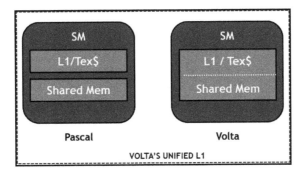

The preceding diagram shows the unification of shared memory and the L1 cache compared to Pascal. It is important to understand that the CUDA programming model has remained almost constant from its inception. Even though the memory's capacity, bandwidth, or latency changes with every architecture, the same CUDA code will run on all architectures. What will definitely change, though, is the impact of performance in terms of these architectural changes. For example, an application that made use of shared memory before Volta and used to see performance gain compared to using global memory might not see such a speedup in Volta because of the unification of L1 and shared memory.

Why do GPUs have caches?

In this evolution process, it is also important to understand that CPU and GPU caches are very different and serve a different purpose. As part of the CUDA architecture, we usually launch hundreds to thousands of threads per SM. Tens of thousands of threads share the L2 cache. So, L1 and L2 are small per thread. For example, at 2,048 threads/SM with 80 SM, each thread gets only 64 bytes at L1 and 38 Bytes at L2 per thread. Caches in GPU cache common data that's accessed by many threads. This is sometimes referred to as spatial locality. A typical example of this is when accesses by threads are unaligned and irregular. The GPU cache can help to reduce the effect of register spills and local memory since the CPU cache is primarily for temporal locality.

Summary

We started this chapter by providing an introduction to the different types of GPU memory. We went into detail about the global, texture, and shared memories, as well as registers. We also looked at what new features the GPU's memory evolution has provided, such as unified memory, which helps to improve the programmer's productivity. We saw how these features are implemented in the latest GPU architectures, such as Pascal and Volta.

In the next chapter, we will go into the details of CUDA thread programming and how to optimally launch different thread configurations to get the best performance out of GPU hardware. We will also be introducing new CUDA Toolkit features such as cooperative groups for flexible thread programming and multi-precision programming on GPUs.

CUDA Thread Programming

3

CUDA has a hierarchical thread architecture so that we can control CUDA threads in groups. Understanding how they work in parallel on a GPU helps you to write parallel programming code and achieve better performance. In this chapter, we will cover CUDA thread operations and their relationship with GPU resources. As a practical experience, we will investigate the parallel reduction algorithm and see how we can optimize CUDA code by using optimization strategies.

In this chapter, you will learn how CUDA threads operate in a GPU: parallel and concurrent thread execution, warp execution, memory bandwidth issues, control overheads, SIMD operation, and so on.

The following topics will be covered in this chapter:

- Hierarchical CUDA thread operations
- Understanding CUDA occupancy
- Data sharing across multiple CUDA threads
- Identifying an application's performance limiter
- Minimizing the CUDA warp divergence effect
- Increasing memory utilization and grid-stride loops
- Cooperative Groups for flexible thread handling
- Warp synchronous programming
- Low-/mixed-precision operations

Technical requirements

This chapter recommends using an NVIDIA GPU card later than Pascal architecture. In other words, your GPU's compute capability should be equal to or greater than 60. If you are unsure of your GPU's architecture, please visit NVIDIA's GPU site at `https://developer.nvidia.com/cuda-gpus`, and confirm your GPU's compute capability.

Sample code was developed and tested with 10.1 when we wrote this book. In general, it is recommended to use the latest CUDA version if applicable.

In this chapter, we'll perform CUDA programming by profiling the code. If your GPU architecture is Turing, it is recommended to install Nsight Compute to profile the code. It is free, and you can download it from `https://developer.nvidia.com/nsight-compute`. When we wrote this book, it was a transition moment of the profiler. You can learn about its basic usage in the *Profiling Kernel with Nsight Compute* section in `Chapter 5`, *CUDA Application Profiling and Debugging*.

CUDA threads, blocks, and the GPU

The basic working unit in CUDA programming is the CUDA thread. The basic CUDA thread execution model is **Single Instruction and Multiple Thread** (**SIMT**). In other words, the body of the kernel function is working descriptions of a single CUDA thread. But, CUDA architecture executes multiple CUDA threads having the same actions.

Conceptually, multiple CUDA threads work in parallel in a group. CUDA thread blocks are collections of multiple CUDA threads. Multiple thread blocks operate concurrently with each other. We call a group of thread blocks a grid. The following diagram shows their relationships:

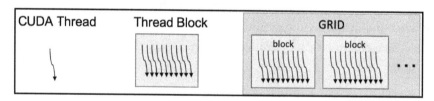

These hierarchical CUDA thread operations match the hierarchical CUDA architecture. When we launch a CUDA kernel, one or multiple CUDA thread blocks execute on each streaming multiprocessor in the GPU. Also, a streaming multiprocessor can run multiple thread blocks depending on resource availability. The number of threads in a thread block varies, and the number of blocks in a grid does too:

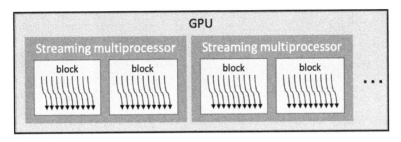

The streaming multiprocessors executes thread blocks arbitrarily and concurrently, executing as many as the GPU resources can afford. Therefore, the number of thread blocks executable in parallel varies depending on how much of the GPU's resources the block requires and the amount of GPU resources available. We will cover this in the following section. The number of streaming multiprocessors varies depending on the GPU specification. For instance, it is 80 for a Tesla V100, and it is 48 for an RTX 2080 (Ti).

The CUDA streaming multiprocessor controls CUDA threads in groups of 32. A group is called a **warp**. In this manner, one or multiple warps configures a CUDA thread block. The following figure shows the relationship:

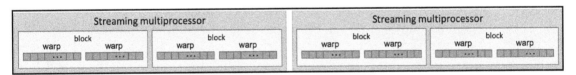

The small green boxes are CUDA threads and they are grouped by a warp. The warp is a basic control unit of GPU architecture. Therefore, its size impacts CUDA programming implicitly or explicitly. For instance, the optimal thread block size is determined among multiple warp sizes that can fully utilize the block's warp scheduling and operations. We call this as occupancy, which will be covered in detail in the next section. Also, CUDA threads in a warp work in parallel and have synchronous operations, inherently. We will talk about this in the *Warp-level primitives programming* section of this chapter.

Exploiting a CUDA block and warp

Now, we will look at CUDA thread scheduling and their implicit synchronization using CUDA's `printf`. The execution of parallel CUDA threads and the blocks operation is concurrent. On the other hand, printing out from the device is a sequential task. So, we can see their execution order easily, since the output will be arbitrary for the concurrent tasks and consistent for the parallel tasks.

We will begin to write kernel code that prints a global thread index, thread block index, warp index, and lane index. For that purpose, the code can be written as follows:

```
__global__ void index_print_kernel() {
    int idx = blockIdx.x * blockDim.x + threadIdx.x;
    int warp_idx = threadIdx.x / warpSize;
    int lane_idx = threadIdx.x & (warpSize - 1);

    if ((lane_idx & (warpSize/2 - 1)) == 0)
        //thread, block, warp, lane
        printf(" %5d\t%5d\t %2d\t%2d\n", idx, blockIdx.x,
                warp_idx, lane_idx);
}
```

This code will help us to understand the concurrency of the warp and CUDA thread scheduling. Let's make our code get arguments from the shell to test various grid and thread block configurations easily.

Then, we will write the host code that calls the kernel function:

```
int main() {
    int gridDim = 4, blockDim = 128;
    puts("thread, block, warp, lane");
    index_print_kernel<<< gridDim, blockDim >>>();
    cudaDeviceSynchronize();
}
```

Finally, let's compile the code, execute it, and see the result:

```
nvcc -m64 -o cuda_thread_block cuda_thread_block.cu
```

The following result is an example of the output result. The actual output might be different:

```
$ ./cuda_thread_block.cu 4 128
thread, block, warp, lane
    64     0     2     0
    80     0     2    16
    96     0     3     0
```

112	0	3	16
0	0	0	0
16	0	0	16
...			
352	2	3	0
368	2	3	16
288	2	1	0
304	2	1	16

From the result, you will see that CUDA threads are launched in warp size and the order is not determined. On the other hand, the lane outputs are in order. From the given result, we can confirm the following facts:

- **Out-of-order block execution:** The second column shows indexes of thread blocks. The result shows that it does not promise in-order execution following the block index.
- **Out-of-order warp index with a thread block:** The third column shows the index of a warp in a block. The warp's order varies across blocks. So, we can infer that there is no guarantee of warp execution order.
- **Grouped threads executed in a warp:** The fourth column shows the lane in a warp. To reduce the number of outputs, the application limits it to printing only two indices. From the in-order output within each warp, we can make an analogy that the `printf` function's output order is fixed so that there is no inversion.

To summarize, CUDA threads are grouped into 32 threads, and their output and the warp's execution have no order. Therefore, programmers have to keep this in mind for CUDA kernel development.

Understanding CUDA occupancy

CUDA occupancy is the ratio of active CUDA warps to the maximum warps that each streaming multiprocessor can execute concurrently. In general, higher occupancy leads to more effective GPU utilization because more warps are available to hide the latency of stalled warps. However, it might also degrade performance due to the increased resource contention between the CUDA threads. Thus, it is crucial for developers to understand this trade-off.

The purpose of finding optimal CUDA occupancy is to make the GPU application issue warps instructions efficiently with the GPU resources. The GPU schedules multiple warps using multiple warp schedulers on a streaming multiprocessor. When multiple warps are scheduled effectively, the GPU can hide latencies between the GPU instructions or memory latencies. Then, the CUDA cores can execute instructions continuously issued from the multiple warps, while the unscheduled warps have to wait until they can issue the next instruction.

Developers can determine CUDA occupancy using two methods:

- **Theoretical occupancy** determined by the CUDA Occupancy Calculator: This calculator is an Excel sheet provided with the CUDA Toolkit. We can determine each kernel's occupancy theoretically from the kernel resource usages and the GPU's streaming multiprocessor.
- **Achieved occupancy** determined by the GPU: The achieved occupancy reflects the true number of concurrent executed warps on a streaming multiprocessor and the maximum available warps. This occupancy can be measured by the NVIDIA profiler with metric analysis.

Theoretical occupancy can be regarded as the maximum upper-bound occupancy because the occupancy number does not consider instructional dependencies or memory bandwidth limitations.

Now, let's see how this occupancy and CUDA C/C++ are related.

Setting NVCC to report GPU resource usages

To begin with, we will use **simple matrix multiplication** (**SGEMM**) kernel code, as follows:

```
__global__ void sgemm_gpu_kernel(const float *A, const float *B,
        float *C, int N, int M, int K, alpha, float beta) {
    int col = blockIdx.x * blockDim.x + threadIdx.x;
    int row = blockIdx.y * blockDim.y + threadIdx.y;

    float sum = 0.f;
    for (int i = 0; i < K; ++i) {
        sum += A[row * K + i] * B[i * K + col];
    }
    C[row * M + col] = alpha * sum + beta * C[row * M + col];
}
```

And, we will call the kernel function using the following kernel code:

```
void sgemm_gpu(const float *A, const float *B, float *C,
            int N, int M, int K, float alpha, float beta) {
    dim3 dimBlock(BLOCK_DIM, BLOCK_DIM);
    dim3 dimGrid(M / dimBlock.x, N / dimBlock.y);
    sgemm_gpu_kernel<<< dimGrid, dimBlock >>>(A, B, C, N, M, K, alpha,
beta);
}
```

You may want to provide appropriate GPU memory and its size information. We will use 2048 for N, M, and K. The memory size is the square of that number. We will set BLOCK_DIM as 16.

Now, let's see how to make the nvcc compiler report the GPU resource usage of the kernel functions.

The settings for Linux

In a Linux environment, we should provide two compiler options, as follows:

- --resource-usage (--res-usage): Setting a verbose option for GPU resource usage
- -gencode: Specifying the target architecture to compile and generate opcodes as follows:
  - Turing: compute_75, sm_75
  - Volta: compute_70, sm_70
  - Pascal: compute_60, sm_60, compute_61, sm_61

If you are not sure which architecture you are using, you can find out from the CUDA GPU website (https://developer.nvidia.com/cuda-gpus). For example, the nvcc compile command can have the compile option as follows:

```
$ nvcc -m 64 --resource-usage \
        -gencode arch=compute_70,code=sm_70 \
        -I/usr/local/cuda/samples/common/inc \
        -o sgemm ./sgemm.cu
```

We can also compile the code to target multiple GPU architectures as follows:

```
$ nvcc -m64 --resource-usage \
    -gencode arch=compute_70,code=sm_70 \
    -gencode arch=compute_75,code=sm_75 \
    -I/usr/local/cuda/samples/common/inc \
    -o sgemm ./sgemm.cu
```

If you want to enable your code to be compatible with the new GPU architecture (Turing), you need to provide an additional option as follows:

```
$ nvcc -m64 --resource-usage \
    -gencode arch=compute_70,code=sm_70 \
    -gencode arch=compute_75,code=sm_75 \
    -gencode arch=compute_75,code=compute_75 \
    -I/usr/local/cuda/samples/common/inc \
    -o sgemm ./sgemm.cu
```

If you want to learn more about these option, you can find the related information in this document: https://docs.nvidia.com/cuda/turing-compatibility-guide/index.html#building-turing-compatible-apps-using-cuda-10-0.

Now, let's compile the source. We can find a resource usage report from NVCC's output. The following result is generated using the preceding commands:

```
ptxas info    : 0 bytes gmem
ptxas info    : Compiling entry function '_Z16sgemm_gpu_kernelPKfS0_Pfiiiff' for 'sm_30'
ptxas info    : Function properties for _Z16sgemm_gpu_kernelPKfS0_Pfiiiff
    0 bytes stack frame, 0 bytes spill stores, 0 bytes spill loads
ptxas info    : Used 32 registers, 364 bytes cmem[0]
```

NVCC reports CUDA kernels resource usage information for each compute capability. In the preceding output screenshot, we can see the number of registers per thread and constant memory usage.

Settings for Windows

When we are developing a Windows application, we can set these settings on the project's properties dialog of Visual Studio. The following the screenshot shows that dialog:

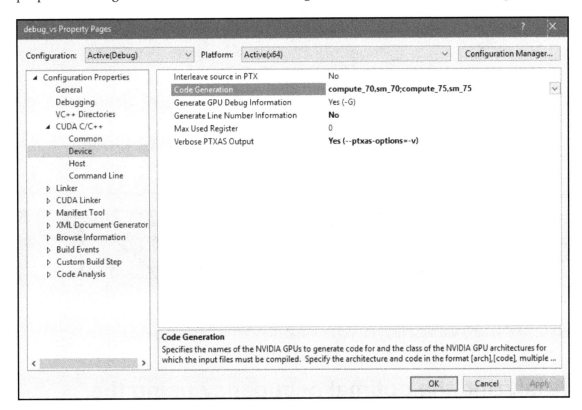

To open this dialog, we should open **debug_vs Property Pages**, then traverse to the **CUDA C/C++ | Device** tab on the left-hand panel. Then, we should set the following options as follows:

- **Verbose PTXAS Output: No | Yes**
- **Code Generation**: Update the option to specify your target architecture as follows:
  - Turing: `compute_75, sm_75`
  - Volta: `compute_70, sm_70`
  - Pascal: `compute_60, sm_60; compute_61, sm_61`

We can specify multiple target architectures using a semi-colon (`;`) for each target.

Now, let's build the source code and we will see NVCC's report on the output panel of Visual Studio. Then, you will see output similar to the following:

```
ptxas info    : 0 bytes gmem
ptxas info    : Compiling entry function '_Z16sgemm_gpu_kernelPKfS0_Pfiiiff' for 'sm_30'
ptxas info    : Function properties for _Z16sgemm_gpu_kernelPKfS0_Pfiiiff
    0 bytes stack frame, 0 bytes spill stores, 0 bytes spill loads
ptxas info    : Used 32 registers, 364 bytes cmem[0]
```

It is the same as the NVCC output in Linux.

Now, let's use the resource usage report to analyze a kernel's occupancy.

Analyzing the optimal occupancy using the Occupancy Calculator

In practice, we can use the CUDA Occupancy Calculator, which is provided with the CUDA Toolkit. Using this, we can obtain theoretical occupancy by providing some kernel information. The calculator is an Excel file, and you can find it in the following, based on the OS you use:

- **Windows:** `C:\Program Files\NVIDIA GPU Computing Toolkit\CUDA\<cuda-version>\tools`
- **Linux:** `/usr/local/cuda/tools`
- **macOS:** `/Developer/NVIDIA/<cuda-version>/tools`

The following is a screenshot of the calculator:

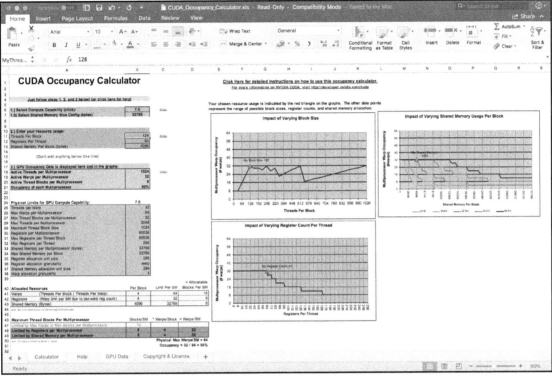

CUDA Occupancy Calculator

This calculator has two parts: kernel information inputs and occupancy information outputs. As input, it requires two kinds of information, as follows:

- The GPU's compute capability (green)
- Thread block resource information (yellow):
    - Threads per CUDA thread block
    - Registers per CUDA thread
    - Shared memory per block

The calculator shows the GPU's occupancy information here:

- GPU occupancy data (blue)
- The GPU's physical limitation for GPU compute capability (gray)
- Allocated resources per block (yellow)
- Maximum thread blocks per stream multiprocessor (yellow, orange, and red)
- Occupancy limit graph following three key occupancy resources, which are threads, registers, and shared memory per block
- Red triangles on graphs, which show the current occupancy data

Now, let's put the obtained information into the calculator. We can edit the green-and orange-colored areas in the Excel sheet:

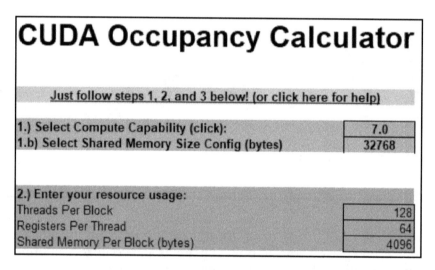

Enter your acquired kernel resource information, and see how the sheet changes.

Depending on compute capability and input data, the occupancy changes, as shown in the following screenshot:

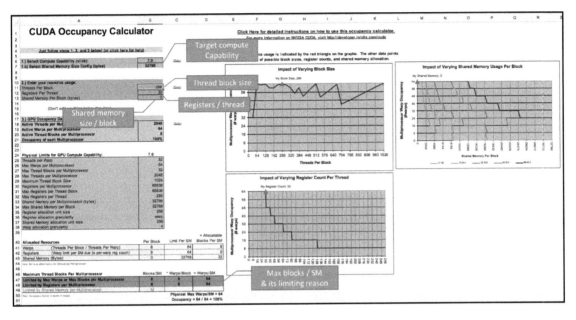

Changes in occupancy depending on compute capability and input data

The blue-colored area shows the kernel function's achieved occupancy. In this screenshot, it shows 100% occupancy achievements. The right-hand side of the sheet presents the occupancy utilization graphs for GPU resources: CUDA threads, shared memory, and registers.

In general, kernel code cannot have 100% theoretical occupancy due to many reasons. However, setting the pick occupancy is the start of utilizing GPU resources efficiently.

Occupancy tuning – bounding register usage

CUDA register usage can increase when the kernel's algorithm is complicated, or the handling datatype is double precision. In that case, the occupancy drops due to the limited active warp size. In that situation, we can increase the theoretical occupancy by limiting the register usage and see whether the performance is enhanced.

One way of resource tuning GPU resource usage is to use the __launch_bound__ qualifier with the kernel function. This informs NVCC to guarantee the minimum thread blocks per stream multiprocessed with the maximum block size. Then, NVCC finds the optimal register size to achieve the given condition. You can use this if you have an idea of the size that makes your algorithm run efficiently at compile time. The identifier can be used as follows:

```
int maxThreadPerBlock = 256;
int minBlocksPerMultiprocessor = 2;
__global__ void
__launch_bound__ (maxThreadPerBlock, minBlocksPerMultiprocessor)
foo_kernel() {
    ...
}
```

Then, the compiler checks the upper-bound resources and reduces the limiting resource usage per block. If its resource usage does not exceed the upper limit, the compiler adjusts the register usage if CUDA can schedule an extra thread block per multiprocessor, if the second parameter is not given. Alternatively, the compiler increases the register usage to hide single-thread instruction latency.

Also, we can simply limit the number of occupied register usages at the application level. The --maxrregcount flag to NVCC will specify the number, and the compiler will reorder the register usages. The following compile command shows how to use that flag in the Linux Terminal:

```
$ nvcc -m64 -I/usr/local/cuda/samples/common/inc -gencode
arch=compute_70,code=sm_70 --resource-usage --maxrregcount 24 -o sgemm
./sgemm.cu
```

But, keep in mind that limiting register usage in this way can introduce thread performance drawn by register throttling. Even the compiler can split the registers into local memory if it cannot set them under the limit, and the local variables are placed in the global memory.

Getting the achieved occupancy from the profiler

Now, we can obtain the achieved occupancy from the profiled metric data using the Visual Profiler. Click the target kernel timeline bar. Then, we can see the theoretical and achieved occupancy in the **Properties** panel. We can also obtain more details from the **Kernel Latency** menu. The following screenshot shows the achieved performance of the example code we used:

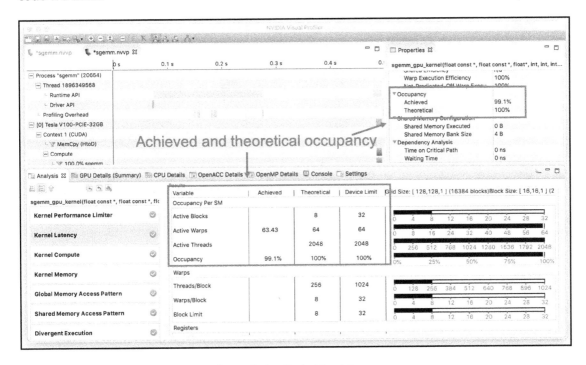

Performance showing achieved and theoretical occupancy

With this occupancy tuning, we can design the CUDA block size to fully utilize warp scheduling in the streaming multiprocessor. However, this does not resolve the 54.75% memory throttling issue, which we found in the previous section. This implies that multiprocessors can stall and cannot conceal memory access latency due to hampered memory requests. We will discuss how to optimize this in this chapter, and in Chapter 7, *Parallel Programming Patterns in CUDA*, we'll discuss matrix-matrix multiplication optimization.

Understanding parallel reduction

Reduction is a simple but useful algorithm to obtain a common parameter across many parameters. This task can be done in sequence or in parallel. When it comes to parallel processing to a parallel architecture, parallel reduction is the fastest way of getting a histogram, mean, or any other statistical values.

The following diagram shows the difference between sequential reduction and parallel reduction:

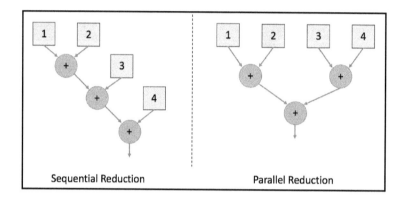

Sequential Reduction   Parallel Reduction

By having the reduction tasks in parallel, the parallel reduction algorithm can reduce the total steps at a log scale. Now, let's begin to implement this parallel reduction algorithm on the GPU. Firstly, we will implement this with a simple design using global memory. Then, we will implement another reduction version using the shared memory. By comparing the two implementations, we will discuss what brings a performance difference.

Naive parallel reduction using global memory

The first basic approach for reduction is to use parallel CUDA threads and share the reduction output using global memory. For every iteration, the CUDA kernel obtains cumulated values from global memory by reducing its size by two. The reduction works as shown in the following diagram, which displays naive parallel reduction with global memory data sharing:

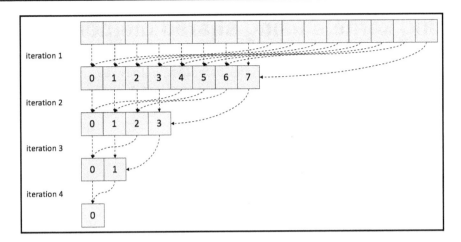

This approach is slow in CUDA because it wastes the global memory's bandwidth and does not utilize any faster on-chip memory. For better performance, it is recommended to use shared memory to save global memory bandwidth and reduce memory-fetch latency. We will discuss how this approach wastes bandwidth later.

Now, let's implement this reduction. Firstly, we will write the reduction kernel function, as follows:

```
__global__ void naive_reduction_kernel
    (float *data_out, float *data_in, int stride, int size) {
    int idx_x = blockIdx.x * blockDim.x + threadIdx.x;
    if (idx_x + stride < size)
        data_out[idx_x] += data_in[idx_x + stride];
}
```

We will call the kernel function while reducing the stride size by half iteratively, until the stride size is one, as follows:

```
void naive_reduction(float *d_out, float *d_in, int n_threads, int size) {
    int n_blocks = (size + n_threads - 1) / n_threads;
    for (int stride = 1; stride < size; stride *= 2)
        naive_reduction_kernel<<<n_blocks, n_threads>>>(d_out, d_in,
    stride, size);
}
```

In this implementation, the kernel code fetches the device memory with stridden addressing and outputs one reduction result. The host code triggers reduction kernels for each step, and the parameter size reduces by half. We cannot have an internal kernel loop since CUDA does not guarantee synchronized operations across thread blocks and streaming multiprocessors.

Reducing kernels using shared memory

In this reduction, each CUDA thread block reduces input values, and the CUDA threads share data using shared memory. For a proper data update, they use the block-level intrinsic synchronization function, __syncthreads(). Then, the next iteration operates on the previous reduction result. Its design is shown in the following diagram, which displays parallel reduction using shared memory:

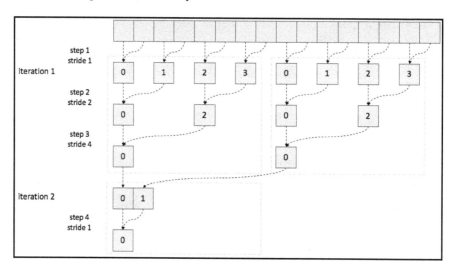

The yellow-dotted boxes represent a CUDA thread block's operation coverage. In this design, each CUDA thread block outputs one reduction result.

Block-level reduction lets each CUDA thread block conduct reduction and outputs a single reduction output. Since it does not require us to save the intermediate result in the global memory, the CUDA kernel can store the transitional value in the shared memory. This design helps to save global memory bandwidth and reduce memory latency.

As we did for global reduction, we will implement the operation. Firstly, we will write the kernel function, as follows:

```
__global__ void reduction_kernel(float* d_out, float* d_in,
                                 unsigned int size) {
    unsigned int idx_x = blockIdx.x * blockDim.x + threadIdx.x;

    extern __shared__ float s_data[];
    s_data[threadIdx.x] = (idx_x < size) ? d_in[idx_x] : 0.f;

    __syncthreads();
```

```
    // do reduction
    for (unsigned int stride = 1; stride < blockDim.x; stride *= 2) {
        // thread synchronous reduction
        if ( (idx_x % (stride * 2)) == 0 )
            s_data[threadIdx.x] += s_data[threadIdx.x + stride];
        __syncthreads();
    }

    if (threadIdx.x == 0)
        d_out[blockIdx.x] = s_data[0];
}
```

Then, we will call the kernel function, as follows:

```
void reduction(float *d_out, float *d_in, int n_threads, int size)
{
    cudaMemcpy(d_out, d_in, size * sizeof(float),
cudaMemcpyDeviceToDevice);
    while(size > 1) {
        int n_blocks = (size + n_threads - 1) / n_threads;
        reduction_kernel
            <<< n_blocks, n_threads, n_threads * sizeof(float), 0 >>>
            (d_out, d_out, size);
        size = n_blocks;
    }
}
```

In this code, we provide n_threads * sizeof (float) bytes, because each CUDA thread will share a single variable for each byte.

Writing performance measurement code

To measure each version's performance, we will use the CUDA sample timer helper function:

```
// Initialize timer
StopWatchInterface *timer;
sdkCreateTimer(&timer);
sdkStartTimer(&timer);

... Execution code ...

// Getting elapsed time
cudaDeviceSynchronize(); // Blocks the host until GPU finishes the work
sdkStopTimer(&timer);
```

```
// Getting execution time in micro-secondes
float execution_time_ms = sdkGetTimerValue(&timer)

// Termination of timer
sdkDeleteTimer(&timer);
```

This function set helps to measure execution time at the microsecond level. Also, it is recommended to call the kernel function ahead of performance measurement to eliminate the device initialization overhead. For a more detailed implementation, visit the implemented code in the `global_reduction.cu` and `reduction.cu` files. These code sets are used across this chapter to evaluate the optimization effect along with the profiler.

Performance comparison for the two reductions – global and shared memory

Now, we can compare the two parallel reduction operations' execution time. Performance can vary depending on GPUs and the implementation environments.Run the following commands for global reduction and reduction using shared memory respectively:

```
# Reduction with global memory
$ nvcc -run -m64 -gencode arch=compute_70,code=sm_70 -
I/usr/local/cuda/samples/common/inc -o reduction_global
./reduction_global.cpp reduction_global_kernel.cu

# Reduction using shared memory
$ nvcc -run -m64 -gencode arch=compute_70,code=sm_70 -
I/usr/local/cuda/samples/common/inc -o reduction_shared
./reduction_shared.cpp reduction_shared_kernel.cu
```

Using my Tesla V100 PCIe card, the estimated performance of both reductions is as follows. The number of elements was 2^{24} items:

Operation	Estimated time (ms)	Speed-up
Original approach (reduction with global memory)	4.609	1.0x
Reduction using shared memory	0.624	7.4x

From this result, we can see how sharing data using shared memory in reduction returns the output quickly. The first implemented version is in `global_reduction.cu`, and the second version is in `shared_reduction.cu`, so you can compare the implementations for yourself.

By dividing the reduction along with the shared memory, we could enhance the performance significantly. However, we cannot determine that it is the maximum performance we could get and do not know what bottleneck our application has. To analyze this, we will cover the performance limiter in the next section.

Identifying the application's performance limiter

Previously, we saw how saving global memory benefits the CUDA kernel's performance. In general, using an on-chip cache is better than using off-chip memory. But, we cannot determine whether much optimization room remains with this simple analogy.

The performance limiter shows the bounding factor, which limits the performance of an application most significantly. Based on its profiling information, it analyzes performance-limiting factors among computing and memory bandwidth. Based on these resources' utilization, an application can be categorized into four types: **Compute Bound**, **Bandwidth Bound**, **Latency Bound**, and **Compute and Latency Bound**. The following graph shows these categories related to compute and memory utilization:

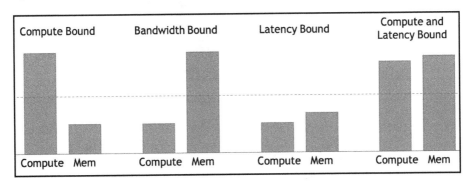

After we identify the limiter, we can use the next optimization strategy. If either resource's utilization is high, we can focus on the optimization of the resource. If both are under-utilized, we can apply latency optimization from I/O aspects of the system. If both are high, we can investigate whether there is a memory operation stalling issue and computing-related issue.

Now let's see how we can obtain that utilization information.

Finding the performance limiter and optimization

Now, let's apply this analysis to both reduction implementations. We will compare them and discuss how shared memory contributes to the performance limiter analysis with improved performance. First, let's profile the global memory-based reduction application with the metric analysis using the following command:

```
$ nvprof -o reduction_global.nvvp ./reduction_global
$ nvprof --analysis-metrics -o reduction_global_metric.nvvp
./reduction_global
```

Then, we will obtain the following chart from NVIDIA profiler, which shows the first global memory-based reduction's performance limiter:

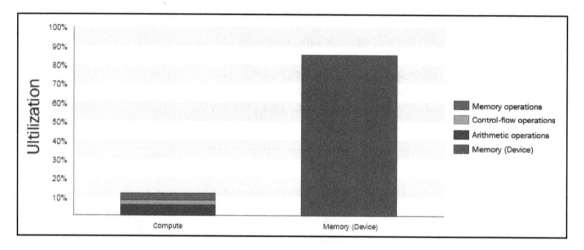

On this chart, we need to review performance execution ratio to see if it is balanced by checking the kernel latency analysis. Because, as you can see in the preceding chart, the utilization gap between **Compute** and **Memory** is large and this could mean there will be a lot of latency in compute due to memory bottleneck. The following graph shows the result of the sampling-based analysis, and we can determine that CUDA cores are starved due to the memory dependency:

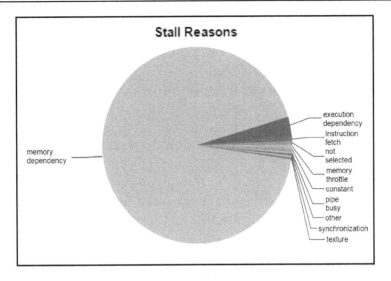

As you can see, the kernel execution is delayed due to memory waiting. Now, let's profile the reduction based on shared memory. We can do this with the following command:

```
$ nvprof -o reduction_shared.nvvp ./reduction_shared
$ nvprof --analysis-metrics -o reduction_shared_metric.nvvp
./reduction_shared
```

Then, we will obtain the following chart, which shows the second shared memory-based reduction's performance limiter:

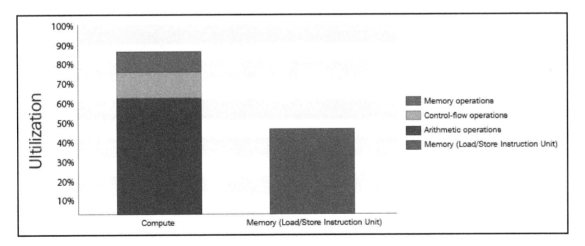

We can determine that it is compute-bounded and memory does not starve the CUDA cores.

Now let's review our kernel operation to optimize computing operations. The following code shows the parallel reduction part in the kernel function:

```
for (unsigned int stride = 1; stride < blockDim.x; stride *= 2) {
    if ( (idx_x % (stride * 2)) == 0 )
        s_data[threadIdx.x] += s_data[threadIdx.x + stride];
    __syncthreads();
}
```

As an arithmetic operation, modular is heavy operation. Since the stride variable is an exponential number of 2, it can be replaced with a bitwise operation, as follows:

```
for (unsigned int stride = 1; stride < blockDim.x; stride *= 2) {
    if ( (idx_x & (stride * 2 - 1)) == 0 )
        s_data[threadIdx.x] += s_data[threadIdx.x + stride];
    __syncthreads();
}
```

Run the following command to see the optimized output:

```
$ nvcc -run -m64 -gencode arch=compute_70,code=sm_70 -
I/usr/local/cuda/samples/common/inc -o reduction_shared
./reduction_shared.cpp reduction_shared_kernel.cu
```

Then, the new estimated time is **0.399 ms**, and we could achieve a more optimized performance, as shown in the following table:

Operation	Estimated time (ms)	Speed-up
Original approach (reduction with global memory)	4.609	1.0x
Reduction using shared memory	0.624	7.4x
Changing conditional operation from % to &	0.399	11.55x

The following graph shows the updated performance limiter:

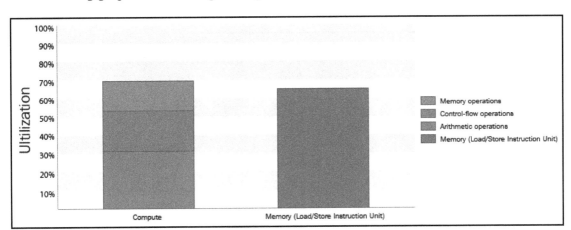

We can identify that its operation is **compute and latency bounded**. So, we can determine that we could increase memory utilization by optimizing computing efficiency.

Minimizing the CUDA warp divergence effect

In a **single instruction, multiple thread** (**SIMT**) execution model, threads are grouped into sets of 32 threads and each group is called a **warp**. If a warp encounters a conditional statement or branch, its threads can be diverged and serialized to execute each condition. This is called **branch divergence**, which impacts performance significantly.

CUDA warp divergence refers to such CUDA threads' divergent operation in a warp. If the conditional branch has an `if-else` structure and a warp has this warp divergence, all CUDA threads have an active and inactive operation part for the branched code block.

The following figure shows a warp divergence effect in a CUDA warp. CUDA threads that are not in the idle condition and reduce the efficient use of GPU threads:

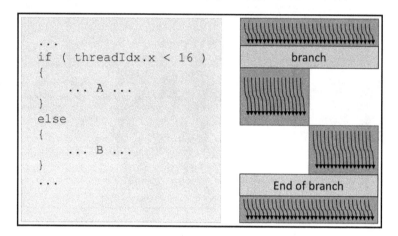

As more of the branched part becomes significant, the GPU scheduling throughput becomes inefficient. Therefore, we need to avoid or minimize this warp divergence effect. There are several options you can choose:

- Divergence avoidance by handling different warps to execute the branched part
- Coalescing the branched part to reduce branches in a warp
- Shortening the branched part; only critical parts to be branched
- Rearranging the data (that is, transposing, coalescing, and so on)
- Partitioning the group using `tiled_partition` in Cooperative Group

Determining divergence as a performance bottleneck

From the previous reduction optimization, you might find a warning about an inefficient kernel due to divergent branches in the computing analysis, as follows:

⚠ **Divergent Branches**

Compute resource are used most efficiently when all threads in a warp have the same branching behavior. When this does not occur the branch is said to be divergent. Divergent branches lower warp execution efficiency which leads to inefficient use of the GPU's compute resources.

Optimization: Select each entry below to open the source code to a divergent branch within the kernel. For each branch reduce the amount of intra-warp divergence.   More...

✓ _ine / File NA
      NA Divergence = 73.4% [3080192 divergent executions out of 4194304 total executions]
      NA Divergence = 12.5% [65536 divergent executions out of 524288 total executions]

73.4 % divergence means that we have an inefficient operation path. We can determine that the reduction addressing is the issue, highlighted next:

```
__global__ void reduction_kernel(float* d_out, float* d_in, unsigned int
size) {
    unsigned int idx_x = blockIdx.x * blockDim.x + threadIdx.x;

    extern __shared__ float s_data[];
    s_data[threadIdx.x] = (idx_x < size) ? d_in[idx_x] : 0.f;

    __syncthreads();

    // do reduction
    for (unsigned int stride = 1; stride < blockDim.x; stride *= 2) {
        // thread synchronous reduction
        if ( (idx_x % (stride * 2 - 1)) == 0 )
            s_data[threadIdx.x] += s_data[threadIdx.x + stride];
        __syncthreads();
    }

    if (threadIdx.x == 0)
        d_out[blockIdx.x] = s_data[0];
}
```

When it comes to reduction addressing, we can select one of these CUDA thread indexing strategies:

- Interleaved addressing
- Sequential addressing

Let's review what they are and compare their performance by implementing these strategies. Since we will just modify the reduction kernel, we can reuse the host code for the next two implementations.

Interleaved addressing

In this strategy, the consecutive CUDA threads to fetch input data using the interleaved addressing strategy. Compared to the previous version, CUDA threads access input data by increasing the stride value. The following diagram shows how CUDA threads are interleaved with reduction items:

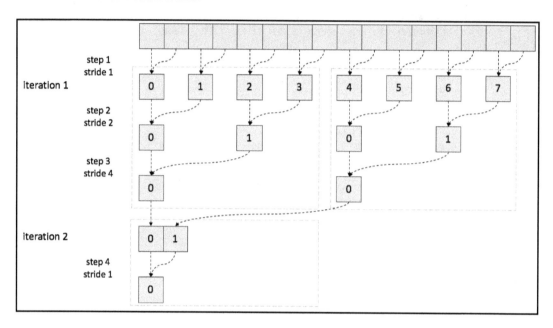

This interleaving addressing can be implemented as follows:

```
__global__ void
 interleaved_reduction_kernel(float* g_out, float* g_in, unsigned int size)
{
    unsigned int idx_x = blockIdx.x * blockDim.x + threadIdx.x;

    extern __shared__ float s_data[];
    s_data[threadIdx.x] = (idx_x < size) ? g_in[idx_x] : 0.f;
    __syncthreads();

    // do reduction
    // interleaved addressing
    for (unsigned int stride = 1; stride < blockDim.x; stride *= 2) {
        int index = 2 * stride * threadIdx.x;
        if (index < blockDim.x)
            s_data[index] += s_data[index + stride];
        __syncthreads();
    }
```

```
        if (threadIdx.x == 0)
            g_out[blockIdx.x] = s_data[0];
    }
```

Run the following command to compile the preceding code:

```
$ nvcc -run -m64 -gencode arch=compute_70,code=sm_70 -
I/usr/local/cuda/samples/common/inc -o reduction ./reduction.cpp
./reduction_kernel_interleaving.cu
```

The measured kernel execution time is **0.446 ms** on the Tesla V100. It is slower than the previous version because each thread block is not fully utilized in this approach. We would be able to get more detail by profiling its metrics.

Now we will try another addressing approach, which is designed so that each thread block computes more data.

Sequential addressing

Compared to previous versions, this has highly coalesced indexing and addressing. This design is more efficient because there is no divergence when the stride size is greater than the warp size. The following diagram shows a coalesced thread operation:

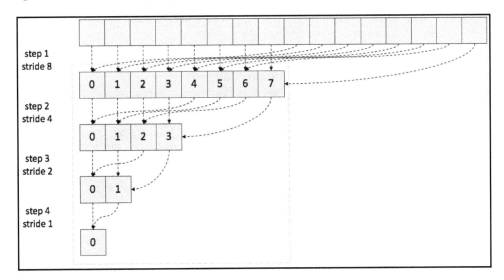

Now, let's write a kernel function to use sequential addressing on the reduction items:

```
__global__ void
 sequantial_reduction_kernel(float *g_out, float *g_in,
                             unsigned int size)
{
    unsigned int idx_x = blockIdx.x * blockDim.x + threadIdx.x;

    extern __shared__ float s_data[];

    s_data[threadIdx.x] = (idx_x < size) ? g_in[idx_x] : 0.f;

    __syncthreads();

    // do reduction
    // sequential addressing
    for (unsigned int stride = blockDim.x / 2; stride > 0;
        stride >>= 1)
    {
        if (threadIdx.x < stride)
            s_data[threadIdx.x] += s_data[threadIdx.x + stride];

        __syncthreads();
    }

    if (threadIdx.x == 0)
        g_out[blockIdx.x] = s_data[0];
}
```

Run the following command to compile the preceding code:

```
$ nvcc -run -m64 -gencode arch=compute_70,code=sm_70 -
I/usr/local/cuda/samples/common/inc -o reduction ./reduction.cpp
./reduction_kernel_sequential.cu
```

Its measured execution time is **0.378 ms** on a Tesla V100 GPU, which is slightly faster than the previous strategy (0.399 ms).

Thanks to the warp divergence avoiding, we could obtain a **12.2x** performance gain on the original compute. The following graph shows the updated performance limiter analysis:

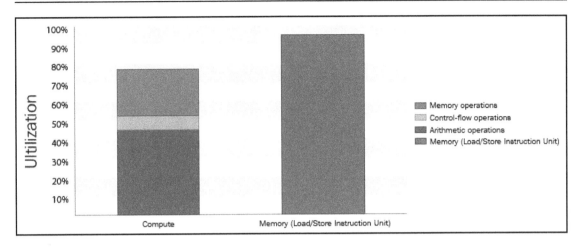

Compared to the previous performance limiter, we can see the reduced control-flow operation and increased memory utilization.

Performance modeling and balancing the limiter

Following the performance limiter analysis, our current reduction performance is bounded by the compute latency due to the memory bandwidth, although the limiter analysis shows the full utilization of each resource. Let's cover why this is an issue and how we can resolve this by following the Roofline performance model.

The Roofline model

The **Roofline model** is an intuitive visual performance analysis model used to provide estimated performance for a given computing kernel on a parallel processing unit. Based on this model, developers in parallel programming can identify what the algorithm should be bounded to and determine which should be optimized.

The following graph shows an example of the Roofline model:

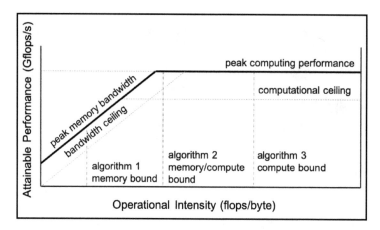

The slanted part means memory-bound, and the flat part means arithmetic-bound. Each parallel algorithm and implementation has its own Roofline model since they have different computing power and memory bandwidth. With this model, algorithms can be placed depending on their operational intensity (flops/bytes). If an implementation does not meet the expected performance of this model, we can determine that this version is bounded by latency.

Considering our parallel reduction's complexity, it must be memory-bound. In other words, it has low operational intensity, so our strategy should maximize memory bandwidth as much as possible.

Therefore, we need to confirm how our reduction kernel function consumes memory bandwidth using the performance analysis in the profiler. The following diagram shows the global memory's bandwidth usages:

Device Memory		
Reads	2097160	326.939 GB/s
Writes	105437	16.437 GB/s
Total	2202597	343.376 GB/s

Idle   Low   Medium   High   Max

As we can see in this diagram, we didn't achieve full utilization of the memory bandwidth. The total bandwidth is 343.376 GB/s on a Tesla V100 GPU, which utilizes about one-third of the bandwidth since this GPU has 900 GB/s bandwidth HBM2 memory. Therefore, the next step is to increase bandwidth usage by letting each CUDA thread digest more data. This will resolve the latency-bound situation and make our application be bounded to memory bandwidth.

Now, let's cover how to increase memory bandwidth.

Maximizing memory bandwidth with grid-strided loops

We can achieve this with a simple idea. The reduction problem allows us to accumulate input data with CUDA threads and start a reduction operation. Previously, our reduction implementation started with the input data size. But now, we will iterate to the input data with a group of CUDA threads, and that size will be the grid size of our kernel function. This style of iteration is called grid-strided loops. This technique has many benefits to control multiple CUDA cores, and they are introduced in this document: https://devblogs.nvidia.com/cuda-pro-tip-write-flexible-kernels-grid-stride-loops.

The following code shows the updated reduction kernel function:

```
__global__ void reduction_kernel(float *g_out, float *g_in,
                                 unsigned int size) {
    unsigned int idx_x = blockIdx.x * blockDim.x + threadIdx.x;
    extern __shared__ float s_data[];

    // cumulates input with grid-stride loop
    // and save to the shared memory
    float input = 0.f;
    for (int i = idx_x; i < size; i += blockDim.x * gridDim.x)
        input += g_in[i];
    s_data[threadIdx.x] = input;
    __syncthreads();

    // do reduction
    for (unsigned int stride = blockDim.x / 2; stride > 0;
         stride >>= 1) {
        if (threadIdx.x < stride)
            s_data[threadIdx.x] += s_data[threadIdx.x + stride];
        __syncthreads();
    }
    if (threadIdx.x == 0)
```

```
            g_out[blockIdx.x] = s_data[0];
    }
```

You will find that this kernel function focuses on accumulating input data first, and then it reduces the loaded data.

Now, we need to determine the grid size. To make our GPU code run on various GPU targets, we have to determine their size at runtime. Also, we need to utilize all the multiprocessors in the GPU. CUDA C provides related functions. We can obtain the occupancy-aware maximum active blocks per multiprocessor using the `cudaOccpancyMaxActiveBlocksPerMultiprocessor()` function. Also, we can obtain the multiprocessor numbers on the target GPU using the `cudaDeviceGetAttribte()` function. The following code shows how we can use those functions and call the kernel function:

```
int reduction(float *g_outPtr, float *g_inPtr, int size, int n_threads)
{
    int num_sms;
    int num_blocks_per_sm;
    cudaDeviceGetAttribute(&num_sms,
                        cudaDevAttrMultiProcessorCount, 0);
    cudaOccupancyMaxActiveBlocksPerMultiprocessor(&num_blocks_per_sm,
            reduction_kernel, n_threads, n_threads*sizeof(float));
    int n_blocks = min(num_blocks_per_sm * num_sms, (size
                    + n_threads - 1) / n_threads);
    reduction_kernel<<<n_blocks, n_threads, n_threads *
                    sizeof(float), 0>>>(g_outPtr, g_inPtr, size);
    reduction_kernel<<<1, n_threads, n_threads * sizeof(float),
                    0>>>(g_outPtr, g_inPtr, n_blocks);
    return 1;
}
```

There is one additional modification in this function. To save the occupancy calculation overhead, it launches the `reduction_kernel()` function once more with a single block. Run the following command:

```
$ nvcc -run -m64 -gencode arch=compute_70,code=sm_70 -
I/usr/local/cuda/samples/common/inc -o reduction ./reduction.cpp
./reduction_kernel.cu
```

The updated reduction performance is **0.278 ms** on a Tesla V100, which is about 100 ms faster than the previous method.

Now, let's review how we could utilize the memory bandwidth. The following diagram shows the memory utilization analysis in the Visual Profiler, and shows how we increased the memory bandwidth twice:

Device Memory			
Reads	2097216	616.386 GB/s	
Writes	87771	25.797 GB/s	
Total	2184987	642.183 GB/s	Idle Low Medium High Max

Although it shows an increased bandwidth, we still have room to increase it further. Let's cover how we can achieve more bandwidth.

Balancing the I/O throughput

From the result we got from the profiler, the local variable input has a substantial amount of load/store requests. Such massive I/O impacts the thread block's scheduling due to the operational dependency. The worst thing in the current data accumulation is that it has a dependency on device memory. So, we will use extra registers to issue more load instructions to ease the dependency. The following code shows how we can do this:

```
#define NUM_LOAD 4
__global__ void
 reduction_kernel(float *g_out, float *g_in, unsigned int size)
{
    unsigned int idx_x = blockIdx.x * blockDim.x + threadIdx.x;

    extern __shared__ float s_data[];

    // cumulates input with grid-stride loop
    // and save to the shared memory
    float input[NUM_LOAD] = {0.f};
    for (int i = idx_x; i < size; i += blockDim.x *
        gridDim.x * NUM_LOAD)
    {
        for (int step = 0; step < NUM_LOAD; step++)
            input[step] += (i + step * blockDim.x * gridDim.x < size) ?
                g_in[i + step * blockDim.x * gridDim.x] : 0.f;
    }
    for (int i = 1; i < NUM_LOAD; i++)
        input[0] += input[i];
    s_data[threadIdx.x] = input[0];
```

```
      __syncthreads();

      // do reduction
      for (unsigned int stride = blockDim.x / 2; stride > 0;
           stride >>= 1)
      {
          if (threadIdx.x < stride)
              s_data[threadIdx.x] += s_data[threadIdx.x + stride];
          __syncthreads();
      }

      if (threadIdx.x == 0) {
          g_out[blockIdx.x] = s_data[0];
      }
  }
```

This code uses three more registers to collect global memory data. The value of `NUM_LOAD` can vary depending on the GPU because it is affected by the GPU's memory bandwidth and the number of CUDA cores in a GPU:

On running the following command, the achieved performance using Tesla V100 card is **0.264** ms:

```
$ nvcc -run -m64 -gencode arch=compute_70,code=sm_70 -
I/usr/local/cuda/samples/common/inc -o reduction ./reduction.cpp
./reduction_kernel_opt.cu
```

Warp-level primitive programming

CUDA 9.0 introduces new warp synchronous programming. This major change aims to avoid CUDA programming relying on implicit warp synchronize operations and handling synchronous targets explicitly. This helps to prevent inattentive race conditions and deadlocks in warp-wise synchronous operations.

Historically, CUDA provided only one explicit synchronization API, `__syncthreads()` for the CUDA threads in a thread block and it relied on the implicit synchronization of a warp. The following figure shows two levels of synchronization of a CUDA thread block's operation:

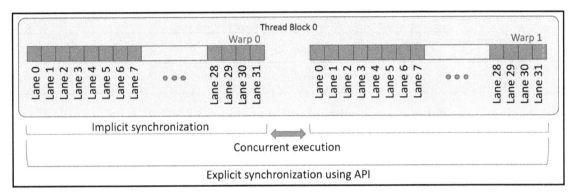

However, the latest GPU architectures (Volta and Turing) have an enhanced thread control model, where each thread can execute a different instruction, while they keep its SIMT programming model. The following diagram shows how it has changed:

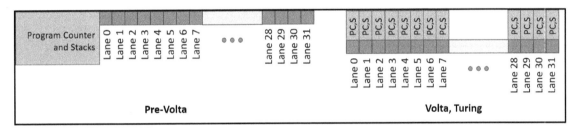

Until the Pascal architecture (left), threads were scheduled at warp level, and they were synchronized implicitly within a warp. Therefore, CUDA threads in a warp synchronized implicitly. However, this had unintended deadlock potential.

The Volta architecture renovated this and introduced **independent thread scheduling**. This control model enables each CUDA thread to have its program counter and allows sets of participating threads in a warp. In this model, we have to use an explicit synchronous API to specify each CUDA thread's operations.

As a result, CUDA 9 introduced explicit warp-level primitive functions:

	Warp-level primitive functions
Identifying active threads	`__activemask()`
Masking active threads	`__all_sync(), __any_sync(), __uni_sync(), __ballot_sync()` `__match_any_sync(), __match_all_sync()`
Synchronized data exchange	`__shfl_sync(), __shfl_up_sync(), __shfl_down_sync(), __shfl_xor_sync()`
Threads synchronization	`__syncwarp()`

There are three categories of warp-wise primitive functions, which are warp identification, warp operations, and synchronization. All these functions implicitly specify synchronization targets to avoid unintended race conditions.

Parallel reduction with warp primitives

Let's see how this can benefit our parallel reduction implementation. This recipe will use the `shfl_down()` function in Cooperative Groups, and `shfl_down_sync()` in warp primitive functions. The following figure shows how shift down operation works with `shfl_down_sync()`:

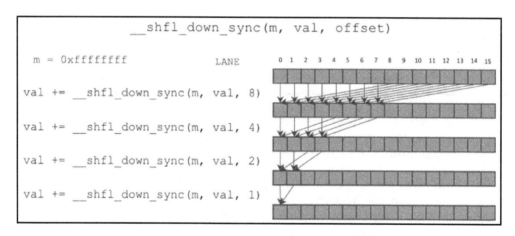

In this collective operation, CUDA threads in a warp can shift a specified register value to another thread in the same warp and synchronize with it. To be specific, the collective operation has two steps (the third one is optional):

1. Identifying, masking, or ballot sourcing CUDA threads in a warp that will have an operation.
2. Letting CUDA thread shift data.
3. All the CUDA threads in a warp are synchronization (optional).

For the parallel reduction problem, we can use warp-level reduction using __shfl_down_sync(). Now, we can enhance our thread block-level reduction with the following figure:

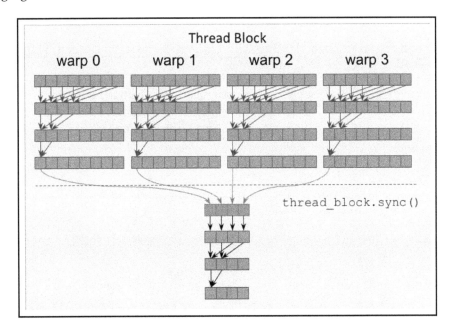

Each warp's reduction result is stored to shared memory to share with other warp. Then, the final block-wise reduction can be obtained by doing warp-wise collection again.

We use __shfl_down_sync() since we need only one thread to have warp-level reduction. If you need to make all the CUDA threads have warp-level reduction, you can use __shfl_xor_sync() instead.

The number of the first block-level reductions is the dimension of the grid, and the outputs are stored in global memory. By calling once again, we can build a parallel reduction kernel using a warp-level synchronous function.

Now, let's implement warp-level reduction using warp-level primitive functions. Firstly, we will write a function that uses warp-shifting functions to make warp-level reductions. The following code shows how this can be implemented:

```
__inline__ __device__ float warp_reduce_sum(float val) {
    for (int offset = warpSize / 2; offset > 0; offset >>= 1) {
        unsigned int mask = __activemask();
        val += __shfl_down_sync(mask, val, offset);
    }
    return val;
}
```

For the warp-shifting, we need to let the CUDA scheduler identify the active threads and let the warp-shifting function do the reduction.

The second step is to write a block-level reduction function using the previous warp-level reduction. We will collect the previous result in the shared memory and make the second reduction from the result. The following code shows how this can be implemented:

```
__inline__ __device__ float block_reduce_sum(float val) {
    // Shared mem for 32 partial sums
    static __shared__ float shared[32];
    int lane = threadIdx.x % warpSize;
    int wid = threadIdx.x / warpSize;

    val = warp_reduce_sum(val); // Warp-level partial reduction
    if (lane == 0)
        shared[wid] = val; // Write reduced value to shared memory
    __syncthreads(); // Wait for all partial reductions

    //read from shared memory only if that warp existed
    if (wid == 0) {
        val = (threadIdx.x < blockDim.x / warpSize) ? shared[lane] : 0;
        val = warp_reduce_sum(val); //Final reduce within first warp
    }
    return val;
}
```

Now, we will implement the reduction kernel function that cumulates input data, and do the reduction from the block-level reduction that we have implemented. Since we just focused on optimizing warp-level optimization, the overall design is the same as the previous version. The following code shows the kernel function:

```
__global__ void
reduction_kernel(float *g_out, float *g_in, unsigned int size) {
    unsigned int idx_x = blockIdx.x * blockDim.x + threadIdx.x;
    // cumulates input with grid-stride loop and save to share memory
    float sum[NUM_LOAD] = { 0.f };
    for (int i = idx_x; i < size; i += blockDim.x * gridDim.x * NUM_LOAD) {
        for (int step = 0; step < NUM_LOAD; step++)
            sum[step] += (i + step * blockDim.x * gridDim.x < size) ?
g_in[i + step * blockDim.x * gridDim.x] : 0.f;
    }
    for (int i = 1; i < NUM_LOAD; i++)
        sum[0] += sum[i];
    // warp synchronous reduction
    sum[0] = block_reduce_sum(sum[0]);

    if (threadIdx.x == 0)
        g_out[blockIdx.x] = sum[0];
}
```

Then, let's compile the code using the following command:

```
$ nvcc -run -m64 -gencode arch=compute_70,code=sm_70 -
I/usr/local/cuda/samples/common/inc -o reduction ./reduction.cpp
./reduction_wp_kernel.cu
```

The following screenshot shows the reduction in execution time:

```
18:03:55  jahan@groot    ...cuda-workspace/03_cuda_thread_programming/07_warp_synchronous_programming
$ nvcc -run -m64 -gencode arch=compute_70,code=sm_70 -I/usr/local/cuda/samples/common/inc -o reduction ./reduction.cpp ./reduction_wp_kernel.cu
Time= 0.259 msec, bandwidth= 259.017578 GB/s
host: 0.996007, device 0.996007
```

No host code modification was available to switch from the warp-primitive to Cooperative Groups. So, we could use the same host code for the two reduction implementations.

We have covered warp synchronous programming in CUDA. Its application is not only limited to reduction but can be used for other parallel algorithms: scan, bitonic sort, and transpose. If you need to learn more, you can checkout the following articles:

- `http://on-demand.gputechconf.com/gtc/2017/presentation/s7622-Kyrylo-perelygin-robust-and-scalable-cuda.pdf`
- `https://devblogs.nvidia.com/using-cuda-warp-level-primitives/`
- `https://devblogs.nvidia.com/faster-parallel-reductions-kepler/`
- `http://on-demand.gputechconf.com/gtc/2013/presentations/S3174-Kepler-Shuffle-Tips-Tricks.pdf`

Cooperative Groups for flexible thread handling

CUDA 9.0 introduces a new CUDA programming feature named **Cooperative Groups**. This introduces a new CUDA programming design pattern for CUDA collective operations by specifying group-wise operations. Using this, programmers can write CUDA code that controls CUDA threads explicitly.

To begin with, let's see what Cooperative Groups is and its programming advantages.

Cooperative Groups in a CUDA thread block

Cooperative Groups provides explicit CUDA thread-grouping objects, which help programmers to write collective operations more clearly and conveniently. For instance, we need to obtain a mask to control the active CUDA threads in a warp to have warp-shifting operations. Cooperative Group objects, on the other hand, bind the available threads as a tile, and we control them as an object. This brings C++ language benefits to the CUDA C programming.

The fundamental type of Cooperative Group is `thread_group`. This enables a C++ class-style type, `thread_group`, which can provide its configuration information with the `is_valid()`, `size()`, and `thread_rank()` functions. Also, this provides collective functions that can apply to all the CUDA threads in a group. These functions are as follows:

	thread_group collective functions
Identifying active threads	`tiled_partition()`, `coalesced_threads()`
Masking active threads	`any()`, `all()`, `ballot()` `match_any()`, `match_all()`
Synchronized data exchange	`shfl()`, `shfl_up()`, `shfl_down()`, `shfl_xor()`
Thread synchronization	`sync()`

These function lists are similar to warp-level primitive functions. So, warp-level primitive operations can be replaced with Cooperative Groups. `thread_group` can be split by a smaller `thread_group`, `thread_block_tile`, or `coalesced_group`.

Cooperative Groups also provides flexibility in thread block programming. Using the following line of code, we can handle a thread block:

```
thread_block block = this_thread_block();
```

`thread_block` provides CUDA built-in keyword wrapping functions, which we use to obtain a block index and thread index:

```
dim3 group_index();   // 3-dimensional block index within the grid
dim3 thread_index();  // 3-dimensional thread index within the block
```

We can obtain a thread block object using `this_thread_block()`, as follows:

```
thread_block block = this_thread_block();
```

Now, let's see what the benefits of Cooperative Groups are compared to traditional CUDA built-in variables.

Benefits of Cooperative Groups

Using Cooperative Groups provides more C++ programmability, rather than using traditional CUDA built-in variables. Using a `thread_block` group, you can switch your kernel code from using built-in variables to Cooperative Group's indexing. But, the real power of Cooperative Groups is more than that. Let's cover its benefits in the following sections.

Modularity

With Cooperative Groups, programmers can modularize their collective operation kernel codes corresponding to the barrier target. This helps to avoid oversights, causing deadlock and race conditions by assuming all threads are running concurrently. The following is an example of a deadlock and normal operations by CUDA thread synchronization:

```
int tid = ...

If (tid < blockDim.x) {
    ... A ...
    __syncthreads()
}
... B ...
```

```
int tid = ...

If (tid < blockDim.x) {
    ... A ...
}
... B ...
__syncthreads()
```

Deadlock
Some branched threads wait for other threads, and the other threads wait for the branched threads

Works without halt
All the threads in a block can meet this __syncthreads() barrier.

For the left-hand side example, the kernel code intends to synchronize a part of the thread in a CUDA thread block. This code minimizes synchronization overhead by specifying barrier targets. However, it introduces a deadlock situation because __syncthreads() invokes a barrier, which waits for all CUDA threads to reach the barrier. However, __synchthroead() cannot meet the others and waits. The right-handed side example shows sound operation since it does not have any deadlock point because all the threads in the thread block can meet __syncthreads().

In the Cooperative Groups API, on the other hand, the CUDA programmers specify thread groups to synchronize. The Cooperative Groups enable explicit synchronization targets so that the programmers can let CUDA threads synchronize explicitly. This item can also be treated as an instance so that we can pass the instance to the device functions.

The following code shows how Cooperative Groups provide explicit synchronization objects and let them be handled as an instance:

```
__device__ bar(thread_group block, float *x) {
    ...
    block.sync();
    ...
}

__global__ foo() {
    bar(this_thread_block(), float *x);
}
```

As you can see in the preceding example code, the kernel code can specify synchronization groups and pass them as a parameter as a `thread_group`. This helps us to specify the synchronize targets in the subroutines. Therefore, programmers can prevent inadvertent deadlock by using Cooperative Groups. Also, we can set different types of groups as a `thread_group` type and reuse synchronization code.

Explicit grouped threads' operation and race condition avoidance

Cooperative Groups support warp-level cooperative operations by tiling threads in a warp. If the tile size matches the warp size, CUDA can omit warps' implicit synchronization, ensuring correct memory operation to avoid race conditions. By eliminating implicit synchronizations, the GPU's performance can be enhanced. Historically, experienced CUDA programmers used separated warps for warp-level synchronizations. This meant the cooperative operations in a warp did not have to sync with other warp operations. This unleashed GPU performance. However, it was risky because it introduces race conditions between cooperative operations.

Dynamic active thread selection

Another benefit of CUDA Cooperative Groups is that the programmers can pick active threads in a warp to avoid a branch divergence effect. Since CUDA is a SIMT architecture, an instruction unit issues a group of threads, and there is no way to disable divergence if they meet a branch. But, from CUDA 9.0 onward, programmer can select active threads that will be active in the branched block using `coalesced_threads()`. This returns coalesced threads by disabling threads that do not take branches. Then, SM's instruction unit issues the next threads that are active in the active thread group.

Applying to the parallel reduction

We will update the previous reduction kernel code to use the Cooperative Group. From the previous kernel code, you can easily apply Cooperative Groups' `thread_block`, as follows:

```
__global__ void
reduction_kernel(float* g_out, float* g_in, unsigned int size)
{
    unsigned int idx_x = blockIdx.x * blockDim.x + threadIdx.x;

    thread_block block = this_thread_block();

    extern __shared__ float s_data[];
```

We don't have to update the data input accumulation part, so let's update the reduction parts for each thread block. The following code shows an example of block-sized reduction:

```
// do reduction
for (unsigned int stride = block.group_dim().x / 2; stride > 0;
    stride >>= 1) {
    if (block.thread_index().x < stride) {
        s_data[block.thread_index().x] +=
            s_data[block.thread_index().x + stride];
        block.sync(); // threads synchronization in a branch
    }
}
}
```

The estimated operation performance is 0.264 ms using the following command:

```
$ nvcc -run -m64 -gencode arch=compute_70,code=sm_70 -
I/usr/local/cuda/samples/common/inc -o reduction_cg -rdc=true
./reduction.cpp ./reduction_cg_kernel.cu
```

The preceding command shows the same performance as in the previous version.

Cooperative Groups to avoid deadlock

Cooperative Groups can support independent CUDA threads scheduling. So, we can control CUDA threads individually with a group, and synchronize them explicitly. The target group can be a predefined tile, but it can also be determined following the conditional branch, as follows:

```
// do reduction
for (unsigned int stride = block.group_dim().x / 2; stride > 0;
    stride >>= 1) {
```

```
    // scheduled threads reduce for every iteration
    // and will be smaller than a warp size (32) eventually.
    if (block.thread_index().x < stride) {
        s_data[block.thread_index().x] += s_data[
                        block.thread_index().x + stride];

        // __syncthreads();  // (3) Error. Deadlock.
        // block.sync();     // (4) Okay. Benefit of Cooperative Group
    }
    // __syncthreads();      // (1) Okay
    block.sync();            // (2) Okay
}
```

This code has four-thread block synchronization options. Options (1) and (2) are equivalent operations with different APIs. On the other hand, options (3) and (4) are not. Option (3) introduces a deadlock of CUDA threads, and the host cannot have the return of the CUDA kernel, because active CUDA threads cannot synchronize with the non-activated CUDA threads. On the other hand, option (4) works thanks to Cooperative Groups' automatic active thread identification. This helps us to avoid unintended errors and develop sophisticated algorithms easily.

> NVIDIA provides detailed descriptions of Cooperative Groups in the following documents:
>
> - https://devblogs.nvidia.com/cuda-9-features-revealed
> - http://on-demand.gputechconf.com/gtc/2017/presentation/s7622-Kyrylo-perelygin-robust-and-scalable-cuda.pdf
>
> You can also learn about its architecture and full API lists from cooperative_groups.h itself.

Loop unrolling in the CUDA kernel

CUDA can also reap the benefits of loop unrolling like other programming languages. With this technique, CUDA threads can reduce or remove loop control overheads such as *the end of loop* tests on each iteration, branch penalties, and so on.

CUDA Compiler unrolls small loops automatically if it can identify the number of iterations for the loops. Programmers can also place the #pragma unroll directive to give a hint to the compiler, or just rewrite the loop code as a group of independent statements. Applying loop unrolling is simple, so you can easily apply this to your current working code.

Let's apply this to our parallel reduction implementation. Like the normal loop unrolling directive in C/C++, we can place the `#pragma` loop unrolling directive on top of `for` loops. The NVCC compiler can unroll the loop since the compiler can obtain the exact size of `group.size()` by itself:

```
template <typename group_t>
__inline__ __device__ float
  warp_reduce_sum(group_t group, float val)
{
    #pragma unroll
    for (int offset = group.size() / 2; offset > 0; offset >>= 1)
        val += group.shfl_down(val, offset);
    return val;
}
```

The estimated operation performance is 0.263 ms using the following command:

```
$ nvcc -run -m64 -gencode arch=compute_70,code=sm_70 -
I/usr/local/cuda/samples/common/inc -o reduction_cg -rdc=true
./reduction.cpp ./reduction_cg_kernel.cu
```

If you prefer to use the warp primitive function, you can write `warp_reduce_sum` like the following. Loop code can be reused by replacing `group.size()` with `warpSize`, but this was slightly faster in this case:

```
#define FULL_MASK 0xFFFFFFFF
__inline__ __device__ float
warp_reduce_sum(float val) {
#pragma unroll 5
    for (int offset = 1; offset < 6; offset++)
        val += __shfl_down_sync(FULL_MASK, val, warpSize >> offset);
    return val;
}
```

Run the following command to compile the preceding code:

```
nvcc -run -m64 -gencode arch=compute_70,code=sm_70 -
I/usr/local/cuda/samples/common/inc -o reduction_wp -rdc=true
./reduction.cpp ./reduction_wp_kernel.cu
```

Its result is 0.263 ms, the same as the previous result.

There is a pitfall of using loop unrolling. The unrolled code execution may result in lower occupancy by the increased register usage. Also, there can be a higher instruction cache miss penalty by the increased code execution size.

Atomic operations

In CUDA programming, programmers can use atomic APIs to update shared resources from multiple CUDA threads. These atomic API guarantee to eliminate race conditions to the shared resource, so we can expect consistent outputs from the parallel execution. This operation is especially useful for getting statistical parameters such as a histogram, mean, sum, and so on. We can also simplify the code implementation. For example, the reduction operation can be written using the atomicAdd() function in the following code:

```
__global__ void
atomic_reduction_kernel(float *data_out, float *data_in, int size)
{
    int idx_x = blockIdx.x * blockDim.x + threadIdx.x;
    atomicAdd(&data_out[0], data_in[idx_x]);
}
```

As you can see, the atomic function simplifies the required operation. However, its performance is slow because the atomic operation serializes all the requests to the shared resource. Run the following command to see the execution time:

```
$ nvcc −run −m64 −gencode arch=compute_70,code=sm_70 −
I/usr/local/cuda/samples/common/inc −o mixed_precision_single
./mixed_precision.cu
```

This kernel function shown took 39 ms on my Tesla V100, which is far slower than the original version (4.609 ms). Therefore, the recommended atomic operation usage is to limit the request only if it is necessary. For the parallel reduction problem, for instance, we can reduce items in parallel at a certain level and use the atomic operation to output the final result.

The following diagram shows another possible approach. This replaces block-wise reduction as `atomicAdd`:

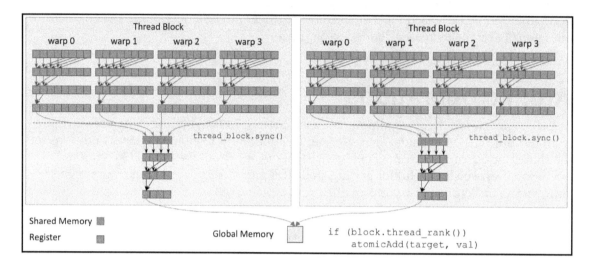

In the preceding diagram, we can see that there are two reduction points: a **warp** and a **thread block**, and, the block-wise reduction result is accumulated by the single global memory variable atomically. As a result, we can eliminate the second reduction iteration. The following screenshot shows the **Kernel Optimization Priorities** (on the left) and the **Performance Limiter Analysis** (on the right) of the second reduction iteration:

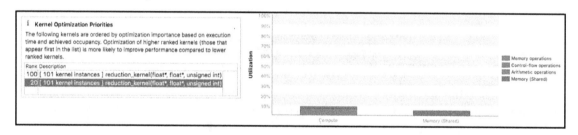

Kernel Optimization Priorities with Performance Limiter Analysis (2nd iteration)

In other words, the second iteration's performance is bounded by the latency due to its small grid size. So, we would be able to reduce the execution time by removing this.

Now let's implement that design and see how the performance can be changed. We just need to update the last part of the reduction kernel function:

```
__global__ void
reduction_kernel(float* g_out, float* g_in, unsigned int size)
```

```
{
    unsigned int idx_x = blockIdx.x * (2 * blockDim.x) + threadIdx.x;

    thread_block block = this_thread_block();

    // cumulates input with grid-stride loop and save to share memory
    float sum[NUM_LOAD] = { 0.f };
    for (int i = idx_x; i < size; i += blockDim.x
        * gridDim.x * NUM_LOAD)
    {
        for (int step = 0; step < NUM_LOAD; step++)
            sum[step] += (i + step * blockDim.x * gridDim.x < size) ?
                         g_in[i + step * blockDim.x * gridDim.x] : 0.f;
    }
    for (int i = 1; i < NUM_LOAD; i++)
        sum[0] += sum[i];
    // warp synchronous reduction
    sum[0] = block_reduce_sum(block, sum[0]);

    sum[0] = block_reduce_sum(sum[0]);

    // Performing Atomic Add per block
    if (block.thread_rank() == 0) {
        atomicAdd(&g_out[0], sum);
    }
}
```

Then, we will remove the second iterative function call. As a result, we can remove kernel call latency and achieve better performance if the atomic operation's latency is shorter than that. Run the following command:

```
$ nvcc -run -m64 -gencode arch=compute_70,code=sm_70 -
I/usr/local/cuda/samples/common/inc -o reduction_atomic_block
./reduction.cpp ./reduction_blk_atmc_kernel.cu
```

Fortunately, the estimated execution time is 0.259 ms on a Tesla V100, so we could achieve a slightly enhanced result.

If you want to learn more about atomic operations in CUDA C, please checkout the programming guide at this link: https://docs.nvidia.com/cuda/cuda-c-programming-guide/index.html#atomic-functions.

Low/mixed precision operations

Mixed precision is a technique for exploring low-precision, and obtains a high accuracy result. This technique computes core operations with low precision and generates output with high-precision operations. Low precision operation computation has the benefits of reduced memory bandwidth and higher computing throughput compared with high-precision computing. If low precision suffices to get target accuracy from an application with high precision, this technique can benefit performance with this trade-off. NVIDIA Developer Blog introduces this programmability: https://devblogs.nvidia.com/mixed-precision-programming-cuda-8.

In these circumstances, CUDA extends its supports to low-precision tools lower than 32-bit data types, such as 8/16-bit integers (INT8/INT16) and 16-bit floating points (FP16). For those low-precision data types, a GPU can use **single instruction, multiple data** (**SIMD**) operations with some specific APIs. In this section, we will look at these two kinds of instructions for low-precision operations for a mixed-precision purpose.

To get benefits from this, you need to confirm that your GPU can support low mixed-precision operations and supporting data types. Supporting low-precision computing is possible in specific GPUs, and the precision varies depending on the GPU chipsets. To be specific, GP102 (Tesla P40 and Titan X), GP104 (Tesla P4), and GP106 support INT8; and GP100 (Tesla P100) and GV100 (Tesla V100) support FP16 (half-precision) operations. The Tesla GV100 is compatible with INT8 operation and has no performance degradation.

CUDA has some special intrinsic functions that enable SIMD operations for low-precision data types.

Half-precision operation

CUDA provides intrinsic functions for the half-sized float data type (FP16) and developers can choose whether CUDA computes one or two values for each instruction. CUDA also provides type conversion functions between single-precision and half-precision. Due to the accuracy limitation of FP16, you must use the conversion intrinsic to work with single-precision values.

Now, let's implement and test the GPU's FP16 operation. GPUs can support the native computing with this type higher than computing capability 5.3. But some GPUs do not support this, so please double-check whether your GPU supports this half-precision operation.

The half-precision datatype in CUDA C is `half`, but you can use the __half type too. For the API, CUDA provides relevant intrinsic functions with this datatype such as __hfma(), __hmul(), and __hadd(). These intrinsic functions also provide native operations with two data at one time using __hfma2(), __hmul2(), and __hadd2(). With these functions, we can write mixed-precision operation kernel code:

```
__global__ void hfma_kernel(half *d_x, half *d_y, float *d_z, int size)
{
    int idx_x = blockIdx.x * blockDim.x + threadIdx.x;
    int stride = gridDim.x * blockDim.x;

    half2 *dual_x = reinterpret_cast<half2*>(d_x);
    half2 *dual_y = reinterpret_cast<half2*>(d_y);
    float2 *dual_z = reinterpret_cast<float2*>(d_z);

    extern __shared__ float2 s_data[];

#if __CUDA_ARCH__ >= 530
    for (int i = idx_x; i < size; i+=stride) {
        s_data[threadIdx.x] = __half22float2(__hmul2(dual_y[i],
                                                     dual_x[i]));
        __syncthreads();
        dual_z[i] = s_data[threadIdx.x];
    }
    #else
    for (int i = idx_x; i < size; i+=stride) {
        s_data[threadIdx.x] = __half22float2(dual_x[i]) *
                              __half22float2(dual_y[i]);
        __syncthreads();
        dual_z[i] = s_data[threadIdx.x];
    }
    #endif
}
```

For those GPUs that do not support native half-precision operations, our code checks CUDA's compute capability at compile time and determines which operation it should take.

The following code calls the kernel function with the half-sized grid size since each CUDA thread will operate two data:

```
int n_threads = 256;
int num_sms;
int num_blocks_per_sm;
cudaDeviceGetAttribute(&num_sms, cudaDevAttrMultiProcessorCount, 0);
cudaOccupancyMaxActiveBlocksPerMultiprocessor(&num_blocks_per_sm,
    hfma_kernel, n_threads, n_threads*sizeof(float2));
```

```
int n_blocks = min(num_blocks_per_sm * num_sms,
                   (size/2 + n_threads - 1) / n_threads);
hfma_kernel<<< n_blocks, n_threads, n_threads * sizeof(float2)
            >>>(X.d_ptr_, Y.d_ptr_, Z.d_ptr_, size/2);
```

Other initialization code and benchmark code is implemented in the sample recipe code, so please review it.

We have covered FMA operations in FP16 precision operations. CUDA C provides various half-precision operations (`https://docs.nvidia.com/cuda/cuda-math-api/group__CUDA__MATH__INTRINSIC__HALF.html`). Please check that for the other operations.

Dot product operations and accumulation for 8-bit integers and 16-bit data (DP4A and DP2A)

For 8-bit/16-bit integers, CUDA provides vectorized dot product operations. These are DP4A (a four element dot product with accumulation) and DP2A (a two element dot product with accumulation). Using these functions, CUDA developers can make faster operations. CUDA 8.0 Development Blog introduces these functions with intuitive figures (`https://devblogs.nvidia.com/mixed-precision-programming-cuda-8/`). The following shows how the GPU's dot product and accumulation operations work:

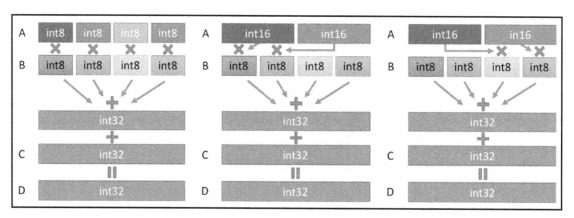

Using this, you can write 8-bit only or 8-bit/16-bit mixed operations with 32-bit integer accumulation. Other operations such as sum, add, and compare are also available with SIMD intrinsic functions.

As discussed previously, there are specific GPUs that can support INT8/INT16 operations with special functions (dp4a and dp2a). The supporting GPUs' compute capability must be higher than 6.1.

Now, let's implement a kernel function that uses the dp4a API, as follows:

```
__global__ void dp4a_kernel(char *d_x, char *d_y, int *d_z, int size)
{
    int idx_x = blockIdx.x * blockDim.x + threadIdx.x;
    int stride = gridDim.x * blockDim.x;

#if __CUDA_ARCH__ >= 610
    char4 *quad_x = (char4 *)d_x;
    char4 *quad_y = (char4 *)d_y;
    for (int i = idx_x; i < size; i+=stride)
        d_z[i] = __dp4a(quad_y[i], quad_x[i], 0);
#else
    for (int i = idx_x; i < size; i+=4*stride) {
        int sum = 0;
        for (int j = 0; j < 4; j++)
            sum += d_y[4 * i + j] * d_x[4 * i + j];
        d_z[i] = sum + 0;
    }
#endif
}
```

In this function, __dp4a fetches two arrays of characters coalescing four items and outputs its dot product outputs. This API is supported since Pascal with CUDA compute capability (version 6.1). But old GPU architectures, lower than version 6.1, need to use the original operations.

The following code shows how we will call the implemented kernel function. Its grid size is reduced by four since each CUDA thread will operate on the four items:

```
int n_threads = 256;
int num_sms;
int num_blocks_per_sm;
cudaDeviceGetAttribute(&num_sms, cudaDevAttrMultiProcessorCount, 0);
cudaOccupancyMaxActiveBlocksPerMultiprocessor(&num_blocks_per_sm,
    dp4a_kernel, n_threads, n_threads*sizeof(int));
int n_blocks = min(num_blocks_per_sm * num_sms, (size/4 + n_threads
                                                - 1) / n_threads);
dp4a_kernel<<< n_blocks, n_threads, n_threads * sizeof(int) >>>
    (X.d_ptr_, Y.d_ptr_, Z.d_ptr_, size/4);
```

Other initialization code and benchmark code is implemented in samples code such as the previous example code.

We have covered the dot operation of INT8, but CUDA C also provides other INT8-type SIMD intrinsic functions (https://docs.nvidia.com/cuda/cuda-math-api/group__CUDA__MATH__INTRINSIC__SIMD.html). Please check this document for the other operations.

Measuring the performance

The sample code has three versions of mixed precision operations: single-precision, half-precision, and INT8. As the precision drops, we can add more operations for each CUDA thread.

Run the following commands for single-precision, half-precision, and INT8 operations:

```
# Single-precision
$ nvcc -run -m64 -gencode arch=compute_70,code=sm_70 -
I/usr/local/cuda/samples/common/inc -o mixed_precision_single
./mixed_precision.cu

# Half-precision
$ nvcc -run -m64 -gencode arch=compute_70,code=sm_70 -
I/usr/local/cuda/samples/common/inc -o mixed_precision_half
./mixed_precision_half.cu

# INT8
$ nvcc -run -m64 -gencode arch=compute_70,code=sm_70 -
I/usr/local/cuda/samples/common/inc -o mixed_precision_int
./mixed_precision_int.cu
```

The following table shows the estimated performance for each precision operation:

Precision	Measured performance
FP32	59.441 GFlops
FP16	86.037 GFlops
INT8	196.225 Gops

Since our implementations are not optimized, the measured performance is quite lower than the theoretical performance of the Tesla V100. When you profile them, they will report that they are highly memory-bounded. In other words, we need to optimize them to be arithmetically bounded to achieve close to the theoretical performance.

Summary

In this chapter, we covered how to configure CUDA parallel operations and optimize them. To do this, we have to understand the relationship between CUDA's hierarchical architecture thread block and streaming multiprocessors. With some performance models—occupancy, performance limiter analysis, and the Roofline model—we could optimize more performance. Then, we covered some new CUDA thread programmability, Cooperative Groups, and learned how this simplifies parallel programming. We optimized parallel reduction problems and achieved 0.259 ms with 2^{24} elements, which is a 17.8 increase in speed with the same GPU. Finally, we learned about CUDA's SIMD operations with half-precision (FP16) and INT8 precision.

Our experience from this chapter focuses on the GPU's parallel processing level programming. However, CUDA programming includes system-level programming. Basically, the GPU is an extra computing resource and works independently from the host. This introduces extra computing power, but can also introduce latency on the other hand. CUDA provides API functions that can utilize this and conceal the latency and enables the full performance of the GPU. We will cover this in the next chapter.

Kernel Execution Model and Optimization Strategies

4

CUDA programming has a procedure for host operations. For example, we need to allocate the global memory, transfer data to the GPU, execute kernel functions, transfer data back to the host, and clean the global memory. That's because the GPU is an extra-processing unit in the system, so we need to care about its execution and data transfer. This is another aspect of GPU programming that's different compared to CPU programming.

In this chapter, we will cover CUDA kernel execution models and CUDA streams, which control CUDA operations. Then, we will discuss optimization strategies at the system level. Then, we will cover CUDA events to measure GPU event time, and how to use CUDA events to measure kernel execution time. After that, we will cover various CUDA kernel executing models and discuss what those features bring to GPU operations.

The following topics will be covered in this chapter:

- Kernel execution with a CUDA streams
- Pipelining GPU execution
- The CUDA callback function
- CUDA streams with priority
- Kernel execution time estimation using CUDA events
- CUDA dynamic parallelism
- Grid-level cooperative groups
- CUDA kernel calls with OpenMP
- Multi-Process Services
- Kernel execution overhead comparison

Technical requirements

This chapter requires us to use a CUDA version later than 9.x, and the GPU architecture should be Volta or Turing. If you use a GPU with Pascal architecture, skip the *Grid-level cooperative groups* section because this feature is introduced for Volta architecture.

Kernel execution with CUDA streams

A stream is a sequence of commands that relate to the GPU in CUDA programming. In other words, all the kernel calls and data transfers are handled by the CUDA stream. By default, CUDA provides a default stream, and all the commands use the stream implicitly. Therefore, we do not have to handle this ourselves.

CUDA supports additional streams, created explicitly. While the operations in a stream are sequential, CUDA can execute multiple operations concurrently by using the multiple streams. Let's learn how to handle streams, and what features they have.

The usage of CUDA streams

The following code shows an example of how CUDA streams can be created, used, and terminated:

```
cudaStream_t stream;
cudaStreamCreate(&stream);
foo_kernel<<< grid_size, block_size, 0, stream >>>();
cudaStreamDestroy(stream);
```

As you can see, we can handle a CUDA stream using `cudaStream_t`. And, we can create this using `cudaStreamCreate()` and terminate it using `cudaStreamDestroy()`. Note that we should provide a pointer to `cudaStreamCreate()`. The created stream is passed to the kernel's fourth argument.

However, we did not provide such a stream previously. That's because CUDA provides a default stream so that all the CUDA operations can operate. Now, let's write an application that uses the default stream and multiple streams. Then, we will see how our application can be changed.

First, let's write an application that uses the default CUDA stream, as follows:

```
__global__ void foo_kernel(int step)
{
    printf("loop: %d\n", step);
}

int main()
{
    for (int i = 0; i < 5; i++)
        // CUDA kernel call with the default stream
        foo_kernel<<< 1, 1, 0, 0 >>>(i);
    cudaDeviceSynchronize();
    return 0;
}
```

As you can see in the code, we call the kernel function with the stream ID as 0, because the identification value of the default stream is 0. Compile the code and see the execution output:

```
$ nvcc -m64 -run -gencode arch=compute_70,code=sm_70 -
I/usr/local/cuda/samples/common/inc -o cuda_default_stream
./1_cuda_default_stream.cu
```

How is the output? We can expect that the output will be the order of the loop index. The following timeline view shows this code's operation:

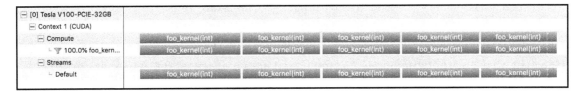

It is to be expected that having loop operations in the same stream shows the order of kernel execution. Then, what can be changed if we use multiple CUDA streams, and each loop step uses different ones? The following code shows an example of printing the loop index from the CUDA kernel function with the different streams:

```
__global__ void foo_kernel(int step)
{
    printf("loop: %d\n", step);
}

int main()
{
    int n_stream = 5;
```

```
cudaStream_t *ls_stream;
ls_stream = (cudaStream_t*) new cudaStream_t[n_stream];

// create multiple streams
for (int i = 0; i < n_stream; i++)
    cudaStreamCreate(&ls_stream[i]);

// execute kernels with the CUDA stream each
for (int i = 0; i < n_stream; i++)
    foo_kernel<<< 1, 1, 0, ls_stream[i] >>>(i);

// synchronize the host and GPU
cudaDeviceSynchronize();

// terminates all the created CUDA streams
for (int i = 0; i < n_stream; i++)
    cudaStreamDestroy(ls_stream[i]);
delete [] ls_stream;

return 0;
}
```

In this code, we have five calls, the same as in the previous code, but here we will use five different streams. To do this, we built an array of `cudaStream_t` and created streams for each. What can you expect with this change? The printed output would be the same as the previous version. Run the following command to compile this code:

```
$ nvcc -m64 -run -gencode arch=compute_70,code=sm_70 -
I/usr/local/cuda/samples/common/inc -o cuda_mutli_stream
./2_cuda_multi_stream.cu
```

However, that does not guarantee that they have the same operation. As we discussed at the beginning, this code shows the concurrency of the multiple streams, as in the following screenshot:

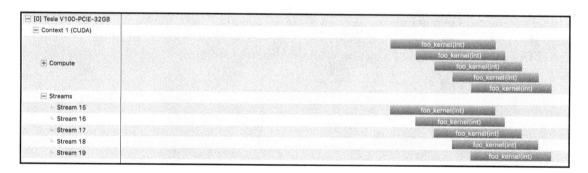

As you can see at the bottom of the screenshot, five individual streams execute the same kernel function concurrently and their operations are overlapped with each other. From this, we can discern two features of the streams, as follows:

1. Kernel executions are asynchronous with the host.
2. CUDA operations in different streams are independent of each other.

Using the concurrency of the stream, we can make extra optimization opportunities by overlapping independent operations.

Stream-level synchronization

CUDA streams provide stream-level synchronization with the `cudaStreamSynchronize()` function. Using this function forces the host to wait until the end of a certain stream's operation. This provides important optimization for the `cudaDeviceSynchronize()` function that we have used so far.

We will discuss how to utilize this feature in the following sections, but let's discuss its basic operations here. The previous example shows concurrent operations without synchronization within the loop. However, we can halt the host to execute the next kernel execution by using the `cudaStreamSynchronize()` function. The following code shows an example of using stream synchronization at the end of the kernel execution:

```
// execute kernels with the CUDA stream each
for (int i = 0; i < n_stream; i++) {
    foo_kernel<<< 1, 1, 0, ls_stream[i] >>>(i);
    cudaStreamSynchronize(ls_stream[i]);
}
```

We can easily predict that the kernel operation's concurrency will vanish due to synchronization. To confirm this, let's profile this and see how this impacts the kernel execution:

```
$ nvcc -m64 -run -gencode arch=compute_70,code=sm_70 -
I/usr/local/cuda/samples/common/inc -o cuda_mutli_stream_with_sync
./3_cuda_multi_stream_with_sync.cu
```

The following screenshot shows the result:

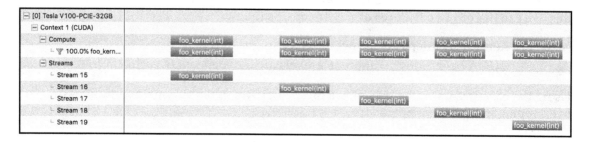

As you can see, all the kernel executions have no overlapping points, although they are executed with the different streams. Using this feature, we can let the host wait for the specific stream operation to start with the result.

Working with the default stream

To have multiple streams operating concurrently, we should use streams we created explicitly, because all stream operations are synchronous with the default stream. The following screenshot shows the default stream's synchronous operation effect:

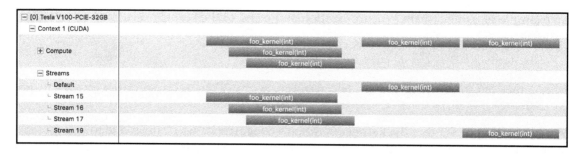

We can achieve this by modifying our multi-stream kernel call operation, like this:

```
for (int i = 0; i < n_stream; i++)
    if (i == 3)
        foo_kernel<<< 1, 1, 0, 0 >>>(i);
    else
        foo_kernel<<< 1, 1, 0, ls_stream[i] >>>(i);
```

Run the following command to compile the code:

```
$ nvcc -m64 -run -gencode arch=compute_70,code=sm_70 -
I/usr/local/cuda/samples/common/inc -o cuda_multi_stream_with_default
./4_cuda_multi_stream_with_default.cu
```

So, we can see that the last operation cannot be overlapped with the previous kernel executions, but that we have to wait until the fourth kernel execution has finished.

Pipelining the GPU execution

One of the major benefits of multiple streams is overlapping the data transfer with the kernel execution. By overlapping the kernel operation and data transfer, we can conceal the data transfer overhead and increase overall performance.

Concept of GPU pipelining

When we execute the kernel function, we need to transfer data from the host to the GPU. Then, we transfer the result back from the GPU to the host. The following diagram shows an example of iterative operations that transfer data between the host and kernel executions:

| Stream 0 | H2D | Kernel | D2H | H2D | Kernel | D2H | H2D | Kernel | D2H |

However, the kernel execution is basically asynchronous in that the host and GPU can operate concurrently with each other. If the data transfer between the host and GPU has the same feature, we would be able to overlap their execution, as we could see in the previous section. The following diagram shows the operation when the data transfer can be executed like a normal kernel operation, and handled along with the stream:

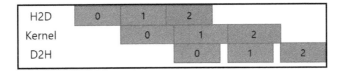

In this diagram, we can see that the data transfer between the host and the device can be overlapped with the kernel execution. Then, the benefit of this overlapped operation is to reduce the application execution time. By comparing the length of the two pictures, you will be able to confirm which operation would have higher operation throughput.

Regarding CUDA streams, all CUDA operations—data transfers and kernel executions—are sequential in the same stream. However, those can operate simultaneously along with the different streams. The following diagram shows overlapped data transfer with the kernel operation for multiple streams:

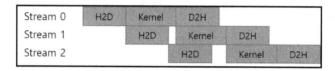

To enable such a pipelining operation, CUDA has three prerequisites:

1. The host memory should be allocated as pinned memory—CUDA provides the `cudaMallocHost()` and `cudaFreeHost()` functions for this purpose.
2. Transfer data between the host and GPUs without blocking the host—CUDA provides the `cudaMemcpyAsync()` function for this purpose.
3. Manage each operation along with the different CUDA streams to have concurrent operations.

Now, let's write a simple application that pipelines the workloads.

Building a pipelining execution

The following code shows a snippet of asynchronous data transfer and the synchronization of a CUDA stream at the end of the execution:

```
cudaStream_t stream;
float *h_ptr, *d_ptr;     size_t byte_size = sizeof(float) * BUF_SIZE;

cudaStreamCreate(&stream);               // create CUDA stream
cudaMallocHost(h_ptr, byte_size);        // allocates pinned memory
cudaMalloc((void**)&d_ptr, byte_size);   // allocates a global memory

// transfer the data from host to the device asynchronously
cudaMemcpyAsync(d_ptr, h_ptr, byte_size, cudaMemcpyHostToDevice, stream);

... { kernel execution } ...
```

```
// transfer the data from the device to host asynchronously
cudaMemcpyAsync(h_ptr, d_ptr, byte_size, cudaMemcpyDeviceToHost, stream);
cudaStreamSynchronize(stream);

// terminates allocated resources
cudaStreamDestroy(stream);
cudaFree(d_ptr);
cudaFreeHost(h_ptr);
```

This code shows how to allocate pinned memory, and transfer data with the user-created stream. By merging this example and the multiple CUDA stream operations, we can have the pipelining CUDA operation.

Now, let's build an application that has the pipelining operation with the data transfer and the kernel execution. In this application, we will use a kernel function that adds two vectors, by slicing the number of streams, and outputs its result. However, the kernel implementation does not require any changes with this since we will do this at the host code level. But, we will iterate the addition operation 500 times to extend the kernel execution time. As a result, the implemented kernel code is as follows:

```
__global__ void
vecAdd_kernel(float *c, const float* a, const float* b)
{
    int idx = blockIdx.x * blockDim.x + threadIdx.x;

    for (int i = 0; i < 500; i++)
        c[idx] = a[idx] + b[idx];
}
```

To handle each stream's operation, we will create a class that manages a CUDA stream and the CUDA operations. This class will allow us to manage the CUDA stream along with the index. The following code shows the basic architecture of the class:

```
class Operator
{
private:
    int index;

public:
    Operator() {
        cudaStreamCreate(&stream);     // create a CUDA stream
    }

    ~Operator() {
        cudaStreamDestroy(stream);     // terminate the CUDA stream
    }
```

```
        cudaStream_t stream;
        void set_index(int idx) { index = idx; }
        void async_operation(float *h_c, const float *h_a,
                             const float *h_b,
                             float *d_c, float *d_a, float *d_b,
                             const int size, const int bufsize);
};  // Operator
```

Now, let's write some sequential GPU execution code that we have used in the previous section, but as a member function of the `Operator` class, as follows:

```
void Operator::async_operation(float *h_c, const float *h_a,
                               const float *h_b,
                               float *d_c, float *d_a, float *d_b,
                               const int size, const int bufsize)
{
    // start timer
    sdkStartTimer(&_p_timer);

    // copy host -> device
    cudaMemcpyAsync(d_a, h_a, bufsize,
                    cudaMemcpyHostToDevice, stream);
    cudaMemcpyAsync(d_b, h_b, bufsize,
                    cudaMemcpyHostToDevice, stream);

    // launch cuda kernel
    dim3 dimBlock(256);
    dim3 dimGrid(size / dimBlock.x);
    vecAdd_kernel<<< dimGrid, dimBlock, 0,
                 stream >>>(d_c, d_a, d_b);

    // copy device -> host
    cudaMemcpyAsync(h_c, d_c, bufsize,
                    cudaMemcpyDeviceToHost, stream);

    printf("Launched GPU task %d\n", index);
}
```

This function's operation is no different to the basic CUDA host programming pattern we have used previously, except we applied `cudaMemcpyAsync()` with the given `_stream`. Then, we write `main()` to work with multiple operator instances and page-locked memory:

```
int main(int argc, char* argv[])
{
    float *h_a, *h_b, *h_c;
    float *d_a, *d_b, *d_c;
    int size = 1 << 24;
```

```
int bufsize = size * sizeof(float);
int num_operator = 4;

if (argc != 1)
    num_operator = atoi(argv[1]);
```

Now, we will allocate host memories using `cudaMallocHost()` to have pinned memories, and initialize them:

```
cudaMallocHost((void**)&h_a, bufsize);
cudaMallocHost((void**)&h_b, bufsize);
cudaMallocHost((void**)&h_c, bufsize);

srand(2019);
init_buffer(h_a, size);
init_buffer(h_b, size);
init_buffer(h_c, size);
```

And, we will have device memories with the same size:

```
cudaMalloc((void**)&d_a, bufsize);
cudaMalloc((void**)&d_b, bufsize);
cudaMalloc((void**)&d_c, bufsize);
```

Now, we will create a list of CUDA operators using the class we used:

```
Operator *ls_operator = new Operator[num_operator];
```

We are ready to execute the pipelining operations. Before we start the execution, let's place a stopwatch to see the overall execution time and see the overlapped data transfer benefit, as follows:

```
StopWatchInterface *timer;
sdkCreateTimer(&timer);
sdkStartTimer(&timer);
```

Let's execute each operator using a loop, and each operator will access the host and the device memory according to their order. We will, also, measure the execution time of the loop:

```
for (int i = 0; i < num_operator; i++) {
    int offset = i * size / num_operator;
    ls_operator[i].set_index(i);
    ls_operator[i].async_operation(&h_c[offset],
                                   &h_a[offset], &h_b[offset],
                                   &d_c[offset],
                                   &d_a[offset], &d_b[offset],
                                   size / num_operator,
```

```
                                                bufsize / num_operator);
    }

    cudaDeviceSynchronize();
    sdkStopTimer(&timer);
```

Finally, we will compare a sample's result and print out the overall measured performance:

```
// prints out the result
int print_idx = 256;
printf("compared a sample result...\n");
printf("host: %.6f, device: %.6f\n", h_a[print_idx] +
        h_b[print_idx], h_c[print_idx]);

// prints out the performance
float elapsed_time_msed = sdkGetTimerValue(&timer);
float bandwidth = 3 * bufsize * sizeof(float) /
                        elapsed_time_msed / 1e6;
printf("Time= %.3f msec, bandwidth= %f GB/s\n",
        elapsed_time_msed, bandwidth);
```

Terminate handles and memories, as follows:

```
sdkDeleteTimer(&timer);
delete [] ls_operator;
cudaFree(d_a);      cudaFree(d_b);      cudaFree(d_c);
cudaFreeHost(h_a); cudaFreeHost(h_b); cudaFreeHost(h_c);
```

To execute the code, let's reuse the host initialization function and GPU kernel function from the previous recipes. We don't have to modify these functions at this moment. Compile the code using the following command:

```
$ nvcc -m64 -run -gencode arch=compute_70,code=sm_70 -
I/usr/local/cuda/samples/common/inc -o cuda_pipelining ./cuda_pipelining.cu
```

You must use your GPU's compute capability version number for the gencode option. The output of the compilation is as follows:

```
Launched GPU task 0
Launched GPU task 1
Launched GPU task 2
Launched GPU task 3
compared a sample result...
host: 1.523750, device: 1.523750
Time= 29.508 msec, bandwidth= 27.291121 GB/s
```

As we can see, GPU tasks are executed following the order of the kernel execution along with the stream.

Now, let's review how the application operates on the inside. By default, the sample code slices the host data into four and executes four CUDA streams concurrently. We can see each kernel's outputs along with the streams' execution. To see the overlapping operation, you need to profile the execution with the following command:

```
$ nvprof -o overlapping_exec.nvvp ./overlapping_exec
```

The following screenshot shows four CUDA streams' operations by overlapping data transfer with kernel execution:

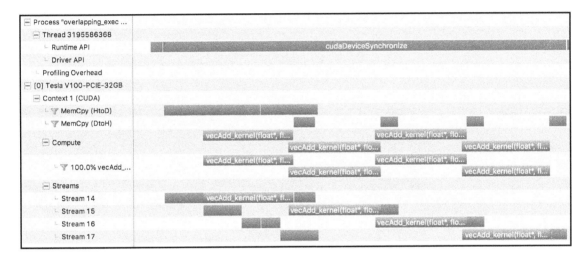

Overlaps between the kernel executions and data transfers

As a result, the GPU can be busy until the last kernel execution is finished, and we can conceal most of the data transfers. This not only enhances the GPU utilization, but also reduces total application execution time.

Between the kernel execution, we can find that none of them have no contention although they belong to different CUDA streams. That's because of the GPU scheduler being aware of the execution requests, and serving the first. However, when the current task is finished, the streaming multiprocessor can serve the next kernel in the other CUDA stream, since they have remained occupancies.

At the end of all the multiple CUDA stream operations, we need to synchronize the host and GPU to confirm that all the CUDA operations on the GPU have finished. To do this, we used `cudaDeviceSynchronize()` right after the loop. This function can synchronize all the selected GPU operations at the calling point.

For the synchronization task, we can replace the `cudaDeviceSynchronize()` function with the following code. To do this, we also have to change the private member `_stream` to be public:

```
for (int i = 0; i < num_operator; i++) {
    cudaStreamSynchronize(ls_operator[i]._stream);
}
```

This can be used when we need to provide specific operations from a single host thread along with the stream after each stream finishes. But, this is not a good operational design since the following operation cannot avoid syncing with the other streams.

What about using `cudaStreamSynchronize()` in the loop? In this case, we cannot perform the overlapping operation that we did before. The following screenshot shows the situation:

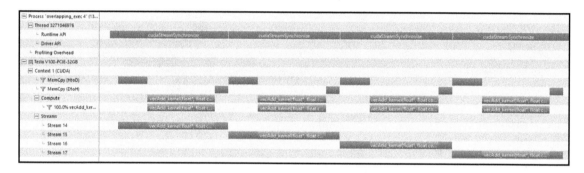

This is because `cudaStreamSynchronize()` will synchronize every iteration and the application will serialize all the CUDA executions, accordingly. In this situation, the execution time was measured as 41.521 ms, which is about 40% slower than the overlapped execution time.

The CUDA callback function

The **CUDA callback function** is a callable host function to be executed by the GPU execution context. Using this, the programmer can specify the host-desired host operation following the GPU operations.

The CUDA callback function has a special datatype named `CUDART_CB`, so it should be defined using this type. With this type, the programmers can specify which CUDA stream launches this function, pass the GPU error status, and provide user data.

To register the callback function, CUDA provides cudaStreamAddCallback(). This function accepts CUDA streams, the CUDA callback function, and its parameters, so that the specified CUDA callback function can be called from the specified CUDA stream and obtain user data. This function has four input parameters, but the last one is reserved. So, we don't use that parameter and it remains as 0.

Now, let's enhance our code to use the callback function and output an individual stream's performance. Duplicate the source code if you want to separate the previous work and this.

First, place these function declarations into the private area of the Operator class:

```
StopWatchInterface *_p_timer;
static void CUDART_CB Callback(cudaStream_t stream, cudaError_t
status, void* userData);
void print_time();
```

The Callback() function will be called after each stream's operation has finished, and the print_time() function will report the estimated performance using the host side timer, _p_timer. The functions' implementations are as follows:

```
void Operator::CUDART_CB Callback(cudaStream_t stream, cudaError_t
status, void* userData) {
    Operator* this_ = (Operator*) userData;
    this_->print_time();
}

void Operator::print_time() {
    sdkStopTimer(&p_timer);      // end timer
    float elapsed_time_msed = sdkGetTimerValue(&p_timer);
    printf("stream %2d - elapsed %.3f ms \n", index,
            elapsed_time_msed);
}
```

To have the right timer operations, we need a timer initializer at the Operator class's constructor and a timer destroyer at the class's terminator. Also, we have to start the timer at the beginning of the Operator::async_operation() function. Then, insert the following code block at the end of the function. This allows the CUDA stream to call the host-side function when it finishes the previous CUDA operations:

```
// register callback function
cudaStreamAddCallback(stream, Operator::Callback, this, 0);
```

Now, let's compile and see the execution result. You must use your GPU's compute capability version number for the `gencode` option:

```
$ nvcc -m64 -run -gencode arch=compute_70,code=sm_70 -
I/usr/local/cuda/samples/common/inc -o cuda_callback ./cuda_callback.cu
```

This is the execution result of our update:

```
stream 0 - elapsed 11.136 ms
stream 1 - elapsed 16.998 ms
stream 2 - elapsed 23.283 ms
stream 3 - elapsed 29.487 ms
compared a sample result...
host: 1.523750, device: 1.523750
Time= 29.771 msec, bandwidth= 27.050028 GB/s
```

Here, we can see the estimated execution time along with the CUDA stream. The callback function estimates its sequence's execution time. Since there is overlapping with other streams and delays for later CUDA streams, we can see the prolonged execution time for the late CUDA streams' execution time. We can confirm those elapsed times by matching with the profiled result, as follows:

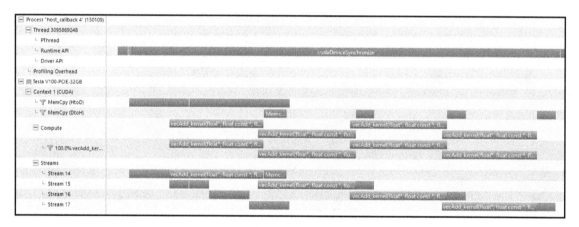

Although their measured elapsed time is extended along with the stream execution, the delta between the streams is regular and we can see these operations from the profiled output.

Therefore, we can conclude that we can write host code that can operate right after each individual CUDA stream's operation has finished. And, this is advanced one against to synchronize each stream from the main threads.

CUDA streams with priority

By default, all CUDA streams have equal priority so they can execute their operations in the right order. On top of that, CUDA streams also can have priorities and can be superseded by a higher prioritized stream. With this feature, we can have GPU operations that meet time-critical requirements.

Priorities in CUDA

To use streams with priorities, we need to obtain the available priorities from the GPU first. We can obtain these using the `cudaDeviceGetStreamPriorityRange()` function. Its output is two numeric values, which are the lowest and highest priority values. Then, we can create a priority stream using the `cudaStreamCreaetWithPriority()` function, as follows:

```
cudaError_t cudaStreamCreateWithPriority(cudaStream_t* pStream, unsigned
int flags, int priority)
```

There are two additional parameters we should provide. The first one determines the created streams' behavior with the default stream. We can make the new stream be synchronous with the default stream, like normal streams, using `cudaStreamDefault`. On the other hand, we can make it operate concurrently with the default stream using `cudaStreamNonBlocking`. Lastly, we can set the stream's priority within the priority range. In CUDA programming, the lowest value has the highest priority.

Also, we can confirm whether the GPU supports this using the following code. But, we don't have to worry too much about this because the priority stream has been available since CUDA compute capability 3.5:

```
cudaDeviceProp prop;
cudaGetDeviceProperties(&prop, 0);
if (prop.streamPrioritiesSupported == 0) { ... }
```

If the device properties value is 0, we should stop the application since the GPU does not support the stream priorities.

Stream execution with priorities

Now, we will reuse the previous multi-stream application with the callback. In this code, we can see that the streams can operate in order, and we will see how this order can be changed with priorities. We will make a derived class from the `Operator` class, and it will handle the priority of the stream. So, we change the member variable stream's protection level from the private member to the protected member. And, the constructor can create the stream optionally since that can be done by the derived class. The change is shown with the following code:

```
... { middle of the class Operator } ...
protected:
    cudaStream_t stream = nullptr;

public:
    Operator(bool create_stream = true) {
        if (create_stream)
            cudaStreamCreate(&stream);
        sdkCreateTimer(&p_timer);
    }
... { middle of the class Operator } ...
```

The derived class, `Operator_with_priority`, will have a function that creates a CUDA stream manually with the given priority. That class configuration is as follows:

```
class Operator_with_priority: public Operator {
public:
    Operator_with_priority() : Operator(false) {}

    void set_priority(int priority) {
        cudaStreamCreateWithPriority(&stream,
            cudaStreamNonBlocking, priority);
    }
};
```

As we handle each stream's operation with the class, we will update the `ls_operator` creation code to use the `Operator_with_priority` class in `main()`, to use the class we wrote before, as follows:

```
Operator_with_priority *ls_operator = new
Operator_with_priority[num_operator];
```

As we update the class, this class does not create streams before we request it to do so. As we discussed before, we need to obtain the available range of priority of the GPU using the following code:

```
// Get priority range
int priority_low, priority_high;
cudaDeviceGetStreamPriorityRange(&priority_low, &priority_high);
printf("Priority Range: low(%d), high(%d)\n", priority_low, priority_high);
```

Then, let's create each operation to have different prioritized streams. To ease this task, we will let the last operation have the highest stream, and see how preemption in CUDA streams works. This can be done with the following code:

```
for (int i = 0; i < num_operator; i++) {
    ls_operator[i].set_index(i);

    // let the latest CUDA stream to have the high priority
    if (i + 1 == num_operator)
        ls_operator[i].set_priority(priority_high);
    else
        ls_operator[i].set_priority(priority_low);
}
```

After that, we will execute each operation, as we did previously:

```
for (int i = 0 ; i < num_operator; i++) {
    int offset = i * size / num_operator;
    ls_operator[i].async_operation(&h_c[offset],
                                   &h_a[offset], &h_b[offset],
                                   &d_c[offset],
                                   &d_a[offset], &d_b[offset],
                                   size / num_operator,
                                   bufsize / num_operator);
}
```

To have the proper output, let's synchronize the host and GPU using the `cudaDeviceSynchronize()` function. And, finally, we can terminate the CUDA streams. The streams with priorities can be terminated with the `cudaStreamDestroy()` function, so we have nothing to do in this application as we already did what was needed.

Now, let's compile the code and see the effect. As always, you need to provide the right GPU compute capability version to the compiler:

```
$ nvcc -m64 -run -gencode arch=compute_70,code=sm_70 -
I/usr/local/cuda/samples/common/inc -o prioritized_cuda_stream
./prioritized_cuda_stream.cu
```

And, the following shows the output of the application:

```
Priority Range: low(0), high(-1)
stream 0 - elapsed 11.119 ms
stream 3 - elapsed 19.126 ms
stream 1 - elapsed 23.327 ms
stream 2 - elapsed 29.422 ms
compared a sample result...
host: 1.523750, device: 1.523750
Time= 29.730 msec, bandwidth= 27.087332 GB/s
```

From the output, you can see that the operation order has been changed. Stream 3 precedes stream 1 and stream 2. The following screenshot shows the profile result of how it changed:

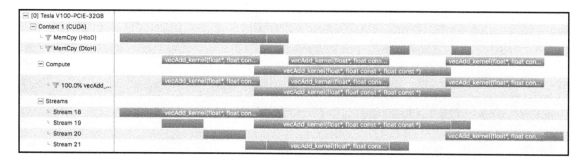

In this screenshot, there was preemption with the second CUDA stream (**Stream 19** in this case) by the prioritized-last CUDA stream (**Stream 21**), so that **Stream 19** could finish its work after **Stream 21** finished execution. Note that the order of data transfer does not change according to this prioritization.

Kernel execution time estimation using CUDA events

The previous GPU operation time estimation has one limitation in that it cannot measure the kernel execution time. That's because we used timing APIs on the host side. So, we need to have synchronized with the host and GPU to measure the kernel execution time, and this is impractical considering the overhead and impact on the application's performance.

This can be resolved using CUDA events. The CUDA event records GPU-side events along with the CUDA stream. CUDA events can be events based on the GPU states and record the scheduled timing. Using this, we can trigger the following operations or estimate the kernel execution time. In this section, we will cover how we can measure the kernel execution time using CUDA events.

The CUDA event is managed with the `cudaEvent_t` handle. We can create a CUDA event handle using `cudaEventCreate()` and terminate it with `cudaEventDestroy()`. To record event time, you can use `cudaEventRecord()`. Then, the CUDA event handle records the event time for the GPU. This function also accepts CUDA streams, so that we can enumerate the event time to the specific CUDA stream. After obtaining the start and end events of kernel execution, you can obtain the elapsed time using `cudaEventElapsedTime()` with millisecond units.

Now, let's cover how we can use CUDA events using those APIs.

Using CUDA events

In this section, we will reuse the previous multi-stream application from the second section. Then, we enumerate each GPU kernel's execution time using CUDA events:

1. We will use a simple vector addition kernel function, as follows:

```
__global__ void
vecAdd_kernel(float *c, const float* a, const float* b) {
    int idx = blockIdx.x * blockDim.x + threadIdx.x;
    for (int i = 0; i < 500; i++)
        c[idx] = a[idx] + b[idx];
}
```

This code has an iteration that extends the kernel execution time.

2. Then, we will use the following snippet to measure the kernel execution time. To compare the result, we will use the host side's timer and CUDA event:

```
... { memory initializations } ...

// initialize the host timer
StopWatchInterface *timer;
sdkCreateTimer(&timer);

cudaEvent_t start, stop;
// create CUDA events
cudaEventCreate(&start);
```

```
cudaEventCreate(&stop);

// start to measure the execution time
sdkStartTimer(&timer);
cudaEventRecord(start);

// launch cuda kernel
dim3 dimBlock(256);
dim3 dimGrid(size / dimBlock.x);
vecAdd_kernel<<< dimGrid, dimBlock >>>(d_c, d_a, d_b);

// record the event right after the kernel execution finished
cudaEventRecord(stop);

// Synchronize the device to measure the execution time from the
host side
cudaEventSynchronize(stop); // we also can make synchronization
based on CUDA event
sdkStopTimer(&timer);
```

As you can see in this code, we can record the CUDA event right after the kernel calls. However, the timer requires synchronization between the GPU and the host. For the synchronization, we use the `cudaEventSynchronize(stop)` function because we can also make the host thread synchronize with the event. Meanwhile, this code only covers handling the timing resources and the kernel execution. But, you also have to initialize the required memory to make it work.

3. After the kernel execution, let's write code that reports the execution time from each timing resource:

```
// print out the result
int print_idx = 256;
printf("compared a sample result...\n");
printf("host: %.6f, device: %.6f\n", h_a[print_idx] +
h_b[print_idx], h_c[print_idx]);

// print estimated kernel execution time
float elapsed_time_msed = 0.f;
cudaEventElapsedTime(&elapsed_time_msed, start, stop);
printf("CUDA event estimated - elapsed %.3f ms \n",
elapsed_time_msed);
```

4. Now, we will finalize our application by terminating the timing resources, using the following code:

```
// delete timer
sdkDeleteTimer(&timer);

// terminate CUDA events
cudaEventDestroy(start);
cudaEventDestroy(stop);
```

5. Let's compile and see the output using the following command:

```
$ nvcc -m64 -run -gencode arch=compute_70,code=sm_70 -
I/usr/local/cuda/samples/common/inc -o cuda_event ./cuda_event.cu
compared a sample result...
host: 1.523750, device: 1.523750
CUDA event estimated - elapsed 23.408 ms
Host measured time= 35.063 msec/s
```

As you can see, we can measure kernel execution time using CUDA events. However, the measured times have gaps between the CUDA event and the timer. We can use NVIDIA Profiler to verify which provides more accurate information. When we use the `# nvprof ./cuda_event` command, the output is as follows:

```
==24298== Profiling result:
           Type  Time(%)      Time     Calls       Avg       Min       Max  Name
GPU activities:   58.32%  23.386ms         1  23.386ms  23.386ms  23.386ms  vecAdd_kernel(float*, float const *, float const *)
                  28.98%  11.620ms         2  5.8101ms  5.8043ms  5.8158ms  [CUDA memcpy HtoD]
                  12.70%  5.0922ms         1  5.0922ms  5.0922ms  5.0922ms  [CUDA memcpy DtoH]
```

As you can see, CUDA events provide accurate results compared to measuring from the host.

Another benefit of using CUDA events is that we can measure multiple kernel execution times simultaneously with multiple CUDA streams. Let's implement an example application and see its operation.

Multiple stream estimation

The `cudaEventRecord()` function is asynchronous to the host. In other words, there is no synchronization to measure the kernel execution time to the example code. To have synchronization with the event and the host, we need to use `cudaEventSynchronize()`. For example, kernel function prints can be placed ahead of asynchronous data transfers from the device to the host by the synchronization effect, when we place this function right after `cudaEventRecord(stop)`.

It is also useful to measure kernel execution time in multiple CUDA stream applications:

1. Let's apply this to the multiple CUDA streams overlapping recipe code in the `04_stream_priority` example code. Update the code with the following code:

```
class Operator
{
private:
    int _index;
    cudaStream_t stream;
    StopWatchInterface *p_timer;
    cudaEvent_t start, stop;

public:
    Operator() {
        cudaStreamCreate(&stream);

        // create cuda event
        cudaEventCreate(&start);
        cudaEventCreate(&stop);
    }

    ~Operator() {
        cudaStreamDestroy(stream);

        // destroy cuda event
        cudaEventDestroy(start);
        cudaEventDestroy(stop);
    }

    void set_index(int idx) { index = idx; }
    void async_operation(float *h_c, const float *h_a,
                         const float *h_b,
                         float *d_c, float *d_a, float *d_b,
                         const int size, const int bufsize);
    void print_kernel_time();
}; // Operator
```

2. Then, we will define the `print_time()` function we included at this time, as follows:

```
void Operator::print_time() {
    float milliseconds = 0;
    cudaEventElapsedTime(&milliseconds, start, stop);
    printf("Stream %d time: %.4f ms\n", index, milliseconds);
}
```

3. Now, insert the `cudaEventRecord()` function calls at the beginning and end of `Operator::async_operation()`, as in the following code:

```
void Operator::async_operation( ... )
{
    // start timer
    sdkStartTimer(&p_timer);

    // copy host -> device
    cudaMemcpyAsync(d_a, h_a, bufsize,
                    cudaMemcpyHostToDevice, stream);
    cudaMemcpyAsync(d_b, h_b, bufsize,
                    cudaMemcpyHostToDevice, stream);

    // record the event before the kernel execution
    cudaEventRecord(start, stream);

    // launch cuda kernel
    dim3 dimBlock(256);
    dim3 dimGrid(size / dimBlock.x);
    vecAdd_kernel<<< dimGrid, dimBlock, 0,
                    stream >>>(d_c, d_a, d_b);

    // record the event right after the kernel execution finished
    cudaEventRecord(stop, stream);

    // copy device -> host
    cudaMemcpyAsync(h_c, d_c, bufsize,
                    cudaMemcpyDeviceToHost, stream);

    // what happen if we include CUDA event synchronize?
    // QUIZ: cudaEventSynchronize(stop);

    // register callback function
    cudaStreamAddCallback(stream, Operator::Callback, this, 0);
}
```

For this function, there is a challenge to place synchronization at the end of the function. Try this after finishing this section. This will impact the application's behavior. It is recommended to try to explain the output to yourself, and then confirm that using the profiler.

Now, let's compile and see the execution time report, as follows; it shows similar performance to the previous executions:

```
$ nvcc -m64 -run -gencode arch=compute_70,code=sm_70 -
I/usr/local/cuda/samples/common/inc -o cuda_event_with_streams
./cuda_event_with_streams.cu
Priority Range: low(0), high(-1)
stream 0 - elapsed 11.348 ms
stream 3 - elapsed 19.435 ms
stream 1 - elapsed 22.707 ms
stream 2 - elapsed 35.768 ms
kernel in stream 0 - elapsed 6.052 ms
kernel in stream 1 - elapsed 14.820 ms
kernel in stream 2 - elapsed 17.461 ms
kernel in stream 3 - elapsed 6.190 ms
compared a sample result...
host: 1.523750, device: 1.523750
Time= 35.993 msec, bandwidth= 22.373972 GB/s
```

In this output, we also can see each kernel's execution time thanks to the CUDA event. From this result, we could see that the kernel execution time is prolonged, as we saw in the previous section.

If you want to learn more about the features of CUDA events, check NVIDIA's CUDA event documention: `https://docs.nvidia.com/cuda/cuda-runtime-api/group__CUDART__EVENT.html`.

Now, we will cover some other aspects of managing CUDA grids. The first item is dynamic parallelism, which enables kernel calls from the GPU kernel function.

CUDA dynamic parallelism

CUDA dynamic parallelism (**CDP**) is a device runtime feature that enables nested calls from device functions. These nested calls allow different parallelism for the child grid. This feature is useful when you need a different block size depending on the problem.

Understanding dynamic parallelism

Like normal kernel calls from the host, the GPU kernel call can make a kernel call as well. The following sample code shows how it works:

```
__global__ void child_kernel(int *data) {
    int idx = blockIdx.x * blockDim.x + threadIdx.x;
    atomicAdd(&data[idx], seed);
}


__global__ void parent_kernel(int *data)
{
    if (threadIdx.x == 0) {
        int child_size = BUF_SIZE/gridDim.x;
        child_kernel<<< child_size/BLOCKDIM, BLOCKDIM >>>
                        (&data[child_size*blockIdx.x], blockIdx.x+1);
    }
    // synchronization for other parent's kernel output
    cudaDeviceSynchronize();
}
```

As you can see in these functions, we need to make sure which CUDA thread makes kernel calls to control the amount that the grid creates. To learn more about this, let's implement the first application using this.

Usage of dynamic parallelism

Our dynamic parallelism code will create a parent grid, and that parent will create a couple of child grids:

1. First, we will write the `parent_kernel()` function and the `child_kernel()` function using the following code:

```
#define BUF_SIZE (1 << 10)
#define BLOCKDIM 256

__global__ void child_kernel(int *data)
{
    int idx = blockIdx.x * blockDim.x + threadIdx.x;
    atomicAdd(&data[idx], 1);
}


__global__ void parent_kernel(int *data)
{
    if (blockIdx.x * blockDim.x + threadIdx.x == 0)
```

```
    {
        int child_size = BUF_SIZE/gridDim.x;
        child_kernel<<< child_size/BLOCKDIM, BLOCKDIM >>> \
                    (&data[child_size*blockIdx.x],
                     blockIdx.x+1);
    }
    // synchronization for other parent's kernel output
    cudaDeviceSynchronize();
}
```

As you can see in this code, the parent kernel function creates child kernel grids as the number of blocks. And, the child grids increment the designated memory by 1 to mark their operation. After the kernel execution, the parent kernel waits until all the child grids finish their jobs using the cudaDeviceSynchronize() function. When we make synchronization, we should determine the range of the synchronization. If we need to synchronize at the block level, we should choose __synchthread() instead.

2. Write the main() function using the following code:

```
#define BUF_SIZE (1 << 10)
#define BLOCKDIM 256
int main()
{
    int *data;
    int num_child = 4;

    cudaMallocManaged((void**)&data, BUF_SIZE * sizeof(int));
    cudaMemset(data, 0, BUF_SIZE * sizeof(int));

    parent_kernel<<<num_child, 1>>>(data);
    cudaDeviceSynchronize();
    // Count elements value
    int counter = 0;
    for (int i = 0; i < BUF_SIZE; i++)
        counter += data[i];

    // getting answer
    int counter_h = 0;
    for (int i = 0; i < num_child; i++)
        counter_h += (i+1);
    counter_h *= BUF_SIZE / num_child;

    if (counter_h == counter)
        printf("Correct!!\n");
    else
        printf("Error!! Obtained %d. It should be %d\n",
```

```
                    counter, counter_h);

        cudaFree(data);
        return 0;
    }
```

As discussed earlier, we will create child grids along with the number of blocks. So, we will execute the parent kernel function with a grid size of 4, whereas the block size is 1.

3. To compile a CDP application, we should provide the `-rdc=true` option to the `nvcc` compiler. Hence, the command to compile the source is as follows:

   ```
   $ nvcc -run -rdc=true -lcudadevrt -gencode
   arch=compute_70,code=sm_70 -o host_callback host_callback.cu -
   I/usr/local/cuda/samples/common/inc
   ```

4. Let's profile this application to understand its operation. The following screenshot shows how this nested call works:

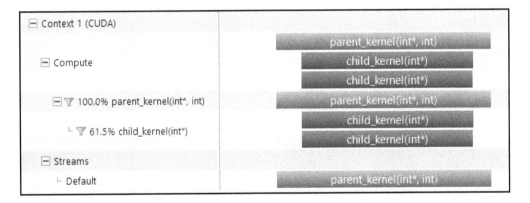

As we can see in this screenshot, the parent kernel creates a child grid, and we can see their relationship with the right angle mark at the left panel. Then, the parent grid (**parent_kernel**) waits for its execution until the child to finish its job. CUDA does not support CDT profiling for SM70 (Volta architecture) at this time, so I have used Tesla P40 to obtain this output.

Recursion

One of the benefits of dynamic parallelism is that we can create a recursion. The following code shows an example of a recursive kernel function:

```
__global__ void recursive_kernel(int *data, int size, int depth) {
    int x_0 = blockIdx.x * size;

if (depth > 0) {
    __syncthreads();
        if (threadIdx.x == 0) {
            int dimGrid = size / dimBlock;
            recursive_kernel<<<dimGrid,
                    dimBlock>>>(&data[x_0], size/dimGrid, depth-1);
            cudaDeviceSynchronize();
        }
        __syncthreads();
    }
}
```

As you can see, there is not much difference from the previous dynamic parallelism kernel function. However, we should use this with caution considering the resource usage and limitations. In general, dynamic parallel kernels can conservatively reserve up to 150 MB of device memory to track pending grid launches and the parent grid status by synchronizing on a child grid launch. In addition, the synchronization must be carefully done across multiple levels, while the depth of nested kernel launches is limited to 24 levels. Finally, the runtime that controls nested kernel launches can affect overall performance.

If you need to learn about the restrictions and limitations of dynamic parallelism, see the following programming guide: https://docs.nvidia.com/cuda/cuda-c-programming-guide/index.html#implementation-restrictions-and-limitations.

We will cover its application for quick sorting implementation in Chapter 7, *Parallel Programming Patterns in CUDA*. To learn more about dynamic parallelism, see the following documentation:

- https://devblogs.nvidia.com/cuda-dynamic-parallelism-api-principles/
- http://on-demand.gputechconf.com/gtc/2012/presentations/S0338-New-Features-in-the-CUDA-Programming-Model.pdf

Grid-level cooperative groups

As discussed in `Chapter 3`, *CUDA Thread Programming*, CUDA provides cooperative groups. Cooperative groups can be categorized by their grouping targets: warp-level, block-level, and grid-level groups. This recipe covers grid-level cooperative groups, and looks at how cooperative groups handle the CUDA grid.

The most prominent benefit of the cooperative group is the explicit synchronization of the target parallel object. Using the cooperative group, the programmer can design their application to synchronize CUDA parallel objects, thread blocks, or grids explicitly. Using the block-level cooperative group covered in `Chapter 3`, *CUDA Thread Programming*, we can write more readable code by specifying which CUDA threads or blocks need to synchronize.

Understanding grid-level cooperative groups

Since version 9.0, CUDA provides another level of cooperative groups, working with grids. To be specific, there are two grid-level cooperative groups: `grid_group` and `multi_grid_group`. Using these groups, the programmer can describe the grid's operation to sync on a single GPU or multiple GPUs.

In this recipe, we will explore the functionality of `grid_group`, which can synchronize grid with reduction problems, as mentioned in `Chapter 3`, *CUDA Thread Programming*, regarding the previous reduction design based on block-level reduction. Each thread block produces its own reduction results and stores them into the global memory. Then, another block-wise reduction kernel launches until we obtain a single reduced value. That's because finishing kernel operation can guarantee that the next **reduction** kernel to read a reduced value from the multiple thread blocks. Its design is described by the diagram on the left:

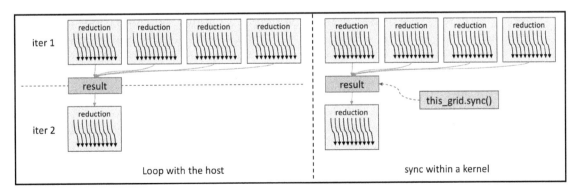

On the other hand, grid-level synchronization enables another kernel design, which synchronizes block-wise **reduction** results internally, so that the host can have only a single kernel call to obtain the reduction **result**. In cooperative groups, `grid_group.sync()` provides such functionality, so we can write the reduction kernel without kernel-level iteration.

To use the `grid_group.sync()` function, we need to call the kernel function using the `cudaLaunchCooperativeKernel()` function. Its interface design is as follows:

```
__host__ cudaError_t cudaLaunchCooperativeKernel
    ( const T* func, dim3 gridDim, dim3 blockDim,
      void** args, size_t sharedMem = 0, cudaStream_t stream = 0 )
```

So, its usage is the same as the `cudaLaunchKernel()` function, which launches a kernel function.

To make all the thread blocks in `grid_group` synchronize, the total number of active thread blocks in the grid should not exceed the number of maximum active blocks for the kernel function and the device. The maximum active block size on a GPU is a multiplication of the maximum amount of active blocks per SM and the number of streaming multiprocessors. The violation of this rule can result in deadlock or undefined behavior. We can obtain the maximum amount of active thread blocks of a kernel function per SM using the `cudaOccupancyMaxActiveBlocksPerMultiprocessor()` function, by passing the kernel function and block size information.

Usage of grid_group

Now, let's apply `grid_group` to the parallel reduction problem and see how the GPU programming can be changed:

1. We will reuse the host code from the previous parallel reduction code in `03_cuda_thread_programming/07_cooperative_groups`. In other words, we will change the GPU's operation with small changes in the host code. You also can use the code in the `07_grid_level_cg` directory.

2. Now, let's write some block-level reduction code. When we have grid-level cooperative groups, all the thread blocks must be active. In other words, we cannot execute multiple thread blocks than the GPU-capable active blocks. So, this reduction will accumulate the input data first to cover all the data with a limited number of thread blocks. Then, it will conduct the parallel reduction at the block level as we covered in Chapter 3, *CUDA Thread Programming*.

The following code shows its implementation:

```
__device__ void
block_reduction(float *out, float *in, float *s_data, int
active_size, int size,
        const cg::grid_group &grid, const cg::thread_block
&block)
{
  int tid = block.thread_rank();

  // Stride over grid and add the values to a shared memory buffer
  s_data[tid] = 0.f;
  for (int i = grid.thread_rank(); i < size; i += active_size)
    s_data[tid] += in[i];
  block.sync();

  for (unsigned int stride = blockDim.x / 2;
      stride > 0; stride >>= 1) {
    if (tid < stride)
      s_data[tid] += s_data[tid + stride];
    block.sync();
  }

  if (block.thread_rank() == 0)
    out[block.group_index().x] = s_data[0];
}
```

3. Then, let's write a kernel function that executes the block-wise reduction
   considering the number of active blocks and `grid_group`. In this function, we
   will call the block-level reduction code and synchronize them at the grid level.
   Then, we will perform parallel reduction from the outputs as we covered in
   `Chapter 3`, *CUDA Thread Programming*. The following code shows its
   implementation:

```
__global__ void
reduction_kernel(float *g_out, float *g_in, unsigned int size)
{
  cg::thread_block block = cg::this_thread_block();
  cg::grid_group grid = cg::this_grid();
  extern __shared__ float s_data[];

  // do reduction for multiple blocks
  block_reduction(g_out, g_in, s_data, grid.size(),
                  size, grid, block);

  grid.sync();
```

```
      // do reduction with single block
      if (block.group_index().x == 0)
        block_reduction(g_out, g_out, s_data, block.size(), gridDim.x,
    grid, block);
    }
```

4. Finally, we will implement the host code that calls the kernel function with the available active thread block dimension. To do this, this function uses the `cudaoccupancyMaxActiveBlocksPerMultiprocessor()` function. Also, the grid-level cooperative group requires us to call the kernel function via the `cudaLaunchCooperativeKernel()` function. You can see the implementation here:

```
int reduction_grid_sync(float *g_outPtr, float *g_inPtr, int size,
int n_threads)
{
    int num_blocks_per_sm;
    cudaDeviceProp deviceProp;

    // Calculate the device occupancy to know
    // how many blocks can be run concurrently
    cudaGetDeviceProperties(&deviceProp, 0);
    cudaOccupancyMaxActiveBlocksPerMultiprocessor(&num_blocks_per_sm,
        reduction_kernel, n_threads, n_threads*sizeof(float));
    int num_sms = deviceProp.multiProcessorCount;
    int n_blocks = min(num_blocks_per_sm * num_sms,
                        (size + n_threads - 1) / n_threads);

    void *params[3];
    params[0] = (void*)&g_outPtr;
    params[1] = (void*)&g_inPtr;
    params[2] = (void*)&size;
    cudaLaunchCooperativeKernel((void*)reduction_kernel,
                                n_blocks, n_threads, params,
                                n_threads * sizeof(float), NULL);

    return n_blocks;
}
```

5. Now, make sure that the host function can be called from the `reduction.cpp` file.

6. Then, let's compile the code and see its operation. The following shell command compiles the code and executes the application. The compute capability should be equal to or greater than 70:

```
$ nvcc -run -m64 -gencode arch=compute_70,code=sm_70 -
I/usr/local/cuda/samples/common/inc -rdc=true -o reduction
./reduction.cpp ./reduction_kernel.cu
Time= 0.474 msec, bandwidth= 141.541077 GB/s
host: 0.996007, device 0.996007
```

The output performance is far behind what we saw in the final result of Chapter 3, *CUDA Thread Programming*. As the block_reduction() function uses high memory throughput at the beginning, it is highly memory bounded:

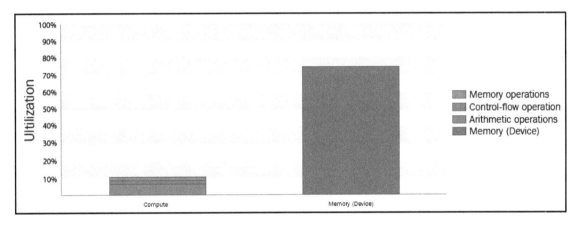

The major impact factor is that we can only use the active thread blocks. So, we cannot hide the memory access time. Actually, the usage of grid_group has other purposes, such as graph search, genetic algorithms, and particle simulation, which requires us to keep the states active for long times for performance.

This grid-level synchronization can provide more benefits to performance and programmability. As this enables the kernel to synchronize itself, we can make the kernel iterate itself. So, it is useful to solve the graph search, genetic algorithms, and practical simulations. To learn more about cooperative groups in grid_groups, please refer to the documentation provided at http://on-demand.gputechconf.com/gtc/2017/ presentation/s7622-Kyrylo-perelygin-robust-and-scalable-cuda.pdf.

CUDA kernel calls with OpenMP

To enlarge the concurrency of the application, we can make kernel calls from the host's parallel tasks. OpenMP, for instance, provides easy parallelism of the multi-core architecture. This recipe covers how CUDA can operate OpenMP.

OpenMP and CUDA calls

OpenMP uses a fork-and-join model of parallelism to target multi-core CPUs. The master thread initiates the parallel operations and creates worker threads. The host threads operate their own jobs in parallel and join after finishing their work.

Using OpenMP, CUDA kernel calls can be executed in parallel with multiple threads. This helps the programmer to not have to maintain individual kernel calls, instead allowing them to have kernel executions depend on the host thread's index.

We will use the following OpenMP APIs in this section:

- `omp_set_num_threads()` sets a number of worker threads that will work in parallel.
- `omp_get_thread_num()` returns an index of worker threads so that each thread can identify their task.
- `#pragma omp parallel {}` specifies a parallel region that will be covered by the worker threads.

Now, let's write some code in which OpenMP calls a CUDA kernel function.

CUDA kernel calls with OpenMP

In this section, we will implement a multi-stream vector add application that uses OpenMP. To do this, we will modify the previous version and see the difference:

1. To test OpenMP with CUDA, we will modify the code from the `03_cuda_callback` directory. We will modify the body of the `main()` function, or you can use the provided sample code placed in the `08_openmp_cuda` directory.

2. Now, let's include the OpenMP header file and modify the code. To use OpenMP in the code, we should use `#include <omp.h>`. And, we will update the code that iterates `for` each stream to use OpenMP:

```
// execute each operator collesponding data
omp_set_num_threads(num_operator);
#pragma omp parallel
{
    int i = omp_get_thread_num();
    printf("Launched GPU task %d\n", i);

    int offset = i * size / num_operator;
    ls_operator[i].set_index(i);
    ls_operator[i].async_operation(&h_c[offset], &h_a[offset],
                                   &h_b[offset],&d_c[offset],
                                   &d_a[offset], &d_b[offset],
                                   size / num_operator, bufsize
                                   / num_operator);
}
```

3. Compile the code with the following command:

```
$ nvcc -run -m64 -gencode arch=compute_70,code=sm_70 -
I/usr/local/cuda/samples/common/inc -Xcompiler -fopenmp -lgomp -o
openmp ./openmp.cu
stream 0 - elapsed 10.734 ms
stream 2 - elapsed 16.153 ms
stream 3 - elapsed 21.968 ms
stream 1 - elapsed 27.668 ms
compared a sample result...
host: 1.523750, device: 1.523750
Time= 27.836 msec, bandwidth= 28.930389 GB/s
```

Whenever you execute this application, you will see that each stream finishes their job out of order. Also, each stream shows a different time. That's because OpenMP can create multiple threads, and the operation is determined at runtime.

To understand its operation, let's profile the application. The following screenshot shows the profiled timeline of the application. This can be different from yours due to the scheduling:

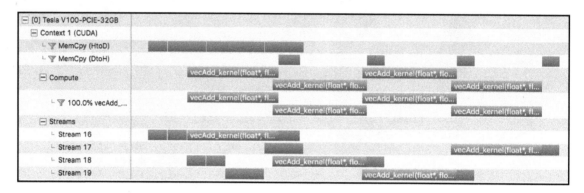

As you can see in this screenshot, you will be able to see that the data transfer has reversed compared to **Stream 17**. For this reason, we can see that the second stream could finish its job at last.

Multi-Process Service

The GPU is capable of executing kernels from concurrent CPU processes. However, by default, they are only executed in a time-sliced manner even though each kernel doesn't fully utilize GPU compute resources. To address this unnecessary serialization, the GPU provides **Multi-Process Service** (**MPS**) mode. This enables different processes to execute their kernels simultaneously on a GPU to fully utilize GPU resources. When it is enabled, the `nvidia-cuda-mps-control` daemon monitors the target GPU and manages process kernel operations using that GPU. This feature is only available on Linux. Here, we can see the MPS in which multiple processes share the same GPU:

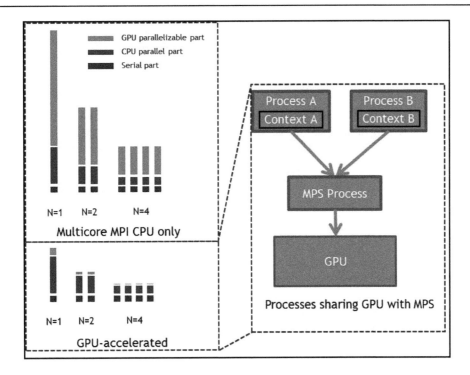

As we can see, each process has a part that runs in parallel in the GPU (green bars), while some part runs on the CPU (blue bars). Ideally, you would need both the blue bars and green bars to get the best performance. This can be made possible by making use of the MPS feature, which is supported by all the latest GPUs.

Please note that multiple MPI processes running on the same GPU are beneficial when one MPI process is unable to saturate the whole GPU and a significant part of the code is also running on the CPU. If one MPI process utilizes the whole GPU, even though the CPU part (blue bar) will reduce, the green bar time will not as the GPU is completely utilized by one MPI process. The other MPI processes will access the GPU one after another in a time-sliced manner based on the GPU architecture. This is similar to the launching-concurrent-kernels scenario. If one kernel utilizes the whole GPU, then the other kernel will either wait for the first kernel to finish or be time-sliced.

The good thing about this is that no changes need to be made to the application to make use of MPS. The MPS process runs as a daemon, as shown in the following commands:

```
$nvidia-smi -c EXCLUSIVE_PROCESS
$nvidia-cuda-mps-control -d
```

After running this command, all the processes submit their commands to the MPS daemon, which takes care of submitting the CUDA commands to GPU. For the GPU, there is only one process accessing the GPU (MPS Daemon) and hence multiple kernels can run concurrently from multiple processes. This can help overlap memory copies from one process with kernel executions from other MPI processes.

Introduction to Message Passing Interface

Message Passing Interface (**MPI**) is a parallel computing interface which enables to trigger multiple processes across the computing units - CPU cores, GPU, and nodes. The typical dense multi-GPU system contains 4-16 GPUs, while the number of CPU cores ranges between 20-40 CPUs. In MPI-enabled code, some parts of the application run in parallel as different MPI processes on multiple cores. Each MPI process will call CUDA. It is very important to understand mapping an MPI process to the respective GPU. The easiest mapping is 1:1, that is, each MPI process gets exclusive access to the respective GPU. Also, we can ideally map multiple MPI processes to a single GPU.

To have the multi-processes application scenario to a single GPU we will use MPI. To use MPI, you need to install OpenMPI for your system. Follow these steps to install OpenMPI for Linux. This operation has been tested on Ubuntu 18.04, so this can vary if you use another distribution:

```
$ wget -O /tmp/openmpi-3.0.4.tar.gz
https://www.open-mpi.org/software/ompi/v3.0/downloads/openmpi-3.0.4.tar.gz
$ tar xzf /tmp/openmpi-3.0.4.tar.gz -C /tmp
$ cd /tmp/openmpi-3.0.4
$ ./configure --enable-orterun-prefix-by-default --with-
cuda=/usr/local/cuda
$ make -j $(nproc) all && sudo make install
$ sudo ldconfig
$ mpirun --version
mpirun (Open MPI) 3.0.4

Report bugs to http://www.open-mpi.org/community/help/
```

Now, let's implement an application that can work with MPI and CUDA.

Implementing an MPI-enabled application

To make an application work with MPI, we need to put some code that can understand MPI commands in the application:

1. We will reuse the OpenMP sample code, so copy the `openmp.cu` file in the `08_openmp_cuda` directory.

2. Insert the `mpi` header `include` statement at the beginning of the code:

   ```
   #include <mpi.h>
   ```

3. Insert the following code right after the stopwatch has been created in the `main()` function:

   ```
   // set num_operator as the number of requested process
   int np, rank;
   MPI_Init(&argc, &argv);
   MPI_Comm_size(MPI_COMM_WORLD, &np);
   MPI_Comm_rank(MPI_COMM_WORLD, &rank);
   ```

4. Slice the required memory size by the number of processes, after the code mentioned in step 3, like this:

   ```
   bufsize /= np;
   size /= np;
   ```

5. We need to make each thread to report their process which they belong. Let's update the `printf()` function in the parallel execution code block, as follows:

   ```
   // execute each operator collesponding data
   omp_set_num_threads(num_operator);
   #pragma omp parallel
   {
       int i = omp_get_thread_num();
       int offset = i * size / num_operator;
       printf("Launched GPU task (%d, %d)\n", rank, i);

       ls_operator[i].set_index(i);
       ls_operator[i].async_operation(&h_c[offset],
                                      &h_a[offset], &h_b[offset],
                                      &d_c[offset], &d_a[offset],
                                      &d_b[offset],
                                      size / num_operator,
                                      bufsize / num_operator);
   }
   ```

6. At the end of `main()`, place the `MPI_Finalize()` function to close the MPI instances.

7. Compile the code with the following command:

```
$ nvcc -m64 -gencode arch=compute_70,code=sm_70 -
I/usr/local/cuda/samples/common/inc -I/usr/local/include/ -
Xcompiler -fopenmp -lgomp -lmpi -o simpleMPI ./simpleMPI.cu
```

You must use your GPU's compute capability version number for the `gencode` option.

8. Test the compiled application using the following command:

```
$ ./simpleMPI 2
```

9. Now, test MPI execution using the following command:

```
$ mpirun -np 2 ./simpleMPI 2
Number of process: 2
Number of operations: 2
Launched GPU task (1, 0)
Launched GPU task (1, 1)
Number of operations: 2
Launched GPU task (0, 0)
Launched GPU task (0, 1)
stream 0 - elapsed 13.390 ms
stream 1 - elapsed 25.532 ms
compared a sample result...
host: 1.306925, device: 1.306925
Time= 25.749 msec, bandwidth= 15.637624 GB/s
stream 0 - elapsed 21.334 ms
stream 1 - elapsed 26.010 ms
compared a sample result...
host: 1.306925, device: 1.306925
Time= 26.111 msec, bandwidth= 15.420826 GB/s
```

Enabling MPS

Enabling MPS in GPUs requires some modification of the GPU operation mode. But, you need to have a GPU architecture later than the Kepler architecture.

Let's follow the steps required to enable MPS as bellow:

1. Enable MPS mode using the following commands:

    ```
    $ export CUDA_VISIBLE_DEVICES=0
    $ sudo nvidia-smi -i 0 -c 3
    $ sudo nvidia-cuda-mps-control -d
    ```

    Or, you can use the `make enable_mps` command for this recipe sample code, which is pre-defined in `Makefile`. Then, we can see the updated compute mode from the `nivida-smi` output:

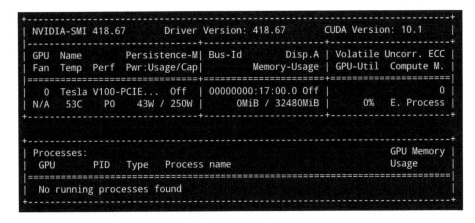

2. Now, test MPI execution with MPS mode using the following command:

    ```
    $ mpirun -np 2 ./simpleMPI 2
    Number of process: 2
    Number of operations: 2
    Launched GPU task (1, 0)
    Launched GPU task (1, 1)
    stream 0 - elapsed 10.203 ms
    stream 1 - elapsed 15.903 ms
    compared a sample result...
    host: 1.306925, device: 1.306925
    Time= 16.129 msec, bandwidth= 24.964548 GB/s
    Number of operations: 2
    Launched GPU task (0, 0)
    Launched GPU task (0, 1)
    ```

```
stream 0 - elapsed 10.203 ms
stream 1 - elapsed 15.877 ms
compared a sample result...
host: 1.306925, device: 1.306925
Time= 15.997 msec, bandwidth= 25.170544 GB/s
```

As you can see, each process' elapsed time has reduced compared to the previous executions.

3. Now, let's recover the original mode. To disable MPS mode, use the following commands:

    ```
    $ echo "quit" | sudo nvidia-cuda-mps-control
    $ sudo nvidia-smi -i 0 -c 0
    ```

    Or, you can use the `make disable_mps` command for this recipe sample code, which is pre-defined in `Makefile`.

To learn more about MPS, please use the following links:

*   `http://on-demand.gputechconf.com/gtc/2015/presentation/S5584-Priyanka-Sah.pdf`
*   `https://docs.nvidia.com/deploy/pdf/CUDA_Multi_Process_Service_Overview.pdf`

Profiling an MPI application and understanding MPS operation

Using MPI, the kernel from multiple processes can share GPU resources at the same time, which enhances overall GPU utilization. Without MPS, the GPU resources are shared inefficiently due to time-sliced sharing and the context-switching overhead.

The following screenshot shows the timeline profile result of multiple processes without MPS:

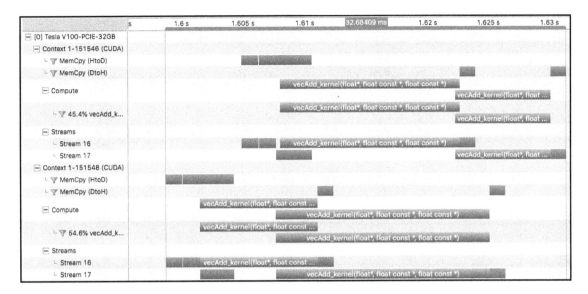

In this profile, we can see that two CUDA contexts share a GPU, and kernel execution times are prolonged due to the time-sharing between the contexts.

On the other hand, MPS mode manages the kernel execution request, so all the kernel executions are launched as though using a single process. The following screenshot shows kernel execution with MPS mode:

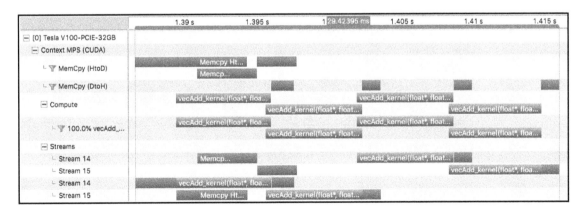

As you can see, only one CUDA stream resides on a GPU and controls all the CUDA streams. Also, all the kernel execution times are stabilized and the total elapsed time is reduced using MPS. In conclusion, using MPS mode benefits overall performance for multiple GPU processes and shares GPU resources.

nvprof supports dumping profiler information for multiple MPI processes in a different file. For example, for an Open MPI-based application, the following command will dump profiling information in multiple files, each with a unique name based on the MPI process rank:

```
$ mpirun -np 2 nvprof -f -o simpleMPI.%q{OMPPI_COMM_WORLD_RANK}_2.nvvp
./simpleMPI 2
```

Or, you can use the following command for the sample recipe code:

```
$ PROCS=2 STREAMS=2 make nvprof
```

Then, you will get two nvvp files for each process.

Now, we will review these nvvp files using NVIDIA Visual Profiler with the following steps:

1. Open the **File** | **Import** menu to create a profiling session by importing the nvvp files:

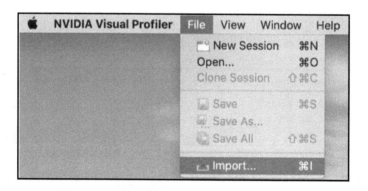

In Windows or Linux, the shortcut key is *Ctrl + I*, and OSX uses *command + I*.

2. Then click the **Next** button after selecting **Nvprof** from the list:

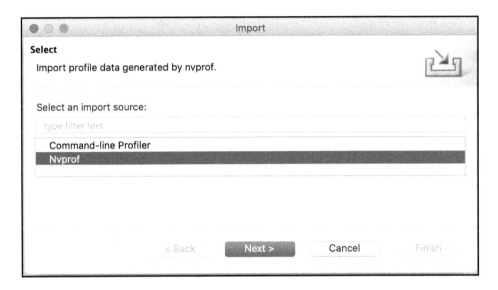

3. From the **Nvprof** option, select **Multiple processes** and click **Next >**:

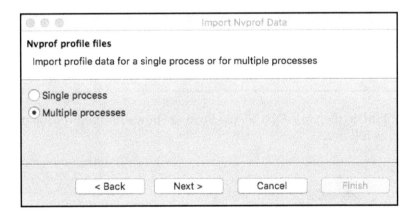

4. From **Import Nvprof Data**, click the **Browse...** button, and select nvvp files, which are generated by nvprof. To profile an application with multi-process, you need to import nvvp files as there are processes:

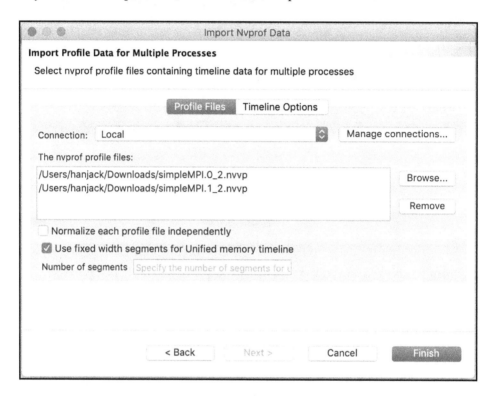

5. Click **Finish**, then NVIDIA Visual Profiler shows profiled results in the timeline view, as follows:

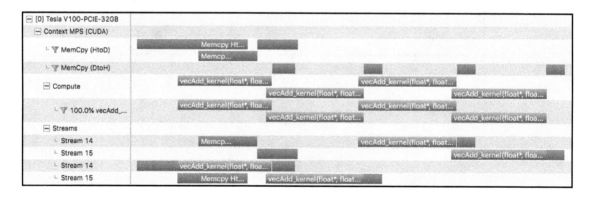

Please note that only the synchronous MPI calls will be annotated by `nvprof`. In the case of an asynchronous MPI API being used, other MPI-specialized profiling tools need to be used. Some of the most famous tools include the following:

- **TAU**: TAU is a performance profiling toolkit and is currently maintained by the University of Oregon.
- **Vampir**: This is a commercially available tool and provides good scalability to hundreds of MPI processes.
- **Intel VTune Amplifier**: Another option when it comes to commercial tools is Intel VTune Amplifier. It is one of the best tools available and can be used for MPI application analysis.

The latest CUDA Toolkits also allow the MPI API to be annotated. For this, the `--annotate-mpi` flag needs to be passed to `nvprof`, as shown in the following command:

```
mpirun -np 2 nvprof --annotate-mpi openmpi -o
myMPIApp.%q{OMPI_COMM_WORLD_RANK}.nvprof ./myMPIApplciation
```

Kernel execution overhead comparison

For iterative parallel GPU tasks, we have three kinds of kernel execution methods: iterative kernel calls, having an inner loop, and having recursions using dynamic parallelism. The best operation is determined by the algorithm and the application. But, you also may consider kernel execution options among them. This recipe helps you to compare those kernel execution overheads and review their programmability.

To begin with, let's determine which operation we will test. This recipe will use a simple SAXPY operation. This helps us to focus and make iterative execution code. In addition, the operation control overhead will become heavier as the operation gets simpler. But, you can try with any other operation you want, of course.

Implementing three types of kernel executions

The following steps cover the performance comparison of three different iterative operations:

1. Create and navigate the `10_kernel_execution_overhead` directory.

2. Write the `simple_saxpy_kernel()` function with the following code:

```
__global__ void
simple_saxpy_kernel(float *y, const float* x, const float alpha,
const float beta)
{
    int idx = blockIdx.x * blockDim.x + threadIdx.x;
    y[idx] = alpha * x[idx] + beta;
}
```

3. Write the `iterative_saxpy_kernel()` function with the following code:

```
__global__ void
iterative_saxpy_kernel(float *y, const float* x,
                       const float alpha, const float beta,
                       int n_loop)
{
    int idx = blockIdx.x * blockDim.x + threadIdx.x;

    for (int i = 0; i < n_loop; i++)
        y[idx] = alpha * x[idx] + beta;
}
```

4. Write the `recursive_saxpy_kernel()` function with the following code:

```
__global__ void
recursive_saxpy_kernel(float *y, const float* x,
                       const float alpha, const float beta,
                       int depth)
{
    int idx = blockIdx.x * blockDim.x + threadIdx.x;

    if (depth == 0)
        return;
    else
        y[idx] = alpha * x[idx] + beta;
    if (idx == 0)
        vecAdd_kernel_C<<< gridDim.x, blockDim.x
                       >>>(y, x, alpha, beta, depth - 1);
}
```

5. Write the host code that launches those CUDA kernel functions. At first, we will have an iterative function call of the `simple_saxpy_kernel()` function:

```
for (int i = 0; i < n_loop; i++) {
    simple_saxpy_kernel<<< dimGrid, dimBlock >>>(
                            d_y, d_x, alpha, beta);
}
```

Secondly, we will call the `iterative_saxpy_kernel()` kernel function, which has an iterative loop inside:

```
iterative_saxpy_kernel<<< dimGrid, dimBlock >>>(
                        d_y, d_x, alpha, beta, n_loop);
```

Lastly, we will call the `recursive_saxpy_kernel()` kernel function, which calls itself in a recursive manner:

```
recursive_saxpy_kernel<<< dimGrid, dimBlock >>>(
                        d_y, d_x, alpha, beta, n_loop);
```

The number of loops is smaller than or equal to 24, since the maximum recursion depth is 24. Other than simple loop operations, you do not have to place a loop operation at the host since it is already defined in the kernel code.

6. Compile the code using the following command:

```
$ nvcc -run -m64 -gencode arch=compute_70,code=sm_70 -
I/usr/local/cuda/samples/common/inc -rdc=true -o cuda_kernel
./cuda_kernel.cu
```

You must use your GPU's compute capability version number for the `gencode` option.

7. Test the compiled application. This result was measured using Tesla P40 because CUDA 9.x does not support **CUDA Dynamic Parallelism** (**CDP**) profile for Volta GPUs:

```
Elapsed Time...
simple loop: 0.094 ms
inner loop : 0.012 ms
recursion : 0.730 ms
```

Comparison of three executions

From the result, we can confirm that the inner loop is the fastest method for the iterative operation. The following screenshot shows a profiled result of this sample application:

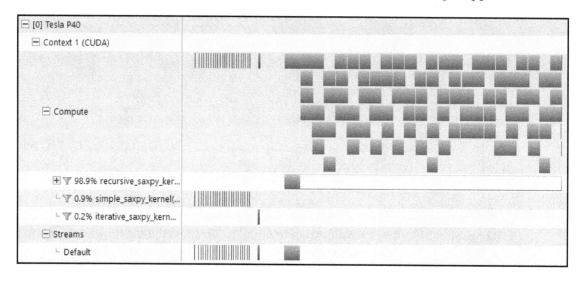

The iterative kernel call shows the kernel launch overhead for each kernel call. The GPU needs to fetch all the required data from the device memory, and needs to schedule the GPU resources, and so on. On the other hand, the inner loop kernel shows one packed operation because all the required resources are pre-located and there's no need to reschedule its execution. The recursive kernel operation shows the most prolonged execution time due to the dynamic parallelism limitations we discussed previously.

In general, using the approach with the least overhead is recommended. However, it is hard to say which kernel call design is superior to the others, since there's more to the algorithm and its problems than what we've covered here. For instance, CDP used to enhance parallelism in certain cases, such as for GPU trees and searches.

Summary

In this chapter, we have covered several kernel execution mechanisms. We covered what CUDA streams are, and how to use them to execute multiple kernel functions concurrently. By utilizing the asynchronous operation between the host and the GPU, we have learned that we can hide the kernel execution time by making the pipelining architecture with data transfer and kernel executions. Also, we can make a CUDA stream call the host function using the callback function. We can create a prioritized stream, and confirm its prioritized execution, too. To measure the exact execution time of a kernel function, we have used CUDA events, and we also learned that CUDA events can be used to synchronize with the host. In the last section, we also discussed the performance of each kernel execution method.

We also covered other kernel operation models: dynamic parallelism and grid-level cooperative groups. Dynamic parallelism enables kernel calls inside the kernel function so we can make recursive operations with that. The grid-level cooperative group enables versatile grid-level synchronization, and we discussed how this feature can be useful in a specific area: graph search, genetic algorithms, and particle simulations.

Then, we expanded our coverage to the host. CUDA kernels can be called from multiple threads or multiple processes. To execute multiple threads, we used OpenMP with CUDA and discussed its usefulness. We used MPI to simulate multiple process operations, and could see how MPS benefits overall application performance.

As we saw in this chapter, choosing the right kernel execution model is an important topic, as is thread programming. This can optimize application execution time. Now, we will expand our discussion to multi-GPU programming to solve big problems.

CUDA Application Profiling and Debugging **5**

CUDA provides many programming tools for developers. These tools are the compilers, profilers, the IDE and its plugins, debuggers, and memory checkers. Learning about these tools will help you analyze your application and help you accomplish the development projects we will be covering. In this chapter, we will cover the basic usage of these tools and discuss how to apply these to application development.

The following topics will be covered in this chapter:

- Profiling focused target ranges in GPU applications
- Visual profiling against the remote machine
- Debugging a CUDA application with CUDA error
- Asserting local GPU values using CUDA Assert
- Debugging a CUDA application with Nsight Visual Studio Edition
- Debugging a CUDA application with Nsight Eclipse Edition
- Debugging a CUDA application with CUDA-GDB
- Runtime validation with CUDA-memcheck

Technical requirements

To complete this chapter, it is recommended that you use an NVIDIA GPU card later than the Pascal architecture. In other words, your GPU's compute capability should be equal to or greater than 60. If you are unsure of your GPU's architecture, please visit NVIDIA's site, `https://developer.nvidia.com/cuda-gpus`, and confirm your GPU's compute capability.

The sample code for this chapter has been developed and tested with version 10.1 of CUDA Toolkit. In general, it is recommended that you use the latest CUDA version if applicable.

Profiling focused target ranges in GPU applications

NVIDIA's Visual Profiler is a handy tool for finding bottlenecks in GPU applications and understanding their operations. Although it provides fluent information of the application operations, those can be redundant if you just want to focus on a specific area of code. In this situation, limiting the range of profiling is more productive.

Profiling targets can be specific code blocks, GPU, and time. Specifying the code blocks is called **focused profiling**. This technique is useful when you want to focus on profiling on a specific kernel function, or profiling on the part of a large GPU application. Targeting GPUs or time will be covered after we cover focused profiling.

Limiting the profiling target in code

To benefit from focused profiling, you may want to include the featured header file in your source code, as follows:

```
#include <cuda_profiler_api.h>
```

Then, you can specify your targeting range of profiling using cudaProfilerStart() and cudaProfilerStop():

```
cudaProfilerStart();
... {target of profile} ...
cudaProfilerStop();
```

Now, you need to profile your application with a specific flag, --profile-from-start.

This option doesn't let the profiler start profiling until the request arrives. If you want to profile your application using NVIDIA Visual Profiler, make sure to tick the **Start execution with profiling enabled** checkbox in the setting view.

The following steps cover how to control the NVIDIA profiler using some simple example code. To make this easier, we will reuse the sample code that we used to operate matrix multiplication in Chapter 3, *CUDA Thread Programming*:

1. Write a CUDA application with two simple SGEMM CUDA kernel functions. The kernel functions are identical but have different names, that is, sgemm_kernel_A() and sgemm_kernel_B().

2. Make two iterative calls, like so:

```
int n_iter = 5;
for (int i = 0; i < n_iter; i++)
    sgemm_gpu_A(d_A, d_B, d_C, N, M, K, alpha, beta);
for (int i = 0; i < n_iter; i++)
    sgemm_gpu_B(d_A, d_B, d_C, N, M, K, alpha, beta);
```

3. Now, let's compile the code and profile using nvprof:

```
$ nvcc -m64 -gencode arch=compute_70,code=sm_70 -o sgemm sgemm.cu
$ nvprof -f -o profile-original.nvvp ./sgemm
```

When you open the generated profile-original.nvvp file using the Visual Profiler, you will have the profiled result, as follows:

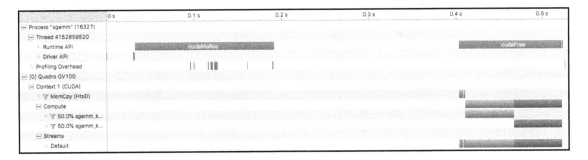

This timeline includes whole profiled information from when the application started. However, we can say that the profiled result contains unnecessary information when we want to optimize our kernel functions.

The following steps cover how to specify the profile focusing area:

1. Place `#include <cuda_profiler_api.h>` on top of the source code to enable focused profile APIs. Then, we can embrace the area we are interested in using `cudaProfilerStart()` and `cudaProfilerStop()`, as follows:

```
cudaProfilerStart();
for (int i = 0; i < n_iter; i++)
    sgemm_gpu_B(d_A, d_B, d_C, N, M, K, alpha, beta);
cudaProfilerStop();
```

2. Compile your code and view the updated profiled result using the Visual Profiler. We have to provide the `--profile-from-start off` option to the profiler, as follows:

```
$ nvcc -m64 -gencode arch=compute_70,code=sm_70 -o sgemm sgemm.cu
$ nvprof -f -o profile-start-stop.nvvp --profile-from-start off
./sgemm
```

When you open the newly generated profile result, the profiler only reports the specified part of the application, as follows:

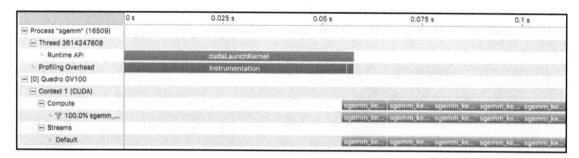

The profile result is restricted. The preceding screenshot shows the kernel's execution from when it started GPU execution. As a result, you can eliminate having to profile an application's initialization and other irrelevant operations.

In conclusion, the focused profile has several benefits, as follows:

- It helps you focus on the module you're currently developing.
- It lets you remove irrelevant operations from the report in the profiler, for example:
  - An external module's behavior that doesn't have any relation to your code
  - Application initialization delay
- It helps you save time when it comes to finding the targeting function in the timeline view.

Limiting the profiling target with time or GPU

The NVIDIA profiler has other options that can limit profile targets. You can use the following options with focused profiling, too:

- The `--timeout <second>` option limits application execution time. This option is useful when you need to profile an application that has a long execution time with iterative operations.
- The `--devices <gpu ids>` option specifies the GPUs to profile. This option helps you narrow down GPU kernel operations in a multiple GPU application.

Also, you don't have to collect all the metrics if you only want to focus on a few kernel functions. You can just stipulate your interest to the profiler with the `--kernels`, `--event`, and `--metrics` options. You can use those options along with other profile options, as follows:

```
$ nvprof -f -o profile_kernels_metric.nvvp --kernels sgemm_kernel_B --
metrics all ./sgemm
```

After importing the collected metrics into the timeline profile result, you will find that the targeted kernels only have metrics information.

There are many other versatile profile features in CPU sampling, such as marking profile range, OpenMP and OpenACC profiles, and so on. If you want to take a look at the features of the NVIDIA profiler, check out the following profiler introduction talk by Jeff Larkin from NVIDIA: `https://www.olcf.ornl.gov/wp-content/uploads/2018/12/summit_workshop_Profilers.pdf`.

NVIDIA's official profiler user guide provides details about the NVIDIA profiler's functions (`https://docs.nvidia.com/cuda/profiler-users-guide/index.html`).

Profiling with NVTX

With focused profiling, we can profile a limited, specific area by using `cudaProfilerStart()` and `cudaProfilerStop()`. However, if we want to analyze functional performance in a complex application, it is limited. For this situation, the CUDA profiler provides timeline annotations via the **NVIDIA Tools Extension** (**NVTX**).

Using NVTX, we can annotate the CUDA code. We can use the NVTX API as follows:

```
nvtxRangePushA("Annotation");
.. { Range of GPU operations } ..
cudaDeviceSynchronization();     // in case if the target code block is
pure kernel calls
nvtxRangePop();
```

As you can see, we can define a range as a group of codes and annotate that range manually. Then, the CUDA profiler provides a timeline trace of the annotation so that we can measure the execution time of code blocks. One drawback of this is that the NVTX APIs are host functions, so we need to synchronize the host and GPU if the target code blocks are pure GPU kernel calls.

To learn more about this, let's apply this NVTX code to the previous focused profiling example. First, we should include an NVTX header file, as follows:

```
#include "nvToolsExt.h"
```

Then, we will insert `nvtxRangePushA()` and `nvtxRangePop()` into several places, as follows:

```
cudaProfileStart();
// copy initial value for gpu memory
nvtxRangePushA("Data Transfer");
cudaMemcpy(d_A, A, N * K * sizeof(float), cudaMemcpyHostToDevice);
cudaMemcpy(d_B, A, K * M * sizeof(float), cudaMemcpyHostToDevice);
cudaMemcpy(d_C, A, N * M * sizeof(float), cudaMemcpyHostToDevice);
nvtxRangePop();

nvtxRangePushA("Kernel Execution");
// do operation
nvtxRangePushA("Kernel A");
for (int i = 0; i < n_iter; i++)
    sgemm_gpu_A(d_A, d_B, d_C, N, M, K, alpha, beta);
cudaDeviceSynchronize();
nvtxRangePop();     // Kernel A

nvtxRangePushA("Kernel B");
for (int i = 0; i < n_iter; i++)
    sgemm_gpu_B(d_A, d_B, d_C, N, M, K, alpha, beta);
cudaDeviceSynchronize();

nvtxRangePop();     // Kernel B
nvtxRangePop();     // Kernel Execution
cudaProfileStop();
```

In the preceding code, we have enlarged the focused profile area to monitor the NVTX operation. We also have `Data Transfer`, `Kernel A`, `Kernel B`, and `Kernel Execution` as NVTX ranges. NVTX supports multi-level annotations, so the `Kernel A` and `Kernel B` ranges will be included in the `Kernel Execution` timeline.

To compile the code, we should provide the `-lnvToolsExt` option to the `nvcc` compiler to provide NVTX API's definition. We can compile the code using the following command:

```
$ nvcc -m64 -gencode arch=compute_70,code=sm_70 -lnvToolsExt -o sgemm
sgemm.cu
```

Then, the NVIDIA profiler can collect NVTX annotations without extra options. We can profile the application using the following command:

```
$ nvprof -f --profile-from-start off -o sgemm.nvvp ./sgemm.nvvp
```

The following screenshot shows the timeline profiled result. In this screenshot, we can see **Markers and Ranges** colored in green. These green bars have the annotations:

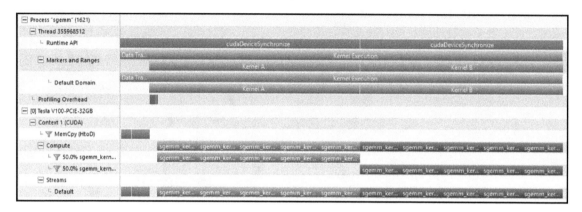

The preceding screenshot provides us with the following information:

- We can identify where the memory copy operation has been called following the NVTX annotation.
- We can divide the functional positions by wrapping the area, for example, `kernel A` and `kernel B`.
- The NVTX annotation can stack multiple levels of annotations. As we can see, `kernel A` and `kernel B` are included in the `kernel execution` annotation.

The following document not only introduces NVTX but also explains how to use different colors using NVTX: `https://devblogs.nvidia.com/cuda-pro-tip-generate-custom-application-profile-timelines-nvtx`. One of the applications of NVTX is to profile deep learning networks with NVTX annotations. This provides insight into network operation bottlenecks. We will discuss this in `Chapter 10`, *Deep Learning Acceleration with CUDA*, of this book.

Visual profiling against the remote machine

The NVIDIA Visual Profiler also can profile remote applications. This feature eases the profiling task when it comes to remote application development, especially when you develop your application on the server-side.

There are several ways of using visual profilers, as follows:

- Profiling on the host with the host CUDA application
- By collecting profile data using the `nvprof` CLI on the target side, copying the file to the host, and opening it using the Visual Profiler
- Profiling the application on the target platform using the host machine

Visual profiling directly in the host machine is convenient and can save development time. Also, remote profiling provides the same user experience that profiling a GPU application on a host machine does. One exception is that we should establish a remote connection. Another benefit OS host-managed visual profiling provides is that the profiler collects metric information on-demand automatically.

The NVIDIA profiler communicates with the NVIDIA profiler in the host machine and collects profiled data. Therefore, you need to confirm that your host machine – desktop or laptop – should connect to the remote machine. The following diagram shows the overview of this connection:

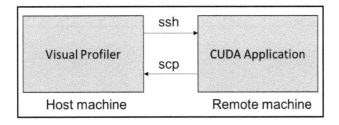

Let's try to profile a GPU application remotely. The following steps cover how to profile a remote GPU application in NVIDIA Visual Profiler:

1. First, go to **File | New session**. When you click the **New Session** menu, you will see the following dialog window:

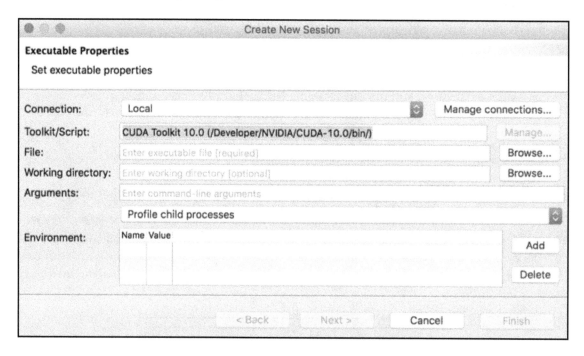

2. Then, we need to add a connection, which we do by going to the **Manage connection...** menu. Then, the **New Remote Connection** dialog will appear. Add your remote machine information by clicking the **Add** button and putting your remote machine information in the appropriate sections. Then, close the dialog by clicking the **Finish** button. When you're finished, you will see the following output:

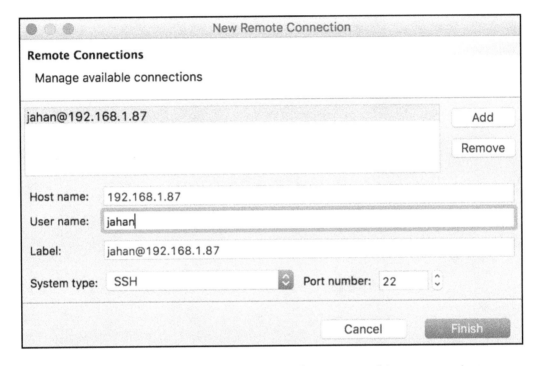

As we discussed previously, the host and remote machine communicate over **SSH**, whose default port number is **22**. If the host machine uses another port for SSH, you have to inform it of that port number in the new remote session creation dialog.

3. Now, we need to set up CUDA Toolkit paths in the remote machine by clicking the **Manage...** button at the right-hand side of **Toolkit/Script**. A good start is to use the **Detect** button. It finds the `nvcc` path and sets up the configuration information automatically. If automatic detection failed, you have to input the configuration information manually. When you've finished with the configuration process, click the **Finish** button, as follows:

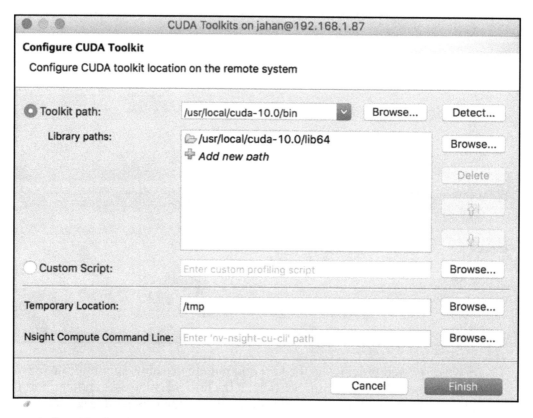

4. Specify the GPU application's binary by clicking the **Browse** button on the right-hand side of the **File** text box. It will ask for your remote machine login password. Find your application path and set the application's path. You can also put the application's arguments if you need to control the application's behavior. When you've finished setting up the application and connection, click the **Next** button to set the profiler's options.

5. Now, we will set up the profiling options. NVIDIA Visual Profiler allows us to set the profiler's options using checkboxes as shown in the following screenshot. By clicking **Finish**, the profiler collects profile data from the application:

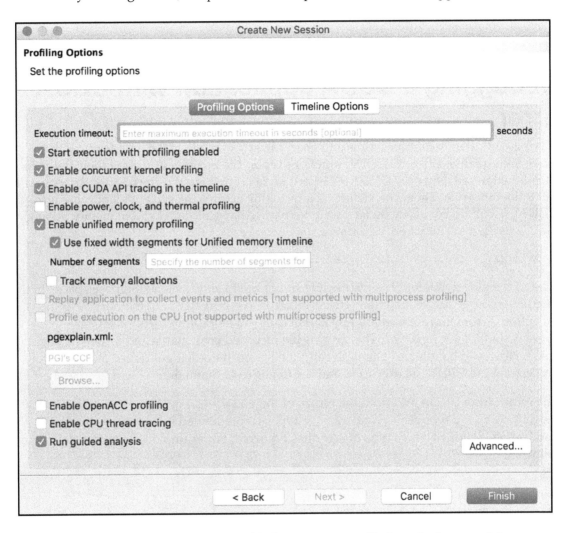

You will see the timelined profiled output, as profiled on the host machine.

4. Finally, analyze the performance of the profiled timeline graph. Click any kernel function you want to analyze. Click the **Perform Kernel Analysis** button; the profiler tool will collect the related metrics information. By doing this, you can quickly get a report regarding the performance limiters and find the bottlenecks of the kernel function.

Debugging a CUDA application with CUDA error

Having dedicated exception checks and checking errors is one of the base features that make high-quality software. CUDA functions report the error by returning their status for each function call. Not only CUDA APIs, but kernel functions and the CUDA library's API call follow this rule. Therefore, detecting a recurring error is the start of identifying errors in CUDA execution. For example, let's assume that we have allocated global memory using the cudaMalloc() function, as follows:

```
cudaMalloc((void**)&ptr, byte_size);
```

What if the global memory has insufficient free space to allocate new memory space? In this case, the cudaMalloc() function returns an error to report an out of memory exception. Errors that are triggered by kernel calls can be captured from the flags using cudaGetLastError(). This returns the recorded error status and resets the flag's value. However, handle this flag with caution: its return doesn't guarantee that the error occurred at the GPU's last execution and the flag is reset manually.

The return from CUDA APIs and the return of the cudaGetLastError() function are of the cudaError_t type. This cudaError_t type is a predefined integer type, and the application identifies which type of error has occurred. For example, this type is defined as follows:

```
Enum cudaErorr_t {
    cudaSuccess = 0,
    cudaErrorMemoryAllocation = 2,
    cudaErrorUnknown = 30,
    cudaErrorNoDevice = 38,
    cudaErrorAssert = 59,
    cudaErrorTooManyPeers = 60,
    cudaErrorNotSupported = 71,
    ....
};
```

Memorizing or translating all of these values is impractical. For this purpose, the CUDA sample code provides a helper function, checkCudaError(), which is located in common/inc/cuda_helper.h. This function prints out the error message when the CUDA function returns errors. Its function definition is as follows:

```
#define checkCudaErrors(err) { \
    if (err != cudaSuccess) {  \

        fprintf(stderr, "checkCudaErrors() API error = %04d \"%s\" from
file <%s>, line %i.\n", \
                err, cudaGetErrorString(err), __FILE__, __LINE__); \
        exit(-1); \
    } \
}
#endif
```

Since this function is defined as a macro, we can identify the line where the error occurred.

There are two ways we can use this function. One is to include the cuda_helper.h file in the source code. Alternatively, we can copy the function code into somewhere in the code.

Then, we will embrace all the CUDA API classes with checkCudaErrors(), as follows:

```
checkCudaErrors(cudaMalloc((void **)&d_A, N * K * sizeof(float)));
checkCudaErrors(cudaMalloc((void **)&d_B, K * M * sizeof(float)));
checkCudaErrors(cudaMalloc((void **)&d_C, N * M * sizeof(float)));
```

For the kernel function call, we will use the cudaGetLastError() function to get the kernel call's error flag, as follows:

```
sgemm_kernel_A<<<dimGrid, dimBlock>>>(A, B, C, N, M, K, alpha, beta);
checkCudaErrors(cudaGetLastError());
```

However, this code has a problem: the kernel operation is asynchronous with the host so that cudaGetLastError() can only catch the host side's return values. It is highly possible that the error was triggered somewhere in the application. To resolve this situation, you can use any host and device synchronization function; for example:

```
sgemm_kernel_A<<<dimGrid, dimBlock>>>(A, B, C, N, M, K, alpha, beta);
checkCudaErrors(cudaDeviceSynchronize());
```

Now, let's test the error detection code by modifying the source code to generate an error. For example, you can request `cudaMemcpy` to copy a larger memory space than the allocated size. In this case, the application returns an error message, as follows:

```
$ nvcc -run -m64 -gencode arch=compute_70,code=sm_70 -
I/usr/local/cuda/samples/common/inc -lnvToolsExt -o sgemm ./sgemm.cu
CUDA error at sgemm.cu:93 code=11(cudaErrorInvalidValue) "cudaMemcpy(d_A,
A, N * K * sizeof(float), cudaMemcpyHostToDevice)"
```

Alternatively, you can pass a `NULL` point for the CUDA kernel so that the kernel accesses the invalid memory space. In this case, the application reports an illegal address error in `cudaDeviceSynchronize()`:

```
$ nvcc -run -m64 -gencode arch=compute_70,code=sm_70 -
I/usr/local/cuda/samples/common/inc -lnvToolsExt -o sgemm ./sgemm.cu
CUDA error at sgemm.cu:104 code=77(cudaErrorIllegalAddress)
"cudaDeviceSynchronize()"
```

This error checking macro is quite useful because it reports where the error occurs in the source code. However, this report has a missing point that its error detected position does not match with the real error occurred position.

The error message should report the position where we copying memory that's larger than the allocated memory results in an illegal value error immediately. So, the developer can identify the error message right after the kernel call. However, this error checking code only works on a host. Therefore, this can confuse the GPU operations if they're not synchronized properly. For example, if we didn't set the synchronization and just checking error, then the `cudaDeviceSynchronize()` function can report an error from the wrong place. In this case, we can set `CUDA_LAUNCH_BLOCKING=1` environment variable to make all the kernel execution to be synchronized with the host:

```
$ ./sgemm
CUDA error at sgemm.cu:104 code=77(cudaErrorIllegalAddress)
"cudaDeviceSynchronize()"

$ CUDA_LAUNCH_BLOCKING=1 ./sgemm
CUDA error at sgemm.cu:36 code=77(cudaErrorIllegalAddress)
"cudaGetLastError()"
```

Line 36 at `sgemm.cu` is the `cudaGetLastError()` call, right after the `sgemm` kernel call. That's where we place an intended error. We can identify the correct error position at runtime.

There are two official documents that can help you learn about the different types of CUDA errors:

- `https://docs.nvidia.com/cuda/cuda-runtime-api/group__CUDART__TYPES.html`
- `include/driver_types.h` in the CUDA Toolkit root path

Asserting local GPU values using CUDA assert

Even though your GPU application works without any systematic errors, you need to check the computed result to make sure that the execution works as it was designed to. For this purpose, CUDA provides the `assert` function, which checks whether the argument value is zero. If it is, this function raises an error flag so that the host can identify that there is an error in the kernel function.

An assertion is used to validate that the operation result is as expected. In CUDA programming, the `assert` function can be called from the device code and can stop the kernel's execution when the given argument is zero:

```
void assert(int expression);
```

This is the declaration of the `assert` function, which is the same as it is for C/C++. When the assertion is triggered, the application stops and reports its error message. If the application is launched by the debugger, it works as a breakpoint so that the developer can debug the given information. For instance, the output message looks like this:

```
$ nvcc -run -m64 -gencode arch=compute_70,code=sm_70 -
I/usr/local/cuda/samples/common/inc -lnvToolsExt -o sgemm ./sgemm.cu
sgemm.cu:29: void sgemm_kernel_A(const float *, const float *, float *,
int, int, int, float, float): block: [16,64,0], thread: [0,0,0] Assertion
`sum == 0.f` failed.
```

Since the output message directs the exact CUDA block and thread index, the developer can analyze the directed CUDA thread's execution easily.

Now, let's apply the assertion and see how it can detect intended errors. We will modify the SGEMM operation code that we used in the *Profiling focused target ranges in GPU applications* section.

First, place the assertion code in the middle of a kernel function. We will see the effect of the expression, which should be false. The assertion code can be written as follows:

```
__global__ void sgemm_kernel_A(const float *A, const float *B, float *C,
int N, int M, int K, float alpha, float beta)
{
    int col = blockIdx.x * blockDim.x + threadIdx.x;
    int row = blockIdx.y * blockDim.y + threadIdx.y;
    float sum = 0.f;
    for (int i = 0; i < K; ++i)
        sum += A[row * K + i] * B[i * K + col];
    if (row == 0 && col == 0)
        assert(sum == 0.f);
    C[row * M + col] = alpha * sum + beta * C[row * M + col];
}
```

You can try other index values or try other possible errors too. Compile the code and run it to see the output. The following code shows the output error of this modification:

```
sgemm.cu:29: void sgemm_kernel_A(const float *, const float *, float *,
int, int, int, float, float): block: [0,0,0], thread: [0,0,0] Assertion
`sum == 0.f` failed.
```

The error message reports that the assertion triggered the code location, the kernel function's name, and GPU's thread index. With this information, we can find out where we should start analyzing easily.

Actually, the usage of the `assert` function is the same as the `assert` function in normal C/C++ programming. One difference is that the `assert` function works in the device code. Therefore, it reports not only the event location and the expression, but also shows the block and thread index.

However, using assertion has an impact on application performance. Therefore, we should only use assertion for debugging purposes. It is recommended to disable it when we're running in a production environment. You can disable assertion at compile time by adding the `NDEBUG` preprocessed macro before including `assert.h`.

Debugging a CUDA application with Nsight Visual Studio Edition

For Windows application developers, the CUDA Toolkit provides Nsight Visual Studio Edition, which enables GPU computing in Visual Studio. This tool works as an extension of Visual Studio, but you can build, debug, profile, and trace GPU applications along with the host. If your working platform is not Windows, the contents in this section won't be applicable, so you can skip it.

The CUDA debugger allows us to monitor the local values on a GPU kernel for each CUDA thread. Like normal host debugging, you can set breakpoints in the kernel code and trigger them. You can also place conditions such as other normal breakpoints. With this feature, you can trigger breakpoints for a specific CUDA thread index and review their local variables.

This tool can be installed along with the CUDA Toolkit. You can obtain the latest version from the website. It is not mandatory, but it is recommended when your development environment is using the old CUDA Toolkit on the latest GPU and its driver. Visit the NVIDIA Nsight web page (`https://developer.nvidia.com/nsight-visual-studio-edition`) to download and install Nsight. You'll need an NVIDIA developer membership to obtain the software. You will also need to install the recommended display driver version.

You can find the CUDA tools by going to **Menu** | **Nsight** in the Visual Studio menu bar. There are several tools in this menu, some of which are as follows:

- **Graphics debugging**: A debugger for graphics (Direct3D, OpenGL, and Vulkan) applications
- **CUDA debugging (Next-Gen)**: A debugger for debugging CPU and GPU code simultaneously (Turing, Volta, and Pascal with the latest drivers)
- **CUDA debugging (Legacy)**: A debugger for GPU kernels only (Pascal with the old drivers, Maxwell, and Kepler)
- **Performance analysis**: For the analysis of the current GPU's application performance
- **CUDA memory checker**: For checking GPU memory violations during runtime (as covered in the previous section)

In this section, we will focus on CUDA debugging (Next-Gen). This is because the Next-Gen debugger can support the latest architectures, including Turing and Volta. The CUDA memory checker will be covered at the end of this chapter.

Now, let's configure a sample project and see how we can debug the application using Nsight Visual Studio Edition. You may use the default sample code or replace the code with the previous CUDA code we covered. You can also use the given sample code in the `05_debug/05_debug_with_vs` file. It is some simple SAXPY code.

Set the project properties to generate the proper device target code. In the project's property page, you can specify the target code version. List the architecture versions you want to use in the **CUDA C/C++ | Code Generation** text box:

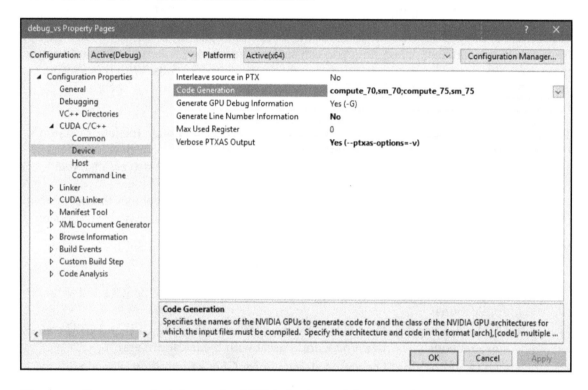

The preceding screenshot shows the CUDA device code's generation property page. You can set several `nvcc` options, such as the target GPU's compute capability, register limitations per thread, and CUDA kernel information that's verbose during compile time.

Place breakpoints at line 34, where the middle of the kernel function is, and at line 75, where we copy data from the host to the device. Then, compile and start debugging using one of these methods:

- Navigate to Nsight in the Visual Studio menu bar and click on **Start CUDA Debugging (Next-Gen)**.
- Right-click on the project in Solution Explorer and choose **Debug** | **Start CUDA Debugging (Next-Gen)**.
- Go to the Nsight CUDA debugging toolbar and click **Start CUDA Debugging (Next-Gen)**.

Window's firewall may ask if you trust and want to allow the network connection of Nsight. This is normal, since Nsight uses the internal network to monitor GPU devices. Click *Accept* and continue the debugging. The current Nsight Visual Studio Edition provides two types of debugging options. It depends on the target GPU architecture version. If your GPU is Volta or Turing, it is recommended to use Next-Gen debugging. If your GPU is Pascal, the proper debugger differs, depending on the driver version. To clarify, please visit the supported GPU list from NVIDIA: `http://developer.nvidia.com/nsight-visual-studio-edition-supported-gpus-full-list`.

The application will stop where the application starts. Continue the trace. The application will stop at line 75 on the host and line 34 on the device. From this, we can learn that the Nsight can trace a GPU application on the host and the device simultaneously.

When the yellow arrow stops in the kernel function, you can review the local variables. The thread index is 0 in global indexes. Since CUDA issues multiple CUDA warps and CUDA threads in parallel, you can review the other threads' local variables by changing `blockIdx` and `threadIdx`. The basic CUDA thread debugging control unit is a warp. In other words, you can control the debugger so that it traverses active warps. The Nsight debugger provides this feature in the **Previous Active Warp/Next Active Warp** menu in the Nsight menu bar.

The following screenshot shows the Nsight debug controls that appear while we're debugging:

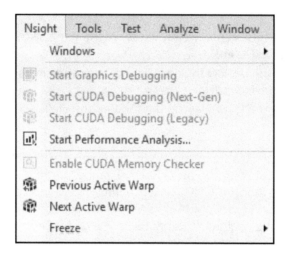

If you change the warp, you will find that the local variables that are monitored in the **Autos** panel update the index, along with the warp. For example, the following screenshot shows the **Autos** window, which reports the local variables of the selected thread in an active warp, that is, the local variable's value that's being monitored by the leading thread:

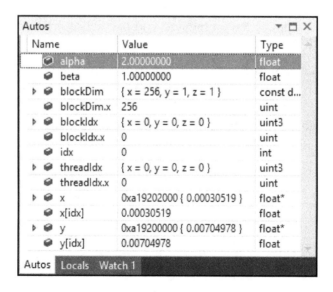

The **Autos** value is updated following the selected thread changes. The following screenshot shows the changes that were made by moving to the next active warp:

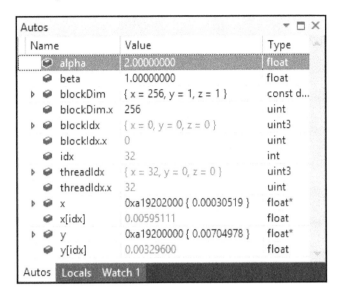

The Next-Gen CUDA debugger provides three types of windows—warp info, lanes, and GPU registers. The yellow arrow denotes current GPU execution, and its information is shown in three aspects:

- The **Warp Info** window provides another way we can select an active warp. You can open the window from **Nsight** | **Window** | **Warp Info** in the menu bar. The window looks as follows:

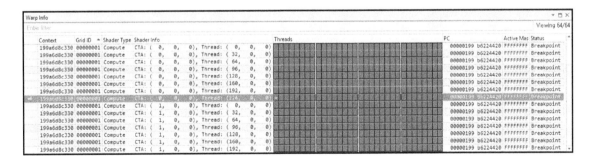

Each row denotes the active warps in the CUDA grid. The fourth column, **Shader Info**, shows each warp's block and leading thread index. The fifth column, threads, shows the CUDA thread's status in the warp. The color of the cell represents each thread's status. They are all red since we are watching them at the breakpoints, but you will see other colors during the debugging process. The following screenshot explains what each color means in terms of thread state:

	Color	Thread State
	Gray	Inactive
	Forest Green	Active
	Light Sea Green	At Barrier
	Red	At Breakpoint
	Orange	At Assert
	Dark Red	At Exception
	Dark Gray	Not Launched
	Light Gray	Exited

Double-click any warp to find out how the local variables in the autos window are updated.

- The **Lanes** window allows you to select specific CUDA threads within the selected active warp. A lane means a single thread in a warp. You can open the window from **Nsight** | **Window** | **Lanes**. By double-clicking one lane, you can find that the local variables in the autos window are updated according to the updated index:

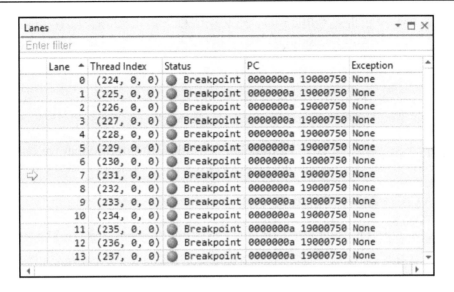

The lanes winn information in an active warp.

The **Registers** window shows the current state of the GPU registers. They will be red if their value is updated.

If you want to learn how to use Nsight Visual Studio Edition, please read the official user guide from NVIDIA. It introduces how to configure a debugging environment, how to use it, and many detailed tips for various situations (`https://docs.nvidia.com/nsight-visual-studio-edition/Nsight_Visual_Studio_Edition_User_Guide.htm`).

Debugging a CUDA application with Nsight Eclipse Edition

For Linux and OSX platform development, the CUDA Toolkit provides Nsight Eclipse Edition. This tool is based on Eclipse, so that developers can easily get used to this tool in CUDA C development.

Nsight Eclipse Edition was built on top of Eclipse for CUDA application development. You can use it to edit, build, debug, and profile your CUDA applications. It makes CUDA C/C++ development in Linux and OSX easy. This tool is installed with the CUDA Toolkit as a package, so you don't have to install this tool separately. However, it is required to configure Java 7 for its operation if you are using Linux.

Nsight Eclipse Edition was built with Eclipse version 4.4.0 (Luna, released in 2014) and was built based on Java 7.

Nsight can be executed with the `nsight` command from a Terminal or from the X window application list.

Now, let's open Nsight from your Terminal or X window desktop so that we can compile and analyze the given example. Either create a new CUDA project or open the provided sample project in `05_debug/06_debug_with_eclipse`. If you want to create a project, select **CUDA C/C++ Project**. **Empty Project** just gives you an empty project, while **CUDA Runtime Project** gives you a project with some sample code inside it. If you want to use the sample project, import it using **File | Import | Existing Projects into Workspace**.

Let's place a breakpoint in the `sgemm` kernel function. Like a normal C/C++ project in Eclipse, you can build and debug the CUDA application in `nsight`. Place a breakpoint at line **23** as a starting point of the kernel function, as follows:

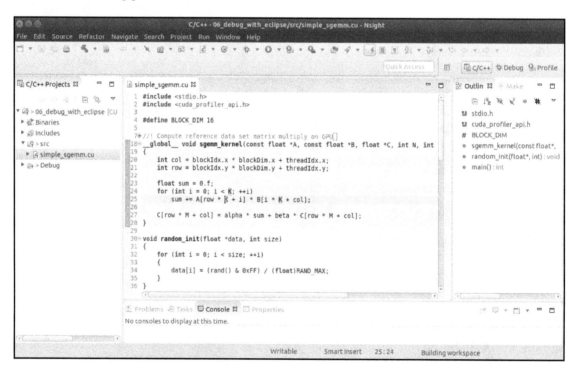

A good starting point for kernel function debugging is right after thread index calculation. Place a breakpoint to halt the GPU's execution. Now, compile and start debugging by clicking the green bug in the menu panel. While the debug window switches the debugging perspectives, click continue until you get to the breakpoint we have placed.

Nsight allows you to monitor local variables and registers in active warps. First, it stops the application at the leading CUDA thread (CUDA thread 0) in the CUDA grid. Then, you can move to the other CUDA active warp from the debug window and inspect each CUDA thread using the CUDA window, like so:

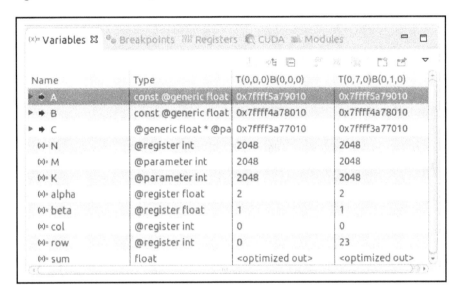

The following screenshot shows the local variable information for a selected CUDA thread. Nsight updates those values whenever they are updated:

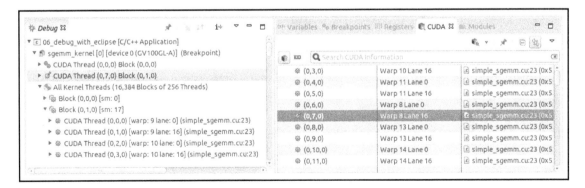

The preceding screenshot shows the **Debug** window and **CUDA** window in Eclipse's debug perspective window. The debug window provides CUDA warp selection among the active warps on the selected GPU and CUDA windows and enables lane selection within the selected active warp.

 NVIDIA also has an Nsight Eclipse Edition user guide. You can learn more about this tool by going to https://docs.nvidia.com/cuda/nsight-eclipse-edition-getting-started-guide/index.html.

Debugging a CUDA application with CUDA-GDB

The CUDA Toolkit provides CUDA-GDB, which supports CUDA C/C++ debugging for programs such as C/C++ GDB. This is useful for directly debugging CUDA C/C++ applications where there's no X window environment or remote debugging.

To debug a GPU application, the Makefile should include the -g debugging flag for the host and the -G debugging flag for the GPU. Basically, CUDA's GDB usage is identical to the host debugging, except there are some extra debugging features alongside the CUDA operations. For example, we can set specific CUDA threads and CUDA-aware breakpoints.

Breakpoints of CUDA-GDB

Let's cover how cuda-gdb can help us detect errors in code. We will set breakpoints in the code and look at the local values on the host and the GPU. For this, move your working directory to 05_debug/07_debug_with_gdb directory. We will check the cuda-gdb operation by matching it with the appropriate line.

To begin with, let's compile the source using the following command:

```
$ nvcc -run -m64 -g -G -Xcompiler -rdynamic -gencode
arch=compute_70,code=sm_70 -I/usr/local/cuda/samples/common/inc -o
simple_sgemm ./simple_sgemm.cu
```

Then, we should execute cuda-gdb so that we can debug the application on the Terminal, as follows:

```
$ cuda-gdb simple_sgemm
```

We can place a breakpoint on a specific line in the code, as follows:

```
(cuda-gdb) break simple_gemm.cu:21
```

Alternatively, we can put a breakpoint on the kernel function's name, as follows. This will trigger the breakpoint at the entry point of the function:

```
(cuda-gdb) break sgemm_kernel
```

Answer y if the cuda-gdb warning states that *the breakpoint wants to make pending on future shared library load*. You can also have breakpoints on the host code.

One problem with using breakpoints is that the breakpoint will be triggered according to how many CUDA threads there are. Therefore, we should provide conditional information to have a breakpoint against specific CUDA threads. The conditional breakpoint is as follows:

```
(cuda-gdb) break sgemm_kernel if blockIdx.y == 2
```

Of course, we can modify the condition of the predefined breakpoint as follows:

```
(cuda-gdb) cond 3 // break 3 is defined previously
```

Let's execute the sample application using the run command. If the application meets any breakpoint, CUDA-GDB provides information about it. The following code shows the cuda-gdb report when the application meets the breakpoint at line 21:

```
(cuda-gdb) run
[Switching focus to CUDA kernel 0, grid 1, block (0,0,0), thread (5,0,0),
device 0, sm 0, warp 0, lane 5]
Thread 1 "simple_sgemm" hit Breakpoint 1,
sgemm_kernel<<<(128,128,1),(16,16,1)>>> (A=0x7fffb6000000,
B=0x7fffb7000000, C=0x7fffb4000000, N=2048, M=2048, K=2048, alpha=2,
beta=1) at simple_sgemm.cu:21
21 int col = blockIdx.x * blockDim.x + threadIdx.x;
```

Now, it's time to use the GDB command to trace the code or monitor the active variables. We can trace the kernel function with next (or n), step (or s), continue (or c), and finish (or fin). However, we should use the continue command when we get to the end of the kernel code and need to switch the target hardware between the host and the device.

Inspecting variables with CUDA-GDB

On the top of the default GDB commands, CUDA-GDB provides debugging features that can work with CUDA kernels. Here's what you can do with CUDA-GDB.

Listing kernel functions

Like a normal function, CUDA-GDB can place breakpoints on the kernel functions. Once your application has been stopped by the breakpoint, you can list them as follows:

```
(cuda-gdb) info cuda kernels
Kernel Parent Dev Grid Status    SMs Mask       GridDim  BlockDim Invocation
*      0      -   0      1 Active 0xffffffff (128,128,1) (16,16,1)
sgemm_kernel(A=0x7ffff5a79010, B=0x7ffff4a78010, C=0x7ffff3a77010, N=2048,
M=2048, K=2048, alpha=2, beta=1)
```

As you can see, the preceding output shows the kernel's configuration information and input parameter variables.

Variables investigation

CUDA-GDB helps us trace specific CUDA threads by selecting a specific thread block index and thread index. With this feature, you can move your current focus to the specified thread. In this example, the block size is 16 and the `col` variable is defined as a CUDA thread index in the x dimension. This following code shows how CUDA-GDB reports the selected local variable's value by changing the thread index:

```
(cuda-gdb) print col
$1 = <optimized out>
(cuda-gdb) cuda kernel 0 block 1,2,0 thread 3,4,0
21 int col = blockIdx.x * blockDim.x + threadIdx.x;
(cuda-gdb) s
22 int row = blockIdx.y * blockDim.y + threadIdx.y;
(cuda-gdb) p col
$2 = 19
```

Check the current focusing thread information:

```
(cuda-gdb) cuda device kernel block thread
kernel 3, block (1,2,0), thread (3,4,0), device 0
```

With the information at hand, we can trace the CUDA thread.

 If you want to learn more about CUDA-GDB, please check the user guide documentation from NVIDIA: https://docs.nvidia.com/cuda/cuda-gdb/index.html.

Runtime validation with CUDA-memcheck

One difficult point of CUDA programming is handling memory space. Since CUDA threads operate in parallel, the boundary condition or unexpected indexing operation can violate valid memory space. CUDA memcheck is a runtime testing tool that validates memory access if any GPU operation exceeds the invalid memory space. This tool detects the following memory errors:

Name	Location	Description	Precise
Memory access error	Device	Invalid memory access (out of bound, misaligned)	O
Hardware exception	Device	Errors from the hardware	X
Malloc/free errors	Device	Incorrect use of `malloc()`/`free()` in CUDA kernels	O
CUDA API errors	Host	The CUDA API's error return	O
cudaMalloc memory leaks	Host	Device memory that's allocated using `cudaMalloc()` did not free by the application	O
Device heap memory leaks	Device	Allocated device memory using `malloc()` in device code is not freed by the application	X

Precise (O) means that memcheck can specify the crashed line and file. On the other hand, imprecise (X) means that the tool can identify the error, but cannot specify the error points due to the concurrency status. `cuda-memcheck` does not require recompilation for the test. However, if we compile with some extra `nvcc` options, we can trace error points. The `nvcc` options including `-lineinfo`, which generates line number information, and `-Xcompiler -rdynamic`, which is used to retain function symbols.

Basically, `cuda-memcheck` is a standalone tool and validates GPU applications at runtime. The following command shows its format in standalone mode:

```
$ cuda-memcheck [options] <application>
```

This tool can also work with CUDA-GDB and help the developer identify errors and debug them. In the CUDA-GDB command line, use the `set cuda memcheck on` command to enable memory checks. This way, CUDA-GDB can identify memory-related exceptions.

Detecting memory out of bounds

Now, let's see how `cuda-memcheck` can detect memory exceptions and work with CUDA-GDB. To ease this, we will make some erroneous code and see how `cuda-memcheck` reports the result. Let's begin with some clean code. You can use the given sample code in `05_debug/08_cuda_memcheck` for this. Let's test the code using `cuda-memcheck` and validate it:

```
$ nvcc -m64 -g -G -Xcompiler -rdynamic -gencode arch=compute_70,code=sm_70
-I/usr/local/cuda/samples/common/inc -o simple_sgemm ./simple_sgemm.cu
$ cuda-memcheck simple_sgemm
========= CUDA-MEMCHECK
Application finished successfully.========= ERROR SUMMARY: 0 errors
```

Now, let's put some erroneous code into the kernel function, as follows. You can put another error if you prefer:

```
For instance, you may add one to the row value.
__global__ void sgemm_kernel(const float *A, const float *B, float *C, int
N, int M, int K, float alpha, float beta)
{
    int col = blockIdx.x * blockDim.x + threadIdx.x;
    int row = blockIdx.y * blockDim.y + threadIdx.y;
    row += 1;

    float sum = 0.f;
    for (int i = 0; i < K; ++i)
        sum += A[row * K + i] * B[i * K + col];
    C[row * M + col] = alpha * sum + beta * C[row * M + col];
}
```

Let's compile and launch the code. The kernel will return a CUDA error and `checkCudaErrors()` will report an error message, as follows:

```
CUDA error at simple_sgemm_oob.cu:78 code=77(cudaErrorIllegalAddress)
"cudaDeviceSynchronize()"
```

However, this information is insufficient if we wish to identify which line in the kernel code is the root cause of the problem. Using `cuda-memcheck`, we can identify which CUDA thread and memory space triggered the error with a stack address:

```
$ cuda-memcheck simple_sgemm_oob
```

The output is as follows:

```
======== CUDA-MEMCHECK
======== Invalid __global__ read of size 4
========      at 0x00000670 in /home/jahan/Dropbox/workspace/CUDA-9x-Cookbook/05_debug/08_memcheck/simple_sgemm_
oob.cu:27:sgemm_kernel(float const *, float const *, float*, int, int, int, float, float)
========      by thread (15,15,0) in block (1,127,0)
========      Address 0x7f2ea7600000 is out of bounds
========      Device Frame:/home/jahan/Dropbox/workspace/CUDA-9x-Cookbook/05_debug/08_memcheck/simple_sgemm_oob.
cu:27:sgemm_kernel(float const *, float const *, float*, int, int, int, float, float) (sgemm_kernel(float const
*, float const *, float*, int, int, int, float, float) : 0x670)
========      Saved host backtrace up to driver entry point at kernel launch time
========      Host Frame:/usr/lib/x86_64-linux-gnu/libcuda.so.1 (cuLaunchKernel + 0x2cd) [0x24f88d]
========      Host Frame:oob [0x22f72]
========      Host Frame:oob [0x23167]
========      Host Frame:oob [0x57525]
========      Host Frame:oob [0x718b]
========      Host Frame:oob [0x7034]
========      Host Frame:oob [0x70b3]
========      Host Frame:oob [0x6cf8]
========      Host Frame:/lib/x86_64-linux-gnu/libc.so.6 (__libc_start_main + 0xe7) [0x21b97]
========      Host Frame:oob [0x672a]
```

The preceding screenshot shows a part of the standalone execution of cuda-memcheck, which shows all the detected errors from the kernel where the error occurred. In this case, cuda-memcheck reports that it detected a memory violation error at line 27. By default, cuda-memcheck stops the application's execution when an error is detected.

In this situation, we can find the root cause easily by inspecting the related variables using cuda-gdb. To do this, we need to launch the application with cuda-gdb and enable cuda-memcheck, as follows:

```
$ cuda-gdb simple_sgemm_oob
(cuda-gdb) set cuda memcheck on
(cuda-gdb) run
```

This procedure makes cuda-gdb report illegal memory access detection from cuda-memcheck:

```
Starting program: /home/jahan/cuda-workspace/CUDA-9X-COOKBOOK/05_debug/08_memcheck/oob
[Thread debugging using libthread_db enabled]
Using host libthread_db library "/lib/x86_64-linux-gnu/libthread_db.so.1".
[New Thread 0x7fffec729700 (LWP 6876)]
[New Thread 0x7fffebf28700 (LWP 6877)]

Illegal access to address (@global)0x7fffc7600000 detected.

Thread 1 "oob" received signal CUDA_EXCEPTION_1, Lane Illegal Address.
[Switching focus to CUDA kernel 0, grid 1, block (0,127,0), thread (0,15,0), device 0, sm 41, warp 20, lane 16]
0x0000555556271ef0 in sgemm_kernel (A=0x7fffc6600000, B=0x7fffae000000, C=0x7fffaf000000, N=2048, M=2048,
    K=2048, alpha=2, beta=1) at simple_sgemm_oob.cu:27
27              sum += A[row * K + i] * B[i * K + col];
```

The preceding screenshot shows a report from cuda-gdb with cuda-memcheck. The developer can easily identify that line 27 in simple_sgemm_oob.cu triggered the reported error. From the given information, we can start to investigate which piece of memory accessed the invalid space, as follows:

```
(cuda-gdb) print A[row * K + i]
Error: Failed to read generic memory at address 0x7fffc7600000 on device 0
sm 41 warp 20 lane 16, error=CUDBG_ERROR_INVALID_MEMORY_SEGMENT(0x7).
(cuda-gdb) print row * K + i
$1 = 4194304
```

Without arduous effort, we can determine that accessing A[row * K + i] triggers an error and that the requested value exceeds the global memory's (A) allocated space. In this manner, you can narrow down the root cause without much effort.

Detecting other memory errors

The CUDA memcheck tool provides additional software validation features, some of which are as follows:

Name	Description	Option
Memory leak	For identifying memory leaks	--leak-check full
Race check	For the analysis of the racing hazard of conflicting access between multiple threads to the shared memory	--tool racecheck
Init check	Identifying device global memory access without initialization	--tool initcheck
Sync check	Validates the correct use of synchronization primitives such as __syncthreads(), __syncwarp(), and cooperative group APIs	--tool synccheck

These tools assume that the memory accesses are correct or verified and do not check for memory errors. Due to this, you need to confirm that no memory errors exist in your application. Other useful memcheck options include --save, which we can use to save the output to a disk, and --print-level, which we can use to control the output detail level.

 NVIDIA provides a user guide for cuda-memcheck. This document will help you validate your application using a GPU and detect unexpected errors (https://docs.nvidia.com/cuda/cuda-memcheck/index.html).

Profiling GPU applications with Nsight Systems

In this section, we will cover the newly introduced CUDA profiler tools, that is, Nsight Systems and Nsight Compute. These profilers support the Volta architecture and onwards GPUs. It is major profiler in the Turing architecture GPU. We will cover the Nsight Systems first, before covering Nsight Compute in the next section.

Nsight Systems (`https://developer.nvidia.com/nsight-systems`) is a system-wide performance analysis tool that can visualize operations in the timeline and easily find optimization points. In terms of the timeline analysis aspects, Nsight Systems provides system-side utilization information so that we can analyze the bottleneck points. We can get Nsight Systems from the NVIDIA website, but CUDA 10 includes Nsight Systems in the toolkit package by default. All we have to do is make sure it is installed correctly.

For the CLI, we should set the `PATH` to ease our operation because its path is separated with ordinary CUDA binaries. Let's include that in the `PATH` environment variable using the following command:

```
export
PATH=$PATH:/usr/local/cuda/bin:/usr/local/cuda-10.1/NsightSystems-2019.3/Target-x86_64/x86_64
```

Nsight Systems provides two interfaces: one for the GUI and one for the CLI. On a host machine, we can collect the application's sampling information by running the application via a GUI. On the remote machine, we can collect the profiled data via a CLI with the following command:

```
$ nsys profile -t osrt,cuda,nvtx,cublas,cudnn -o baseline -w true <command>
```

This option can be interpreted as follows:

	Option	Switches
Tracing	-t/--trace	cuda: For tracing CUDA operations, nvtx: For tracing nvtx tags, cublas, cudnn, opengl, openacc: For tracing the API operation, osrt: For tracing OS runtime libraries, none: No API trace
Output file	-o/--output	Output filename
Show output	-w/--show-output	true/false: Prints out the behavior of the profiler on the Terminal

For example, we can obtain a profiled file named sgemm.qdrep from the 02_nvtx SGEMM application. Let's compare the profiled output between Nsight Systems and the NVIDIA Visual Profiler. We can collect the Nsight System's profile data with the following command:

```
$ nsys profile -t osrt,cuda,nvtx -o sgemm -w true ./sgemm
```

This is the profiled timeline view from Nsight Systems:

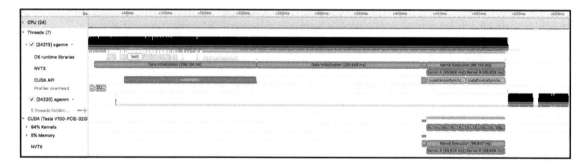

The following screenshot shows the profiled timeline view from the NVIDIA Visual Profiler:

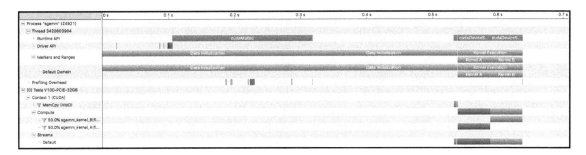

The Visual Profiler shows the operation event blocks, but Night Systems shows the system utilization together. Therefore, we can easily see which resource—CPU core, GPU, or PCIe bus—has an impact on performance. Also, Nsight Systems provides a more interactive profiling experience. When you double-click any function operation, the Nsight Systems Viewer expands the timeline to fit the window and helps us inspect the operation. In addition, Nsight Systems makes it easy for us to discover the number of kernel executions that are occurring under a certain NVTX area. In the Visual Profiler timeline view, the kernel executions look like a single execution, but Nsight Systems shows the separated execution.

Now that we have determined that a function should be optimized, we can move on to Nsight Compute, which is another new profiler that inspects the GPU operations of the kernel function.

Profiling a kernel with Nsight Compute

Nsight Compute is a kernel-level profiler for computations. It collects GPU metric information and helps us focus on the CUDA kernel's optimization. In other words, this tool covers the Visual Profiler's performance analysis features.

Nsight Compute provides two interfaces: the GUI and the CLI. The GUI supports the host and the remote application profile, while the CLI works on the target machine. However, we can get the profiled data and review the results using the GUI.

Profiling with the CLI

For ease of using the Nsight Compute CLI, we need to set the `PATH` environment variable for the Nsight Compute path in `/usr/local/cuda-10.1/NsightCompute-2019.3/nv-nsight-cu-cli`. Then, we can collect profile data using the following command:

```
$ nv-nsight-cu-cli -o <output filename> <application command>
```

This command collects GPU execution metric information and saves the data to the specified file. If we don't provide an output filename, Nsight Compute reports the collected metric reports to the console, which provides a fast metric performance report over the console.

Since we can specify the profiling target, we can limit Nsight Compute to collect the following information:

- `--kernel-regex`: Specifies the kernel to the profile
- `--devices`: Focuses on profiling a specific GPU

This feature is useful when we have to look at the report on the console.

Profiling with the GUI

By opening a new project in Nsight Compute, we can initiate the profile operation. The following screenshot shows the profile configuration. For host application development, make a connection to the localhost. Alternatively, you can specify the target GPU server we want to profile:

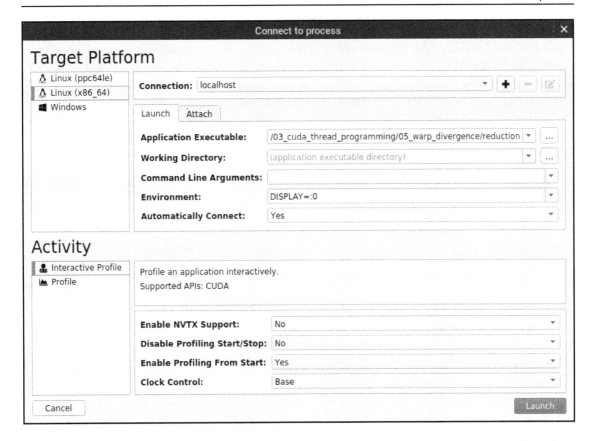

Of course, we can also open the `nsight-cuprof-report` file, which was generated with the CLI tool over the target machine. For example, we can make the sgemm profiled file with the following command:

```
$ nv-nsight-cu-cli -o reduction reduction
```

For OSX users, Nsight Systems will require the target `glib` library for remote profiling. In this case, we should copy the library from the Nsight Compute installation image. It provides the required libraries as a directory named target and copies that directory to the `Applications/NVIDIA Nsight Compute.app/target` directory.

For the ease of this lab, we will use a reduction sample code from Chapter 3, *CUDA Thread Programming*. It has two parallel reduction implementations with different addressing. You can find the code from 03_cuda_thread_programming/05_warp_divergence directory. Click the **Launch** button when you finish to set the connection and application Executable text bar as shown in the connect to progress diagram. Then, put *Ctrl + I, Ctrl + K* key to run to next kernel function, and then the profiler will stop at reduction_kernel_1. Put *Ctrl + I, Ctrl + P* key to profile this kernel. Then you'll get the following output. This picture shows Nsight Compute's GUI-based profiling for the first kernel profiling:

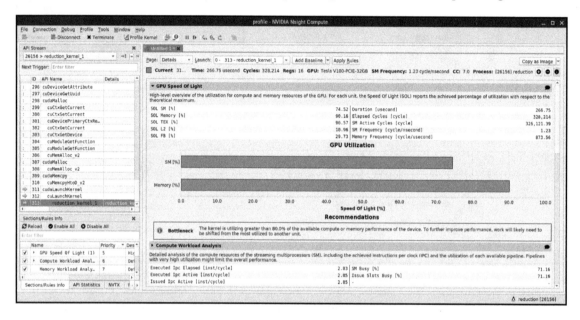

Output showing GUI-based profiling (for the first kernel profiling)

It provides interactive profiling and debugging. Using the step control debug buttons, we can debug the CUDA API and kernel functions. We can also move to the next kernel function or the next profile range using the control button on the left side API stream panel. On the right panel, you can get the detail profiled information of the kernel.

We also can get the profiled result automatically by enabling the auto profile with the following procedure—go to the **Menu** bar and select **Profile | Auto Profile**. Then, proceed with the application. Nsight Systems will profile all the kernel functions. Alternatively, you can profile the kernel function manually by clicking the **Profile Kernel** button on the top of the window. When we use the CLI's collected profiled results, we will just see profiled data from all the kernel functions.

Performance analysis report

As we could see on the right panel in the interactive profile window, the Nsight Compute provides a performance analysis report. From the report, we can identify the performance limiters and investigate the underutilized resources. Also, Nsight Compute provides optimization recommendations based on resource utilization statistics. We can also identify them from direct profile.

Also, Nsight Compute provides optimization recommendations by analyzing the GPU components utilizations. It finds a bottleneck and suggests a recommended investigation to optimize the kernel.

This report page provides each component's utilizations such as compute, memory, scheduler, instruction, warp, and so on. Furthermore, you can get even more details by extending the left top arrow for each component. The following picture shows an example report of the Memory Workload Analysis:

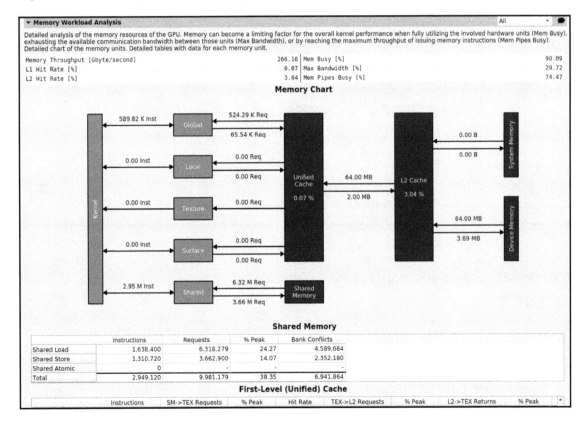

In the Nsight Compute, we can get such detailed information easily. In the previous profiler, NVIDIA Profiler, we should execute each analysis to obtain such information.

Baseline compare

During the optimization process, we should compare the new result from the baseline operation. To make this task easy for us, Nsight Compute provides the **baseline compare** feature. Click the **Add baseline** button at the top of the performance report panel and change it to the other kernel function. Then, we can use the Nsight Compute to compare kernel function utilizations. The following screen shows this:

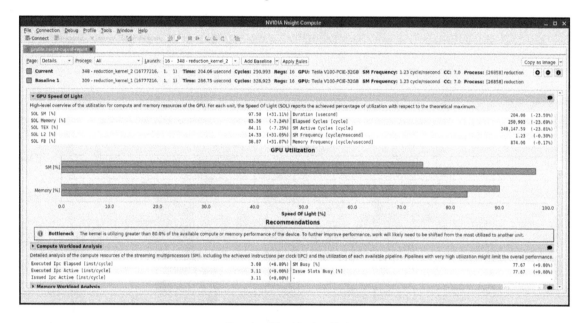

Comparison of kernel function utilizations

This is useful if we wish to trace our optimization efforts and identify the effective components.

Source view

Nsight Compute provides various pages that we can investigate. One of its useful pages is the **Source** page. If the CUDA application is built with -lineinfo option, Nsight Compute can show correlated information with CUDA C/C++ source with CUDA SASS code. Then, we can analyze the bottleneck code and investigate how it is related to the SASS code level.

Also, it provides a **Live Registers** number so that we can investigate the number of required registers in the kernel function. The following screenshot shows the **Source** page:

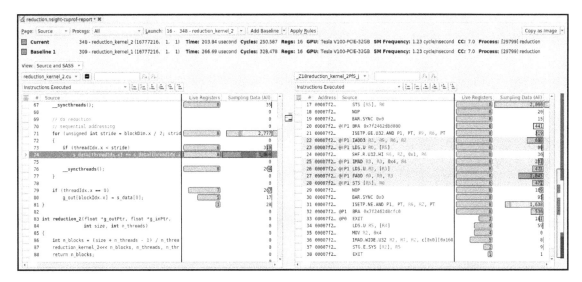

If you need to learn more about this feature, you can find the related information in this document—https://docs.nvidia.com/nsight-compute/NsightCompute/index.html#profiler-report-source-page.

Nsight Compute provides a CUDA kernel performance analysis centric operation that we can use to verify that Night Systems and Nsight Compute have a different optimization scope.

Summary

In this chapter, we have covered how to profile a GPU application and debug it. Understanding these CUDA tools will help you develop efficiently and effectively as they help you find bottlenecks pragmatically and find errors and bugs in a short time.

Up until now, we have focused on single GPU application development. However, many GPU applications use multiple GPUs to achieve better performance. In the next chapter, we will cover how to write code that works on multiple GPUs and aim for scalable performance. You will learn what can make an impact on performance and how to achieve good performance levels. You will also be able to apply the tools that we covered in this chapter on the next chapter's problems to reinforce multiple GPU systems and their experiences.

6
Scalable Multi-GPU Programming

So far, we have concentrated on getting optimal performance on a single GPU. Dense nodes with multiple GPUs have become a pressing need for upcoming supercomputers, especially since the ExaFLOP (a quintillion operations per sec) system is becoming a reality. GPU architecture is energy-efficient and hence, in recent years, systems with GPUs have taken the majority of the top spots in the Green500 list (`https://www.top500.org/green500`). In Green500's November 2018 list, seven out of the top 10 systems were based on the NVIDIA GPU.

The DGX system from NVIDIA now has 16 V100 32 GB in one server. With the help of unified memory and interconnect technologies such as NVLink and NvSwitch, developers can see all GPUs as one big GPU with 512 GB memory (16 GPU * 32 GB each). In this chapter, we will go into the details of writing CUDA code and make use of CUDA-aware libraries to efficiently get scalability in a multi-GPU environment within and across nodes.

In this chapter, we will cover the following topics:

- Solving a linear equation using Gaussian elimination
- GPUDirect peer to peer
- A brief introduction to MPI
- GPUDirect RDMA
- CUDA streams
- Additional tricks

Technical requirements

A Linux PC with a modern NVIDIA GPU (Pascal architecture onward) is required for this chapter, with all necessary GPU drivers and the CUDA Toolkit (10.0 onward) installed. If you are unsure of your GPU's architecture, please visit NVIDIA GPU's site (`https://developer.nvidia.com/cuda-gpus`) and confirm your GPU's architecture. This chapter's code is also available on GitHub at `https://github.com/PacktPublishing/Learn-CUDA-Programming`.

The sample code examples in this chapter have been developed and tested with CUDA version 10.1. However, it is recommended you use the latest version (CUDA) or a higher one.

Since this chapter needs to showcase multi-GPU interactions, we will need a minimum of two GPUs of the same type and architecture. Also, note that some features, such as GPUDirect RDMA and NVLink, are only supported on Tesla cards of NVIDIA. If you don't have a Tesla card such as the Tesla P100 or Tesla V100, don't be disheartened. You can safely ignore some of these features. There will be a change in performance numbers compared to what we show here, but the same code will work as-is.

In the next section, we will look at an example of the popular Gaussian algorithm to solve a series of linear equations to demonstrate how to write multi-GPUs.

Solving a linear equation using Gaussian elimination

To demonstrate the usage of multiple GPUs within and across nodes, we will start with some sequential code and then convert it into multiple GPUs within and across nodes. We will be solving a linear system of equations containing M equations and N unknowns. The equation can be represented as follows:

$$A \times x = b$$

Here, A is a matrix with M rows and N columns, x is a column vector (also referred to as a solution vector) with N rows, and b is also a column vector with M rows. Finding a solution vector involves computing vector x when A and b are given. One of the standard methods for solving a linear system of equations is Gaussian elimination. In Gaussian elimination, first matrix A is reduced to either the upper or lower triangular matrix by performing elementary row transformations. Then, the resulting triangular system of equations is solved by using the back substitution step.

The following pseudocode explains the steps that are involved in solving the linear equation:

```
1. For iteration 1 to N (N: number of unknowns)
     1.1 Find a row with non-zero pivot
     1.2 Extract the pivot row
     1.3 Reduce other rows using pivot row
  2 Computing the solution vector through back substitution
```

Let's take a look at an example in order to understand the algorithm. Let's say the system of equations is as follows:

System of Equation	Row Elimination	Augmented Matrix
x-2y+z=0 2x+y-3z=5 4x-7y+z=-1		1 -2 1 0 2 1 -3 5 4 -7 1 -1
	Row2 - 2*Row1 → Row2 Row3 - 4*Row1 → Row3	1 -2 1 | 0 0 5 -5 | 5 0 1 -3 | -1
	Row3 - 1/5*Row2 → Row3	1 -2 1 | 0 0 5 -5 | 5 0 0 -2 | -2

The matrix is now in Triangular form. With back substitution we get the following results:

z = 1
y = 2
x = 3

First, we will try to set the baseline system, as follows:

1. Prepare your GPU application. This code can be found in the `06_multigpu/gaussian` folder in this book's GitHub repository.

2. Compile your application with the nvcc compiler, as follows:

```
$ nvcc -o gaussian_sequential.out gaussian_sequential.cu
$ nvcc -o gaussian_single_gpu.out gaussian_single_gpu.cu
$ $ time ./gaussian_sequential.out
$ time ./gaussian_single_gpu.out
```

The preceding steps compile and run two versions of the code that are present in this chapter:

- The CPU code, which runs sequentially
- The CUDA code, which runs on a single GPU

Now, let's take a look at the hotspots in the single GPU implementation of Gaussian elimination.

Single GPU hotspot analysis of Gaussian elimination

Let's try to understand and profile sequential and single GPU code to set a baseline. Over this baseline, we will enhance and add support for running on multi-GPUs.

Sequential CPU code: The following code shows the extracted code of sequential implementation:

```
for( int n = 0; n < N; n++ ){
// M: number of equations, N: number of unknowns
    for( int pr = 0; pr < M; pr++ ){
        // finding the pivot row
        //if pr satisfies condition for pivot i.e. is non zero
        break;
    }
    for( int r = 0; r < M; r++ ){
        // reduce all other eligible rows using the pivot row
        double ratio = AB[r*N+n]/AB[pr*N+n]
        for( int nn = n; nn < N + 1; nn++ ){
            AB[r * N + nn] -= (ratio*AB[pr * N + nn]);
        }
    }
}
```

Visually, the operation that takes place is as follows:

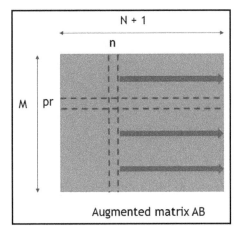

Here, in this Gaussian elimination, the number of rows is equal to the number of equations and the number of columns is equal to the number of unknowns. The **pr** row shown in the preceding diagram is the pivot row and will be used to reduce other rows using the pivot element.

The first observation that we can make is that we are operating on an augmented matrix to merge the *A* matrix with the *b* vector. Hence, the size of unknowns is *N+1* as an augmented matrix has the last column as the *b* vector. Creating an augmented matrix helps us work on just one data structure, that is, a matrix. You can profile this code using the following command. The profiling results will show you that the guassian_elimination_cpu() function takes the most time to complete:

```
$ nvprof --cpu-profiling on ./guassian_sequential.out
```

CUDA single GPU code: After going through the previous chapters, we expect you to have familiarized yourself with how to write optimal GPU code and hence we will not go into the details of the single GPU implementation. The following extract shows that, in a single GPU implementation, the three steps are known as three kernels for finding *N* unknowns:

- findPivotRowAndMultipliers<<<...>>>: The kernel finds the pivot row and multiplier, which should be used for row elimination.
- extractPivotRow<<<>>>: The kernel extracts the pivot row, which is then used to perform row elimination.
- rowElimination<<<>>>: This is the final kernel call, and does the row elimination in parallel on the GPU.

The following code snippet shows the three kernels called iteratively after the data has been copied to the GPU:

```
<Copy input augmented matrix AB to GPU>
...
for( int n = 0; n < N; n++ ){
// M: number of equations, N: number of unknowns
    findPivotRowAndMultipliers<<<...>>>();
    extractPivotRow<<<...>>>();
    rowElimination<<<...>>>();

}
```

The focus of this chapter is on how this single GPU implementation can be enhanced to support multiple GPUs. However, to fill in the missing pieces from the GPU implementation, we need to make some optimization changes to the single GPU implementation:

- The performance of the Gaussian elimination algorithm is heavily influenced by the memory access pattern. Basically, it depends on how the AB matrix is stored:
  - Finding the pivot row prefers the column-major format as it provides coalesced access if the matrix is stored in a column major format.
  - On the other hand, extracting a pivot row prefers the row-major format.
- No matter how we store the *AB* matrix, one coalesced and one strided/non-coalesced access to memory is unavoidable.
- The column major format is also beneficial for row elimination kernels and hence, for our Gaussian elimination kernel, we decided to store the transpose of the AB matrix instead of AB. The AB matrix gets transposed once, at the beginning of the code in the `transposeMatrixAB()` function.

In the next section, we will enable multi-GPU P2P access and split the work among multiple GPUs.

GPUDirect peer to peer

The GPUDirect technology was created to allow high-bandwidth, low-latency communication between GPUs within and across different nodes. This technology was introduced to eliminate CPU overheads when one GPU needs to communicate with another. GPUDirect can be classified into the following major categories:

- **Peer to peer (P2P) transfer between GPU**: Allows CUDA programs to use high-speed **Direct Memory Transfer** (**DMA**) to copy data between two GPUs in the same system. It also allows optimized access to the memory of other GPUs within the same system.
- **Accelerated communication between network and storage**: This technology helps with direct access to CUDA memory from third-party devices such as InfiniBand network adapters or storage. It eliminates unnecessary memory copies and CPU overhead and hence reduces the latency of transfer and access. This feature is supported from CUDA 3.1 onward.
- **GPUDirect for video**: This technology optimizes pipelines for frame-based video devices. It allows low-latency communication with OpenGL, DirectX, or CUDA and is supported from CUDA 4.2 onward.
- **Remote Direct Memory Access (RDMA)**: This feature allows direct communication between GPUs across a cluster. This feature is supported from CUDA 5.0 and later.

In this section, we will be converting our sequential code to make use of the P2P feature of GPUDirect so that it can run on multiple GPUs within the same system.

The GPUDirect P2P feature allows the following:

- **GPUDirect transfers**: `cudaMemcpy()` initiates a DMA copy from GPU 1's memory to GPU 2's memory.
- **Direct access**: GPU 1 can read or write GPU 2's memory (load/store).

The following diagram demonstrates these features:

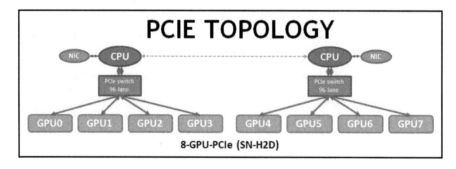

To understand the advantage of P2P, it is necessary to understand the PCIe bus specification. This was created with the intention of optimally communicating through interconnects such as InfiniBand to other nodes. This is different when we want to optimally send and receive data from individual GPUs. The following is a sample PCIe topology where eight GPUs are being connected to various CPUs and NIC/InfiniBand cards:

In the preceding diagram, P2P transfer is allowed between GPU0 and GPU1 as they are both situated in the same PCIe switch. However, GPU0 and GPU4 cannot perform a P2P transfer as PCIe P2P communication is not supported between two **I/O Hubs** (**IOHs**). The IOH does not support non-contiguous bytes from PCI Express for remote peer-to-peer MMIO transactions. The nature of the QPI link connecting the two CPUs ensures that a direct P2P copy between GPU memory is not possible if the GPUs reside on different PCIe domains. Thus, a copy from the memory of GPU0 to the memory of GPU4 requires copying over the PCIe link to the memory attached to CPU0, then transferring it over the QPI link to CPU1 and over the PCIe again to GPU4. As you can imagine, this process adds a significant amount of overhead in terms of both latency and bandwidth.

The following diagram shows another system where GPUs are connected to each other via an NVLink interconnect that supports P2P transfers:

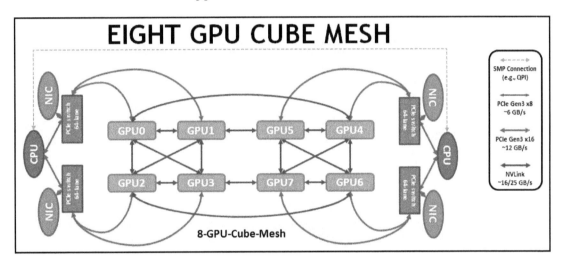

The preceding diagram shows a sample NVLink topology resulting in an eight-cube mesh where each GPU is connected to another GPU with a max 1 hop.

The more important query would be, *How can we figure out this topology and which GPUs support P2P transfer?* Fortunately, there are tools for this. `nvidia-smi` is one such tool that gets installed as part of the NVIDIA driver's installation. The following screenshot shows the output of running `nvidia-smi` on the NVIDIA DGX server whose network topology is shown in the preceding diagram:

```
$ nvidia-smi topo -m
         GPU0   GPU1   GPU2   GPU3   GPU4   GPU5   GPU6   GPU7   mlx5_0  mlx5_2  mlx5_1  mlx5_3  CPU Affinity
GPU0      X     NV1    NV1    NV1    NV1    SYS    SYS    SYS    PIX     SYS     PHB     SYS     0-19
GPU1     NV1     X     NV1    NV1    SYS    NV1    SYS    SYS    PIX     SYS     PHB     SYS     0-19
GPU2     NV1    NV1     X     NV1    SYS    SYS    NV1    SYS    PHB     SYS     PIX     SYS     0-19
GPU3     NV1    NV1    NV1     X     SYS    SYS    SYS    NV1    PHB     SYS     PIX     SYS     0-19
GPU4     NV1    SYS    SYS    SYS     X     NV1    NV1    NV1    SYS     PIX     SYS     PHB     20-39
GPU5     SYS    NV1    SYS    SYS    NV1     X     NV1    NV1    SYS     PIX     SYS     PHB     20-39
GPU6     SYS    SYS    NV1    SYS    NV1    NV1     X     NV1    SYS     PHB     SYS     PIX     20-39
GPU7     SYS    SYS    SYS    NV1    NV1    NV1    NV1     X     SYS     PHB     SYS     PIX     20-39
mlx5_0   PIX    PIX    PHB    PHB    SYS    SYS    SYS    SYS     X      SYS     PHB     SYS
mlx5_2   SYS    SYS    SYS    SYS    PIX    PIX    PHB    PHB    SYS      X      SYS     PHB
mlx5_1   PHB    PHB    PIX    PIX    SYS    SYS    SYS    SYS    PHB     SYS      X      SYS
mlx5_3   SYS    SYS    SYS    SYS    PHB    PHB    PIX    PIX    SYS     PHB     SYS      X

Legend:

  X    = Self
  SYS  = Connection traversing PCIe as well as the SMP interconnect between NUMA nodes (e.g., QPI/UPI)
  NODE = Connection traversing PCIe as well as the interconnect between PCIe Host Bridges within a NUMA node
  PHB  = Connection traversing PCIe as well as a PCIe Host Bridge (typically the CPU)
  PXB  = Connection traversing multiple PCIe switches (without traversing the PCIe Host Bridge)
  PIX  = Connection traversing a single PCIe switch
  NV#  = Connection traversing a bonded set of # NVLinks
```

The preceding screenshot represents the result of the `nvidia-smi topo -m` command being run on the DGX system, which has 8 GPUs. As you can see, any GPU that is connected to another GPU via SMP interconnect (`QPI/UPI`) cannot perform P2P transfer. For example, GPU0 will not be able to do P2P with GPU5, GPU6, and GPU7. Another way is to figure out this transfer via CUDA APIs, which we will be using to convert our code in the next section.

Now that we have understood the system topology, we can start converting our application into multiple GPUs in a single node/server.

Single node – multi-GPU Gaussian elimination

Prepare your multi-GPU application. This code can be found at `06_multigpu/gaussian` in this book's GitHub repository. Compile your application with the `nvcc` compiler, as follows:

```
$ nvcc -o gaussian_multi_gpu_p2p.out gaussian_multi_gpu_p2p.cu
$ time ./gaussian_multi_gpu_p2p.out
```

Going from a single-to multi-GPU implementation, the three kernels we defined in the previous subsection will be used as-is. However, the linear system is split into a number of parts equal to the number of GPUs. These parts are distributed one part per GPU. Each GPU is responsible for performing the operation on the part that's been assigned to that GPU. The matrix is split column-wise. This means each GPU gets an equal number of consecutive columns from all the rows. The kernel for finding the pivot is launched on the GPU that holds the column containing the pivot element. The row index of the pivot element is broadcasted to other GPUs. The extracted pivot row and row elimination kernels are launched on all the GPUs, with each GPU working on its own part of the matrix. The following diagram shows the rows being split among multiple GPUs and how the pivot row needs to be broadcasted to the rest of the processes:

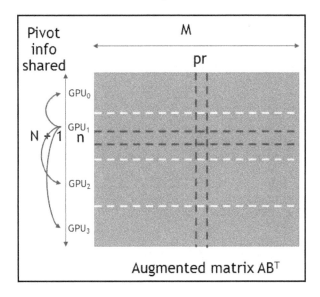

The preceding diagram represents the division of work across multiple GPUs. Currently, the pivot row belongs to **GPU1** and is responsible for broadcasting the pivot row to other GPUs.

Let's try to understand these code changes, as well as the CUDA API that was used to enable the P2P feature:

1. Enable P2P access between the supported GPUs. The following code shows the first step in this:s enabling P2P access between GPUs:

```
for( int i = 0; i < nGPUs; i++ ){
    // setup P2P
    cudaSetDevice(i);
    for( int j = 0; j < nGPUs; j++ ) {
```

```
        if (i == j) continue;
        cudaDeviceCanAccessPeer(&canAccessPeer, i, j);
        if (canAccessPeer)
            cudaDeviceEnablePeerAccess(j, 0);
    }
}
```

The key APIs that were used in the preceding code are as follows:

- `cudaDeviceCanAccessPeer()`: Checks if the current GPU can do P2P access to the GPU whose ID is sent as a parameter
- `cudaDeviceEnablePeerAccess()`: If `cudaDeviceCanAccessPeer()` returns `True`, enable P2P access

2. Split and transfer the content to the respective GPUs:

```
for( int g = 0; g < nGPUs; g++ ){
    cudaSetDevice(g);
    //Copy  part 'g' of ABT to GPU 'g';
}
```

The key API that was used in the preceding code is `cudaSetDevice()`. This sets the current context to the GPU ID that was passed as an argument.

3. Find the pivot row and broadcast it via P2P:

```
for( int n = 0; n < N; n++ ){
    gp = GPU that holds n;
    cudaSetDevice(gp);
    findPivotRowAndMultipliers<<<...>>>();
    for( int g = 0; g < nGPUs; g++ ){
        if (g == gp) continue;
        cudaMemcpyPeer(pivotDatag, g, pivotDatagp, gp, numBytes);
    } ...
```

The API that's used to broadcast the transfer to GPUs is `cudaMemcpyPeer()`.

4. Extract the pivot row and perform row elimination:

```
for( int n = 0; n < N; n++ ){
    ...
    for( int g = 0; g < nGPUs; g++ ){
        cudaSetDevice(g);
        extractPivotRow<<<...>>>();
        rowElimination<<<...>>>();
    }
}
```

As you can see, we are still reusing the same kernels. The only difference is that we use the `cudaSetDevice()` API to tell the CUDA runtime which GPU the kernel should be launched on. Note that `cudaSetDevice()` is a costly call, especially on older generation GPUs. Therefore, it is advised that you call the for loop for nGPUs in parallel on the CPU by making use of `OpenMP/OpenACC` or any other threading mechanism on the CPU.

5. Copy the data back from the respective CPU:

```
for( int g = 0; g < nGPUs; g++ ){
    cudaSetDevice(g);
    Copy  part 'g' of reduced ABT from GPU 'g' to Host;
}
```

These five steps complete the exercise of converting a single GPU implementation into a multiple GPU on a single node.

CUDA samples that get shipped as part of CUDA's installation include some sample code that tests P2P bandwidth performance. It can be found in the `samples/1_Utilities/p2pBandwidthLatencyTest` folder. It is advised that you run this application on your system so that you understand the P2P bandwidth and latency of your system.

Now that we've achieved multi-GPU implementation on a single node, we'll change gear and run this code on multiple GPUs. But before converting our code into multiple GPUs, we will provide a short primer on MPI programming, which is primarily used for internode communication.

Brief introduction to MPI

The **Message Passing Interface** (**MPI**) standard is a message-passing library standard and has become the industry standard for writing message-passing programs on HPC platforms. Basically, MPI is used for message passing across multiple MPI processes. MPI processes that communicate with each other may reside on the same node or across multiple nodes.

The following is an example Hello World MPI program:

```
#include <mpi.h>
int main(int argc, char *argv[]) {
    int rank,size;
    /* Initialize the MPI library */
    MPI_Init(&argc,&argv);
    /* Determine the calling process rank and total number of ranks */
    MPI_Comm_rank(MPI_COMM_WORLD,&rank);
    MPI_Comm_size(MPI_COMM_WORLD,&size);
    /* Compute based on process rank */
    /* Call MPI routines like MPI_Send, MPI_Recv, ... */
    ...
    /* Shutdown MPI library */
    MPI_Finalize();
    return 0;
}
```

As you can see, the general steps that are involved in the MPI program are as follows:

1. We include the header file, mpi.h, which includes the declaration of all MPI API calls.
2. We initialize the MPI environment by calling MPI_Init and passing the executable arguments to it. After this statement, multiple MPI ranks are created and start executing in parallel.
3. All MPI processes work in parallel and communicate with each other using message-passing APIs such as MPI_Send(), MPI_Recv(), and so on.
4. Finally, we terminate the MPI environment by calling MPI_Finalize().

We can compile this code using different MPI implementation libraries such as OpenMPI, MVPICH, Intel MPI, and so on:

```
$ mpicc -o helloWorldMPI helloWorldMPI.c
$ mpirun -n 4 --hostfile hostsList ./helloWorldMPI
```

We are making use of the `mpicc` compiler to compile our code. `mpicc` is basically is a wrapper script that internally expands the compilation instructions to include the paths to the relevant libraries and header files. Also, running an MPI executable requires it to be passed as an argument to `mpirun`. `mpirun` is a wrapper that helps set up the environment across multiple nodes where the application is supposed to be executed. The `-n 4` argument says that we want to run four processes and that these processes will run on nodes with the hostname stored in the file hosts list.

In this chapter, our goal is to integrate GPU kernels with MPI to make it run across multiple MPI processes. However, we will not be covering the details of MPI programming. Those of you who are not familiar with MPI programming should take a look at `https://computing.llnl.gov/tutorials/mpi/` to understand distributed parallel programming before moving on to the next section.

GPUDirect RDMA

In a cluster environment, we would like to make use of GPUs across multiple nodes. We will allow our parallel solver to integrate CUDA code with MPI to utilize multi-level parallelism on multi-node, multi-GPU systems. A CUDA-aware MPI is used to leverage GPUDirect RDMA for optimized inter-node communication.

GPUDirect RDMA allows direct communication between GPUs across a cluster. It was first supported by CUDA 5.0 with the Kepler GPU card. In the following diagram, we can see the GPUDirect RDMA, that is, **GPU 2** in **Server 1** communicating directly with **GPU 1** in **Server 2**:

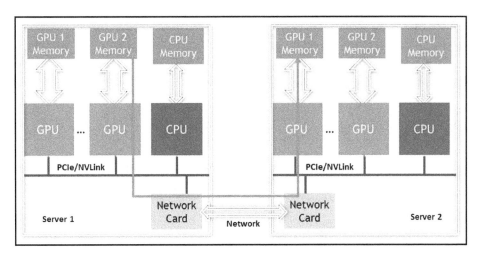

The only theoretical requirement for GPUDirect RDMA to work is that the **Network Card** and **GPU** share the same root complex. The path between the GPU and a third-party device such as a network adapter decides whether RDMA is supported or not. Let's revisit the output of the `nvidia-smi topo -m` command on the DGX system that we ran in the previous section:

```
$ nvidia-smi topo -m
          GPU0  GPU1  GPU2  GPU3  GPU4  GPU5  GPU6  GPU7  mlx5_0  mlx5_2  mlx5_1  mlx5_3  CPU Affinity
GPU0      X     NV1   NV1   NV1   NV1   SYS   SYS   SYS   PIX     SYS     PHB     SYS     0-19
GPU1      NV1   X     NV1   NV1   SYS   NV1   SYS   SYS   PIX     SYS     PHB     SYS     0-19
GPU2      NV1   NV1   X     NV1   SYS   SYS   NV1   SYS   PHB     SYS     PIX     SYS     0-19
GPU3      NV1   NV1   NV1   X     SYS   SYS   SYS   NV1   PHB     SYS     PIX     SYS     0-19
GPU4      NV1   SYS   SYS   SYS   X     NV1   NV1   NV1   SYS     PIX     SYS     PHB     20-39
GPU5      SYS   NV1   SYS   SYS   NV1   X     NV1   NV1   SYS     PIX     SYS     PHB     20-39
GPU6      SYS   SYS   NV1   SYS   NV1   NV1   X     NV1   SYS     PHB     SYS     PIX     20-39
GPU7      SYS   SYS   SYS   NV1   NV1   NV1   NV1   X     SYS     PHB     SYS     PIX     20-39
mlx5_0    PIX   PIX   PHB   PHB   SYS   SYS   SYS   SYS   X       SYS     PHB     SYS
mlx5_2    SYS   SYS   SYS   SYS   PIX   PIX   PHB   PHB   SYS     X       SYS     PHB
mlx5_1    PHB   PHB   PIX   PIX   SYS   SYS   SYS   SYS   PHB     SYS     X       SYS
mlx5_3    SYS   SYS   SYS   SYS   PHB   PHB   PIX   PIX   SYS     PHB     SYS     X

Legend:

  X    = Self
  SYS  = Connection traversing PCIe as well as the SMP interconnect between NUMA nodes (e.g., QPI/UPI)
  NODE = Connection traversing PCIe as well as the interconnect between PCIe Host Bridges within a NUMA node
  PHB  = Connection traversing PCIe as well as a PCIe Host Bridge (typically the CPU)
  PXB  = Connection traversing multiple PCIe switches (without traversing the PCIe Host Bridge)
  PIX  = Connection traversing a single PCIe switch
  NV#  = Connection traversing a bonded set of # NVLinks
```

If we look at the GPU4 row, it shows that the GPU4 to mlx5_2 connection type is PIX (traversal via PCIe switch). We can also see that the GPU4 to mlx_5_0 connection type is SYS (traversal via QPI). This means that GPU4 can perform RDMA transfers via Mellanox InfiniBand Adapter mlx_5_2 but not if the transfer needs to happen from mlx_5_0 as QPI does not allow RDMA protocols.

CUDA-aware MPI

All the latest versions of the MPI libraries support the GPUDirect feature. MPI libraries that support for NVIDIA GPUDirect and **Unified Virtual Addressing** (**UVA**) enable the following:

- MPI can transfer the API to copy data directly to/from GPU memory (RDMA).
- The MPI library can also differentiate between device memory and host memory without any hints from the user and hence it becomes transparent to the MPI programmer.
- The programmer's productivity increases as less application code needs to be changed for data transfers across multiple MPI ranks.

As we mentioned earlier, CPU memory and GPU memory are different. Without a CUDA-aware MPI, the developer can only pass pointers pointing to CPU/host memory to MPI calls. The following code is an example of using non-CUDA-aware MPI calls:

```
//MPI rank 0:Passing s_buf residing in GPU memory
// requires it to be transferred to CPU memory
cudaMemcpy(s_buf_h,s_buf_d,size,cudaMemcpyDeviceToHost);
MPI_Send(s_buf_h,size,MPI_CHAR,1,100,MPI_COMM_WORLD);

//MPI rank 1: r_buf received buffer needs to be
// transferred to GPU memory before being used in GPU
MPI_Recv(r_buf_h,size,MPI_CHAR,0,100,MPI_COMM_WORLD, &status);
cudaMemcpy(r_buf_d,r_buf_h,size,cudaMemcpyHostToDevice);
```

With a CUDA-aware MPI library, this is not necessary; the GPU buffers can be directly passed to MPI, as shown in the following code:

```
//MPI rank 0
MPI_Send(s_buf_d,size,MPI_CHAR,1,100,MPI_COMM_WORLD);

//MPI rank n-1
MPI_Recv(r_buf_d,size,MPI_CHAR,0,100,MPI_COMM_WORLD, &status);
```

For example, for Open MPI, CUDA-aware support exists in the Open MPI 1.7 series and later. To enable this feature, the Open MPI library needs to be configured with CUDA support at the time of compilation, as follows:

```
$ ./configure --with-cuda
```

Having a CUDA-aware MPI does not mean that the GPUDirect RDMA is always used. The GPUDirect feature is used if the data transfer happens between the network card and the GPU that share the same root complex. Nonetheless, even if RDMA support is not enabled, having a CUDA-aware MPI makes the application more efficient by making use of features such as message transfers, which can be pipelined as shown in the following diagram:

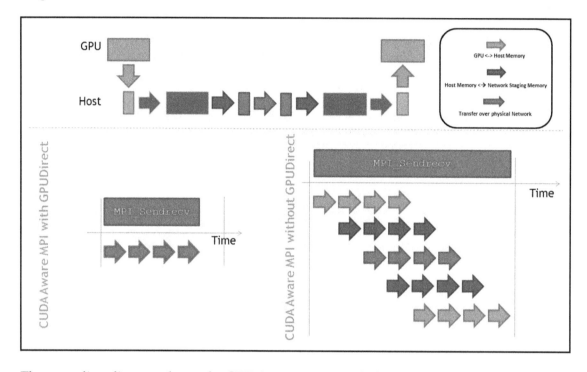

The preceding diagram shows the CUDA-aware MPI with GPUDirect versus the CUDA-aware MPI without GPUDirect. Both calls are from the CUDA-aware MPI, but the left-hand side is with GPUDirect transfer and the right-hand side is without GPUDirect transfer.

Non-GPUDirect transfer has the following stages:

- Node 1: Transfer from GPU1 to host memory
- Node 1: Transfer from host memory to the network adaptor staging area
- Network: Transfer over the network
- Node 2: Transfer from the network staging area to host memory
- Node 2: Transfer from host memory to GPU memory

If GPUDirect RDMA is supported, the transfer from the GPU happens directly over the network and the additional copies involving host memory are all removed.

Now that we have grasped this concept, let's start converting the code to enable Multi-GPU support using CUDA-aware MPI programming.

Multinode – multi-GPU Gaussian elimination

Prepare your GPU application. This code can be found at `06_multigpu/gaussian` in this book's GitHub repository. Compile and run your application with the `nvcc` compiler, as follows:

```
$ mpicc-o gaussian_multi_gpu_rdma.out gaussian_multi_gpu_rdma.cu
$ mpirun -np 8 ./gaussian_multi_gpu_rdma.out
```

We are using `mpicc` instead of `nvcc` to compile the MPI program. We run the executable using the `mpirun` command instead of running the compiled executable directly. The results that you will see in this section are the output of running on the DGX system with 8 V100 on the same system. We make use of the 8 max MPI process as we map 1 MPI process per GPU. To understand how to map multiple MPI processes onto the same GPU, please read the *MPS* subsection later in the chapter. For this exercise, we have used Open MPI 1.10, which has been compiled to support CUDA as described in the previous section.

The steps that are involved in the multi-GPU implementation are as follows:

1. Rank 0 of the MPI process generates data for the linear system (matrices A, B).
2. The transposed augmented matrix (AB^T) is split row-wise by the root among the MPI processes using `MPI_Scatterv()`.

3. Each MPI process computes on its part of the input in parallel:
   - Processing the three kernels happens on the GPU.
   - The consensus of the pivot is achieved after the `findPivot` operation using `MPI_Send()/Recv()`.

4. The reduced **transposed augmented matrix (ABT)** is gathered on the root using `MPI_Gatherv()`.

5. The root performs back substitution to compute solution X.

The extracted sample Gaussian code which showcases the preceding code is as follows:

```
void gaussianEliminationOnGPU() {
    cudaSetDevice(nodeLocalRank); //Set CUDA Device based on local rank
    //Copy  chuck of AB Transpose from Host to GPU;
    for( int n = 0; n < N; n++ ){
        prank = MPI rank that holds n;
        if (myRank == prank)
            findPivotRowAndMultipliers<<<...>>>();
        bCastPivotInfo(); // from prank to other ranks
        extractPivotRow<<<...>>>();
        rowElimination<<<...>>>();
    //Copy  myPartOfReducedTransposeAB from GPU to Host;
}
```

Now, let's add multi-GPU support:

1. **Set the CUDA device per MPI rank**: In Open MPI, you can get the local rank of the MPI process by making use of `MPI_COMM_TYPE_SHARED` as a parameter to `MPI_Comm_split_type`, as shown in the following code:

   ```
   MPI_Comm loc_comm;
   MPI_Comm_split_type(MPI_COMM_WORLD, MPI_COMM_TYPE_SHARED, rank,
   MPI_INFO_NULL, &loc_comm);
   int local_rank = -1;
   MPI_Comm_rank(loc_comm, &local_rank);
   MPI_Comm_free(&loc_comm);
   ```

Now that we have the local rank, each MPI process uses it to set the current GPU by using `cudaSetDevice()`, as shown in the following diagram:

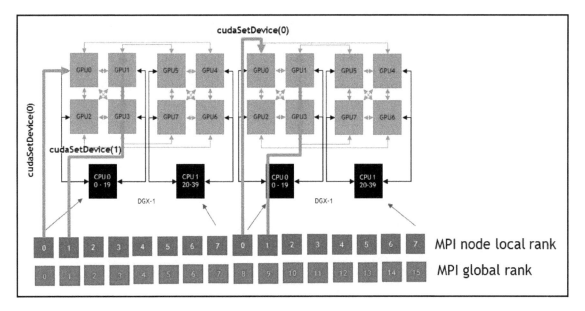

2. Split and distribute the inputs to different MPI processes using `MPI_Scatter`:

```
void distributeInputs() {
    MPI_Scatterv(transposeAB, ..., myPartOfTransposeAB, recvCount,
MPI_UNSIGNED, 0, MPI_COMM_WORLD);
}
```

3. Perform Gaussian elimination on the GPU:

```
void gaussianEliminationOnGPU() {
    cudaSetDevice(nodeLocalRank);
    for( int n = 0; n < N; n++ ){
        prank = MPI rank that holds n;
        if (myRank == prank)
            findPivotRowAndMultipliers<<<...>>>();
        MPI_Bcast(...); // from prank to other ranks
        extractPivotRow<<<...>>>();
        rowElimination<<<...>>>();
    }
}
```

Before performing any operation, the current GPU is set based on local rank. Then, the pivot row is extracted by the process which is responsible for that row, followed by the pivot row being broadcasted to all the other MPI ranks, which we use for elimination.

The overall performance of the transfer time can be improved by making use of asynchronous MPI calls instead of using broadcast APIs such as MPI_Bcast. In fact, the use of a broadcast API is discouraged; it should be replaced with MPI_Isend and MPI_Irecv, which are asynchronous versions that can achieve the same functionality. Please note that making the calls asynchronous adds complexity to other aspects such as debugging. Due to this, the user needs to write additional code to send and receive data.

 This chapter provides the best coding practices when it comes to adding GPU support to an existing MPI program and should not be considered an expert guide on the best programming practices for MPI programming.

CUDA streams

Streams act in a FIFO manner, where the sequence of operations is executed in the order of when they were issued. Requests that are made from the host code are put into First-In-First-Out queues. Queues are read and processed asynchronously by the driver, and the device driver ensures that the commands in a queue are processed in sequence. For example, memory copies end before kernel launch, and so on.

The general idea of using multiple streams is that CUDA operations that are fired in different streams may run concurrently. This can result in multiple kernels overlapping or overlapping memory copies within the kernel execution.

To understand CUDA streams, we will be looking at two applications. The first application is a simple vector addition code with added streams so that it can overlap data transfers with kernel execution. The second application is of an image merging application, which will also be used in Chapter 9, *GPU Programming Using OpenACC*.

To start, configure your environment according to the following steps:

1. Prepare your GPU application. As an example, we will be merging two images. This code can be found in the 06_multi-gpu/streams folder in this book's GitHub repository.
2. Compile your application with the nvcc compiler as follows:

```
$ nvcc --default-stream per-thread -o vector_addition -Xcompiler -
fopenmp -lgomp vector_addition.cu
$ nvcc --default-stream per-thread -o merging_muli_gpu -Xcompiler -
fopenmp -lgomp scrImagePgmPpmPackage.cu image_merging.cu
$ ./vector addition
$ ./merging_muli_gpu
```

The preceding commands will create two binaries named `vector_addition` and `merging_multi_gpu`. As you might have observed, we are using additional arguments in our code. Let's understand them in more detail:

- `--default-stream per-thread`: This flag tells the compiler to parse the OpenACC directives provided in the code.
- `-Xcompiler -fopenmp -lgomp`: This flag tells `nvcc` to pass these additional flags to the CPU compiler underneath to compile the CPU part of the code. In this case, we are asking the compiler to add OpenMP-related libraries to our application.

We will divide this section into two parts. Application 1 and application 2 demonstrate using streams in single and multiple GPUs, respectively.

Application 1 – using multiple streams to overlap data transfers with kernel execution

The steps that we need to follow to overlap data transfers with kernel execution or to launch multiple kernels concurrently are as follows:

1. Declare the host memory to be pinned, as shown in the following code snippet:

```
cudaMallocHost(&hostInput1, inputLength*sizeof(float));
cudaMallocHost(&hostInput2, inputLength*sizeof(float));
cudaMallocHost(&hostOutput, inputLength*sizeof(float));
```

Here, we are making use of the `cudaMallocHost()` API to allocate vectors as pinned memory.

2. Create a `Stream` object, as shown in the following code snippet:

```
for (i = 0; i < 4; i++) {
  cudaStreamCreateWithFlags(&stream[i],cudaStreamNonBlocking);
```

Here, we make use of the `cudaStreamCreateWithFlags()` API, passing `cudaStreamNonBlocking` as the flag to make this stream non-blocking.

3. Call the CUDA kernel and memory copies with the `stream` flag, as shown in the following code snippet:

```
for (i = 0; i < inputLength; i += Seglen * 4) {
    for (k = 0; k < 4; k++) {
        cudaMemcpyAsync(... , cudaMemcpyHostToDevice, stream[k]);
        cudaMemcpyAsync(... , cudaMemcpyHostToDevice, stream[k]);
        vecAdd<<<Gridlen, 256, 0, stream[k]>>>(...);
    }
}
```

As we can see, instead of performing the vector addition in one shot by copying the whole array once, instead we chunk the array into segments and copy the segments asynchronously. Kernel execution is also done asynchronously in the respective streams.

When we run this code through Visual Profiler, we can see the following characteristics:

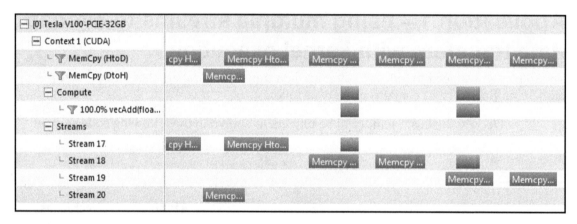

The preceding profiler screenshot shows that the blue bars (which are basically `vector_addition` kernels) overlap the memory copies. Since we created four streams in our code, there are four streams in the profiler as well.

Every GPU has two memory copy engines. One is responsible for the host to device transfer while the other is responsible for the device to host transfer. Hence, the two memory copies, which happen in opposite directions, can be overlapped. Also, the memory copies can be overlapped with the compute kernels. This can result in *n*-way concurrency, as shown in the following diagram:

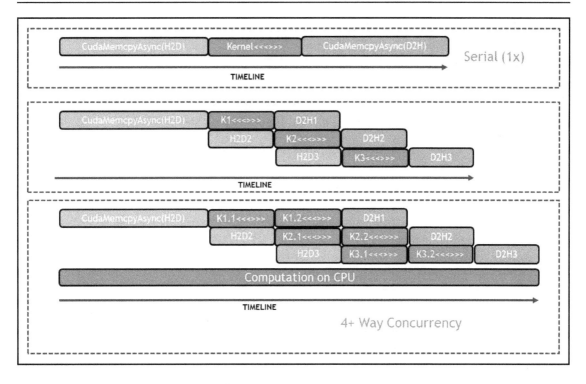

Every GPU architecture comes with certain constraints and rules based on which we will see these overlaps at execution time. In general, the following are some guidelines:

- CUDA operations must be in different, non-0 streams.
- cudaMemcpyAsync with the host should be pinned using cudaMallocHost() or cudaHostAlloc().
  - Sufficient resources must be available
  - cudaMemcpyAsyncs in different directions
  - Device resources (SMEM, registers, blocks, and so on) to launch multiple concurrent kernels

Application 2 – using multiple streams to run kernels on multiple devices

To run kernels and overlap memory transfers across multiple devices, the steps that we followed previously remain the same, except for one additional step: setting the CUDA device to create the stream. Let's have a look at the following steps:

1. Create streams equal to the number of CUDA devices present in the system, as shown in the following code snippet:

```
cudaGetDeviceCount(&noDevices);
cudaStream_t *streams;
streams = (cudaStream_t*) malloc(sizeof(cudaStream_t) * noDevices);
```

We make use of the `cudaGetDeviceCount()` API to get the number of CUDA devices.

2. Create the stream in the respective device, as shown in the following code snippet:

```
#pragma omp parallel num_threads(noDevices)
{
    int block = omp_get_thread_num();
    cudaSetDevice(block);
    cudaStreamCreate(&streams[block]);
```

We are launching OpenMP threads equal to the number of CUDA devices so that each CPU thread can create its own CUDA stream for its respective devices. Each CPU thread executes `cudaSetDevice()` to set the current GPU based on its ID and then creates the stream for that device.

3. Launch the kernel and memory copies in that stream, as follows:

```
cudaMemcpyAsync(... cudaMemcpyHostToDevice,streams[block]);
cudaMemcpyAsync(..., cudaMemcpyHostToDevice, streams[block]);
merging_kernel<<<gridDim,blockDim,0,streams[block]>>>(...);
cudaMemcpyAsync(...,streams[block]);
```

The output after running the code in the profiler can be seen in the following screenshot, which represents the Visual Profiler's timeline view. This shows an overlapping memory copy for one GPU with the kernel execution of the other GPU:

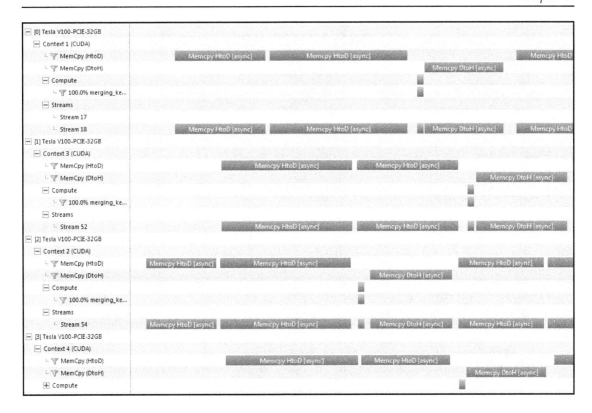

As you can see, we ran this code on the multi-GPU system with four V100s. The memory copies and kernels in the different GPUs overlap each other. In this code, we demonstrated making use of OpenMP to call CUDA kernels in parallel on different devices. This can also be done by making use of MPI to launch multiple processes that utilize different GPUs.

In the next section, we will take a look at some additional topics that can improve the performance of multi-GPU applications and help developers profile and debug their code.

Additional tricks

In this section, we will cover some additional topics that will help us understand the additional characteristics of the multi-GPU system.

Benchmarking an existing system with an InfiniBand network card

Different benchmarks are available for testing the RDMA feature. One such benchmark for the InfiniBand adapter can be found at `https://www.openfabrics.org/`. You can test your bandwidth by executing the following code:

```
$ git clone git://git.openfabrics.org/~grockah/perftest.git
$ cd perftest
$ ./autogen.sh
$ export CUDA_H_PATH=<<Path to cuda.h>>
$ ./configure –prefix=$HOME/test
$ make all install
```

Then, you can run the following commands to test the bandwidth:

```
For example host to GPU memory (H-G) BW test:
server$ ~/test/bin/ib_write_bw –n 1000 –O –a --use_cuda
client $ ~/test/bin/ib_write_bw –n 1000 –O –a server.name.org

//GPU to GPU memory (G-G) BW test:
server$ ~/test/bin/ib_write_bw –n 1000 –O –a --use_cuda
client $ ~/test/bin/ib_write_bw –n 1000 –O –a --use_cuda server.name.org
```

NVIDIA Collective Communication Library (NCCL)

The NCCL provides an implementation of communication primitives that are commonly used in domains such as deep learning. NCCL 1.0 started with the implementation of communication primitives across multiple GPUs within the same node and evolved to support multiple GPUs in multiple nodes. Some key features of the NCCL library include the following:

- Supports calls from multiple threads and multiple processes
- Supports the multiple ring and tree topology for better bus utilization within and across nodes
- Supports InfiniBand inter-node communication
- The source package is free to download from GitHub (`https://github.com/nvidia/nccl`)

NCCL can be scaled up to 24,000 GPUs, well below the 300 microsecond latency. Note that NCCL has proven to be a really useful and handy library for deep learning frameworks but has its limitation when used for HPC applications as it does not support point-to-point communication. NCCL supports collective operations, which are used in deep learning applications such as the following:

- `AllReduce`
- `AllGather`
- `ReduceScatter`
- `Reduce`
- `Broadcast`

All NCCL calls run as CUDA kernels for faster access to GPU memory. It makes use of fewer threads that are implemented as one block. This ends up running only on one GPU SM and hence does not affect the utilization of other GPUs. Let's have a look at the following code:

```
ncclGroupStart();
for (int i=0; i<ngpus; i++)
{
    ncclAllGather(..., comms[i], streams[i]);
}
ncclGroupEnd();
```

As we can see, NCCL calls are simple and can be called with ease.

Collective communication acceleration using NCCL

The **NVIDIA Collective Communication Library** (**NCCL**) provides a performance-optimized collective of communication primitives for multiple NVIDIA GPUs. In this section, we will see how this library works and how we can benefit from using it.

It isn't difficult to find deep learning models that use multiple GPUs to train the network. Since two GPUs compute the neural network in parallel, we can easily imagine that this technique will increase training performance along with the GPU numbers. Unfortunately, the world is not that simple. The gradients should be shared across multiple GPUs and the weight update procedure in one GPU should wait for the others' gradients to update its weights. This is the general procedure of deep learning training with multiple GPUs, and is shown in the following diagram:

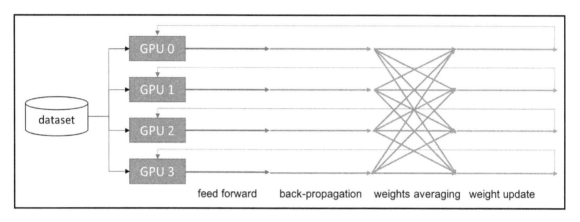

feed forward   back-propagation   weights averaging weight update

Collective communication has many types: all-reduce, broadcast, reduce, all gather, reduce scatter, and so on. In deep learning, each GPU collects another GPU's data while it transfers its own to the other GPUs. Therefore, we can determine that deep learning needs all types of reducing style communication in their communication.

In the HPC community, collective communication, including all-reduce, is quite a common topic. Communication between the processor from inter- and intra-nodes was a challenging but crucial issue because it's directly related to scalability. As we mentioned in Chapter 6, *Scalable Multi-GPU Programming*, in the *Multiple GPU programming* section, it requires a lot of consideration to communicate with each GPU. The developer should design and implement collective communication in GPUs, even though MPI already supports such communication patterns.

NCCL provides such a collective that's aware of the GPU topology configuration. By using a variety of grouping and communication commands, you can apply the required communication task.

One prerequisite is that your system needs to have more than one GPU because NCCL is a communication library that works with multiple GPUs.

The following steps cover how to call `ncclAllReduce()` as a test and measure the system's GPU network bandwidth. The sample code is implemented in `04_nccl`:

1. Let's define a type that will contain, send, and receive, a buffer and `cudaStream` for each GPU device, as follows:

```
typedef struct device
{
    float *d_send;
    float *d_recv;
    cudaStream_t stream;
} device_t;
```

2. At the beginning of the application, we need to prepare some handles so that we can control multiple GPUs:

```
cudaGetDeviceCount(&num_dev);
ncclComm_t *ls_comms = new ncclComm_t[num_dev];
int *dev_ids = new int[num_dev];
for (int i = 0; i < num_dev; i++)
    dev_ids[i] = i;
```

3. Then, we will create a buffer, assuming that we have data. For each device, we will initialize each device's items, as follows:

```
unsigned long long size = 512 * 1024 * 1024; // 2 GB

// allocate device buffers and initialize device handles
device_t *ls_dev = new device_t[num_dev];
for (int i = 0; i < num_dev; i++) {
    cudaSetDevice(i);
    cudaMalloc((void**)&ls_dev[i].d_send, sizeof(float) * size);
    cudaMalloc((void**)&ls_dev[i].d_recv, sizeof(float) * size);
    cudaMemset(ls_dev[i].d_send, 0, sizeof(float) * size);
    cudaMemset(ls_dev[i].d_recv, 0, sizeof(float) * size);
    cudaStreamCreate(&ls_dev[i].stream);
}
```

4. Before starting the NCCL communication, we need to initialize the GPU devices so that they are aware of their rank across the GPU group. Since we will be testing the bandwidth with a single process, we are safe to call a function that initializes all the devices:

```
ncclCommInitAll(ls_comms, num_dev, dev_ids);
```

5. If we are testing the bandwidth with multiple processes, we need to call `ncclCommInitRank()`. We will need to provide GPU IDs for counting the process IDs and GPU ranks.

6. Now, we can complete the all-reduce operations with NCCL. The following code is an example implementation of `ncclAllReduce`:

```
ncclGroupStart();
for (int i = 0; i < num_dev; i++) {
    ncclAllReduce((const void*)ls_dev[i].d_send,
                  (void*)ls_dev[i].d_recv,
        test_size, ncclFloat, ncclSum,
        ls_comms[i], ls_dev[i].stream);
}
ncclGroupEnd();
```

For each device, we need to trigger the traffic. For this, we need to start and close NCCL group communication. Now, we have implemented some test code that uses `ncclAllReduce()`. Let's cover how NCCL works by micro-benchmarking our system.

Let's test this code on a multi-GPU system, run the following command:

```
$ nvcc -run -m64 -std=c++11 -I/usr/local/cuda/samples/common/inc -gencode
arch=compute_70,code=sm_70 -lnccl -o nccl ./nccl.cu
```

The following diagram shows the performance that was measured using four V100 32G GPUs in DGX Station. The blue line denotes the NVLink-based bandwidth, while the orange line denotes PCIe-based bandwidth, which it does by setting `NCCL_P2P_DISABLE=1` `./ncd` and turning off peer-to-peer GPUs:

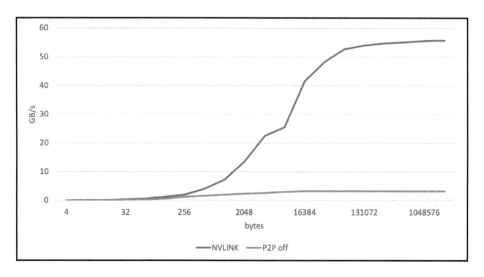

This NCCL test can be impacted by the system's configuration. This means that the result can vary, depending on your system's GPU topology.

This shows the difference between PCI express-based and NVLINK-based all-reduce performance. We can see its communication using `nvprof`. The following screenshot shows NCCL's all-reduce communication in DGX Station via NCCL 2.3.7:

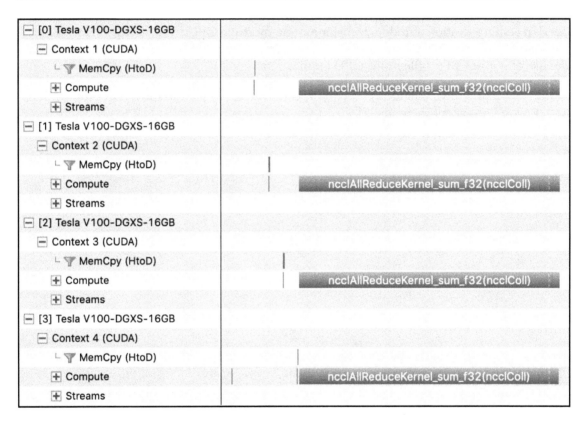

NCCL is getting faster and faster. By introducing new GPU interconnects with NVLink and NVSwitch, our experience with NCCL is increasing, so much so that we can achieve scalable performance.

 The following link provides a discussion about NCCL: `https://developer.nvidia.com/gtc/2019/video/S9656/video`.

Summary

In this chapter, we covered different approaches to multi-GPU programming. With the help of an example Gaussian elimination, we saw how a single GPU application workload can be split across multiple GPUs, first into a single node and then into multiple nodes. We saw how system topology plays an important role in making use of features such as P2P transfer and GPUDirect RDMA. We also saw how multiple CUDA streams can be used to overlap communication and data transfer among multiple GPUs. We also briefly covered some additional topics that can help CUDA programmers optimize code such as MPS and the use of `nvprof` to profile multi-GPU applications.

In the next chapter, we will look at common patterns that appear in most HPC applications and how to implement them in GPUs.

7
Parallel Programming Patterns in CUDA

In this chapter, we will cover parallel programming algorithms that will help you understand how to parallelize different algorithms and optimize CUDA. The techniques we will cover in this chapter can be applied to a variety of problems, for example, the parallel reduction problem we looked at in `Chapter 3`, *CUDA Thread Programming*, which can be used to design an efficient softmax layer in neural network operations.

In this chapter, we will cover the following topics:

- Matrix multiplication optimization
- Image convolution
- Prefix sum
- Pack and split
- N-body operation
- QuickSort in CUDA using dynamic parallelism
- Radix sort
- Histogram calculation

Technical requirements

To complete this chapter, it is recommended that you use an NVIDIA GPU card later than the Pascal architecture. In other words, your GPU's compute capability should be equal to or greater than 60. If you are unsure of your GPU's architecture, please visit NVIDIA GPU's site (`https://developer.nvidia.com/cuda-gpus`) and confirm your GPU's compute capability.

The same codes in this chapter have been developed and tested with CUDA version 10.1. In general, it is recommended to use the latest CUDA version if applicable.

Matrix multiplication optimization

Although we have used matrix multiplication code in many examples, we didn't investigate whether the operation was optimized. Now, let's review its operation and how we can find an opportunity for optimization.

Matrix multiplication is a group of dot product operations from two matrices. We can simply parallelize the operations that are done by all the CUDA threads to generate a dot product of elements. However, this operation is inefficient in terms of memory usage because the data that's loaded from memory isn't reused. To confirm our analogy, let's measure the performance limiter. The following chart shows the GPU utilization for a Tesla V100 card using Nsight Compute:

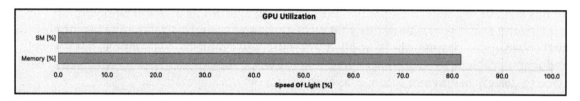

Based on our performance limiter analysis, this utilization ratio can be categorized as memory bounded. Therefore, we should review the memory utilization to mitigate utilization. The following screenshot shows the memory workload analysis section:

▶ Memory Workload Analysis		All	▾	◯
Detailed analysis of the memory resources of the GPU. Memory can become a limiting factor for the overall kernel performance when fully utilizing the involved hardware units (Mem Busy), exhausting the available communication bandwidth between those units (Max Bandwidth), or by reaching the maximum throughput of issuing memory instructions (Mem Pipes Busy). Detailed chart of the memory units. Detailed tables with data for each memory unit.				
Memory Throughput [Gbyte/second]	169.45	Mem Busy [%]		81.66
L1 Hit Rate [%]	88.25	Max Bandwidth [%]		54.90
L2 Hit Rate [%]	58.11	Mem Pipes Busy [%]		54.42

From this analysis, we can see that the L2 cache hit rate is low and that the max bandwidth is low. We can presume that this is because the original matrix multiplication operation does not reuse loaded data, as we mentioned earlier. This can be resolved by using shared memory, that is, reusing the loaded data and mitigating global memory usage. Now, let's review matrix multiplication and how we can optimize this to use shared memory that has a small memory space.

Matrix multiplication is a group of dot product operations with some small size matrices and a cumulation of output. The small matrices are called tiles and they map to the matrices along the output matrix. Each tile will compute its own output in parallel. This operation can be implemented in the following steps:

1. Determine the tile size for two input and output matrices.
2. Traverse the input tiles, along with their direction (matrix A goes to the right, and matrix B goes down).
3. Compute matrix multiplication within the tile.
4. Continue the second step until the tile reaches the end.
5. Flush the output.

The following diagram shows the concept of tiled matrix multiplication:

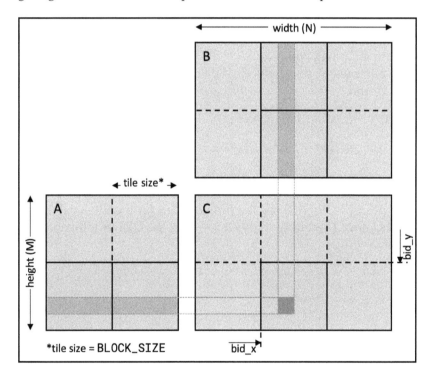

In the preceding diagram, we compute a matrix multiplication, $C = AB$. We compute a smaller matrix multiplication as a tile, in green, from matrix A and matrix B. Then, we traverse the input tile position, respectively. The operation result is accumulated to the previous output to generate the matrix multiplication's output.

This operation provides an optimization opportunity because we can break down the large matrix operation with the small problems and place it in the small memory space. In CUDA programming, we place the small matrices in shared memory and mitigate global memory access. In our implementation, we will match the tile with the CUDA thread block. The tile's position will be determined by its block index, which is done with the `tid_*` variable.

Implementation of the tiling approach

Now, let's implement an optimized matrix multiplication using the tiled approach. We will reuse the previous matrix multiplication sample code that we used in Chapter 3, *CUDA Thread Programming*. After optimization, we will look at how performance can be enhanced. Follow these steps to get started:

1. Let's create a kernel function that will be our optimized version of matrix multiplication. We will name the kernel function `v2` in the `sgemm` operation. This kernel function will compute $C = \alpha AB + \beta C$, so we should provide the related parameters, respectively. We will also pass the matrix size information with `M`, `N`, and `K`:

    ```
    __global__ void sgemm_kernel_v2(const float *A, const float *B,
    float *C,
        int M, int N, int K, float alpha, float beta) {}
    ```

2. For this operation, we will use the block index and the thread index separately. As we discussed earlier, we need to use the block index separately to designate the tile position. We will use the thread index for the tile-level matrix multiplication. Therefore, we need to create the CUDA index parameter, as follows:

    ```
    int bid_x = blockIdx.x * blockDim.x;
    int bid_y = blockIdx.y * blockDim.y;
    int tid_x = threadIdx.x;
    int tid_y = threadIdx.y;
    ```

3. After that, we will use shared memory as tiles and use a local register to save the output value:

    ```
    float element_c = 0.f;
    __shared__ float s_tile_A[BLOCK_DIM][BLOCK_DIM];
    __shared__ float s_tile_B[BLOCK_DIM][BLOCK_DIM];
    ```

4. Then, we will write a loop that controls the tiles' position. Here is the for loop code that controls a loop based on its block size. Be aware that the loop size is determined by K considering how many times blocks should be traversed:

```
for (int k = 0; k < K; k += BLOCK_DIM)
{
    ... {step 5 and 6 will cover } ...
}
```

5. Now, we will write code that feeds data in the second loop. As we discussed earlier, each tile has its own moving direction, along with the matrices; tile A traverses the column of matrix A and tile B traverses the row of matrix B. We place them according to the diagram shown in the *Matrix multiplication optimization* section. After that, we should place __syncthreads() after copying data from global memory to shared memory to avoid un-updated data from the previous iteration:

```
// Get sub-matrix from A
s_tile_A[tid_y][tid_x] = A[ (bid_y + tid_y) * K + tid_x + k ];
// Get sub-matrix from B
s_tile_B[tid_y][tid_x] = B[ k * N + bid_x + tid_x ];

__syncthreads();
```

6. Then, we can write matrix multiplication code from the tiles. The local variable known as element_c will cumulate the result:

```
for (int e = 0; e < BLOCK_DIM; e++)
    element_c += s_tile_A[tid_y][e] * s_tile_B[e][tid_x];
```

7. We will write the result into global memory. The following operation should be placed after the second loop finishes:

```
C[(bid_y + tid_y) * N + (bid_x + tid_x)] = \
 alpha * element_c + beta * C[(bid_y + tid_y) * N + (bid_x +
tid_x)];
```

8. Now, let's review how this tiling approach benefits the matrix multiplication operation. By using shared memory in our tiled matrix multiplication, we can expect that we will reduce the global memory traffic by using the input data and thus enhancing performance. We can confirm this with the profile result easily:

```
$ nvcc -m64 -I/usr/local/cuda/samples/common/inc -gencode
arch=compute_70,code=sm_70 -o sgemm ./sgemm.cu
$ nvprof ./sgemm
```

```
         Type Time(%)     Time Calls     Avg      Min      Max Name
GPU activities: 47.79% 9.9691ms      1 9.9691ms 9.9691ms 9.9691ms
sgemm_kernel(...)
                32.52% 6.7845ms      1 6.7845ms 6.7845ms 6.7845ms
sgemm_kernel_v2(...)
```

9. Since we designed the kernel to reuse input data, the increased block size may help with performance. For instance, a 32 x 32 block size can be optimal considering the warp size and the number of shared memory banks to avoid bank conflicts. We can easily obtain its experiment result using the profile:

```
         Type Time(%)     Time Calls     Avg      Min      Max
Name
GPU activities: 46.52% 8.1985ms      1 8.1985ms  8.1985ms  8.1985ms
sgemm_kernel(...)
                31.24% 5.4787ms      1 5.4787ms  5.4787ms  5.4787ms
sgemm_kernel_v2(...)
```

As you can see, the increased tile size benefits the matrix multiplication operation's performance. Now, let's analyze its performance.

Performance analysis of the tiling approach

Previously, we looked at the tiling approach and how it can achieve good performance. Let's review what the tiling approach resolves and look at what steps we can take next. Covering this part is optional in general because NVIDIA provides the cuBLAS and CUTLASS libraries for the GEMM (short for **General Matrix Multiply**) operation to provide optimized performance.

The following chart shows the updated GPU utilization report from Nsight Compute. The updated utilization output from the lower profile is a result of the upper profile:

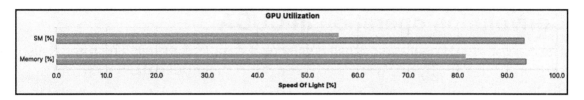

As both resources scored high utilization, we should review each one's resource usage. First of all, let's review the memory workload. The following screenshot shows the updated result:

▸ Memory Workload Analysis				All	
Detailed analysis of the memory resources of the GPU. Memory can become a limiting factor for the overall kernel performance when fully utilizing the involved hardware units (Mem Busy), exhausting the available communication bandwidth between those units (Max Bandwidth), or by reaching the maximum throughput of issuing memory instructions (Mem Pipes Busy). Detailed chart of the memory units. Detailed tables with data for each memory unit.					
Memory Throughput [Gbyte/second]	7.69	(−95.46%)	Mem Busy [%]	93.80	(+14.87%)
L1 Hit Rate [%]	36.47	(−58.67%)	Max Bandwidth [%]	85.18	(+55.14%)
L2 Hit Rate [%]	98.33	(+69.22%)	Mem Pipes Busy [%]	92.63	(+70.23%)

From this result, we can see that global memory access is optimized from maximized memory bandwidth and reduced memory throughput. Also, the L2 cache hit rate is enhanced. So, our tiling approach transforms matrix multiplication from global memory into the on-chip-level operation.

However, this does not mean that we achieved the most optimized performance. From the memory workload analysis, we can see that the memory pipes are too busy. This is due to our element-wise multiplication from shared memory. To resolve this issue, we need to remap the data in shared memory. We will not cover that in this book, but you can learn about it in this article: https://github.com/NervanaSystems/maxas/wiki/SGEMM.

As we discussed earlier, the cuBLAS library shows much faster performance. We will cover its usage in the *cuBLAS* section in Chapter 8, *Programming with Libraries and Other Languages*. However, understanding the tiling approach at this stage is useful so that we can understand how GPUs can begin optimization.

Convolution

The convolutional operation (or filtering) is another common operation in many applications, especially in image and signal processing, as well as deep learning. Although this operation is based on the product of sequential data from the input and filter, we have a different approach for matrix multiplication.

Convolution operation in CUDA

The convolutional operation consists of source data and a filter. The filter is also known as a kernel. By applying the filter against the input data, we can obtain the modified result. A two-dimensional convolution is shown in the following diagram:

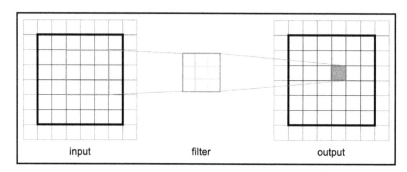

We need to consider a couple of concepts when we implement convolution operation, that is, kernel and padding. The kernel is a set of coefficients that we want to apply to the source data. This is also known as a filter. The padding is extra virtual space around the source data so that we can apply kernel functions to the edge. When the padding size is 0, we don't allow the filter to move beyond the source space. However, in general, the padding size is half the size of the filter.

To start easily, we can design the kernel function with the following in mind:

- Each CUDA thread generates one filtered output.
- Each CUDA thread applies the filter's coefficients to the data.
- The filter shape is a box filter.

Following these conditions, we can have a simple convolutional operation filter like this:

```
__global__ void
convolution_kernel_v1(float *d_output, float *d_input, float *d_filter, int
num_row, int num_col, int filter_size)
{
    int idx_x = blockDim.x * blockIdx.x + threadIdx.x;
    int idx_y = blockDim.y * blockIdx.y + threadIdx.y;

    float result = 0.f;
    // iterates over the every value in the filter
    for (int filter_row = -filter_size / 2;
        filter_row <= filter_size / 2; ++filter_row)
```

```
    {
        for (int filter_col = -filter_size / 2;
            filter_col <= filter_size / 2; ++filter_col)
        {
            // Find the global position to apply the given filter
            // clamp to boundary of the source
            int image_row = min(max(idx_y + filter_row, 0),
                            static_cast<int>(num_row - 1));
            int image_col = min(max(idx_x + filter_col, 0),
                            static_cast<int>(num_col - 1));

            float image_value = static_cast<float>(
                            d_input[image_row * num_col +
                            image_col]);
            float filter_value = d_filter[(filter_row +
                                        filter_size / 2) *
                                        filter_size
                                        + filter_col +
                                        filter_size / 2];

            result += image_value * filter_value;
        }
    }

    d_output[idx_y * num_col + idx_x] = result;
}
```

This kernel function fetches input data and a filter for the very operation and does not reuse all the data. Considering the performance impact from memory inefficiency, we need to design our kernel code so that we can reuse the loaded data. Now, let's write the optimized version of convolution.

Optimization strategy

First of all, the convolution filter is a read-only matrix and is used by all the CUDA threads. In this case, we can use CUDA's constant memory to utilize its cache operation with the broadcasting operation.

In convolution implementation design, we use the tiling approach, and each tile will generate the filtered output to the mapped position. Our tile design has extra space to consider the convolution filter size, which provides the required data for the convolution operation. This extra space is called **padding**. The following diagram shows an example of a thread block with a 6 x 6 dimension and a filter that's 3 x 3 size.

Then, we need to have an 8 x 8 sized tile on shared memory for each thread block, as follows:

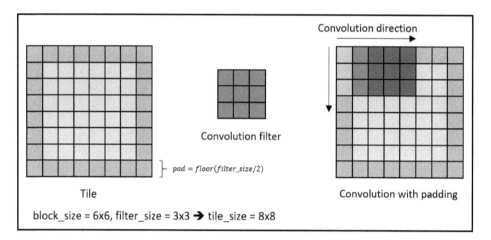

Convolution direction

Convolution filter

$pad = floor(filter\_size/2)$

Tile

Convolution with padding

block_size = 6x6, filter_size = 3x3 ➜ tile_size = 8x8

The pad area can be input data when the source's addresses are invalid memory space, or they are filled with zero (zero-padding approach). By doing this, we can make the tile replace the input global memory with no additional effect on the boundary elements. To fill the tile, we iterate over the tile with the thread block size, and determine which value should be filled by checking the boundary condition of the input data. Our implementation sets the input data as a multiple of the tile size so that the boundary condition matches with the pad space of each thread block's tile. A brief diagram of mapping the source data to the tile is as follows:

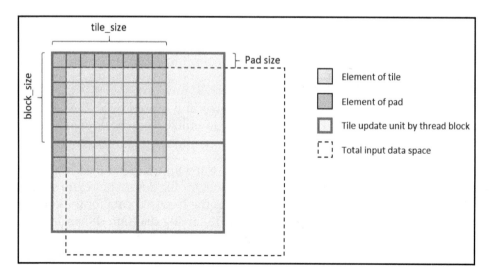

tile_size

block_size

Pad size

Element of tile

Element of pad

Tile update unit by thread block

Total input data space

In this design, the number of iterations we need to do to fill the tile is four. However, this should be changed depending on the filter size. This way, the number of iterations to fill the tile is determined by the number of the ceiling of tile size, divided by the thread block size. Its implementation is simple, as shown in the following code:

```
for (int row = 0; row <= tile_size / BLOCK_DIM; row++) {
    for (int col = 0; col <= tile_size / BLOCK_DIM; col++) {
        ... (filter update operation) ...
    }
}
```

Now, let's implement the optimized convolution operation using shared memory as a box filter.

Filtering coefficients optimization using constant memory

Firstly, we will learn how to optimize filter coefficient data usage.

We will make a modified version of `convolution_kernel()`. Let's duplicate the kernel code and rename one of them as `convolution_kernel_v2()`:

1. First, we will create a constant memory space to store the filter coefficients. The constant memory's size is limited and we can't make modifications to the kernel code. However, we can use this constant memory since our convolutional filter is suitable for this condition. We can use constant memory like so:

   ```
   #define MAX_FILTER_LENGTH 128
   __constant__ float c_filter[MAX_FILTER_LENGTH * MAX_FILTER_LENGTH];
   ```

2. Then, we can place our convolutional filter coefficients in constant memory using the `cudaMemcpyToSymbol()` function:

   ```
   cudaMemcpyToSymbol(c_filter, h_filter, filter_size * filter_size *
   sizeof(float));
   ```

3. Let's switch the filter operation so that we can use constant memory. The whole kernel implementation is as follows. As you can see, only one variable's usage has changed:

```
__global__ void
convolution_kernel_v2(float *d_output, float *d_input, float
*d_filter, int num_row, int num_col, int filter_size)
{
    int idx_x = blockDim.x * blockIdx.x + threadIdx.x;
    int idx_y = blockDim.y * blockIdx.y + threadIdx.y;

    float result = 0.f;
    for (int filter_row = -filter_size / 2;
        filter_row <= filter_size / 2; ++filter_row)
    {
        for (int filter_col = -filter_size / 2;
            filter_col <= filter_size / 2; ++filter_col)
        {
            int image_row = idx_y + filter_row;
            int image_col = idx_x + filter_col;

            float image_value = (image_row >= 0
                                && image_row < num_row
                                && image_col >= 0
                                && image_col < num_col) ?
                                d_input[image_row * num_col
                                    + image_col] : 0.f;
            float filter_value = c_filter[(filter_row
                                    + filter_size / 2)
                                  * filter_size
                                  + filter_col
                                  + filter_size / 2];

            result += image_value * filter_value;
        }
    }

    d_output[idx_y * num_col + idx_x] = result;
}
```

4. Now, we can confirm the performance enhancement thanks to the filter data reusing nvprof:

```
$ nvcc -run -m64 -I/usr/local/cuda/samples/common/inc -gencode
arch=compute_70,code=sm_70 -o convolution ./convolution.cu
$ nvprof ./convolution
            Type Time(%) Time Calls Avg Min Max Name
                 12.85% 442.21us     1 442.21us 442.21us 442.21us
```

```
convolution_kernel_v1(...)
                    11.97% 412.00us    1 412.00us 412.00us 412.00us
convolution_kernel_v2(...)
```

From this result, we can see a reduced kernel execution time.

Tiling input data using shared memory

Now, we will optimize input data usage using shared memory. To differentiate our next optimization step, let's duplicate the previous convolution kernel function and name it `convolution_kernel_v3()`:

1. First, we need to preprepare the shared memory space so that it can store the input data. To get the benefit of the filter operation from shared memory, we need to have extra input data. To create sufficient memory space, we need to modify the kernel call, as follows:

   ```
   int shared_mem_size = (2*filter_size+BLOCK_DIM) *
   (2*filter_size+BLOCK_DIM) * sizeof(float);
   convolution_kernel_v3<<<dimGrid, dimBlock, shared_mem_size, 0
   >>>(d_output, d_input, d_filter, num_row, num_col, filter_size);
   ```

2. In the kernel code, we can declare the shared memory space as follows:

   ```
   extern __shared__ float s_input[];
   ```

3. Then, we can copy the input data to shared memory, which will be calculated by the thread block. First, let's declare some variables that help control the memory operation:

   ```
   int pad_size = filter_size / 2;
   int tile_size = BLOCK_DIM + 2 * pad_size;
   ```

4. Now, we can copy the load input data to shared memory by following the tiling design we discussed previously:

   ```
   for (int row = 0; row <= tile_size / BLOCK_DIM; row++) {
       for (int col = 0; col <= tile_size / BLOCK_DIM; col++) {
           int idx_row = idx_y + BLOCK_DIM * row - pad_size;
           // input data index row
           int idx_col = idx_x + BLOCK_DIM * col - pad_size;
           // input data index column
           int fid_row = threadIdx.y + BLOCK_DIM * row;
           // filter index row
           int fid_col = threadIdx.x + BLOCK_DIM * col;
   ```

```
            // filter index column
            if (fid_row >= tile_size || fid_col >= tile_size) continue;

            s_input[tile_size * fid_row + fid_col] = \
                (idx_row >= 0 && idx_row < num_row && idx_col >= 0
                  && idx_col < num_col) ?
                    d_input[num_col * idx_row + idx_col] : 0.f;
        }
    }

    __syncthreads();
```

5. Since the input memory has changed, our convolution code should be updated. We can write the convolution code as follows:

```
float result = 0.f;
    for (int filter_row = -filter_size / 2;
         filter_row <= filter_size / 2; ++filter_row)
    {
        for (int filter_col = -filter_size / 2;
             filter_col <= filter_size / 2; ++filter_col)
        {
            // Find the global position to apply the given filter
            int image_row = threadIdx.y + pad_size + filter_row;
            int image_col = threadIdx.x + pad_size + filter_col;

            float image_value = s_input[tile_size
                                        * image_row + image_col];
            float filter_value = c_filter[(filter_row
                                        + filter_size / 2)
                                        * filter_size
                                        + filter_col
                                        + filter_size / 2];

            result += image_value * filter_value;
        }
    }
```

6. Finally, we can measure the performance gain using `nvprof`. From the result, we can confirm that we have accelerated about 35% faster than the original operation:

```
$ nvcc -run -m64 -I/usr/local/cuda/samples/common/inc -gencode
arch=compute_70,code=sm_70 -o convolution ./convolution.cu
$ nvprof ./convolution
Processing Time (1) -> GPU: 0.48 ms
Processing Time (2) -> GPU: 0.43 ms
Processing Time (3) -> GPU: 0.30 ms
Processing Time -> Host: 4104.51 ms
... (profiler output) ...
                type Time(%)     Time Calls .     Avg      Min .     Max
Name
   GPU activities: 66.85% 2.3007ms     3 766.91us 1.1840us 2.2979ms
[CUDA memcpy HtoD]
                12.85% 442.21us     1 442.21us 442.21us 442.21us
convolution_kernel_v1()
                11.97% 412.00us     1 412.00us 412.00us 412.00us
convolution_kernel_v2()
                8.33% 286.56us     1 286.56us 286.56us 286.56us
convolution_kernel_v3()
```

Now, we have covered how to utilize loaded data so that we can reuse it with other on-chip caches instead of global memory. We'll talk about this in more detail in the next section.

Getting more performance

If the filter is the symmetric filter or separable filter, we can break down the box filter as two filters: a horizontal filter and a vertical filter. Using two directional filters, we can have more optimization in shared memory usage: memory space and memory utilization. If you want to learn more about this, have a look at a CUDA sample named `convolutionSeparable` in the `3_Imaging/convolutionSeparable` directory. Its detailed explanation is also included in the same directory as `doc/convolutionSeparable.pdf`.

Prefix sum (scan)

Prefix sum (scan) is used to obtain a cumulative number array from the given input numbers array. For example, we can make a prefix-sum sequence as follows:

Input numbers	1	2	3	4	5	6	...
Prefix sums	1	3	6	10	15	21	...

It differs from parallel reduction since reduction just generates the total operation output from the given input data. On the other hand, scan generates outputs from each operation. The easiest way to solve this problem is to iterate all the inputs to generate the output. However, it would take a long time and would be inefficient in GPUs. Hence, the mild approach can parallelize the prefix-sum operation, as follows:

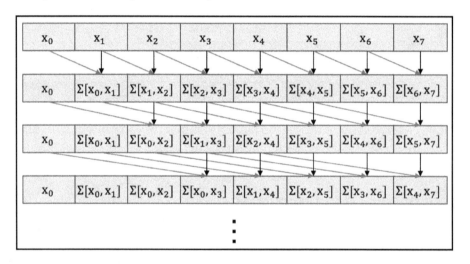

In this approach, we can obtain the output using multiple CUDA cores. However, this method does not reduce the total number of iterations because the first input element should be added for all the outputs one by one. Also, we cannot predict the output result when the array is sufficiently large, so multiple thread blocks should be launched. This is because all the scheduled CUDA threads are not launched at the same time in the CUDA architecture and there would be conflicts in multiple CUDA threads. To avoid this, we need a double buffer approach for the array, which is another inefficiency. The following code shows its implementation:

```
__global__ void
scan_v1_kernel(float *d_output, float *d_input, int length, int offset) {
    int idx = blockDim.x * blockIdx.x + threadIdx.x;
    float element = 0.f;
```

```
for (int offset = 0; offset < length; offset++) {
    if (idx - offset >= 0)
        element += d_input[idx - offset];
}
d_output[idx] = element;
}
```

There is another optimized approach named **Blelloch scan**. This method generates prefix-sum outputs by increasing and decreasing the strides exponentially. This method's procedure is shown in the following diagram:

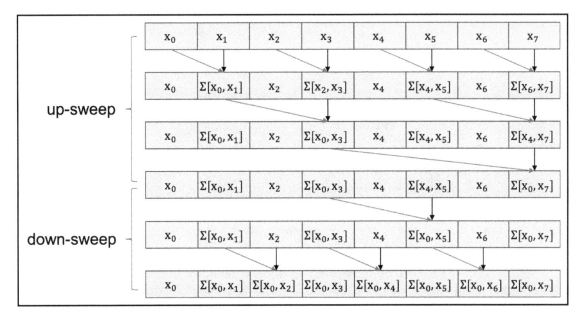

There are two steps based on the stride controls. While increasing the stride, it obtains the partial summations accordingly. Then, it obtains the partial summations while reducing the stride accordingly. Each step has a different operation pattern, but they can be figured out with the stride size. Now, let's cover the Blelloch scan's implementation and check out the updated performance.

Blelloch scan implementation

The following steps will show you how to implement the optimized parallel scan algorithm:

1. Let's create a kernel function that can accept input and output memories, along with their size:

```
__global__ void scan_v2_kernel(float *d_output, float *d_input, int
length)
{
    ...
}
```

2. Then, we will create a CUDA thread index and a global index to handle the input data:

```
int idx = blockDim.x * blockIdx.x + threadIdx.x;
int tid = threadIdx.x;
```

3. To speed up the iteration, we will use shared memory. This algorithm can generate outputs that are double the size of CUDA threads, so we will load extra block-sized input data into shared memory:

```
extern __shared__ float s_buffer[];
s_buffer[threadIdx.x] = d_input[idx];
s_buffer[threadIdx.x + BLOCK_DIM] = d_input[idx + BLOCK_DIM];
```

4. Before we start the iteration, we will declare the offset variable that counts the gap between the left-hand operand and the right-hand operand:

```
int offset = 1;
```

5. Then, we will add up the input data until the offset becomes larger than the input's length:

```
while (offset < length)
{
    __syncthreads();
    int idx_a = offset * (2 * tid + 1) - 1;
    int idx_b = offset * (2 * tid + 2) - 1;
    if (idx_a >= 0 && idx_b < 2 * BLOCK_DIM) {
        s_buffer[idx_b] += s_buffer[idx_a];
    }
    offset <<= 1;
}
```

6. After that, we will iterate again while we reduce the reduction size by two:

```
offset >>= 1;
while (offset > 0) {
    __syncthreads();
    int idx_a = offset * (2 * tid + 2) - 1;
    int idx_b = offset * (2 * tid + 3) - 1;
    if (idx_a >= 0 && idx_b < 2 * BLOCK_DIM) {
        s_buffer[idx_b] += s_buffer[idx_a];
    }
    offset >>= 1;
}
__syncthreads();
```

7. Finally, we will store the output value in global memory using the kernel function:

```
d_output[idx] = s_buffer[tid];
d_output[idx + BLOCK_DIM] = s_buffer[tid + BLOCK_DIM];
```

8. Now, we can call this scan kernel function as follows:

```
void scan_v2(float *d_output, float *d_input, int length)
{
    dim3 dimBlock(BLOCK_DIM);
    dim3 dimGrid(1);
    scan_v2_kernel<<<dimGrid, dimBlock,
                    sizeof(float) * BLOCK_DIM * 2>>>
                (d_output, d_input, length);
    cudaDeviceSynchronize();
}
```

You can also write a naïve scan version with the same function interface. Now, let's review how fast our new version is, and if there are any other optimization opportunities we can take advantage of.

9. The following code shows the profiled result of the naïve scan's and Blelloch scan's performance:

```
$ nvcc -m64 -std=c++11 -I/usr/local/cuda/samples/common/inc -
gencode arch=compute_70,code=sm_70 -L/usr/local/cuda/lib -o scan
./scan.cu ./scan_v1.cu ./scan_v2.cu
$ nvprof ./scan
            Type Time(%)      Time Calls      Avg      Min      Max
Name
 GPU activities:   68.96% 22.751us      1 22.751us 22.751us 22.751us
scan_v1_kernel(float*, float*, int)
                   12.71% 4.1920us      1 4.1920us 4.1920us 4.1920us
scan_v2_kernel(float*, float*, int)
```

As you can see, the Blolloch scan is about five times faster than the naive scan algorithm due to reduced overhead. We can also validate the operation result by comparing the output of the different implementations:

```
input         :: -0.4508 -0.0210 -0.4774  0.2750 ... 0.0398 0.4869
result[cpu]   :: -0.4508 -0.4718 -0.9492 -0.6742 ... 0.3091 0.7960
result[gpu_v1]:: -0.4508 -0.4718 -0.9492 -0.6742 ... 0.3091 0.7960
SUCCESS!!
result[cpu]   :: -0.4508 -0.4718 -0.9492 -0.6742 ... 0.3091 0.7960
result[gpu_v2]:: -0.4508 -0.4718 -0.9492 -0.6742 ... 0.3091 0.7960
SUCCESS!!
```

Up until now, we have covered how to design and implement the optimized parallel prefix-sum operation on a single block size. To use the prefix-sum operation on the input data, which has more data than the block size, we need to build a block-level prefix-sum operation based on our block-level reduction code. We'll talk about this in more detail in the following section.

Building a global size scan

Our implemented prefix-sum operation works within a single thread block. Since the first step has two inputs and the maximum CUDA threads we can have in a thread block is 1,024, the maximum available size is 2,048. Without considering other thread block operations, the thread block does up-sweeping and down-sweeping.

However, this operation can be enlarged if we perform a block-wise scan operation. To do this, you will need extra steps that collect the last prefix-sum result, scan them, and add each thread block's result with each block's block-level scanned value. This procedure can be implemented as follows:

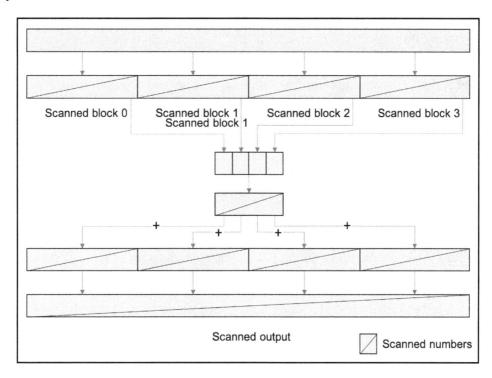

The pursuit of better performance

Our implementation code performs the optimal operation. However, we can make further optimizations by reducing the shared memory's bank conflicts. In our implementation, the CUDA threads access the same memory banks at certain points. NVIDIA's GPU Gem3 introduced prefix-sum (scan) in *Chapter 39, Parallel Prefix Sum (Scan) with CUDA* (https:// developer.nvidia.com/gpugems/GPUGems3/gpugems3_ch39.html), and points out this issue in *39.2.3 Avoiding Bank Conflicts*. You can adapt the solution to our implementation, but you should update NUM_BANKS to 32 and LOG_NUM_BANKS to 5 if you do. Nowadays, the CUDA architecture has 32 shared memory banks.

Other applications for the parallel prefix-sum operation

Dr. G.E. Blelloch published an article about his prefix-sum named *Prefix Sums and Their Application* (https://www.cs.cmu.edu/~guyb/papers/Ble93.pdf) in 1993. You can learn more about the parallel prefix-sum algorithm and its applications by reading his article. The applications are compact, split, segmented scan, quick sort, radix sort, and merge sort.

Dr. Ahmed Sallm's video lecture, *Intro to Parallel Processing with CUDA - Lecture 4 Part 2\3* (https://youtu.be/y2HzWKTqo3E), provides a good introduction to these. It provides conceptual introductions to how the prefix-sum algorithm can be used to clip graphics and build a sparse matrix. He also provides instructions regarding how to use the sort algorithms.

Compact and split

Previously, we covered how to parallelize the sequential prefix sum algorithm and discussed how it can be used for other applications. Now, let's cover some of those applications: compact and split. The compact operation is an algorithm that can consolidate values that fulfill the given condition from an array. On the other hand, the split operation is an algorithm that distributes the values to the designated place. In general, these algorithms work sequentially. However, we will see how the parallel prefix-sum operation can improve how it functions.

The compact operation is used to collect specific data that meets a certain condition into an array. For example, if we want to use the compact operation for the positive elements in an array, then the operation is as follows:

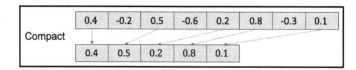

In parallel programming, we have a different approach that can utilize multiple cores using the parallel prefix-sum operation. First, we mark the data to check whether it meets the condition or not (that is, predicate), and then we do the prefix-sum operation. The output of prefix-sum will be the index of the marked values, so we can obtain the gathered array by copying them. The following diagram shows an example of a compact operation:

input	0.4	-0.2	0.5	-0.6	0.2	0.8	-0.3	0.1
predicate	1	0	1	0	1	1	0	1
scan	1	1	2	2	3	4	4	5
address	0		1		2	3		4
gather	0.4	0.5	0.2	0.8	0.1			

Since all of these tasks can be done in parallel, we can obtain the gathered array in four steps.

On the other hand, split means to distribute the data to a number of different places. In general, we distribute the data from where it was initially. The following diagram shows an example of its operation:

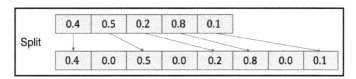

This example shows that the gathered array elements are distributed where they were from. We can also do this in parallel using prefix-sum. Firstly, we refer to the predicate array and do the prefix-sum. Since the outputs are each element's address, we can distribute them easily. The following diagram shows how this operation can be done:

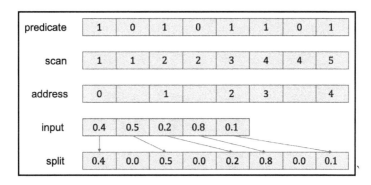

Now, let's implement this and discuss their performance limiters and their application.

Implementing compact

The compact operation is a sequence of predicate, scan, addressing, and gather. In this implementation, we will build an array of positive numbers from an array of randomly generated numbers. The initial version can only afford a single thread block operation since we will only use a single block-sized prefix-sum operation. However, we can learn how prefix-sum is useful for other applications and extend this operation to larger arrays with the extended prefix-sum operation.

To implement a compact operation, we will write several kernel functions that can do the required operation for each step and call those last:

1. Let's write a kernel function that can make a predicate array by checking whether each element's value is greater than zero or not:

    ```
    __global__ void
    predicate_kernel(float *d_predicates, float *d_input, int length)
    {
        int idx = blockDim.x * blockIdx.x + threadIdx.x;

        if (idx >= length) return;

        d_predicates[idx] = d_input[idx] > FLT_ZERO;
    }
    ```

2. Then, we have to perform a prefix-sum operation for that predicate array. We will reuse the previous implementation here. After that, we can write a kernel function that can detect the address of the scanned array and gather the target elements as output:

    ```
    __global__ void
    pack_kernel(float *d_output, float *d_input, float *d_predicates,
    float *d_scanned, int length)
    {
        int idx = blockDim.x * blockIdx.x + threadIdx.x;

        if (idx >= length) return;

        if (d_predicates[idx] != 0.f)
        {
            // addressing
            int address = d_scanned[idx] - 1;
    ```

```
                // gather
                d_output[address] = d_input[idx];
        }
    }
```

3. Now, let's call them all together to make a compact operation:

```
// predicates
predicate_kernel<<< GRID_DIM, BLOCK_DIM >>>(d_predicates, d_input,
length);
// scan
scan_v2(d_scanned, d_predicates, length);
// addressing & gather (pack)
pack_kernel<<< GRID_DIM, BLOCK_DIM >>>(d_output, d_input,
d_predicates, d_scanned, length);
```

4. Now, we have an array of positive numbers that were gathered from a randomly generated array:

```
$ nvcc -run -m64 -std=c++11 -I/usr/local/cuda/samples/common/inc -
gencode arch=compute_70,code=sm_70 -L/usr/local/cuda/lib -o
pack_n_split ./pack_n_split.cu
input     :: -0.4508 -0.0210 -0.4774  0.2750 ....  0.0398  0.4869
pack[cpu]::   0.2750  0.3169  0.1248  0.4241 ....  0.3957  0.2958
pack[gpu]::   0.2750  0.3169  0.1248  0.4241 ....  0.3957  0.2958
SUCCESS!!
```

By using the parallel prefix-sum operation, we can implement the compact operation in parallel easily. Our implementation compacts the positive values from the given array, but we can switch this to the other condition and apply the compact operation without difficulty. Now, let's cover how to distribute these compact elements to the original array.

Implementing split

The split operation is a sequence of predicate, scan, address, and split. In this implementation, we will reuse the address array we created in the previous section. Therefore, we can skip the previous steps and just implement the split operation from the address array:

1. Let's write the split kernel function, as follows:

```
__global__ void
split_kernel(float *d_output, float *d_input, float *d_predicates,
float *d_scanned, int length)
{
```

```
int idx = blockDim.x * blockIdx.x + threadIdx.x;

if (idx >= length) return;

if (d_predicates[idx] != 0.f)
{
    // address
    int address = d_scanned[idx] - 1;

    // split
    d_output[idx] = d_input[address];
}
}
```

2. Now, we can call the kernel function, as follows:

```
cudaMemcpy(d_input, d_output, sizeof(float) * length,
cudaMemcpyDeviceToDevice);
    cudaMemset(d_output, 0, sizeof(float) * length);
    split_kernel<<<GRID_DIM, BLOCK_DIM>>>(d_output, d_input,
d_predicates, d_scanned, length);
```

3. Since we'll be using the output of the scan from the previous step, we will copy it to the input and clear the original array. In total, we can do a parallel compact and split using CUDA. Here is the output of our implementation. You can confirm that it operates as desired:

```
$ nvcc -run -m64 -std=c++11 -I/usr/local/cuda/samples/common/inc -
gencode arch=compute_70,code=sm_70 -L/usr/local/cuda/lib -o
pack_n_split ./pack_n_split.cu
input      :: -0.4508 -0.0210 -0.4774  0.2750 ....  0.0398  0.4869
pack[cpu]::    0.2750  0.3169  0.1248  0.4241 ....  0.3957  0.2958
pack[gpu]::    0.2750  0.3169  0.1248  0.4241 ....  0.3957  0.2958
SUCCESS!!
split[gpu]     0.0000  0.0000  0.0000  0.2750 ....  0.0398  0.4869
SUCCESS!!
```

In our implementation, we generated a compact array and a split array for the positive elements. Thanks to the parallel prefix-sum, we can also do this in parallel. One of the major limitations of our version is that it only supports less than 2,048 elements since our implementation is based on our previous parallel prefix-sum implementation.

N-body

Any N-body simulation is a simulation of the dynamical system that evolves under the influence of physical forces. Numerical approximation is done as the bodies continuously interact with each other. N-body simulation is done extensively in physics and astronomy, for example, so that scientists can understand the dynamics of particles in the Universe. N-body simulations are used in many other domains, including computational fluid dynamics in order to understand turbulent fluid flow simulation.

A relatively easy method for solving N-body simulation is to make use of a brute-force technique that has $O(N^2)$ complexity. This approach is embarrassingly parallel in nature. There are various optimizations at algorithmic scale that can reduce the compute complexity. Instead of applying all-pairs to the whole simulation, it can be used to determine forces in close-range interactions. Even in this case, creating a kernel for solving the forces on CUDA is very useful as it will also improve the performance of far-field components. Accelerating one component will offload work from the other components, so the entire application benefits from accelerating one kernel.

Implementing an N-body simulation on GPU

The algorithm is basically an all-pairs algorithm calculating force, f_{ij}, for an N×N grid. The total force/acceleration, F_i, on a body, i, is the result of a summation of all the entries in row i. From a parallelism point of view, this is an embarrassingly parallel task of $O(N^2)$.

From a performance point of view, the application is memory bound and would be limited by memory bandwidth. The good part is that much of the data can be reused and stored in high bandwidth and low latency memory such as shared memory. Data reuse and storage in shared memory reduces the load on global memory and hence helps in reaching peak compute performance.

The following diagram shows the strategy that we will be using:

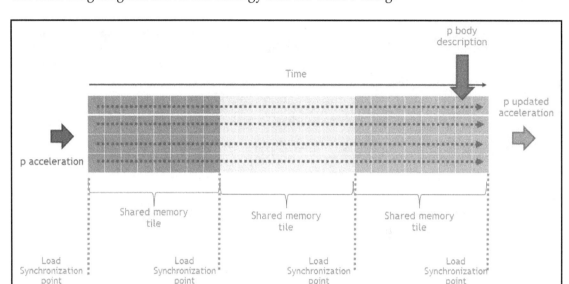

Instead of loading the memory again and again from global memory, we make use of tiling. We've already demonstrated the use of tiling for matrix multiplication and looked at its use in imaging applications in previous chapters. The preceding diagram shows that each row is evaluated in parallel. The tile size is defined by the maximum number of elements that can be stored in shared memory that don't affect the occupancy of the kernel. Each block loads the data into shared memory, followed by performing synchronization. Once the data has been loaded into shared memory, the force/acceleration calculation is done in every block. It is visible that even though a separate row is calculated in parallel, to achieve optimal data reuse, the interaction in each row is done sequentially.

Overview of an N-body simulation implementation

Let's review the implementation of this in pseudocode format, followed by explaining its logic. In this example, we use gravitational potential to illustrate the basic form of computation in an all pairs N-body simulation. The implemented code can be found in 07_parallel_programming_pattern/05_n-body. Follow these steps to get started:

1. Initialize n-space with random variables:

```
data[i] = 2.0f * (rand() / max) - 1.0f
```

2. Declare and store the data in an intermediate shared memory space for efficient reuse. Synchronize it to guarantee that all the threads within the block see the updated values in shared memory:

```
for (int tile = 0; tile < gridDim.x; tile++) {
...
__shared__ float3 shared_position[blockDim.x];
float4 temp_position = p[tile * blockDim.x + threadIdx.x];
shared_position[threadIdx.x] = make_float3(temp_position.x,
temp_position.y, temp_position.z);
__syncthreads();
...
}
```

3. Calculate the force by iterating every block:

```
for (int j = 0; j < BLOCK_SIZE; j++) {
    //Calculate Force
    __syncthreads();
}
```

4. Finally, compile the application with the `nvcc` compiler with the following command:

```
$nvcc -run --gpu-architecture=sm_70 -o n-body n_body.cu
```

As you can see, implementing an N-body simulation is an embarrassingly parallel task and quite straightforward. While we have implemented the basic version of code here, there are various algorithmic variations that exist. You can make use of this version as a template that you can improve, based on changes that are made to the algorithm.

Histogram calculation

In an embarrassingly parallel job, ideally, you would assign computation to each thread working on independent data, resulting in no data races. By now, you will have realized that some patterns don't fit this category. One such pattern is when we're calculating a histogram. The histogram pattern displays the frequency of a data item, for example, the number of times we used the word CUDA in each ch apter, the number of times each letter occurred in this chapter, and so on. A histogram takes the following form:

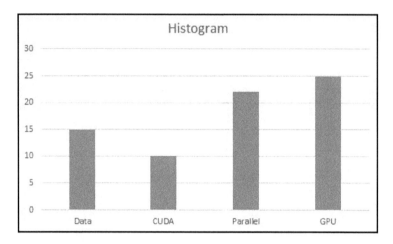

In this section, we will make use of atomic operations to serialize access to data in order to get the correct results.

Compile and execution steps

The histogram provides important features about the datasets at hand, as well as useful insights about the same. For example, out of the whole image, there are only a few regions where regions of interest may lie. Creating a histogram is sometimes used to figure out where in the image the region of interest may be. In this example, we will be making use of calculating a histogram on an image where the whole image is divided into chunks. Let's get started:

1. Prepare your GPU application. This code can be found at `07_parallel_programming_pattern/08_histogram`.
2. Compile your application with the `nvcc` compiler with the following command:

```
$ nvcc -c scrImagePgmPpmPackage.cpp
$ nvcc -c image_histogram.cu
$ nvcc -run -o image_histogram image_histogram.o
scrImagePgmPpmPackage.o
```

The `scrImagePgmPpmPackage.cpp` file provides the source code that we can use to read and write images with `.pgm` extensions. The histogram calculation code can be found in `image_histogram.cu`.

Understanding a parallel histogram

Patterns such as the histogram demand atomic operation, which means updating a value at a specific address in a serialized fashion to remove contention from multiple threads, thereby updating the same address. This requires coordination among multiple threads. In this seven-step process, you might have observed that we made use of privatization. Privatization is a technique that makes use of low latency memory such as shared memory to reduce throughput and decrease latency, as shown in the following diagram:

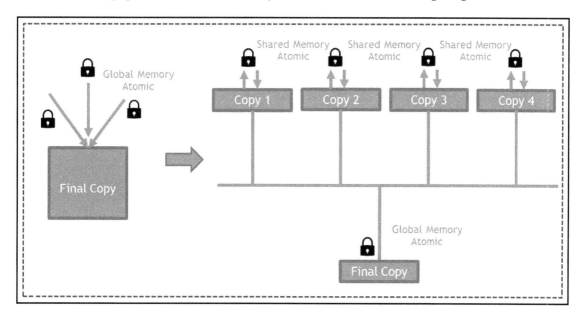

Basically, instead of making use of atomic operations on global memory, we make use of atomics on shared memory. The reason should be quite obvious to you by now. Atomic operations on global memory are more costly compared to doing the same on shared memory/an L1 cache. From the Maxwell architecture onward, atomic operations are hardware supported. The privatized shared memory implementation should ideally give you 2x performance from the Maxwell architecture onward. However, please note that atomic operations are limited to specific functions and data sizes.

Calculating a histogram with CUDA atomic functions

Primarily, we are going to make use of the `atomicAdd()` operation on shared memory to calculate a histogram for each block in shared memory. Follow these steps to calculate the histogram in a kernel:

1. Allocate shared memory per block equal to the size of the histogram per block. Since it is a char image, we expect the elements to be in the range of 0-255:

   ```
   __shared__ unsigned int histo_private[256];
   ```

2. Initialize the shared memory array to 0 per block:

   ```
   if(localId <256)
       histo_private[localId] = 0;
   ```

3. Synchronize this to make sure all the threads within a block see initialized array:

   ```
   __syncthreads();
   ```

4. Read the data of the image from the global/texture memory:

   ```
   unsigned char imageData = tex2D<unsigned
   char>(texObj,(float)(tidX),(float)(tidY));
   ```

5. Do an `atomicAdd()` operation on shared memory:

   ```
   atomicAdd(&(histo_private[imageData]), 1);
   ```

6. Synchronize across the block before writing to global memory:

   ```
   __syncthreads();
   ```

7. Write the histogram per block to global memory:

   ```
   if(localId <256)
       imageHistogram[histStartIndex+localId] =
   histo_private[localId];
   ```

Now, we have finished implementing the histogram calculation on the GPU.

To summarize, histograms are easy to implement with shared atomic memory. This approach can attain high performance on Maxwell onward cards due to its native support for shared atomic memory in hardware.

Quicksort in CUDA using dynamic parallelism

One of the key algorithms that's a fundamental building block for any application is sorting. There are many sorting algorithms available that have been studied extensively. The worst time complexity, best time complexity, input data characteristics (is the data almost sorted or random? Is it a key-value pair? Is it an integer or a float?), in-place or out of place memory requirements, and so on define which algorithm is suitable for which application. Some of the sorting algorithms fall into the category of divide and conquer algorithms. These algorithms are suitable for parallelism and suit architectures such as GPU where data to be sorted can be divided for sorting. One such algorithm is Quicksort. As we stated earlier, Quicksort falls into the category of divide and conquer. It is a three-step approach, as follows:

1. Pick an element from an array that needs to be sorted. This element acts as a pivot element.
2. The second step is partitioning where all the elements go. All the elements that are less than the pivot are shifted to the left and all the elements greater than or equal to the pivot are shifted to the right of the pivot element. This step is also known as partitioning.
3. Recursively do steps 1 and 2 until all the sub-arrays have been sorted.

Quicksort worst-case complexity is O(N^2), which may not seem ideal compared to other sorting processes whose worst-case complexity is O($Nlog(N)$), such as merge sort and heap sort). However, Quicksort is seen to be effective in practice. The choice of the pivot element can be chosen with consideration and sometimes randomly so that worst-case complexity hardly occurs. Also, Quicksort is seen to have less memory load and requirements compared to other sorting algorithms, such as merge sort, which requires extra storage. More practical implementations of Quicksort use a randomized version. The randomized version has the expected time complexity of O($Nlog(N)$). Worst-case complexity is also possible in the randomized version, but it doesn't occur for a particular pattern (such as a sorted array) and randomized Quicksort works well in practice.

While we can write a whole chapter on the characteristics of the sorting algorithm, we plan to cover only the features of CUDA that will help you to implement Quicksort efficiently on GPU. In this section, we will be making use of dynamic parallelism, which was introduced from CUDA 6.0 and GPUs with a 3.5 architecture onwards.

Now, let's review how dynamic parallelism contributes to the sorting algorithm.

Quicksort and CUDA dynamic parallelism

The Quicksort algorithm demands launching kernels recursively. So far, the algorithms we have seen call the kernel once via the CPU. After the kernel has finished executing, we return to the CPU thread and then relaunch it. Doing this results in giving back control to the CPU, and may also result in data transfer between CPU and GPU, which is a costly operation. It used to be very difficult to efficiently implement algorithms such as Quicksort on GPUs that demand features such as recursion. With the GPU architecture 3.5 and CUDA 5.0 onwards, a new feature was introduced called dynamic parallelism.

Dynamic parallelism allows the threads within a kernel to launch new kernels from the GPU without returning control back to the CPU. The word dynamic comes from the fact that it is dynamically based on the runtime data. Multiple kernels can be launched by threads at once. The following diagram simplifies this explanation:

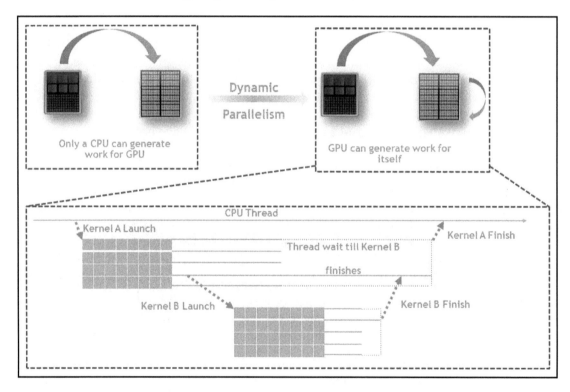

If we were to translate this concept to how Quicksort is executed, it would look something like this:

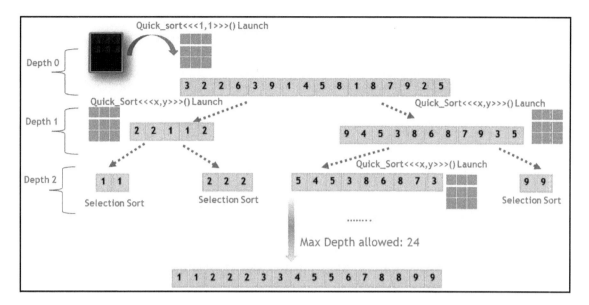

Depth 0 is the call from the CPU. For each subarray, we launch two kernels: one for the left array and one for the right array. Recursion stops after the max depth of the kernel has been reached or the number of elements is less than 32, which is the warp size. For the kernel's launch to be in a non-zero stream and asynchronous so that the subarray kernel gets launched independently, we need to create a stream before every kernel launch:

```
cudaStream_t s;
cudaStreamCreateWithFlags( &s, cudaStreamNonBlocking );
cdp_simple_quicksort<<< 1, 1, 0, s >>>(data, left, nright, depth+1);
cudaStreamDestroy( s );
```

This is a really important step because, otherwise, the kernel's launch may get serialized. For more details on streams, please refer to the multi-GPU kernel.

Quicksort with CUDA

For our Quicksort implementation, we are going to make use of dynamic parallelism to launch the GPU kernel recursively. The major steps involved in implementing Quicksort are as follows:

1. **The CPU launches the first kernel**: The kernel is launched with one block and one thread. The left element is the start of the array, while the right is the last element of the array (basically the whole array):

   ```
   int main(int argc, char **argv)
   { ...
       cdp_simple_quicksort<<< 1, 1 >>>(data, left, right, 0);
   }
   ```

2. **Limit check**: Check the two criteria before launching the kernel from inside a kernel. First, check if we have reached the max allowed limit of depth by the hardware. Second, we need to check whether the number of elements to be sorted in a sub-array is less than the warp size (32). If one of them is true, then we have to do a selection sort sequentially rather than launch a new kernel:

   ```
   __global__ void cdp_simple_quicksort( unsigned int *data, int left,
   int right, int depth )
   { ...

   if( depth >= MAX_DEPTH || right-left <= INSERTION_SORT )
     {
         selection_sort( data, left, right );
         return;
     }
   ```

3. **Partitioning**: If the preceding conditions are met, then partition the array into two sub-arrays and launch two new kernels, one for the left array and another for the right array. If you look closely at the following code, you'll see we are launching a kernel from inside the kernel:

   ```
   __global__ void cdp_simple_quicksort( unsigned int *data, int left,
   int right, int depth ) {
   ...
   while(lptr <= rptr)
     {
         // Move the left pointer as long as the
         // pointed element is smaller than the pivot.
         // Move the right pointer as long as the
         // pointed element is larger than the pivot.
         // If the swap points are valid, do the swap!
   ```

```
        // Launch a new block to sort the left part.
        if(left < (rptr-data))
        { // Create a new stream for the eft sub array
            cdp_simple_quicksort<<< 1, 1, 0, s
                                >>>(data, left, nright, depth+1);
        }
        // Launch a new block to sort the right part.
        if((lptr-data) < right)
        {//Create stream for the right sub array
            cdp_simple_quicksort<<< 1, 1, 0, s1
                                >>>(data, nleft, right, depth+1);
        }
    }
```

4. **Executing the code**: The implemented code can be found at `07_parallel_programming_pattern/06_quicksort`. Compile your application with the `nvcc` compiler with the following command:

```
$nvcc -o quick_sort --gpu-architecture=sm_70 -rdc=true
quick_sort.cu
```

As you can see, we have added two flags to the compilation:

- `-- gpu-architecture=sm_70`: This flag tells the `nvcc` to compile and generate the binary/`ptx` for the Volta GPU. If you specifically do not add this flag, the compiler tries to compile the code compatible from `sm_20`, that is, Fermi generation cards, until the new architecture, which is `sm_70`, that is, Volta. The compilation will fail since dynamic parallelism is not supported by older generation cards.
- `-rdc=true`: This is a key argument that enables dynamic parallelism on the GPU.

Dynamic parallelism guidelines and constraints

Though dynamic parallelism provides us with an opportunity to port algorithms such as Quicksort on GPU, there are some fundamental rules and guidelines that need to be followed.

Programming model rules: Basically, all the CUDA programming model rule apply:

- The kernel launches are asynchronous per thread.
- Synchronization is only allowed per block.
- Streams that are created are shared within a block.
- Events can be used to create inter-stream dependencies.

Memory consistency rules:

- The child kernel sees the parent kernel's state at the time of the launch.
- The parent kernel can see the changes that have been made by the child kernel, but only after the synchronization.
- Local and shared memory is, as usual, private, and cannot be passed or accessed by the parent kernel.

Guidelines:

- It is also important to understand that there is latency that gets added per kernel launch. The latency of launching a kernel from inside another kernel has gradually reduced over time with the new architecture.
- While launch throughput is an order of magnitude higher than from the host, limits can be placed on the maximum depth. The max depth that's allowed is 24 for the latest generation cards.
- Performing `cudaDeviceSynchronize()` from inside the kernel is a very costly operation and should be avoided as much as possible.
- There is additional memory preallocated on global memory so that we can store kernels before they are launched.
- If the kernel fails, the error is only visible from the host. Hence, you are advised to make use of the `-lineinfo` flag along with `cuda-memcheck` to locate the error's location.

Radix sort

Another very popular sorting algorithm is radix sort as it is really fast on sequential machines. The fundamental policy of radix sort is that each element is sorted digit by digit. Let's look at a simple example to explain the steps involved in radix sort:

Suppose the elements to be sorted are as follows:

Value	7	14	4	1

The equivalent binary values of these numbers are as follows:

Bits	0111	1110	0100	0001

The first step is to sort based on bit 0. Bit 0 for the numbers are as follows:

0th Bit	1	0	0	1

To sort based on the 0th bit basically means that all the zeroes are on the left. All the ones are on the right while preserving the order of elements:

Sorted value on 0th bit	14	4	7	1
Sorted bits based on 0th bit	1110	0100	0111	0001

After the 0th bit is done, we move on to the first bit. The result after sorting based on the first bit is as follows:

Sorted value on the first bit	4	14	7	1
Sorted bits based on the first bit	0100	1110	0111	0001

Then, we move on to the next higher bit until all the bits are over. The final result is as follows:

Sorted value on all bits	1	4	7	1
Sorted bits based on all bits	0001	0100	0111	1110

As you can see, the upper limit that we set in this example was 4 bits. For larger numbers, such as integers, this will continue until 32 bits as integers are 32-bit.

Now that we have understood this algorithm, let's look at how this can be implemented in the GPU. Compared to the other sections in this chapter, we will take two approaches to showcase the CUDA ecosystem so that we can implement/use radix sort.

Option 1: We are going to make use of a warp level to do radix sort on just 32 elements. The reason for this is that we want to make use of radix sort to introduce you to warp-level primitives.

Option 2: We will be making use of the Thrust library, which is part of the CUDA Toolkit. It implements a generic radix sort. The best implementation is reuse. Since Thrust already provides one of the best implementations of radix sort, we will use that.

Two approaches

To ease your understanding, let's begin with the example code. In this example, we will be making use of warp-level primitives and the Thrust library to implement/use the radix sort. The example code can be found at `07_parallel_programming_pattern/07_radixsort`.

Compile your application with the `nvcc` compiler with the following command:

- Warp-level primitive version:

```
$ nvcc -run -o radix_warp_sort radix_warp_sort.cu
```

- Thrust library version:

```
$ nvcc -run -o radix_thrust_sort thrust_radix_sort.cu
```

These two examples show the sorted output that's given by the GPU. Now, let's review how these operations are implemented in detail.

Approach 1 – warp-level primitives

Let's look at how CUDA warp-level primitives are used to implement our algorithm in the code:

1. First, load the data from global memory to shared memory:

   ```
   __shared__ unsigned int s_data[WARP_SIZE*2];
   ```

   The size of the memory is equal to the warp size, `*2`, so that it can implement the ping pong buffer.

2. Loop through from the lower bit to the upper bit:

   ```
   for (int i = MIN_BIT_POS; i <= MAX_BIT_POS; i++){ ... }
   ```

3. Get the current bitmask:

   ```
   unsigned int bit  = data&bit_mask;
   ```

4. Get the number of ones and zeroes (histogram):

```
unsigned int active = __activemask();
unsigned int ones = __ballot_sync(active,bit);
unsigned int zeroes = ~ones;
```

5. Get the positions of the threads that have zero (0) in the current bit (Prefix Sum).
6. Get the positions of the threads that have one (1) in the current bit (Prefix Sum):

```
if (!bit) // threads with a zero bit
  // get my position in ping-pong buffer
  pos = __popc(zeroes&thread_mask);
else // threads with a one bit
  // get my position in ping-pong buffer
  pos = __popc(zeroes)+__popc(ones&thread_mask);
```

7. Store the data in the ping pong shared buffer memory:

```
s_data[pos-1+offset] = data;
```

8. Repeat steps 2-6 until the upper bit has been reached.
9. Store the final result in global memory from shared memory:

```
d_data[threadIdx.x] = s_data[threadIdx.x+offset];
```

It may not be clear to you where the histogram and prefix sum appeared all of a sudden. Let's talk about this implementation in detail so that we can understand how we use warp-level primitives to implement the same.

At the beginning of this section, we described how we sort using an example. What we did not cover, however, was how to find out the position of the element that needs to be swapped. Radix sort can be implemented using fundamental primitives such as histogram and prefix-sum and, hence, can easily be implemented in the GPU.

Let's revisit the example we looked at and gather its details, included the steps of the histogram and prefix sum. The following table shows various calculations that were done at each bit iteratively:

Value	7	14	4	1
Binary	0111	1110	0100	0001
Bit 0	1	0	0	1
Histogram prefix sum	2	0	2	2
Offset	0	0	1	1
New index (prefix Sum and Offset)	2	0	1	3

Let's explain each and every calculation shown in the preceding table, as follows:

1. First, we build a histogram for the number of elements with 0 in the 0th-bit position and the number of elements with 1 in the 0th-bit position:

Histogram: zero-bits (2 values), one-bits (2 values)

2. Then, we perform an exclusive prefix sum on these values. The prefix sum can be defined as the sum of all the previous values. In our case, we do this separately for both 0th-bits and 1st-bits.
3. Finally, we move the elements based on the prefix sum values.

The warp-level primitives we used to find the histogram and prefix sum were `__ballot_sync()` and `__popc()`, respectively.

The `__ballot_sync()` API evaluates the predicates for all the active threads of the warp and returns an integer whose Nth bit is set if, and only if, the predicate evaluates to non-zero for the Nth thread of the warp. `__popc()`, which counts the number of integers, was set to one.

In the CUDA programming model, we have seen that the minimum execution unit is a warp (32 threads). CUDA provides various warp-level primitives with fine-grained control that, in many applications, can result in better performance. We covered one such primitive, `__bllot__sync()`, in the previous section. Other important warp-level primitives include `shuffle` instructions, which are used for doing warp-level reduction in particular. `shuffle` instructions have already been covered in this book. If you have reached ninja programmer level proficiency in CUDA, then we recommend that you look at the CUDA API guide to understand more of these warp-level primitives.

This completes describing radix sort using warp-level primitives. Now, let's look at the Thrust-based library implementation.

Approach 2 – Thrust-based radix sort

Thrust-based radix sort is a generic implementation of radix sort and works pretty well for different types of data, such as integer, float, or key-value pairs. We would like to reemphasize the fact that sorting is a heavily studied algorithm and so has its parallel implementation. Therefore, we recommend that you reuse existing libraries before implementing one on your own.

The steps involved in making use of Thrust for radix sort are as follows:

1. Import the relevant header files (Thrust is a header-only library, similar to STL):

    ```
    #include <thrust/device_vector.h>
    #include <thrust/sort.h>
    ```

2. Declare and initialize a device vector:

    ```
    //declare a device vector of size N
    thrust::device_vector<int> keys(N);
    //Generate a random number generator engine
    thrust::default_random_engine r(12);
    //create a distribution engine which will create integer values
    thrust::uniform_int_distribution<int> d(10, 99);
    //Fill the array with randon values
    for(size_t i = 0; i < v.size(); i++)
        v[i] = d(r);
    ```

3. Perform sorting on the initialized device vector:

    ```
    thrust::sort(keys.begin(), keys.end());
    ```

Using this library provides an easier and robust approach. Thrust provides different types of sorting methods, including radix sort for integers and floats. Alternatively, you can create a custom comparator to do customized sortings, such as sorting all the event numbers followed by odd numbers, sorting in descending order, and so on. You are advised to look at sample examples that have been provided by CUDA if you want to learn more about Thrust-based sorting examples.

Now, we have looked at both approaches to implementing radix sort on GPUs.

Summary

In this chapter, we looked at the implementation of commonly used algorithms and patterns in CUDA. These algorithms and patterns are commonly available. We covered basic optimization techniques in matrix multiplication and convolution filtering. Then, we expanded our discussion on how to parallelize the problem by using prefix sum, N-body, histogram, and sorting. To do this, we have used dedicated GPU knowledge, libraries, and lower-level primitives.

Many of the algorithms we have covered are implemented in CUDA libraries. For example, matrix multiplication is in the cuBLAS library, while convolution is in the CUDNN library. In addition, we have covered two approaches in the radix sort implementation: using the Thrust library or warp-level primitives for histogram computation.

Now that you've seen how these patterns can be implemented in commonly used libraries, the next logical step is to see how we can use these libraries. This is what we will be doing in the next chapter.

Programming with Libraries and Other Languages

This chapter covers other GPU programming methods—programming with GPU accelerated libraries and other languages. Programming using the GPU accelerated libraries enables us to develop applications with the optimized kernels. Also, we can develop the CUDA software using other programming languages, which are aware of CUDA acceleration. Both ways improve programmability and productivity. Also, we don't have to spend our time optimizing the common operations, which are already optimized.

The CUDA Toolkit provides many GPU accelerated libraries in linear algebra, image and signal processing, and random processing. They are cuBLAS (Basic Linear Algebra Subroutines), cuFFT (Fast Fourier Transform), cuRAND (Random Number Generation), NPP (image and signal processing), cuSPARSE (Sparse Linear Algebra), nvGRAPH (Graph Analysis), cuSolver (LAPACK in GPU), Thrust (STL in CUDA), and so on. We also can write GPU accelerated programs with the OpenCV library. We will cover some of these libraries in this chapter.

We also can use GPU accelerations using R, MATLAB, Octave, and Python. Nowadays, Python integration is popular and powerful, as GPU can accelerate many machine learning and data science tasks. We also cover these languages as an entry-level.

The following topics will be covered in this chapter:

- Linear algebra operation using cuBLAS
- Mixed-precision operation using cuBLAS
- cuRAND for parallel random number generation
- cuFFT for Fast Fourier Transformation in GPU
- NPP for image and signal processing with GPU
- Writing GPU accelerated code in OpenCV

- Writing Python code that works with CUDA
- NVBLAS for zero coding acceleration in Octave and R
- CUDA acceleration in MATLAB

Linear algebra operation using cuBLAS

The cuBLAS library is a GPU-optimized, standard implementation of **Basic Linear Algebra Subroutines** (**BLAS**). Using its APIs, the programmers can write GPU-optimized, compute-intensive code to a single GPU or multiple GPUs. There are three levels in cuBLAS. Level-1 performs the vector-vector operation, level-2 does the matrix-vector operation, and level-3 does the matrix-matrix operation.

Covering each level is out of the scope of this book. We are just focusing on how to use cuBLAS APIs and extend its performance for multiple GPUs. To be specific, this receipt will cover a **Single Precision Floating Matrix Multiplication** (**SGEMM**) operation—a level-3 operation.

The cuBLAS library is a part of CUDA Toolkit, so you can use cuBLAS without extra installation. Also, you can use the `cc` or `cpp` file extensions, rather than `.cu`, because you do not need to use CUDA-specific built-in keywords such as `__global__` or `threadIdx`. This following code snippet shows the basic application of the cuBLAS function (`cubalsSgemm`):

```
cublasHandle_t handle;
cublasCreate(&handle);

.. { data operation } ..

cublasSgemm(...);

.. { data operation } ..

cublasDestroy(handle);
```

As you can see, cuBLAS APIs work with the `cublasHandle_t` type handle.

cuBLAS SGEMM operation

The GEMM operation can be denoted by the following equation:

$$C = alpha \operatorname{op}(A) \operatorname{op}(B) + beta \operatorname{op}(C)$$

Where *alpha* and *beta* are scalas and *A*, *B*, and *C* are matrices in column-major format. This matches with the cuBLAS function interface in the following box:

```
cublasStatus_t cublasSgemm(cublasHandle_t handle,
                           cublasOperation_t transa,
                           cublasOperation_t transb,
                           int m, int n, int k,
                           const float *alpha,
                           const float *A, int lda,
                           const float *B, int ldb,
                           const float *beta,
                           float *C, int ldc);
```

Before using this GEMM function, let's look at the details of the parameters:

- `transa` and `transb`: Instruction to the cuBLAS functions whether the matrices *A* and *B* should be transposed or not for the operation.
- `m`, `n`, and `k`: The dimensional size of the matrices.
- `alpha` and `beta`: Parameters that determine how to configure the output value from the source.
- `*A`, `*B`, and `*C`: Linear buffer for the matrix data.
- `lda`: Leading column dimension of matrix *A*. cuBLAS aligns the matrix elements with this value.
- `ldb`: Leading column dimension of matrix *B*. cuBLAS aligns the matrix elements with this value.

To transfer the data between the host and the device, you can use cuBLAS's `cublasSetMatrix()` and `cublasGetMatrix()` helper functions. They are wrapper functions of `cudaMemcpy()`, but have the matrices' dimensional information, so that they help to enhance the code readability; you can simply use `cudaMemcpy()` instead, of course.

Let's just implement an application that has the GEMM operation using cuBLAS SGEMM function. We will include `cublas_v2.h` to use the updated cuBLAS API. For convenience, we will use the `getMatrix()` function to get a randomly generated matrix from the given dimension, and the `printMatrix()` function to print the matrix elements. The codes are implemented in the given example codes. In the main function, we will initialize three matrices—A, B, and C—from the given M, N, and K. Then we will compute `cublasSgemm()` as follows:

```
cublasHandle_t handle;

// Prepare input matrices
float *A, *B, *C;
```

```
int M, N, K;
float alpha, beta;

M = 3;    N = 4;    K = 7;
alpha = 1.f;    beta = 0.f;

// create cuBLAS handle
cublasCreate(&handle);

srand(2019);
A = getMatrix(K, M);
B = getMatrix(N, K);
C = getMatrix(M, N);

std::cout << "A:" << std::endl;
printMatrix(A, K, M);
std::cout << "B:" << std::endl;
printMatrix(B, N, K);
std::cout << "C:" << std::endl;
printMatrix(C, M, N);

// Gemm
cublasSgemm(handle, CUBLAS_OP_T, CUBLAS_OP_T,
    M, N, K, &alpha, A, K, B, N, &beta, C, M);

cudaDeviceSynchronize();
std::cout << "C out:" << std::endl;
printMatrix(C, M, N);

cublasDestroy(handle);
cudaFree(A);    cudaFree(B);    cudaFree(C);
return 0;
```

Compile the code with nvcc by linking the cuBLAS library:

```
$ nvcc -run -gencode arch=compute_70,code=sm_70 -lcublas -o cublasSgemm
./cublasSgemm.cpp
```

The following code snippet shows the output of the execution:

```
A:
  0.0492 0.4790 0.0226
  0.7750 0.2794 0.8169
  0.3732 0.6248 0.2636
  0.9241 0.5841 0.8532
  0.7188 0.5052 0.5398
  0.9869 0.6572 0.0520
  0.6815 0.7814 0.5988
```

```
B:
   0.8957 0.0481 0.7958 0.7825 0.3264 0.5189 0.5018
   0.4559 0.6342 0.0759 0.5051 0.1132 0.0985 0.2802
   0.3926 0.9153 0.6534 0.0174 0.1790 0.5775 0.6015
   0.0322 0.2963 0.1068 0.5720 0.2832 0.7640 0.6240
C:
   0.9647 0.5454 0.2229 0.8604
   0.5935 0.0186 0.6430 0.9198
   0.5375 0.1448 0.3757 0.1718
C out:
   1.1785 2.5682 2.4854 0.6066
   0.5817 0.8091 1.1724 2.0773
   2.0882 1.4503 2.1331 1.8450
```

As described in the `cublasSgemm()` function call, matrices *A* and *B* are transposed matrices. We passed the original leading column size to the `cublasSgemm()` function as `lda`, `ldb`, and `ldc`, and we could see that the operation works as expected.

Multi-GPU operation

The cuBLAS library's cuBLAS-XT API provides cuBLAS's level-3 operation when it is working on multiple GPUs. With this API, your application can use multi-GPU computing operation. This snippet shows the basic operation for using cuBLAS-XT:

```
cublasXtHandle_t handle;
cublasXtCreate(&handle);

cudaGetDeviceCount(&num_of_total_devices);
devices = (int *)calloc(num_of_devices, sizeof(int));
for (int i = 0; i < num_of_devices; i++)
    devices[i] = i;
cublasXtDeviceSelect(handle, num_of_devices, devices);

cublasXtSgemm( ... );

cublasXtDestroy(handle);
```

The `cublasXtSgemm()` interface is the same as the `cublasSgemm()` function, so we can use multiple GPU's computing performances at ease. For example, we can obtain the following result using the sample code in the repository with two GPUs. This performance can vary depending on your GPU and system configuration:

```
$ nvcc -run -gencode arch=compute_70,code=sm_70 -lcublas -o cublasXtSgemm ./cublasXtSgemm.cpp
Elapsed Time on 2 GPUs: 8.30685 ms, 23.6682 GFlops.
196608000
```

The cuBLAS library provides a lot of versatile linear algebra operations. So you should check how your necessary function is provided in the library. Also, you will need an example of how to use that function. The following items are the links to the document and examples. So, it is recommended that you check both documents frequently when you need to implement an application based on cuBLAS:

- NVIDIA's cuBLAS programming guide—A reference guide: `https://docs.nvidia.com/cuda/cublas/index.html`
- *Matrix computations on the GPU: CUBLAS, CUSOLVER, and MAGMA by example* by Andrzej Chrzęszczyk and Jacob Anders: `https://developer.nvidia.com/sites/default/files/akamai/cuda/files/Misc/mygpu.pdf`

Mixed-precision operation using cuBLAS

The cuBLAS library supports mixed-precision computation. This computation means an operation that operates with different precisions, for instance, computation with single and half-precision variables, or with single and characters (`INT8`). This technique is useful when we need to achieve a higher performance using lowered precision, while also obtaining a higher accuracy in the result.

The cuBLAS library provides `cublasGemmEx()` and `cublas{S/C}gemmEx()` to support GEMM operation for the mixed-precision operations. They are extensions of `cublas<t>gemm()`, which accepts specified data types for each *A*, *B*, and *C* matrices. The following table shows the precision support matrix for `cublasGemmEx()`, and other replaceable APIs in cuBLAS library:

Compute type	A type / B type	C type	Replaceable APIs
CUDA_R_16F	CUDA_R_16F	CUDA_R_16F	cublasHgemm()
CUDA_R_32I	CUDA_R_8I	CUDA_R_32I	N/A
CUDA_R_32F	CUDA_R_16F	CUDA_R_16F	cublasSgemmEx()
	CUDA_R_8I	CUDA_R_32F	
	CUDA_R_16F	CUDA_R_32F	
	CUDA_R_32F	CUDA_R_32F	
CUDA_R_64F	CUDA_R_64F	CUDA_R_64F	cublasDgemm()
CUDA_C_32F	CUDA_C_8I	CUDA_C_32F	cublasCgemmEx()
	CUDA_C_32F	CUDA_C_32F	
CUDA_C_64F	CUDA_C_64F	CUDA_C_64F	cublasZgemm()

You can see that `cublasGemmEx()` can cover the `cublas{S/C}gemmEx()` function's operation. Therefore, we will cover `cublasGemmEx()` in this section.

The last parameter of the `cublasGemmEx()` function, `cublasGemmAlgo_t`, specifies the algorithm for matrix-matrix multiplication. With this parameter, we can choose whether to use TensorCore or not. `CUBLAS_GEMM_DEFAULT` selects the GEMM algorithm and runs on CUDA cores. On the other hand, `CUBLAS_GEMM_DEFAULT_TENSOR_OP` selects algorithms that use tensor cores. If TensorCore is unavailable for the given condition, cuBLAS selects an algorithm that uses CUDA cores. This condition can be for the GPUs having no tensor cores or matrix size, which does not fit with how the TensorCore operates—in multiples of four (* 4).

GEMM with mixed precision

Now, let's try the mixed-precision using the cuBLAS GEMM operation. After the implementation, we will cover how the matrix size can affect the operations. The fully implemented version is in `02_sgemm_mixed_precision/cublasGemmEx.cu`:

1. This code uses a custom memory managing class, `CBuffer`, to ease the handling of mixed precisions and copy, but it can use unified memory instead. For the cuBLAS operation, we should include `cublas_v2.h` in our code:

   ```
   #include <cublas_v2.h>
   #include "helper.cuh"    // for CBuffer and printMatrix()
   ```

2. Now, let's implement the `main()` function. First, we will create and initialize A, B, and C matrices. The following snippet shows how to use the `CBuffer` class and initialize the matrices:

   ```
   int M = 4, N = 5, K = 6;
   CBuffer<half> A, B;
   CBuffer<float> C;

   A.init(K * M, true);
   B.init(N * K, true);
   C.init(N * M, true);
   ```

3. To specify the precision types of A, B, and C, and to test the various precisions together, we need to specify some CUDA data type parameters:

```
cudaDataType TYPE_A, TYPE_B, TYPE_C;
if (typeid(*A.h_ptr_) == typeid(float)) {
    TYPE_A = TYPE_B = CUDA_R_32F;
}
else if (typeid(*A.h_ptr_) == typeid(half)) {
    TYPE_A = TYPE_B = CUDA_R_16F;
}
else if (typeid(*A.h_ptr_) == typeid(int8_t)) {
    TYPE_A = TYPE_B = CUDA_R_8I;
}
else {
    printf("Not supported precision\n");
    return -1;
}

if (typeid(*C.h_ptr_) == typeid(float)) {
    TYPE_C = CUDA_R_32F;
}
else if (typeid(*C.h_ptr_) == typeid(int)) {
    TYPE_C = CUDA_R_32I;
}
else {
    printf("Not supported precision\n");
    return -1;
}
```

4. For the cuBLAS operation, we should initialize cublas_handle, alpha, and beta:

```
float alpha = 1.f, beta = 0.f;
cublasHandle_t cublas_handle;
cublasCreate(&cublas_handle);
```

5. Then, we copy the data to the GPU:

```
A.cuda(true);
B.cuda(true);
C.cuda(true);
```

6. We then call `cublasGemmEx()` function as follows:

```
cublasGemmEx(cublas_handle,
             CUBLAS_OP_N, CUBLAS_OP_N,
             M, N, K,
             &alpha, A.d_ptr_, TYPE_A, M, B.d_ptr_, TYPE_B, K,
             &beta,  C.d_ptr_, TYPE_C, M, TYPE_C,
             CUBLAS_GEMM_DEFAULT);
```

7. To review the matrix values, we can use `printMatrix()`, which is defined in `helper.h`:

```
std::cout << "A:" << std::endl;
printMatrix(A.h_ptr_, K, M);
std::cout << "B:" << std::endl;
printMatrix(B.h_ptr_, N, K);
```

8. The `printMatrix()` is defined using the function overriding method to allow the printing of half-precision values with the same format in other data types. Part of the definitions is as follows:

```
template <typename T>
void printMatrix(const T *matrix, const int ldm, const int n) {
    std::cout << "[" << __FUNCTION__ << "]::
                Not supported type request" << std::endl;
}
void printMatrix(const float *matrix, const int ldm, const int n) {
    for (int j = 0; j < n; j++) {
        for (int i = 0; i < ldm; i++)
            std::cout << std::fixed << std::setw(8) <<
                        std::setprecision(4) <<
                        matrix[IDX2C(i, j, ldm)];
        std::cout << std::endl;
    }
}
void printMatrix(const half *matrix, const int ldm, const int n) {
    for (int j = 0; j < n; j++) {
        for (int i = 0; i < ldm; i++)
            std::cout << std::fixed << std::setw(8) <<
                        std::setprecision(4) <<
__half2float(matrix[IDX2C(i, j, ldm)]);
        std::cout << std::endl;
    }
}
... ( functions for other data types ) ...
```

9. Then, the code will have a GEMM operation to the given A, B, and C matrices. The following shows an example of the output when M is 4, N is 5, and M is 6:

```
$ nvcc -run -m64 -std=c++11 -I/usr/local/cuda/samples/common/inc -
gencode arch=compute_70,code=sm_70 -lcublas -o cublasGemmEx
./cublasGemmEx.cu
A:
  0.0049 0.0479 0.0023 0.0775 0.0279 0.0817
  0.0373 0.0625 0.0264 0.0924 0.0584 0.0853
  0.0719 0.0505 0.0540 0.0987 0.0657 0.0052
  0.0682 0.0781 0.0599 0.0896 0.0048 0.0796
B:
  0.0624 0.0965 0.0545 0.0223 0.0861
  0.0594 0.0019 0.0643 0.0920 0.0537
  0.0145 0.0376 0.0172 0.0221 0.0881
  0.0285 0.0319 0.0161 0.0677 0.0235
  0.0814 0.0695 0.0414 0.0392 0.0296
  0.0446 0.0688 0.0403 0.0018 0.0971
C:
  0.0509 0.0117 0.0877 0.0445 0.0830
  0.0742 0.0242 0.0136 0.0625 0.0681
  0.0362 0.0046 0.0265 0.0963 0.0638
  0.0070 0.0446 0.0516 0.0194 0.0089
C out:
  0.0153 0.0228 0.0143 0.0292 0.0113
  0.0200 0.0118 0.0214 0.0081 0.0138
  0.0098 0.0168 0.0132 0.0199 0.0125
  0.0269 0.0120 0.0222 0.0085 0.0228
```

Now, let's try with the other data types and see how `cublasGemmEx()` operates to the given matrices. The provided example also outputs the operation's execution time to measure the performance:

- What should we modify if matrix *A* or matrix *B* is the transposed matrix?
- Is there any preferable matrix size to the operation? Compare the execution time by changing the size.
- Is there any preferable matrix size for each data type? If you try the INT8 precision, you will see errors. How this can be fixed? Change the size and see how the INT8 operation can be supported in `cublasGemmEx()`.

GEMM with TensorCore

TensorCore provides the accelerated performance of tensor's dot operations. It supports FP16 in the Volta architecture, and `INT8` and `INT4` in the Turing architecture. Therefore, we should use reduced precision or mixed precision to use TensorCore.

Previously we used `CUBLAS_GEMM_DEFAULT` as the cuBLAS GEMM algorithm, which uses CUDA cores in their operation. To use TensorCore, we should use `CUBLAS_GEMM_DEFAULT_TENSOR_OP`. To utilize the TensorCore, each dimension of your operand matrices should be a multiple of 4. That is the unit size of TensorCore's **WMMA** (short for, **Warp Matrix Multiply Accumulate**) operation optimization internally. For instance, matrix-matrix multiplication with *A* (8,192 × 8,192) and *B* (8,192 × 8,192) shows a much higher performance against the operation with *A* (8,192 × 8,192) and *B* (8,192 × 8,190). You can also confirm this operation via a profile.

The following timeline is a result of a matrix multiplication using matrix *A* (8,192 × 8,192) and matrix *B* (8,192 × 8,190):

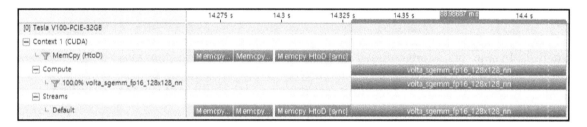

Furthermore, this timeline image is a result of a matrix multiplication from matrix *A* (8,192 × 8,192) and matrix *B* (8,192 × 8,192):

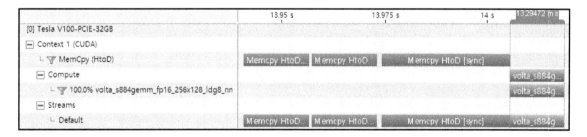

Both tests use `CUBLAS_GEMM_DEFAULT_TENSOR_OP` in CUDA C/C++, but the GEMM operation with TensorCore is 6.7x faster than with CUDA cores. As TensorCore is available based on the matrix size, `nvcc` compiles the code with the special kernel functions, starting with `volta_s884g`. In conclusion, pad your matrices to align with 4, if you want to get benefits of TensorCore. This can be an overhead, but performance gain from TensorCore may overwhelm the overhead.

NVIDIA provides how-to programming TensorCores using the cuBLAS library in their development blog site (`https://devblogs.nvidia.com/programming-tensor-cores-cuda-9`). This document also introduces other available methods. But, using the cuBLAS library provides the fastest performance for you, as proven following a paper from Oak Ridge National Laboratory—*NVIDIA Tensor Core Programmability, Performance and Precision* (`https://arxiv.org/pdf/1803.04014.pdf`).

cuRAND for parallel random number generation

Many applications use the pseudo-random number for their simulation or probabilistic analysis. In spite of its conventional usages, a large number of random number generation procedure took much time. One solution is to generate random numbers in parallel, but each multiple thread should have different random seeds in order to generate random numbers independently.

The cuRAND library enables GPU to generate a number of random numbers from GPU. This library is available from the host or from the device code. The host API enables the generation of random numbers only using the host code. Therefore, you can use the generated data directly for other kernel functions. The device API enables the generation of random numbers in kernel code, so you can make CUDA threads that have their own randomly generated numbers during the execution.

cuRAND host API

First, you need to create a new generator of the desired type, using curandGenerator(). Then, set the generator options of the desired seed and order. For example, you can generate the pseudo-random generator using curandSetPseudoRandomGeneratorSeed():

```
curandGenerator_t curand_gen;
curandCreateGenerator(&curand_gen, CURAND_RNG_PSEUDO_DEFAULT);
curandSetPseudoRandomGeneratorSeed(curand_gen, 2019UL);
```

Then, you can generate random numbers using curandGenerate(). There are nine different generation functions. For example, you can generate uniformly distributed floating-point values using curandGenerateUnifrom():

```
curandGenerateUniform(curand_gen, random_numbers_on_device_memory, length);
```

 The cuRAND programming guide provides descriptions of various kinds of generation functions: https://docs.nvidia.com/cuda/curand/host-api-overview.html#generation-functions.

After the use of random number generation, you can terminate the cuRAND generator with the destroyer function:

```
curandDestroyGenerator(curand_gen);
```

Now, let's implement an application that generates random numbers using several cuRAND APIs. The fully implemented version is 03_curand/curand_host.cpp. So, you can modify the code and test other functions as you need.

At first, we should include curand.h for the cuRAND host APIs and other CPP-related header files as follows:

```
#include <iostream>
#include <iomanip>
#include <curand.h>
```

Let's assume that we will create a matrix that is initialized with random numbers. We need to implement the `printMatrix()` function in order to review the generated random numbers as follows:

```
#define IDX2C(i, j, ld) (((j) * (ld)) + (i))

template <typename T>
void printMatrix(const T *matrix, const int ldm, const int n)
{
    for (int j = 0; j < ldm; j++) {
        for (int i = 0; i < n; i++)
            std::cout << std::fixed << std::setw(12)
                      << std::setprecision(4) << matrix[IDX2C(i, j, ldm)];
        std::cout << std::endl;
    }
}
```

Then, we will allocate the required memory space as follows. Now, we will implement the `main()` function that initializes random numbers and prints the result using `printMatrix()`. First, we will initialize the cuRAND handle for the operation as follows:

```
// create curand generator & set random seed
curandGenerator_t curand_gen;
curandCreateGenerator(&curand_gen, CURAND_RNG_PSEUDO_DEFAULT);
curandSetPseudoRandomGeneratorSeed(curand_gen, 2019UL);
```

You can change the random seed as you want. The next thing is to allocate memory space. To ease the evaluation of the operation, we will use a unified memory, because cuRAND functions will generate random numbers on GPU:

```
size_t size = M * N;
unsigned int *np_random;
float *fp_random;
cudaMallocManaged((void**)&np_random, sizeof(*np_random) * size);
cudaMallocManaged((void**)&fp_random, sizeof(*fp_random) * size);
```

Next, we will generate random numbers to the given memory space. We will use the integer memory space (`np_random`) for random number generation, and floating memory space (`fp_random`) for uniformly distributed random numbers, as follows:

```
// random number generation
std::cout << "Generated random numbers" << std::endl;
curandGenerate(curand_gen, np_random, size);
cudaDeviceSynchronize();
printMatrix(np_random, M, N);

// uniform distributed random number generation
std::cout << "Generated uniform random numbers" << std::endl;
curandGenerateUniform(curand_gen, fp_random, size);
cudaDeviceSynchronize();
printMatrix(fp_random, M, N);
```

Because we are using a unified memory, we can allow the GPU and the host to share the same memory address, and we can review the output values by synchronizing them. Finally, we can terminate the cuRAND handle and memories as follows:

```
// terminates used resources
curandDestroyGenerator(curand_gen);
cudaFree(np_random);
cudaFree(fp_random);
```

Now, its time to compile and run the code. Compiling the code using cuRAND APIs should provide `-lcurand` for the `nvcc` compiler. When `M = 3` and `N = 5`, the outputs are as follows:

```
$ nvcc -run -gencode arch=compute_70,code=sm_70 -lcurand -o curand_host
curand_host.cpp
Generated random numbers
   3395652512 793372546 2133571103 595847267 2461872808
    595847267 2461872808 500895635 498154070 2385617847
    498154070 2385617847 196336856 388563169 745758309
Generated uniform random numbers
        0.7134 0.0830 0.1458 0.2099 0.6066
        0.2099 0.6066 0.3078 0.5122 0.8856
        0.5122 0.8856 0.3530 0.8477 0.8370
```

We have covered how CUDA can generate random numbers using the host API, but, in some cases, it is better to design the CUDA kernels to generate random numbers. We call this the device API, and we can obtain random numbers from each CUDA thread.

cuRAND device API

Using the device API, we can set the generator seed and generate random numbers on your CUDA device.

Firstly, we need to prepare a device memory space of `curandState_t`, in order to store generator seeds to provide the random seed to the CUDA threads in parallel. This can be done like a normal device memory allocation code as follows:

```
cudaMalloc((void **)&devStates, length * sizeof(curandState_t));
```

In your kernel code, we need to initialize random seeds using `curand_init()`. This function requires seed, sequence number, and offset. Then, this function sets up the state. For the same seed, cuFFT always generates the same state. To generate random values, use the `curand()` function. Like the host's generation function, the device API has various generation functions. For example, uniformly distributed random number generation can be done like this:

```
int idx = blockIdx.x * blockDim.x + threadIdx.x;
curand_init(2019UL, idx, 0, &state[idx]);
generated_out[idx] = curand_uniform(&state[idx]);
```

The cuRAND library provides various generation functions for the various data types and stochastic distributions. To find your desired generation function, check the cuRAND developer guide's device API overview. After the random number generation, the device states buffer should be terminated like normal memory, as follows:

```
cudaFree(devStates);
```

Now, we will create an application that uses cuRAND device APIs. The fully implemented codes are `curand_device.cu`, so you can modify and test the code too. Firstly, we should include the `curand_kernel.h` file with other C++ required header files as follows:

```
#include <iostream>
#include <iomanip>
#include <curand_kernel.h>
```

We will write `setup_kernel()` that initializes a random seed for each CUDA thread as follows:

```
__global__ void setup_kernel(curandState_t *state)
{
    int idx = blockIdx.x * blockDim.x + threadIdx.x;
    // Each thread gets same seed,
    // a different sequence number, no offset */
    curand_init(2019UL, idx, 0, &state[idx]);
}
```

Write two random number generation functions: `generate_kernel()` and `generate_uniform_kernel()`. We will generate a 32-bit integer and a single floating point with uniformly distributed random numbers:

```
__global__ void generate_kernel(unsigned int *generated_out,
                                  curandState_t *state)
{
    int idx = blockIdx.x * blockDim.x + threadIdx.x;
    generated_out[idx] = curand(&state[idx]) & 0xFF;
}
__global__ void generate_uniform_kernel(float *generated_out,
                                         curandState_t *state)
{
    int idx = blockIdx.x * blockDim.x + threadIdx.x;
    generated_out[idx] = curand_uniform(&state[idx]);
}
```

Now, we will implement the `main()` function and initialize the device states buffer:

```
cudaMalloc((void **)&devStates, sizeof(curandState) * size);
setup_kernel<<<(size + BLOCK_DIM - 1) / BLOCK_DIM, BLOCK_DIM>>>(devStates);
```

Then, generate random numbers using `generate_kernel()`. For convenience, we will use unified memory for space and validate the output from the host. After that, we will print out the result as follows:

```
// random number generation
std::cout << "Generated random numbers" << std::endl;
cudaMallocManaged((void**)&np_random, sizeof(*np_random) * size);
generate_kernel<<<(size + BLOCK_DIM - 1) / BLOCK_DIM, BLOCK_DIM>>>
                (np_random, const_cast<curandState_t *>(devStates));
cudaDeviceSynchronize();
printMatrix(np_random, M, N);
```

In the same way, we will create uniformly distributed random numbers using `generate_uniform_kernel()` as follows:

```
// uniform distributed random number generation
std::cout << "Generated uniform random numbers" << std::endl;
cudaMallocManaged((void**)&fp_random, sizeof(*fp_random) * size);
generate_uniform_kernel<<<(size + BLOCK_DIM - 1) / BLOCK_DIM, BLOCK_DIM>>>
                (fp_random, const_cast<curandState_t *>(devStates));
cudaDeviceSynchronize();
printMatrix(fp_random, M, N);
```

Because we are using unified memory, we can allow the GPU and the host to share the same memory address, and we can review the output values by synchronizing them. Finally, we can terminate the cuRAND handle and memories as follows:

```
// terminates used resources
curandDestroyGenerator(curand_gen);
cudaFree(np_random);
cudaFree(fp_random);
```

Now, its time to compile and run the code. In order to compile the code using cuRAND, APIs should provide `-lcurand` for the `nvcc` compiler. When M equals 3 and N equals 5, the outputs are as follows:

```
$ nvcc -run -gencode arch=compute_70,code=sm_70 -lcurand -o curand_device
curand_device.cpp
Generated random numbers
   3395652512 793372546 2133571103 595847267 2461872808
    595847267 2461872808 500895635 498154070 2385617847
    498154070 2385617847 196336856 388563169 745758309
Generated uniform random numbers
        0.8064 0.2783 0.2971 0.2386 0.7491
        0.2386 0.7491 0.4782 0.1060 0.2922
        0.1060 0.2922 0.1823 0.6199 0.9137
```

When you compare the output numbers from the host API and the device API, the generated random numbers are the same, whereas the uniform random numbers are not. This can be resolved if you reset the random seed ahead of the second random number generation.

cuRAND with mixed precision cuBLAS GEMM

Previously, we have used the C++ random number generator to initialize matrices for a GEMM operation. This function is handy when we want to generate random numbers in general. However, you may find that this function took a long time to generate large random numbers in the last section. In this section, we will cover how cuRAND API can work with the cuBLAS GEMM operations. The fully implemented version is the `gemm_with_curand_host.cpp` file. Let's see how this was implemented:

1. Currently, we don't have a low-precision random number generator in the cuRAND library. Also, we need to convert the half-precision numbers to float in order to evaluate the output. For these reasons, we need to create type conversion functions on GPU as follows:

```
namespace fp16{
__global__ void float2half_kernel(half *out, float *in)
{
    int idx = blockIdx.x * blockDim.x + threadIdx.x;
    out[idx] = __float2half(in[idx]);
}
void float2half(half *out, float *in, size_t length)
{
    float2half_kernel<<< (length + BLOCK_DIM - 1) / BLOCK_DIM,
BLOCK_DIM >>>(out, in);
}
```

2. Now, we will write a random number generation function that uses the cuRAND host API. As we discussed before, we should convert the generated random numbers from float to half, when we need to use half-precision data. This function can be implemented as follows:

```
template <typename T>
typename std::enable_if<(std::is_same<T, float>::value),
float>::type
*curand(curandGenerator_t generator, size_t length)
{
    T *buffer = nullptr;
    cudaMalloc((void **)&buffer, length * sizeof(float));
    curandGenerateUniform(generator, buffer, length);
    return buffer;
}
template <typename T>
typename std::enable_if<std::is_same<T, half>::value, half>::type
*curand(curandGenerator_t generator, size_t length)
{
    T *buffer = nullptr;
```

```
        float *buffer_fp32;
        cudaMalloc((void **)&buffer_fp32, length * sizeof(float));
        curandGenerateUniform(generator, buffer_fp32, length);
        cudaMalloc((void **)&buffer, length * sizeof(T));
        fp16::float2half(buffer, buffer_fp32, length);
        cudaFree(buffer_fp32);
        return buffer;
    }
```

3. Define some local variables that control GEMM operations in the `main()` function:

```
void *d_A, *d_B, *d_C;
cudaDataType AType, BType, CType, computeType;
int M = 8192, N = 8192, K = 8192;
float alpha = 1.f, beta = 1.f;
std::string precision = "fp32";
bool tensor_core = true;
```

In this code, we determine the GEMM operation size, data type, and operation type.

4. Now, let's create input buffer arrays, and set parameters, along with the operation precision:

```
if (precision == "fp32") {
    auto *a = curand<float>(curand_gen, M * K);
    auto *b = curand<float>(curand_gen, K * N);
    auto *c = curand<float>(curand_gen, M * N);
    AType = BType = CType = CUDA_R_32F;
    computeType = CUDA_R_32F;
    d_A = a, d_B = b, d_C = c;
}
else if (precision == "fp16") {
    auto *a = curand<half>(curand_gen, M * K);
    auto *b = curand<half>(curand_gen, K * N);
    auto *c = curand<float>(curand_gen, M * N);
    AType = BType = CUDA_R_16F, CType = CUDA_R_32F;
    computeType = CUDA_R_32F;
    d_A = a, d_B = b, d_C = c;
}
else {
    exit(EXIT_FAILURE);
}
```

5. Create cuRAND and cuBLAS handles as follows:

```
cublasCreate(&cublas_handle);
curandCreateGenerator(&curand_gen, CURAND_RNG_PSEUDO_DEFAULT);
curandSetPseudoRandomGeneratorSeed(curand_gen, 2019UL);
```

6. Then, we should determine the operation type in order to use TensorCores:

```
cublasGemmAlgo_t gemm_algo = (tensor_core) ?
                            CUBLAS_GEMM_DEFAULT_TENSOR_OP :
CUBLAS_GEMM_DEFAULT;
```

7. Then, we can call the `cublasGemmEx()` function that affords FP32 and FP16 operations as follows:

```
cublasGemmEx(cublas_handle, CUBLAS_OP_N, CUBLAS_OP_N,
            M, N, K,
            &alpha, d_A, AType, M, d_B, BType, K,
            &beta,  d_C, CType, M,
            computeType, gemm_algo);
```

The GEMM operation should show a similar performance when compared to the previous version. But, you may find that the whole application speed is enhanced, since the parallel random number generation on the GPU is much faster than the generation from the host.

The cuRAND developer guide will help you to find other random number generators, options, and distributions. This document is located at `https://docs.nvidia.com/pdf/CURAND_Library.pdf`.

cuFFT for Fast Fourier Transformation in GPU

The cuFFT library provides GPU accelerated operations for the **FFT** (short for, **Fast Fourier Transform**) algorithm. The programmers can transform real or complex data using GPU computing power, and apply GPU kernel operations for the transformed signal. Also, the supported functions are matched with the FFTW library, so we can migrate the host project to the GPU.

To handle the FFT sample's dimensional information, cuFFT is required to create a plan handle using `cufftPlan1D()`, `cufftPlan2D()`, or `cufftPlan3D()`, accordingly. If sample data has a batched and stride layout, we should use `cufftPlanMany()`. If the sample size is greater than 4 GB, we should use `64` as a suffix to the plan functions to support that size. For example, `cufftPlanMany64()` supports larger samples on top of the `cufftPlanMany()` function.

The cuFFT library supports multi-GPU operations. First, you need to create an empty plan using `cufftCreate()`. Then, we can specify the list of GPUs that will carry out the operation using `cufftXtSetGPUs()`. After that, we can generate a plan using normal plan generation functions, which we have previously covered. The following table shows the plan generation function categories:

	Basic plans	Multi-GPU plans
Simple plan	`cufftPlan{1d,2d,3d}()`	`cufftMakePlan{1d,2d,3d}()`
Advanced data layout	`cufftPlanMany()`	`cufftMakePlanMany()`
FP16 operation	`cufftXtMakePlanMany()`	

Then you can forward (FFT) and inverse (IFFT) to your sample data using the `cufftExec()` function. The cuFFT library provides three kinds of data transformation: complex-to-complex, real-to-complex, and complex-to-real. Its operation data type can be a float or a double:

Transform direction	Float	Double
Complex-to-complex	`cufftExecC2C()` `cufftXtExecDescriptorC2C()`	`cufftExecZ2Z()` `cufftXtExecDescriptorZ2Z()`
Real-to-complex	`cufftDExecR2C()` `cufftXtExecDescriptorR2C()`	`cufftExecD2Z()` `cufftXtExecDescriptorD2Z()`
Complex-to-real	`cufftExecC2R()` `cufftXtExecDescriptorC2R()`	`cufftExecZ2D()` `cufftXtExecDescriptorZ2D()`
All	`cufftXtExec()` / `cufftXtExecDesciptor()`	

The cuFFT operation is either *forward* or *inverse,* and the operation should be paired with the other direction.

The functions that transform between the real data and the complex data, such as `R2C` and `C2R`, have implicit directional information in their function name. This feature helps you to avoid having to have an additional operation in order to convert your data in the real domain to a complex data type. Meanwhile, you have to create an additional plan since each plan has transformation direction information.

On the other hand, you have to provide the transform direction information for the complex-to-complex transformation, such as C2C and Z2Z. For the inversion operation, you don't have to create another cuFFT handle, because the plan should be the same data type operation.

The cufftXtExec() and cufftXtExecDescriptor() functions can perform transformation on any given data type, since every input data should be provided with their data type information when you create a cuFFT plan.

Basic usage of cuFFT

Now let's try to use cuFFT. The fully implemented version is the 04_cufft/cufft.1d.cpp file. Let's discuss how this is implemented:

1. Firstly, start with some header files: C++, CUDA, cuRAND, and cuFFT:

```
#include <iostream>
#include <iomanip>
#include <cuda_runtime.h>
#include <cufft.h>
#include <curand.h>
```

2. In this FFT operation, we will have both real-to-complex and complex-to-real transformations. Therefore, let's declare some custom data types, Real and Complex, in order to simplify the code. This can be done as follows:

```
typedef cufftReal Real;
typedef cufftComplex Complex;
```

3. Now, let's begin with the main() function. For the input sample data, we will use unified memory in order to ease the data transfer between the host and the GPU. The transformed data may only be used on the GPU. Therefore, memory space can be allocated as follows:

```
cudaMallocManaged((void**)&p_sample, sizeof(Real) * sample_size *
batch_size);
cudaMalloc((void**)&d_freq, sizeof(Complex) * sample_size *
batch_size);
```

4. Then, we will use the cuRAND host API to initialize the input data as follows:

```
curandGenerator_t curand_gen;
curandCreateGenerator(&curand_gen, CURAND_RNG_PSEUDO_DEFAULT);
curandSetPseudoRandomGeneratorSeed(curand_gen, 2019UL);
curandGenerateUniform(curand_gen, p_sample, sample_size *
batch_size);
```

5. And, we should initialize the cuFFT plan for forward and inverse transforms. Since they have different data types we should create two plans, respectively, for real-to-complex and complex-to-real transformations:

```
int rank = 1;
int stride_sample = 1, stride_freq = 1;
int dist_sample = sample_size, dist_freq = sample_size / 2 + 1;
int embed_sample[] = {0};
int embed_freq[] = {0};
cufftPlanMany(&plan_forward, rank, &sample_size,
                            embed_sample, stride_sample,
                            dist_sample,
                            embed_freq, stride_freq, dist_freq,
                            CUFFT_R2C, batch_size);
cufftPlanMany(&plan_inverse, rank, &sample_size,
                            embed_freq, stride_freq, dist_freq,
                            embed_sample, stride_sample,
                            dist_sample,
                            CUFFT_C2R, batch_size);
```

6. Now, we can have forward or inverse transforms, with the given cuFFT plans. In order to measure the execution time, we can embrace these operations using CUDA events:

```
cufftExecR2C(plan_forward, p_sample, d_freq);
cufftExecC2R(plan_inverse, d_freq, p_sample);
```

7. Then, we can compile the code with the following commands:

```
$ nvcc -run -gencode arch=compute_70,code=sm_70 -lcufft -lcurand -o
cufft.1d cufft.1d.cpp
```

The `cufft.1d` command will report its transform time for each step as follows:

```
FFT operation time for 1048576 elements with 512 batch..
Forward (ms): 21.5322
Inverse (ms): 21.4
```

cuFFT with mixed precision

The cuFFT library provides extended CUDA computing features, such as the FP16 FFT operation. The full version is the `cufft.half.cpp` file. Let's discuss its implementation.

In this code, we should use `cufftXtMakePlanMany()` for the plan creation and the `cufftXtExec()` function for the transformation. `cufftXtMakePlanMany()` allows the passing of input and output data types if they are FP16 or FP32. Also, we should create two plans for forward and inverse transformation, in order to cover real-to-complex and complex-to-real transformations. To an empty cuFFT plan, `cufftXtMakePlanMany()` can specify the sample size, the input data format and type, the batch size, and so on. For example, plan creations can be implemented as follows:

```
int rank = 1;
int stride_sample = 1, stride_freq = 1;
long long int dist_sample = sample_size, dist_freq = sample_size / 2 + 1;
long long embed_sample[] = {0};
long long embed_freq[] = {0};
size_t workSize = 0;
cufftCreate(&plan_forward);
cufftXtMakePlanMany(plan_forward,
        rank, &sample_size,
        embed_sample, stride_sample, dist_sample, CUDA_R_16F,
        embed_freq, stride_freq, dist_freq, CUDA_C_16F,
        batch_size, &workSize, CUDA_C_16F);
cufftCreate(&plan_inverse);
cufftXtMakePlanMany(plan_inverse,
        rank, &sample_size,
        embed_freq, stride_freq, dist_freq, CUDA_C_16F,
        embed_sample, stride_sample, dist_sample, CUDA_R_16F,
        batch_size, &workSize, CUDA_R_16F);
```

In this implementation, we also have to consider whether to provide the input data in half-precision. You may use the host random function and convert them into half-precision data, but, this code shows you how the cuRAND host API can be used for this purpose, as follows:

```
template <typename T>
typename std::enable_if<std::is_same<T, half>::value>::type
curand(curandGenerator_t generator, T *buffer, size_t length) {
    float *buffer_fp32;

    cudaMalloc((void **)&buffer_fp32, length * sizeof(float));
    curandGenerateUniform(generator, buffer_fp32, length);

    // convert generated single floating to half floating
```

```
fp16::float2half(buffer, buffer_fp32, length);
cudaFree(buffer_fp32);
}
```

So, we can provide half-precision on uniformly distributed random numbers for FFT, and we can use `cufftXtExec()` for the forward and inverse transformations. Transformation performance is as follows:

```
FFT operation time for 1048576 elements with 512 batch..
Forward (ms): 15.3236
Inverse (ms): 15.4881
```

cuFFT for multi-GPU

Another usage of cuFFT is having a large FFT operation using multiple GPUs. To do this, we have to create an empty cuFFT plan using `cufftCreate()`, and provide GPU numbers using `cufftXtSetGPUs()`. For example, this can be done as follows:

```
cufftHandle cufft_plan;
int n_gpu = 2, devices[2] = {0,1};
cufftCreaet(&cufft_plan); // create an empty plan
cufftXtSetGPUs(cufft_plan, n_gpu, devices); // set multi-gpu information
```

The total number of GPUs can vary depending on the system. Now, we can generate the cuFFT plan using `cufftXtMakePlanMany()` to specify the sample information. For instance, `cufftXtMakePlanMany()` can be called like this:

```
size_t *work_size = (size_t*) new size_t[num_gpus];
cufftXtMakePlanMany(cufft_plan, 1 &sample_size,
                    nullptr, 1, 1, CUDA_C_32F,
                    nullptr, 1, 1,  CUDA_C_32F,
                    batch_size, work_size, CUDA_C_32F);
```

The cuFFT library provides `cufftXtMalloc()`, which prepares the GPU memory space for the target GPUs. Then, we can copy our data to the allocated memory using the `cufftXtMemcpy()` function. For example, this can be implemented as follows:

```
cudaLibXtDesc *d_sample;
cufftXtMalloc(cufft_plan, &d_sample, CUFFT_XT_FORMAT_INPLACE);
cufftXtMemcpy(cufft_plan, d_sample, h_sample, CUFFT_COPY_HOST_TO_DEVICE);
```

Then, we can execute FFT on multi-GPUs with the `cufftXtExecDesciptor()` function:

```
cufftXtExecDesciptor(cufft_plan, d_sample, d_sample, CUFFT_FORWARD);
```

Using `nvidia-smi`, we can monitor the distributed memory allocation and execution across the GPUs. The elapsed time can be different, depending on your GPUs and system configuration.

If you want to learn more about the cuFFT library and its functions, the cuFFT library user guide (`https://docs.nvidia.com/cuda/cufft/index.html`) is a good reference for you.

CUDA sample code is another good reference for learning how to use cuFFT functions. The sample codes are placed in the `NVIDIA_CUDA-10.x_Samples/7_CUDALibraries/CUFFT*` directory. You can learn how to apply filter operations using CUDA kernel code, and by working with cuFFT's forward/backward transformations.

NPP for image and signal processing with GPU

The **NPP** (short for, **NVIDIA Performance Primitive**) library is a default CUDA library with a set of GPU accelerated processing functions that focus on imaging and video processing. While it enables flexible development in these fields, the developers can save their application development time.

The NPP library has two functional parts: imaging-processing APIs, and signal-processing APIs. The image-processing APIs include tools relating to image filtering, compression/decompression, color transformation, resizing, color conversion, statistical operations, and so on. The signal-processing APIs are filtering, conversion, and so on. You can visit the NPP's document (`https://docs.nvidia.com/cuda/npp`), and see its configurations and the full list of functionalities.

CUDA provides many NPP-based samples. In this section, we will cover the basic use of the NPP library and discuss its application.

Image processing with NPP

First, we will cover how the NPP library can ease an image-processing task. Before doing this, we should install the FreeImage library in order to be able to load and write a JPEG compressed image file easily. There are three options that can be used to prepare the library:

1. Installation from the Ubuntu archive:

```
$ sudo apt-get install libfreeimage-dev
```

2. Build from the source code and install:

```
$ wget http://downloads.sourceforge.net/freeimage/FreeImage3180.zip
$ unzip FreeImage3180.zip
$ cd FreeImage && make -j && sudo make install
```

3. Use the library that has already been installed with the CUDA Toolkit. An NPP sample code, 7_CUDALibraries/freeImageInteropNPP, in CUDA sample code uses the FreeImage library. For this sample, NPP header files and library files are installed at 7_CUDALibrires/common/FreeImage in the CUDA sample directory. You may use this if you prefer not to install other binaries into your machine.

Now, let's implement the NPP-based image-processing application. The fully implemented code is 05_npp/imageFilter.cpp. This file begins with the header files:

```
#include <iostream>
#include <iomanip>
#include <cassert>
#include <cstring>
#include <cuda_runtime.h>
#include <npp.h>
#include <FreeImage.h>
#include <helper_timer.h>
```

In this application, it has the ImageInfo_t structure to easily manage image information and data:

```
struct ImageInfo_t
{
    /* image information */
    FIBITMAP* dib; // FreeImage bitmap
    int nHeight;   // image height size
    int nWidth;    // image width size
    int nPitch;    // image pitch size
    int nBPP;      // Bit Per Pixel (i.e. 24 for BGR color)
    int nChannel;  // number of channels
    BYTE* pData;   // bytes from freeimage library
    /* CUDA */
    Npp8u *pDataCUDA; // CUDA global memory for nppi processing
    int nPitchCUDA;   // image pitch size on CUDA device
};
```

Write the `LoadImage()` function in order to load a JPEG image. The `FreeImage` library supports any other image format, so you can try other images as you want. Then, we will fill the source image information managing structure with the loaded image data. The `loadImage()` function is implemented as follows:

```
void LoadImage(const char *szInputFile, ImageInfo_t &srcImage) {
    FIBITMAP *pSrcImageBitmap = FreeImage_Load(FIF_JPEG, szInputFile,
JPEG_DEFAULT);
    if (!pSrcImageBitmap) {
        std::cout << "Couldn't load " << szInputFile << std::endl;
        FreeImage_DeInitialise();
        exit(1);
    }

    srcImage.dib = pSrcImageBitmap;
    srcImage.nWidth = FreeImage_GetWidth(pSrcImageBitmap);
    srcImage.nHeight = FreeImage_GetHeight(pSrcImageBitmap);
    srcImage.nPitch = FreeImage_GetPitch(pSrcImageBitmap);
    srcImage.nBPP = FreeImage_GetBPP(pSrcImageBitmap);
    srcImage.pData = FreeImage_GetBits(pSrcImageBitmap);
    assert(srcImage.nBPP == (unsigned int)24); // BGR color image
    srcImage.nChannel = 3;
}
```

Then, write some NPPI helper functions that provide the NPPI image size and the NPPI ROI size data from the image structure as follows:

```
NppiSize GetImageSize(ImageInfo_t imageInfo)
{
    NppiSize imageSize;
    imageSize.width = imageInfo.nWidth;
    imageSize.height = imageInfo.nHeight;
    return imageSize;
}
NppiRect GetROI(ImageInfo_t imageInfo)
{
    NppiRect imageROI;
    imageROI.x = 0;      imageROI.y = 0;
    imageROI.width = imageInfo.nWidth;
    imageROI.height = imageInfo.nHeight;
    return imageROI;
}
```

Then, let's implement the NPPI-based image resizing function as follows. In this function, we will use `nppiResize_8u_C3R()`, which was discussed at the beginning. NPP APIs have naming convention rules to explicitly clarify their operation. Depending on their functional categories, their naming starts with `nppi` for the image processing, and `npps` for the signal processing. For instance, an NPP image-processing function, `nppiResize_8u_C3R()`, begins with the `nppi` prefix, and it resizes input data with an unsigned char data type in three channels to the given ROI (you can learn more detail about this convention in the document):

```
int ResizeGPU(ImageInfo_t &dstImage, ImageInfo_t &srcImage,
              NppiSize &dstSize, NppiRect &dstROI,
              NppiSize &srcSize, NppiRect &srcROI, scale)
{
    // update output image size
    dstSize.width = dstROI.width = dstImage.nWidth;
    dstSize.height = dstROI.height = dstImage.nHeight;

    nppiResize_8u_C3R(srcImage.pDataCUDA, srcImage.nPitchCUDA,
              srcSize, srcROI,
              dstImage.pDataCUDA, dstImage.nPitchCUDA,
              dstSize, dstROI,
              NPPI_INTER_LANCZOS);
    return 0;
}
```

To compare the performance with the CPU, we will use a FreeImage's function, as follows:

```
void ResizeCPU(const char* szInputFile, ImageInfo_t &dstImage) {
    FreeImage_Rescale(dib, dstImage.nWidth, dstImage.nHeight,
FILTER_LANCZOS3);
}
```

Now, let's implement the `main()` function. At first, we should initialize the FreeImage library and load an image:

```
FreeImage_Initialise();
ImageInfo_t srcImage, dstImage;
LoadImage(szInputFile, srcImage);
```

Then, we will initialize the GPU memory space for the input image, as follows. In this procedure, we initialize the global memory space with an NPPI function and transfer the loaded image into the global memory using `cudaMemcpy2D()`:

```
// copy loaded image to the device memory
srcImage.pDataCUDA =
            nppiMalloc_8u_C3(srcImage.nWidth, srcImage.nHeight,
                    &srcImage.nPitchCUDA);
```

```
cudaMemcpy2D(srcImage.pDataCUDA, srcImage.nPitchCUDA,
             srcImage.pData, srcImage.nPitch,
             srcImage.nWidth * srcImage.nChannel * sizeof(Npp8u),
             srcImage.nHeight,
             cudaMemcpyHostToDevice);
```

After that, we will initialize the output memory space with the resized image size information as follows:

```
std::memcpy(&dstImage, &srcImage, sizeof(ImageInfo_t));
dstImage.nWidth *= scaleRatio;
srcImage.nHeight *= scaleRatio;
dstImage.pDataCUDA =
              nppiMalloc_8u_C3(dstImage.nWidth, dstImage.nHeight,
                               &dstImage.nPitchCUDA);
```

Then, we call the `ResizeGPU()` and `ResizeCPU()` functions, which we have implemented already. For each operation, we will use `cudaEvent` to measure the execution time on the GPU:

```
RunNppResize(dstImage, srcImage, dstImageSize, dstROI, srcImageSize,
srcROI, scaleRatio);
RunCpuResize(szInputFile, dstImage);
```

For verification, we will save the result to the file. To do this, we should create a FreeImage bitmap, and copy the resized image into the memory space. Then, we can save an output image, as follows:

```
// Save resized image as file from the device
FIBITMAP *pDstImageBitmap =
              FreeImage_Allocate(dstImage.nWidth, dstImage.nHeight,
                                 dstImage.nBPP);
dstImage.nPitch = FreeImage_GetPitch(pDstImageBitmap);
dstImage.pData = FreeImage_GetBits(pDstImageBitmap);
cudaMemcpy2D(dstImage.pData, dstImage.nPitch,
             dstImage.pDataCUDA, dstImage.nPitchCUDA,
             dstImage.nWidth * dstImage.nChannel * sizeof(Npp8u),
             dstImage.nHeight, cudaMemcpyDeviceToHost);
FreeImage_Save(FIF_JPEG, pDstImageBitmap, szOutputFile, JPEG_DEFAULT);
```

After that, we can finally terminate the related resources:

```
nppiFree(srcImage.pDataCUDA);
nppiFree(dstImage.pDataCUDA);
FreeImage_DeInitialise();
```

Compile the code using `nvcc` with the linked NPP and FreeImage library:

```
$ nvcc -run -m64 -std=c++11 -I/usr/local/cuda/samples/common/inc -gencode
arch=compute_70,code=sm_70 -lnppc -lnppif -lnppisu -lnppig -lnppicom -lnpps
-lfreeimage -o imageFilter ./imageFilter.cpp
```

As a result, when the scale factor is 0.5 f, the image size is reduced like this:

```
$ ls -alh *.jpg
-rw-rw-r-- 1 ubuntu ubuntu 91K Nov 13 22:31 flower.jpg
-rw-rw-r-- 1 ubuntu ubuntu 23K Nov 17 02:46 output.jpg
```

The measured elapsed time is `0.04576 ms` using V100. Its time can vary depending on the GPU:

```
Rescale flower.jpg in 0.5 ratio.
CPU: 23.857 ms
GPU: 0.04576 ms
Done (generated output.jpg)
```

For more detail on the use of NPP for image processing, visit and see the linked document: `http://on-demand.gputechconf.com/gtc/2014/presentations/HANDS-ON-LAB-S4793-image-processing-using-npp.pdf`.

Signal processing with NPP

NPP also provides signal-processing features. The main difference to image-processing APIs is that they do not require image-shape-related information. As we continue to cover the basic usage of NPP functions, we will find out how we can obtain the sum, min/max, mean, and L2 normalized distribution value from the given arrays. The fully written code is `05_npp/statisticsNPP.cpp`.

First, let's begin with the required header file:

```
#include <iostream>
#include <cuda_runtime.h>
#include <npp.h>
```

As an input data, we will use randomly generated numbers:

```
void GetData(float** buffer, size_t size)
{
    (*buffer) = (float*) new float[size];
```

```
        for (int i = 0; i < size; i++) {
            (*buffer)[i] = float(rand() % 0xFFFF) / RAND_MAX;
        }
    }
```

Before we call the statistical operation functions, we need a temporary memory space for their operations. We can obtain the required size using other NPP functions that are related to the operations, and we can create a common workspace memory space:

```
int GetWorkspaceSize(int signalSize)
{
    int bufferSize, tempBufferSize;

    nppsSumGetBufferSize_32f(signalSize, &tempBufferSize);
    bufferSize = std::max(bufferSize, tempBufferSize);
    nppsMinGetBufferSize_32f(signalSize, &tempBufferSize);
    bufferSize = std::max(bufferSize, tempBufferSize);
    nppsMaxGetBufferSize_32f(signalSize, &tempBufferSize);
    bufferSize = std::max(bufferSize, tempBufferSize);
    nppsMeanGetBufferSize_32f(signalSize, &tempBufferSize);
    bufferSize = std::max(bufferSize, tempBufferSize);
    nppsNormDiffL2GetBufferSize_32f(signalSize, &tempBufferSize);
    bufferSize = std::max(bufferSize, tempBufferSize);

    return bufferSize;
}
```

Let's begin with the main() function. At first, we will begin with input data preparation, and getting to know the required workspace memory space. We will prepare two input data types, and compare their differences using NPP:

```
GetData(&h_input1, buf_size);
GetData(&h_input2, buf_size);
workspace_size = GetWorkspaceSize(buf_size);
```

After that, we will allocate GPU memory space for the input/output and workspace. We will also transfer the input data as follows:

```
cudaMalloc((void **)&d_input1, buf_size * sizeof(float));
cudaMalloc((void **)&d_input2, buf_size * sizeof(float));
cudaMalloc((void **)&d_output, sizeof(float));
cudaMalloc((void **)&d_workspace, workspace_size * sizeof(Npp8u));
```

Now, let's do some simple statistical operations, using NPP functions:

```
nppsSum_32f(d_input1, buf_size, d_output, d_workspace);
cudaMemcpy(&h_output, d_output, sizeof(float), cudaMemcpyDeviceToHost);
std::cout << "Sum: " << h_output << std::endl;
```

```
nppsMin_32f(d_input1, buf_size, d_output, d_workspace);
cudaMemcpy(&h_output, d_output, sizeof(float), cudaMemcpyDeviceToHost);
std::cout << "Min: " << h_output << std::endl;

nppsMax_32f(d_input1, buf_size, d_output, d_workspace);
cudaMemcpy(&h_output, d_output, sizeof(float), cudaMemcpyDeviceToHost);
std::cout << "Max: " << h_output << std::endl;

nppsMean_32f(d_input1, buf_size, d_output, d_workspace);
cudaMemcpy(&h_output, d_output, sizeof(float), cudaMemcpyDeviceToHost);
std::cout << "Mean: " << h_output << std::endl;
```

NPP also provides functions that report the differences between the two inputs as follows:

```
nppsNormDiff_L2_32f(d_input1, d_input2, buf_size, d_output, d_workspace);
cudaMemcpy(&h_output, d_output, sizeof(float), cudaMemcpyDeviceToHost);
std::cout << "NormDiffL2: " << h_output << std::endl;
```

Then, we terminate the used memories. After that, let's compile the code with the following command:

```
$ nvcc -run -m64 -std=c++11 -I/usr/local/cuda/samples/common/inc -gencode
arch=compute_70,code=sm_70 -lnppc -lnppif -lnppisu -lnppig -lnppicom -lnpps
-o statisticsNPP ./statisticsNPP.cpp
```

As a result, we obtain the result as follows:

```
Sum: 0.00100016
Min: 1.30432e-06
Max: 3.04836e-05
Mean: 1.56275e-05
NormDiffL2: 9.46941e-05
```

Applications of NPP

In this section, we have covered the filtering in image processing, and statistical operations in signal processing. Although we have tried simple applications, we may find that NPP programming is much easier than kernel implementation. For this reason, NPP is applied to many media transcoding filters, bath image-processing applications, pre-processing of images in computer vision or deep learning, and so on.

Writing GPU accelerated code in OpenCV

The OpenCV library is quite a popular library in computer vision. It supports GPU programming in order to benefit performance at higher resolutions in the computer vision area. In this section, we will cover how to use a GPU with OpenGL.

CUDA-enabled OpenCV installation

To start OpenCV programming with CUDA, you need to compile the OpenCV library with the CUDA feature enabled. Follow this to enable OpenCV in Ubuntu:

```
$ sudo apt-get install -y --no-install-recommends \
    cmake git libgtk2.0-dev pkg-config libavcodec-dev \
    libavformat-dev libswscale-dev \
    libatlas-base-dev gfortran libeigen3-dev \
    libgtkglext1 libgtkglext1-dev
```

If your system can use X window (not a server), install other packages to enable the GTK dialog:

```
$ sudo apt-get install -y —no-install-recommends \
    Libgtkglext1 libgtkglext1-dev
```

Download the source code and untar them using the following commands. This was tested with OpenCV, which were the latest OpenCV versions at the time of writing:

```
# We are install OpenCV 4.1.1
OPENCV_VERSION=4.1.1
OPENCV_DIR=opencv

# Download OpenCV and contrib source codes
mkdir -p ${OPENCV_DIR}
wget -O ${OPENCV_DIR}/opencv-${OPENCV_VERSION}.tar.gz
https://github.com/opencv/opencv/archive/${OPENCV_VERSION}.tar.gz
wget -O ${OPENCV_DIR}/opencv_contrib-${OPENCV_VERSION}.tar.gz
https://github.com/opencv/opencv_contrib/archive/${OPENCV_VERSION}.tar.gz

# Untar the files
tar -C ${OPENCV_DIR} -xzf ${OPENCV_DIR}/opencv-${OPENCV_VERSION}.tar.gz
tar -C ${OPENCV_DIR} -xzf ${OPENCV_DIR}/opencv_contrib-
${OPENCV_VERSION}.tar.gz
```

Now, let's compile the downloaded source code using the following commands. You can put other options if you want. Its compilation takes a while:

```
# Build the codes and install
cd ${OPENCV_DIR}/opencv-${OPENCV_VERSION}
mkdir build
cd build
cmake -D CMAKE_BUILD_TYPE=RELEASE \
    -D CMAKE_INSTALL_PREFIX=/usr/local \
    -D ENABLE_PRECOMPILED_HEADERS=OFF \
    -D OPENCV_GENERATE_PKGCONFIG=ON \
    -D WITH_CUDA=ON -D WITH_CUVID=OFF -D BUILD_opencv_cudacodec=OFF \
    -D ENABLE_FAST_MATH=1 \
    -D CUDA_FAST_MATH=1 \
    -D OPENCV_EXTRA_MODULES_PATH=../../opencv_contrib-
${OPENCV_VERSION}/modules \
    -D WITH_CUBLAS=1 \
    -D PYTHON_DEFAULT_EXECUTABLE=`which python3` \
    -D INSTALL_PYTHON_EXAMPLES=ON \
    -D BUILD_EXAMPLES=ON ..
make -j$(nproc)
sudo make install -j$(nproc)
```

To confirm the installation use the following command:

```
$ pkg-config —cflags opencv4 -I/usr/local/include/opencv4/opencv -
I/usr/local/include/opencv4
```

In OpenCV 4, CUDA-related functions and classes are defined in CUDA namespaces. For instance, you can create a CUDA global memory space using this command:

```
cv::cuda::GpuMat cuda_mem = cv::cuda::GpuMat(src.rows, src.cols, CV_8UC1);
```

Then, the device `cuda_mem` memory space can be handled like a normal CPU memory type (`cv::Mat`).

Implementing a CUDA-enabled blur filter

Now, we will implement a tiny GPU-enabled OpenCV application and compare its performance. Let's begin by including the required header files:

```
#include <iostream>
#include <string>
#include "opencv2/opencv.hpp"
```

Here is the host blur filter implementation using OpenCV:

```
void BlurHost(std::string filename)
{
    cv::Mat src = cv::imread(filename, 1);
    cv::Mat dst;
    cv::TickMeter tm;
    tm.reset();
    tm.start();
    cv::bilateralFilter(src, dst, 10, 50, 50);
    tm.stop();
    std::cout << "CPU Time: " << tm.getTimeMilli() << " ms." << std::endl;
    cv::imwrite("result_host.jpg", dst);
}
```

And this is the CUDA-enabled blur filter implementation:

```
void BlurCuda(std::string filename)
{
    cv::Mat src = cv::imread(filename, 1);
    cv::Mat dst;
    cv::cuda::GpuMat src_cuda = cv::cuda::GpuMat(src.rows,
                                            src.cols, CV_8UC1);
    cv::cuda::GpuMat dst_cuda = cv::cuda::GpuMat(src.rows,
                                            src.cols, CV_8UC1);
    cv::TickMeter tm;
    // warm-up
    cv::cuda::bilateralFilter(src_cuda, dst_cuda, 10, 50, 50);
    tm.reset();
    tm.start();
    src_cuda.upload(src);
    cv::cuda::bilateralFilter(src_cuda, dst_cuda, 10, 50, 50);
    dst_cuda.download(dst);
    tm.stop();
    std::cout << "GPU Time: " << tm.getTimeMilli()
                << " ms." << std::endl;
    cv::imwrite("result_cuda.jpg", dst);
}
```

This receipt code shows how the `bilateralFilter()` operation matches with the host, and how CUDA matches with the CUDA namespace. For the CUDA memory manipulation, `cv::cuda::GpuMat` is used for the device memory, and the device memory provides `upload()` and `download()` member functions, such as `cudaMemcpy()`. To measure the elapsed time, `cv::TickMeter` was used. Then, `main()` calls both implementations, as follows:

```
int main(int argc, char *argv[])
{
    std::string filename("flower.JPG");
    BlurHost(filename);
    BlurCuda(filename);
    return 0;
}
```

Now, let's compile the code. We should include the OpenCV header files and libraries using `pkg-config --cflag opencv` in your compilation option. For example, the compilation option can be written like this:

```
$ nvcc -run -m64 -gencode arch=compute_70,code=sm_70 -
I/usr/local/cuda/samples/common/inc `pkg-config opencv4 --cflags --libs` -o
blur ./blur.cpp
```

Then, the output result is as follows:

```
CPU Time: 57.6544 ms.
GPU Time: 2.97784 ms.
```

The execution time can be different depending on your system and the GPU.

Enabling multi-stream processing

In OpenCV, the CUDA stream is managed with `cv::cuda::Stream`. Using this, we can have multi-stream-based pipelining GPU operations:

1. As we know, the host memory should be a pinned memory in order to have asynchronous data transfer:

   ```
   Mat::setDefaultAllocator(cuda::HostMem::getAllocator(cuda::HostMem:
   :PAGE_LOCKED));
   ```

2. Then, we will create multiple streams, as follows:

```
const int num_stream = 4;
cuda::Stream stream[num_stream];
```

3. And, we load the source image and initialize the GPU memory based on the loaded image information as follows:

```
Mat src = imread(filename, 1);
Mat dst;
cuda::GpuMat src_cuda[num_stream], dst_cuda[num_stream];
for (int i = 0; i < num_stream; i++)
    src_cuda[i] = cuda::GpuMat(src);
```

4. Now, we will transfer the image to the GPU, blur the image, and transfer it back to the host with each stream:

```
for (int i = 0; i < num_stream; i++) {
    src_cuda[i].upload(src, stream[i]);
    cuda::bilateralFilter(src_cuda[i], dst_cuda[i], 21, 150.f,
                        150.f, BORDER_DEFAULT, stream[i]);
    dst_cuda[i].download(dst, stream[i]);
}
```

5. Then, we have to synchronize the host and the GPU. To do this, we will use the `cv::Stream.waitForCompletion()` function that can synchronize for each stream after they finish the data transfer to the host:

```
for (int i = 0; i < num_stream; i++)
    stream[i].waitForCompletion();
```

6. To compare the performance with the CPU, we also call `cv::bilateralFilter()` as follows:

```
bilateralFilter(src, dst, 21, 150, 150);
```

Its execution time is as follows. The GPU execution time is the average of the measured time from the multi-stream execution loop to synchronization:

```
$ nvcc -run -m64 -gencode arch=compute_70,code=sm_70 -
I/usr/local/cuda/samples/common/inc `pkg-config opencv4 --cflags --
libs` -o blur ./blur.cpp
CPU Time: 84.8649 ms.
GPU Time: 1.60979 ms.
```

7. In order to confirm the multi-stream operation, we can profile the operation. The following screenshot shows this:

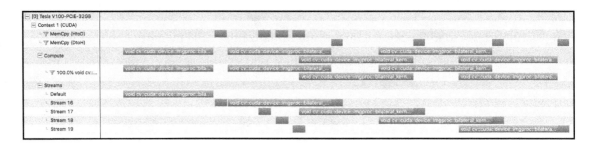

Profiling the operation

The first operation on the default stream is warp-up execution, and a four-multi-stream operation follows. Here, we can see that the GPU operations are overlapped. For this reason, the average execution time is shorter than for a one-stream execution.

We have only covered bilateral filtering in OpenCV. However, many OpenCV features support CUDA acceleration, so that you can get the benefits of GPU computing. Its interface is consistent with the CPU version, so you can easily migrate your CPU version to the GPU.

As an introductory level, there are some useful materials from GTC:

- http://on-demand.gputechconf.com/gtc/2013/webinar/opencv-gtc-express-shalini-gupta.pdf
- http://on-demand.gputechconf.com/gtc/2013/webinar/gtc-express-itseez-opencv-webinar.pdf
- http://developer.download.nvidia.com/GTC/PDF/1085_Fung.pdf

It is recommended that you start with OpenCV's reference guide: https://docs.opencv.org/4.1.1/d2/dbc/cuda_intro.html.

Writing Python code that works with CUDA

Nowadays, many people use CUDA with Python. It works not only as a glue of binaries, but it also enables to us write GPU accelerated code directly. As a glue language, Python can call the APIs from the CUDA C/C++ libraries, using `pybind11` (`https://github.com/pybind/pybind11`) or SWIG (`http://swig.org/`). However, we have to write CUDA C/C++ codes and integrate them into the Python application.

However, there are Python packages—Numba, CuPy, and PyCUDA—that enable GPU programming with Python. They provide native accelerated APIs and wrappers for CUDA kernels. In other words, we don't have to write C/C++ code and spend our time performing integration. Numba provides a vectorization and CUDA **just-in-time** (**jit**) compiler to accelerate its operation. It is compatible with NumPy, so you can accelerate your numerical computing code based on NumPy. You can also write flexible CUDA code in Python thanks to the jit compiler. CuPy is also NumPy compatible and accelerates linear algebra algorithms. It provides Pythonic programmability and transparent custom kernel programming, such as Numba. PyCUDA provides a CUDA C/C++ interface, so that you can write and use the CUDA kernel function in your Python code.

Numba – a high-performance Python compiler

Numba (`https://numba.pydata.org/`) translates Python functions for execution on the GPU without any C/C++ programming.

In Numba, you can easily write vectorized functions by applying the Numba decorator to the target function:

```
from numba import vectorize
@vectorize(["float32(float32, float32, float32)"], target='cuda')
def saxpy(scala, a, b):
return scala * a + b
```

As you can see, the decorator specifies the parameters and return data types, and the target specifies which architecture that code will operate. There are three kinds of targets:

Target	Description	Recommended data size and operation
cuda	Targeting NVIDIA GPU	Larger than 1 MB, compute-intensive operation
parallel	Optimized for multi-core CPU	Less than 1 MB, normal operation
cpu	Optimized for single thread operation	Less than 1 KB, low compute-intensive operation

If your function does not return a value, use @guvectorize, and specify the parameter as the vectors.

Another use of Numba is with the @cuda.jit decorator. This enables you to write CUDA-specific operations like the following:

```
from numba import cuda

@cuda.jit
def matmul(d_c, d_a, d_b):
    x, y = cuda.grid(2)
    if (x < d_c.shape[0] and y < d_c.shape[1]):
        sum = 0
        for k in range(d_a.shape[1]):
            sum += d_a[x, k] * d_b[k, y]
        d_c[x, y] = sum
```

The cuda.grid() keyword provides the CUDA threads index in grid-level, so that you can write the kernel code, such as CUDA C/C++ code, in the Python way. Calling the CUDA kernel function can be done as follows:

```
matmul[dimGrid, dimBlock](d_c, d_a, d_b)
```

Now, let's install this package and try some examples.

Installing Numba

To use Numba in your Python code, you need to install the package, and configure the environment variables:

```
$ pip3 install numba
$ export NUMBAPRO_NVVM=/usr/local/cuda/nvvm/lib64/libnvvm.so
$ export NUMBAPRO_LIBDEVICE=/usr/local/cuda/nvvm/libdevice/
```

You would need to put the environment variable settings at the end of .bashrc or .zshrc, for the ease of future use. If they are not set, Python will return this message:

```
numba.cuda.cudadrv.error.NvvmSupportError: libNVVM cannot be found. Do
`conda install cudatoolkit`:
library nvvm not found
```

Using Numba with the @vectorize decorator

We will test the `@vectorize` decorator with a simple `saxpy` operation. This converts a specific function to work in parallel:

1. Create `numba_saxpy.py`.

2. Import `numba`, `numpy`, and any other required packages:

   ```
   import numpy as np
   from numba import vectorize
   from timeit import default_timer as timer
   ```

3. Write a `saxpy` code with the `@vectorize` decorator and target with `'cuda'` in order to work on a CUDA device:

   ```
   @vectorize(["float32(float32, float32, float32)"], target='cuda')
   def saxpy_cuda(scala, a, b):
       return scala * a + b
   ```

4. Write a saxpy code with the `@vecotrize` decorator and target with `'parallel'` to work on a multi-core processor (host):

   ```
   @vectorize(["float32(float32, float32, float32)"],
   target='parallel')
   def saxpy_host(scala, a, b):
       return scala * a + b
   ```

5. Write an operation code to call the functions with some NumPy-generated input data:

   ```
   scala = 2.0
   np.random.seed(2019)
   print("size \t\t CUDA \t\t CPU")
   for i in range(16,20):
       N = 1 << i
       a = np.random.rand(N).astype(np.float32)
       b = np.random.rand(N).astype(np.float32)
       c = np.zeros(N, dtype=np.float32)

       # warm-up
       c = saxpy_cuda(scala, a, b)

       # measuring execution time
       start = timer()
       c = saxpy_host(scala, a, b)
       elapsed_time_host= (timer() - start) * 1e3
   ```

```
start = timer()
c = saxpy_cuda(scala, a, b)
elapsed_time_cuda = (timer() - start) * 1e3
print("[%d]: \t%.3f ms\t %.3f ms" % (N, elapsed_time_cuda,
elapsed_time_host))
```

This code reports the elapsed time with the various operand sizes:

```
size            CUDA            CPU
[65536]:      1.174 ms      0.199 ms
[131072]:     1.362 ms      0.201 ms
[262144]:     2.240 ms      0.284 ms
[524288]:     2.384 ms      0.337 ms
```

In this situation, CUDA shows slower performance than the CPU, because the operation is simple, but data transfer overhead is heavy.

Using Numba with the @cuda.jit decorator

We also can write sophisticated operations to work on the GPU with Numba using the `@cuda.jit` decorator:

1. Create `numba_matmul.py`.

2. Import `numpy`, `numba`, and any other required packages:

```
import numpy as np
from numba import cuda
from timeit import default_timer as timer
```

3. Write a matrix multiplication code with the `@cuda.jit` decorator:

```
@cuda.jit
def matmul(d_c, d_a, d_b):
    x, y = cuda.grid(2)
    if (x < d_c.shape[0] and y < d_c.shape[1]):
        sum = 0
        for k in range(d_a.shape[1]):
            sum += d_a[x, k] * d_b[k, y]
        d_c[x, y] = sum
```

In this code, we use `cuda.grid(dimension_size)` to specify the CUDA thread index among the grid, so, we can specify the index of the CUDA threads in Python.

4. Create the `a` and `b` matrices as a NumPy matrix:

```
N = 8192
a = np.random.rand(N, N).astype(np.float32)
b = np.random.rand(N, N).astype(np.float32)
```

5. Copy the NumP- generated data to the device:

```
d_a = cuda.to_device(a)
d_b = cuda.to_device(b)
```

6. Create the `c` matrix that will be placed in the CUDA device memory:

```
d_c = cuda.device_array((N, N))
```

7. Call the matrix multiplication kernel function:

```
start = timer()
matmul[dimGrid, dimBlock](d_c, d_a, d_b)
elapsed_time_gpu = (timer() - start) * 1e3
```

8. Copy the output to the host:

```
c = d_c.copy_to_host()
```

9. Compare the CUDA operation with the host:

```
# matrix multiplication (cpu)
start = timer()
c_host = np.matmul(a, b)
elapsed_time_cpu = (timer() - start) * 1e3

# print elapse times
print("Elapsed Time")
print("GPU: %.3f ms" % elapsed_time_gpu)
print("CPU: %.3f ms" % elapsed_time_cpu)

if (np.allclose(c_host, c)):
print("Done.")
else:
print("GPU and host results are mismatching.")
```

With a `@cuda.jit` decorator and the built-in `cuda.grid()` keywords, this sample code shows how simple it is to implement Numba into the matrix multiplication in Python. This code reports the operation-elapsed time on both the device and the host:

```
Elapsed Time
GPU: 104.694 ms
CPU: 1539.005 ms
Done.
```

Now, let's cover the CuPy that enables more Pythonic programming in CUDA programming.

CuPy – GPU accelerated Python matrix library

CuPy (`https://cupy.chainer.org`) enables linear algebra accelerations using Python and fully utilizes GPUs by using CUDA libraries. It is NumPy compatible and provides enjoyable Pythonic programmability.

Let's cover its installation, basic usage, and manual kernel developments.

Installing CuPy

We can use `pip` to install CuPy using the following command. Then it also installs the `cupy` package and the CUDA dependencies:

```
$ pip3 install cupy-cuda101    # CUDA 10.1
$ pip3 install cupy-cuda101    # CUDA 10.0
$ pip3 install cupy-cuda902    # CUDA 9.2
```

Now, let's cover the basic usage of CuPy.

Basic usage of CuPy

We can write a saxpy operation as follows:

```
>>> x = cp.arange(5).astype('f')
>>> x
array([0., 1., 2., 3., 4.], dtype=float32)
>>> y = cp.arange(5).astype('f')
>>> 0.5 * x + y
array([0. , 1.5, 3. , 4.5, 6. ], dtype=float32)
```

We also can use the `matmul()` function for the matrix multiplication as follows:

```
>>> x = cp.random.uniform(0, 1, (2, 4)).astype('float32')
>>> y = cp.random.uniform(0, 1, (4, 2)).astype('float32')
>>> cp.matmul(x, y)
array([[0.6514087, 0.826463 ],
       [0.7826104, 0.2878886]], dtype=float32)
```

As we discussed earlier, CuPy is compatible with NumPy. Basically, the previous CuPy's object is CuPy's array type:

```
>>> x = cp.random.uniform(0, 1, (2, 4)).astype('float32')
>>> type(x)
<class 'cupy.core.core.ndarray'>
```

However, we can convert that using the `cupy.asnumpy()` function to convert to the NumPy array as follows:

```
type(cp.asnumpy(x))
<class 'numpy.ndarray'>
```

The reverse is also available using `cupy.ascupy()` function. Therefore, we can do the following operation based on this compatibility:

```
>>> gpu = cp.random.uniform(0, 1, (2, 4)).astype('float32')
>>> cpu = np.random.uniform(0, 1, (2, 4)).astype('float32')
>>> gpu + cp.asarray(cpu)
array([[0.8649391 , 1.1412742 , 1.1280626 , 0.38262686],
       [0.44767308, 0.738155 , 0.8397665 , 1.5165564 ]], dtype=float32)
>>> cpu + cp.asnumpy(gpu)
array([[0.8649391 , 1.1412742 , 1.1280626 , 0.38262686],
       [0.44767308, 0.738155 , 0.8397665 , 1.5165564 ]], dtype=float32)
```

As you can see, we can easily switch the target computing process, and we can benefit from each platform's advantages. Now, let's cover the custom kernel implementation using CuPy.

Implementing custom kernel functions

CuPy provides three types of custom kernel function: elementwise, reduction and raw kernels. The elementwise kernel helps with the automatic indexing for each element. Therefore, we can just write an element's operation. The reduction kernel carries out the reduction operation, while also performing the user-defined operation. The raw kernel enables direct CUDA C/C++ kernel programming on Python codes, so that we can define any operation on it. In this section, we will not cover all of them. However, you can learn more from the relevant documentation—https://docs-cupy.chainer.org/en/stable/tutorial/kernel.html.

Let's discuss the user-defined elementwise kernel implementation. Here is an example of elementwise operation:

```
>>> squared_diff = cp.ElementwiseKernel(
...        'float32 x, float32 y',
...        'float32 z',
...        'z = (x - y) * (x - y)',
...        'squared_diff')
```

Then, we can do the elementwise operation without the explicit indexing operation:

```
>>> x = cp.random.uniform(0, 1, (2, 4)).astype('float32')
>>> y = cp.random.uniform(0, 1, (2, 4)).astype('float32')
>>> squared_diff(x, y)
array([[0.54103416, 0.01342529, 0.01425287, 0.67101586],
       [0.04841561, 0.09939388, 0.46790633, 0.00203693]], dtype=float32)
>>> squared_diff(x, 0.5)
array([[0.23652133, 0.22603741, 0.08065639, 0.00647551],
       [0.00029328, 0.07454127, 0.00666 , 0.18399356]], dtype=float32)
```

As you can see, CuPy provides a highly Pythonic interface and is easy to learn. There are lots of internal routines, which are also compatible with NumPy—https://docs-cupy.chainer.org/en/stable/reference/routines.html. In other words, we can consider using CuPy when we need accelerated computations in NumPy.

Now, we will cover PyCUDA, which provides direct kernel programming and implicit memory management wrappers.

PyCUDA – Pythonic access to CUDA API

PyCUDA (https://documen.tician.de/pycuda/) enables us to write CUDA C/C++ codes in Python codes, and execute them without compilation. In this way, you can write CUDA C/C++ codes that are CUDA-specific operations. But, you have to optimize this code yourself, since PyCUDA doesn't optimize your kernel functions.

This is a snippet of code that was produced using PyCUDA:

```python
import pycuda.autoinit      # initialize CUDA devices
from pycuda import driver, compiler, gpuarray
from string import Template

kernel_code_template = Template("""
__global__ void matmul_kernel(float *d_C, float *d_A, float *d_B)
{
    int idx_x = blockIdx.x * blockDim.x + threadIdx.x;
    ...
}
""")

mod = compiler.SourceModule(kernel_code_template.substitute(MATRIX_SIZE=N))
matmul_kernel = mod.get_function("matmul_kernel")
matmul_kernel(driver.Out(C), driver.In(A), driver.In(B), block=(dimBlock,
dimBlock, 1), grid=(dimGrid, dimGrid))
```

As you can see in this code, we can write the kernel code using the same Python code. We also can retain signs of required data transfer using `driver.In()` and `driver.Out()`. These indicate that PyCUDA should transfer the data before invoking the kernel. The data transfers automatically, and we also can transfer the data as follows:

```python
d_A = driver.to_device(A) # cudaMemcpyHostToDevice
A = driver.from_device_like(d_A) # cudaMemcpyDeviceToHost
```

Now, let's install PyCUDA and try some simple examples.

Installing PyCUDA

To use PyCUDA, you also need to install the package. Download the PyCUDA source file from the website (`https://pypi.org/project/pycuda/`). At the moment, version 2019.1.1 is in use.

Then install the dependencies as follows:

```
$ sudo apt-get install build-essential python-dev python-setuptools
libboost-python-dev libboost-thread-dev

$ tar -xzf pycuda-2019.1.2.tar.gz
$ cd pycuda-2019.1.2
$ python3 ./configure.py --cuda-root=/usr/local/cuda --cudadrv-lib-
dir=/usr/lib \
    --boost-inc-dir=/usr/include --boost-lib-dir=/usr/lib \
    --boost-python-libname=boost_python-py36 --boost-thread-
libname=boost_thread
$ python3 setup.py build
$ sudo python3 setup.py install
```

If you want to use Python 2, skip using Python 3 for the `configure.py` command. The configuration command can be different depending on your Python version.

Matrix multiplication using PyCUDA

We can perform matrix multiplication using PyCUDA in the following manner:

1. Create a `pycuda_matmul.py` file.

2. Import the required packages as follows:

```
import pycuda.autoinit
from pycuda import driver, compiler, gpuarray
import numpy as np
from string import Template
import timeit
```

3. Write a CUDA kernel function code:

```
kernel_code_template = Template("""
__global__ void matmul_kernel(float *d_C, float *d_A, float *d_B)
{
    int idx_x = blockIdx.x * blockDim.x + threadIdx.x;
    int idx_y = blockIdx.y * blockDim.y + threadIdx.y;
```

```
        float sum = 0.f;
        for (int e = 0; e < ${MATRIX_SIZE}; e++)
            sum += d_A[idx_y * ${MATRIX_SIZE} + e] * d_B[e *
${MATRIX_SIZE} + idx_x];
        d_C[idx_y * ${MATRIX_SIZE} + idx_x] = sum;
    }
""")
```

4. Generate input/output matrices using NumPy:

```
N = 8192
np.random.seed(2019)
A = np.random.rand(N, N).astype(np.float32)
B = np.random.rand(N, N).astype(np.float32)
C = np.zeros((N, N), dtype=np.float32)
```

5. Compile the kernel code:

```
mod = compiler.SourceModule( \
        kernel_code_template.substitute(MATRIX_SIZE=N))
```

6. Get the kernel function from the compiled module:

```
matmul_kernel = mod.get_function("matmul_kernel")
```

7. Create device memories with the input data that is generated from the host:

```
d_A = gpuarray.to_gpu(A)
d_B = gpuarray.to_gpu(B)
d_C = gpuarray.zeros((N, N), dtype=np.float32)
```

8. Configure the grid and block dimensions:

```
dimBlock = 16
dimGrid = int((N + dimBlock - 1) / dimBlock)
```

9. Prepare to get the GPU events:

```
start = driver.Event()
stop = driver.Event()
```

10. Call the kernel function:

```
print("Started GPU operation...")
start.record()

matmul_kernel(d_C, d_A, d_B,
    block=(dimBlock, dimBlock, 1),
    grid=(dimGrid, dimGrid))
```

```
stop.record()
stop.synchronize()
gpu_time = stop.time_since(start)
print("GPU Execution Time: %.3f ms" % (gpu_time))
```

11. Launch the matrix multiplication from the host, and compare this with the result from the device:

```
print("Started Host operation...")
start = timeit.default_timer()
c_host = np.matmul(A, B)
host_time = timeit.default_timer() - start

print("CPU Execution Time: %.3f ms" % (host_time * 1e3))

if (np.allclose(c_host, d_C.get())):
    print("Done.")
else:
    print("GPU and host results are mismatching.")
```

This code also reports an estimated time on the device and the host:

```
Started GPU operation...
GPU Execution Time: 657.547 ms
Started Host operation...
CPU Execution Time: 1531.133 ms
Done.
```

While PyCUDA exposes the CUDA C/C++ kernel code, this result gives a hint that manual kernel optimization is required, due to the lack of performance against the operation that was carried out by Numba.

NVBLAS for zero coding acceleration in Octave and R

NVBLAS is a CUDA library for the BLAS operation for other packages, such as Octave and R. By replacing the operations carried out OpenBLAS, the Octave or developers and data scientists can easily enjoy GPU performance. In this chapter, we will cover how to accelerate Octave and R using NVBLAS.

NVBLAS is a dynamic library on top of the cuBLAS operation. The cuBLAS library is a GPU implementation of linear algebra operations. It replaces BLAS libraries, so that we can easily accelerate any application with zero coding effort. Let's see how this can be done from GEMM example codes.

Configuration

To use NVBLAS in Octave and R, we need to provide some working environment variables to NVBLAS. To do this, let's create an nvblas.conf file, where the directory, which we will work with Octave and R code examples, can be found. The nvblas.conf file can be written as follows:

```
NVBLAS_CPU_BLAS_LIB libopenblas.so
NVBLAS_LOGFILE nvblas.log
NVBLAS_GPU_LIST 0
NVBLAS_AUTOPIN_MEM_ENABLED
```

In this file, we can see that NVBLAS needs to be aware of the CPU side's BLAS library. We will use OpenBLAS in this session, so we need to install it with the following command in Ubuntu:

```
$ sudo apt-get install libopenblas-base libopenblas-dev
```

Also, we can get a multi-GPU performance by providing multiple GPU IDs for NVBLAS_GPU_LIST. This book provides results from a GPU execution result, but try to provide multiple IDs if you have multiple GPUs.

To use NVBLAS in Octave and R, we should set an environment—LD_PRELOAD=libnvblas.so—with your application execution:

- For Octave code, execute your code as follows:

```
$ LD_PRELOAD=libnvblas.so octave sgemm.m
```

- For the R script, execute your script as follows:

```
$ LD_PRELOAD=libnvblas.so Rscript sgemm.R
```

Of course, the `libnvblas.so` file should be accessible from the working directory. It is located in `/usr/local/cuda/lib64/`.

NVBLAS is compatible with the archived packages. Therefore, using Octave- and R-installed ones with the following commands works well with our test:

```
$ sudo apt-get install octave # for octave installation
$ sudo apt-get install r-base # for R installation
```

Now, let's try using NVBLAS using the Octave and R languages.

Accelerating Octave's computation

First, we will try NVBLAS using Octave. The fully implemented code is `08_nvblas/sgemm.m`. This is implemented as follows:

```
for i = 1:5
    N = 512*(2^i);
    A = single(rand(N,N));
    B = single(rand(N,N));
    start = clock();
    C = A * B;
    elapsedTime = etime(clock(), start);
    gFlops = 2*N*N*N/(elapsedTime * 1e+9);
    printf("Elapsed Time [%d]: %.3f ms, %.3f GFlops\n", N, elapsedTime,
gFlops);
end
```

For the GPU operation, execute the Octave script using the following command, and compare the performance with GPU, with the NVBLAS environment library and CPU by default:

```
$ LD_PRELOAD=libnvblas.so octave sgemm.m
```

Then, we can launch this with the `octave sgemm.m` command. The output results are as follows:

CPU	GPU V100
•Elapsed Time [1024]: 0.011 ms, 188.909 GFlops	•Elapsed Time [1024]: 0.010 ms, 208.346 GFlops
•Elapsed Time [2048]: 0.075 ms, 228.169 GFlops	•Elapsed Time [2048]: 0.024 ms, 721.731 GFlops
•Elapsed Time [4096]: 0.212 ms, 647.022 GFlops	•Elapsed Time [4096]: 0.094 ms, 1465.538 GFlops
•Elapsed Time [8192]: 1.158 ms, 949.763 GFlops	•Elapsed Time [8192]: 0.582 ms, 1889.193 GFlops
•Elapsed Time [16384]: 7.292 ms, 1206.241 GFlops	•Elapsed Time [16384]: 4.472 ms, 1967.037 GFlops

As you can see, GPU shows higher computational throughput as the matrices' size get larger.

Accelerating R's compuation

Now, we will try NVBLAS for the R language, with the help of the following steps:

1. First, let's write a `sgemm.R` file which carries out a dot operation:

```
set.seed(2019)
for(i in seq(1:5)) {
    N = 512*(2^i)
    A = matrix(rnorm(N^2, mean=0, sd=1), nrow=N)
    B = matrix(rnorm(N^2, mean=0, sd=1), nrow=N)
    elapsedTime = system.time({C = A %*% B})[3]
    gFlops = 2*N*N*N/(elapsedTime * 1e+9);
    print(sprintf("Elapsed Time [%d]: %3.3f ms, %.3f GFlops", N,
elapsedTime, gFlops))
}
```

2. Execute the R script using the following command and compare the performance:

```
$ LD_PRELOAD=libnvblas.so Rscript sgemm.R
```

The sample code operates several times, while increasing the data size. The following table shows the outputs of the previous commands:

CPU	GPU V100
• Elapsed Time [1024]: 0.029 ms, 74.051 GFlops	• Elapsed Time [1024]: 0.034 ms, 63.161 GFlops
• Elapsed Time [2048]: 0.110 ms, 156.181 GFlops	• Elapsed Time [2048]: 0.063 ms, 272.696 GFlops
• Elapsed Time [4096]: 0.471 ms, 291.802 GFlops	• Elapsed Time [4096]: 0.286 ms, 480.556 GFlops
• Elapsed Time [8192]: 2.733 ms, 402.309 GFlops	• Elapsed Time [8192]: 1.527 ms, 720.047 GFlops
• Elapsed Time [16384]: 18.291 ms, 480.897 GFlops	• Elapsed Time [16384]: 9.864 ms, 891.737 GFlops

From the results, we can see the performance gap between the CPU and GPU. Also, we are able to identify that the performance gain of GPU increases when we increase the sample size.

If you are interested in R acceleration with GPU, please visit an NVIDIA development blog: https://devblogs.nvidia.com/accelerate-r-applications-cuda/

CUDA acceleration in MATLAB

MATLAB is a productive, high-level numerical analysis tool with various tools and functions. This tool supports CUDA from the early stages with their **Parallel Computing Toolbox**. This section will show us how to generate CUDA code using this tool.

To enable GPU acceleration, we need to install MATLAB with the Parallel Computing Toolbox. If you already have MATLAB, check if your license covers the Parallel Computing Toolbox. If you don't, you can try the MATLAB evaluation code. From MATLAB's evaluation site, you may download any kind of package, except the control systems. Most packages contain the Parallel Computing Toolbox, so you may try this. But if you are not considering using MATLAB, you may skip this section.

When we use MATLAB code to work on GPU, you need to create a device memory using gpuArray. In the same way that *Numba* and *PyCUDA* send their host data to the device, MATLAB's gpuArray() creates a device memory and transfers the given host data to the device:

```
d_A = gpuArray(A);
```

This session will assume that you have already installed MATLAB and the Parallel Computing Toolbox. In this section, we will focus on implementing the sample code, and compare the performances of the host and GPU:

1. Let's write a host.m file, which can work on the CPU. The code is as follows:

```
N = 8192;
A = single(rand(N,N));
B = single(rand(N,N));

start = clock();
C = A * B;
elapsedTime = etime(clock(), start);
gFlops = 2*N*N*N/(elapsedTime * 1e+9);
fprintf("Elapsed Time: %.3f ms, %.3f GFlops\n", elapsedTime,
gFlops);
```

Now, let's execute both implementations with the following commands. This is the command to MATLAB, and its output:

```
$ matlab -r "run('host.m'); exit;" -nodisplay
Elapsed Time: 6.421 ms, 171.243 Gflops
```

2. Then, let's write a cuda.m file, which works on the GPU. We just apply gpuArray() to the input matrices as follows:

```
N = 8192;
A = single(rand(N,N));
B = single(rand(N,N));
d_A = gpuArray(A);      'GPU memory allocation
d_B = gpuArray(B);      'GPU memory allocation
start = clock();
d_C = d_A * d_B;
elapsedTime = etime(clock(), start);
gFlops = 2*N*N*N/(elapsedTime * 1e+9);
fprintf("Elapsed Time: %.3f ms, %.3f GFlops\n", elapsedTime,
gFlops);
```

This is the GPU version execution code, and the execution result:

```
$ matlab -r "run('cuda.m'); exit;" -nodisplay
Elapsed Time: 0.179 ms, 6140.739 Gflops.
```

As we can see, GPU shows a higher performance against the CPU.

MathWorks provides plenty of examples of GPU computing with MATLAB. Please visit their site if you want to learn more: `https://www.mathworks.com/examples/parallel-computing/category/gpu-computing`.

Summary

In this chapter, we have covered the CUDA programming methods using CUDA libraries, and other compatible languages. We have also covered the basic use of cuBLAS and its mixed-precision operation feature. Also, we explored the cuRAND, cuFFT, NPP, and OpenCV libraries. Thanks to these libraries, we could implement GPU applications with little effort, as discussed at the beginning of the chapter.

We have implemented some GPU applications using other languages that are compatible with CUDA. Firstly, we covered several Python packages, which enable Python and CUDA interops. They provide Pythonic programmabilities and compatibilities with other Python features. Then, we covered CUDA accelerations in other scientific computing languages, such as Octave, R, and MATLAB.

Now, we have one more GPU programming method to cover—OpenACC. With this we can covert the original C/C++ and Fortran host codes to work on GPUs using directives such as `#pragma acc kernels`. We will cover this in the next chapter.

GPU Programming Using OpenACC

9

Every processor architecture provides different approaches to writing code to run on the processor. CUDA is no exception; it also provides different approaches to coding. One such approach, which has become very popular in recent years, is making use of OpenACC, which fundamentally is directive-based programming.

OpenACC is basically a standard which exposes heterogeneous computing as a first-class citizen. The standard fundamentally dictates that there are two kinds of processor, that is, a host and a device/accelerator, which is very similar to the concepts that the CUDA programming model states.

CUDA programming, using languages such as C, C++, Fortran, and Python, is the preferred way to express parallelism for programmers who want to get the best performance. Programming languages require a programmer to recreate their sequential program from scratch, while maintaining both serial and parallel versions of their key operations. Programmers can micromanage everything about their program and often use device-specific features, which are too specific for higher-level approaches, to achieve the best performance. Parallel programs created in a parallel programming language tend to only work on a very small number of platforms.

Compiler directives blend the flexibility of programming languages with the easy use of libraries. The programmer annotates the code with high-level instructions that a compiler can use to parallelize the code, or can safely ignore. This means that code with compiler directives can be compiled for many different parallel platforms, and there's no need to maintain separate serial and parallel versions of the code. Also, there is sometimes a need to quickly test and prototype an application to run on a GPU. One such example is converting code bases such as weather code, which has millions of lines of code, to run on a GPU; doing this using popular languages will take a lot of effort. In such a scenario, OpenACC becomes a logical choice. In OpenACC the developers provide hints to the compiler in the form of directives. The compiler takes these hints and generates an architecture-specific accelerator code.

The OpenACC standard also provides vendor neutrality to the developers of code. Single-source code with OpenACC directives can be recompiled for different devices. For example, the PGI compiler currently supports OpenACC backends such as Intel CPU multi-core, NVIDIA GPU, Intel Xeon Phi, and **Field-Programmable Gate Array (FPGA)** / **Application Specific Integrated Circuit (ASIC)** architectures. This is a really attractive proposition to developers who want to write vendor-neutral code. Key applications in **high-processing computing (HPC)** such as **Vienna Ab-initio Simulation Package (VASP)** (molecular dynamics/quantum chemistry), **Weather Research and Forecasting (WRF)**, and ANSYS Fluent **Computational Fluid Dynamics (CFD)** make use of the OpenACC programming model to target the NVIDIA GPU.

To summarize the key takeaways for OpenACC:

- The OpenACC standard was developed when heterogeneous computing was considered to be the new programming model.
- OpenACC provides performance portability across various accelerators.
- OpenACC is not an alternative to the CUDA programming language. When the targeted processor is chosen as NVIDIA, the OpenACC compilers generate CUDA code behind the scenes.

In recent years, the OpenMP standard has also started incorporating heterogeneous computing APIs. But to date, there is no compiler that supports different processor architectures, and so we have chosen with stick to OpenACC in this book.

We will cover the following topics in this chapter:

- OpenACC directives
- Asynchronous programming in OpenACC
- Additional important directives and clauses

Technical requirements

A Linux/Windows PC with a modern NVIDIA GPU (Pascal architecture onward) is required for this chapter.

As mentioned in the introduction, OpenACC is a standard and this standard is implemented by different compilers such as the GCC, PGI, and CRAY compilers. The compiler that we will be using for this chapter is PGI. The PGI compiler has been really popular in the Fortran community and has always been ahead of the curve in implementing the OpenACC latest specifications, and it provides a community edition, which can be downloaded from the PGI website for free. The good part is that fundamentally there is no change in functionality between the community edition and a paid-for version of the PGI compiler. For this chapter, you will be required to download the PGI community edition.

This chapter's code is also available on GitHub at: `https://github.com/PacktPublishing/Learn-CUDA-Programming`.

Sample code examples are developed and tested with version 19.4 of the PGI community edition. But it is recommended you use the latest PGI version.

Image merging on a GPU using OpenACC

In order to understand the OpenACC concept, we have chosen a simple computer vision algorithm for merging two images. Fundamentally in this code, we are trying to merge two images, shown as follows:

The preceding image demonstrates a computer vision algorithm merging two images.

We will talk more about the code structure later in the chapter. To start, configure the environment according to the following steps:

1. Prepare your GPU application. As an example, we will use a kernel algorithm for merging two images. This code can be found at `09_openacc/`.
2. Compile your application with the `pgc++` compiler:

```
$ pgc++ -c -acc -ta=tesla:pinned scrImagePgmPpmPackage.cpp
$ pgc++ -c -acc -ta=tesla:pinned -Minfo=accel image_merging.cpp
$ pgc++ -o merging.out -acc -ta=tesla:pinned -Minfo=accel
scrImagePgmPpmPackage.o image_merging.o
$ ./merging.out
```

The preceding commands will create a binary named `blurring.out`. As you might have observed we are using the `pgc++` compiler to compile our code. Also, we pass a few arguments to our code. Let's understand them in more detail:

- `-acc`: This flag tells the compiler to parse the OpenACC directives provided in the code.
- `-ta`: Stands for the target architecture that the device code should be generated for. Note that `-ta=tesla` means we are targeting a NVIDIA GPU. Some examples of other targets include `-ta=multi-core`, which targets multi-core as the device, `-ta=radeaon`, which targets AMD GPUs, and a few others. Additionally, we can add device-specific flags; for example, we added a pinned flag to a GPU that allocates all CPU memory as pinned (non-pageable).
- `-Minfo`: This option tells the compiler to provide us with more information about steps taken by the compiler to make our code parallel. By saying `-Minfo-accel`, we are asking the compiler to provide us with more information related to the accelerator region only. We can change the flag to `-Minfo=all` to provide details of the non-accelerator region also. The following output shows part of the output of adding a `Minfo` flag to our code:

```
.... < More compiler output above>
merge_parallel_pragma(unsigned char *, unsigned char *, unsigned
char *, long, long):
     30, Generating copyin(in1[:w*h])
     Generating copyout(out[:w*h])
     Generating copyin(in2[:w*h])
     Accelerator kernel generated
     Generating Tesla code
     30, #pragma acc loop gang /* blockIdx.x */
     32, #pragma acc loop vector(128) /* threadIdx.x */
```

```
        32, Loop is parallelizable
   ... < More compile output below >
```

To understand this compilation output, we need to understand OpenACC pragmas, which we will do in the next section. We will revisit this compilation output later. Further details on other available flags can be found using `pgc++ --help`.

The sample output after running the binary is as follows:

```
$ ./merging.out
Reading image width height and width [1536][2048]
Time taken for serial merge: 0.0028 seconds
Time taken for OpenACC merge(data+kernel): 0.0010 seconds
Time taken for OpenACC merge(kernel only) with Blocking: 0.0002 seconds
        Time taken for OpenACC merge(data _kernel) with blocking: 0.0014
seconds
Time taken for OpenACC merge (data+kernel)with Pipeline Async: 0.0008
seconds
```

The preceding output shows that we are reading an image of size 1536*2048. The code has one serial implementation and three parallel implementations using OpenACC pragmas. The timings of each of the implementations are shown in the preceding output. The last implementation with the pipeline approach shows the best timing: `0.0008 seconds`. We will take an incremental approach and go into the details of each implementation in the next sections.

The serial implementation of this algorithm is very simple, and shown in the following code snippet:

```
void merge_serial(unsigned char *in1, unsigned char*in2, unsigned char
*out, long w, long h)
{
    long x, y;
    for(y = 0; y < h; y++) {
        for(x = 0; x < w; x++) {
            out[y * w + x] = (in1[y * w + x]+in2[y * w + x])/2;
        }
    }
}
```

There is nothing fancy about the code; basically, it takes two input image data (`in1` and `in2`), performs the average operation to merge both inputs, and finally stores the output. The key thing for us, with respect to parallelism, is that the loop is embarrassingly parallel and suitable for architecture such as GPUs. As shown in the preceding code output, serial implementation took `0.0028` seconds. Please note that the timings may vary slightly, based on the system that you are running the code on.

In the next section, we will introduce you to the OpenACC directives necessary to convert the sample code to run on a GPU.

OpenACC directives

In this section, we will try to understand the syntax of OpenACC pragmas, and implement basic parallel and data directives for the merge operation. The basic syntax of the OpenACC pragma is as follows:

```
#pragma acc <directive> <clauses>
!$acc parallel [clause [[,] clause]...]
```

The preceding command is explained as follows:

- `#pragma` in C/C++ is what's known as a "compiler hint." These are very similar to programmer comments; however, the compiler will actually read our pragmas. If the compiler does not understand the pragma, it can ignore it, rather than throw a syntax error.
- `acc` is an addition to our pragma. It specifies that this is an OpenACC pragma. Any non-OpenACC compiler will ignore this pragma.
- `directive` is a command in OpenACC that will tell the compiler to perform some operation. For now, we will only use directives that allow the compiler to parallelize our code.
- `clauses` are additions/alterations to our directives. These include, but are not limited to, optimizations.

There are three directives we will cover in this section: *parallel*, *loop*, and *data*. We will showcase each of them and finally apply them to our merge algorithm.

Parallel and loop directives

The parallel directive is the most straightforward of the directives. It will mark a region of the code for parallelization (this usually only involves parallelizing a single `for` loop), as shown in the following code:

```
#pragma acc parallel loop
for (int i = 0; i < N; i++ ) {
    //loop code
}
```

We may also define a parallel region. The parallel region may have multiple loops (though this is often not recommended!). The parallel region is everything contained within the outer most curly braces, as shown in the following code snippet:

```
#pragma acc parallel
{
    #pragma acc loop
    for (int i = 0; i < N; i++ )
    {
        < loop code >
    }
}
```

It is extremely important to include the loop; otherwise, you will not be parallelizing the loop properly. The parallel directive tells the compiler to parallelize the code redundantly, shown as follows:

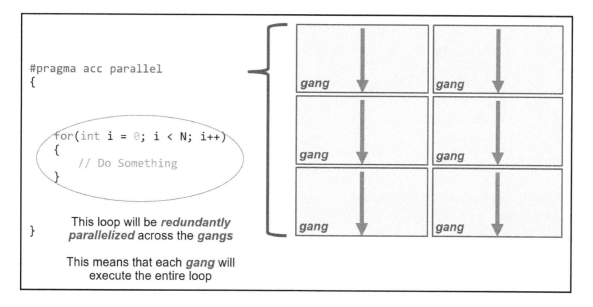

The loop directive specifically tells the compiler that we want the loop parallelized, as shown in the following screenshot:

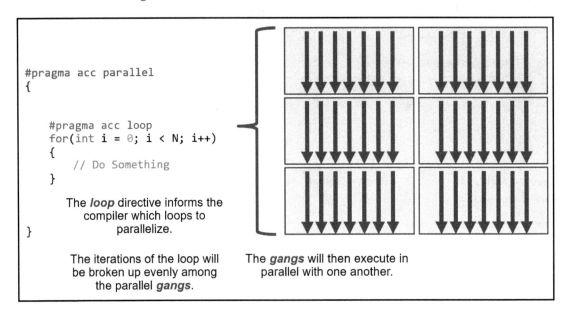

```
#pragma acc parallel
{

    #pragma acc loop
    for(int i = 0; i < N; i++)
    {
        // Do Something
    }
```

The *loop* directive informs the compiler which loops to parallelize.

```
}
```

The iterations of the loop will be broken up evenly among the parallel *gangs*.

The *gangs* will then execute in parallel with one another.

The loop directive has two major uses:

- To mark a single loop for parallelization
- To allow us to explicitly define optimizations/alterations for the loop

We will cover loop optimizations later on in the chapter, along with gang and vector; for now, we will focus on the parallelization aspect. For the loop directive to work properly, it must be contained within the parallel directive:

```
#pragma acc parallel loop
for (int i = 0; i < N; i++ )
{
    //loop code
}
```

When using the parallel directive, you must include the loop directive for the code to function properly. We may also use the loop directive to parallelize multidimensional loop nests. In the following code snippet, we see a nested loop and we mention the loop clause explicitly for the second loop:

```
#pragma acc parallel loop
for (int i = 0; i < N; i++ )
{
    #pragma acc loop
    for( int j = 0; j < M; j++ )
    {
        //loop code
    }
}
```

Note that, in the preceding code snippet, we do not put the parallel clause again in the inner loop as we have already mentioned it in the scope that starts from the outer loop.

Data directive

The OpenACC parallel model states that we have a host, which runs our sequential code (mostly it would be a CPU). Then we have our device, which is some sort of parallel hardware. The host and device usually (though not always) have separate memories, and the programmer can use OpenACC to move data between the two memories.

As discussed in the first chapter, the GPU and CPU architectures are fundamentally different. The GPU, being a throughput-based architecture, has a high number of computational units along with high-speed memory bandwidth. The CPU, on the other hand, is a latency-reducing architecture, has a large cache hierarchy, and also provides a large main memory. Any data that needs to be operated on needs to be first copied to the GPU memory. (Note that even in the case of unified memory the data gets copied behind the scenes in the form of pages by the driver.)

As illustrated in the following diagram, the data transfer between the two architectures (CPU and GPU) happens via an I/O bus:

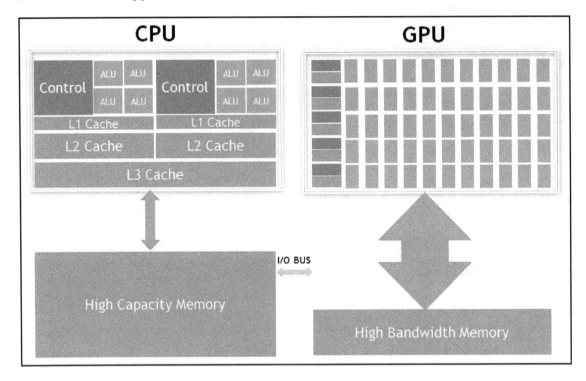

Our goal when using a GPU as the target architecture in OpenACC is to only use it to offload our parallel code, and the sequential code will continue to run on our CPU. The OpenACC standard allows the programmer to explicitly define data management by using the OpenACC **data directive and data clauses**. Data clauses allow the programmer to specify data transfers between the host and device (or, in our case, the CPU and the GPU).

Implicit data management: We can leave the transfer of data to the compiler as shown in the following example:

```
int *A = (int*) malloc(N * sizeof(int));

#pragma acc parallel loop
for( int i = 0; i < N; i++ )
{
    A[i] = 0;
}
```

In the preceding code, the compiler will understand that the A vector needs to be copied from the GPU, and generate an implicit transfer for the developer.

Explicit data management: It is good practice to make use of explicit data transfers to gain more control over the transfers, as shown in the following code where we are using the copy data clause:

```
int *a = (int*) malloc(N * sizeof(int));
#pragma acc parallel loop copy(a[0:N])
for( int i = 0; i < N; i++ )
{
    a[i] = 0;
}
```

In the preceding code snippet we make use of the copy data clause. The following diagram explains the steps executed when runtime reached the copy data directive:

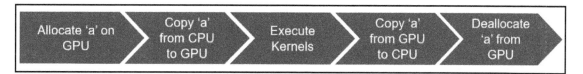

We will go into the details of these steps with the help of the merge code where we will be applying the data clauses.

Other available data clauses are as listed as follows:

Data clause	Description	Key usage
copy(list)	• Allocates memory on the device • Copies data from the host to the device when entering the region • Copies data to the host when exiting the region	This is the default for input data structures that are modified and then returned from function
copyin(list)	• Allocates memory on the device • Copies data from the host to the device when entering the region	Vectors that are just input to a subroutine

copyout (list)	• Allocates memory on the device • Copies data to the host when exiting the region	A result that doesn't overwrite the input data structure
create(list)	• Only allocates memory on the device • No copy is made	Temporary arrays

To maximize performance, the programmer should avoid all unnecessary data transfers, and hence explicit memory management is preferred over implicit data management.

Array shaping: Array shaping is how you specify the size of the array. If you do not specify a shape, then the compiler will try to assume the size. This works well in Fortran, since Fortran tracks the size of the array; however, it will most likely not work in C/C++. Array shaping is also the only way to copy a portion of data from the array (for example, if you only need to copy half of the array, this can be a performance boost, cutting out unnecessary copies), as shown in the following code snippet:

```
#pragma acc parallel loop copy(A[1:N-2])
```

This would copy all of the elements of A except for the first and last elements.

Applying the parallel, loop, and data directive to merge image code

Let's now try to apply the parallel, loop, and data directive to the merge sequential code:

```
void merge_parallel_pragma(unsigned char *in1, unsigned char*in2,unsigned
char *out, long w, long h)
{
    long x, y;
    #pragma acc parallel loop gang copyin(in1[:h*w],
                                          in2[:h*w])
                                    copyout(out[:h*w])
    for(y = 0; y < h; y++) {
        #pragma acc loop vector
        for(x = 0; x < w; x++) {
            out[y * w + x] = (in1[y * w + x]+in2[y * w + x])/2;
        }
    }
}
```

We have made both the loops (height: y and width: x) parallel using the parallel loop directive. Also, we have explicitly added data clauses to copy the data. Note that, since the `in1` and `in2` vectors are input only, they are copied using the `copyin()` data clause. The `out` vector is the output and is copied using the `copyout()` data clause. Let's try to understand the compiler output for this function:

```
merge_parallel_pragma(unsigned char *, unsigned char *, unsigned char *,
long, long):
    30, Generating copyin(in1[:w*h])
        Generating copyout(out[:w*h])
        Generating copyin(in2[:w*h])
        Accelerator kernel generated
        Generating Tesla code
        30, #pragma acc loop gang /* blockIdx.x */
        32, #pragma acc loop vector(128) /* threadIdx.x */
    32, Loop is parallelizable
```

The preceding compiler output shows that for the `merge_parallel_pragma` function the following actions have been generated by the compiler:

- At line 30, `copyin` was generated for the `in1` and `in2` variables. The array size copied to the GPU before the kernel launch will be `[0:w*h]`.
- At line 30, `copyout` was generated for the `out` variable. The array size that will be copied after the GPU kernel launch will be `[0:w*h]`.
- At lines 30 and 32, Tesla kernel code was generated:
  - At line 30, the outer loop was parallelized with gang-level parallelism.
  - At line 32, the inner loop was parallelized with vector-level parallelism

When the code is run on V100, the time taken by this whole kernel is `0.0010s`. This is basically approximately twice as fast as the serial code. This may not sound impressive. The reason for that is that most time is spent on data transfers rather than kernel computation. In order to confirm this, let's make use of `nvprof`:

```
$ nvprof ./merging.out
==26601== DoneProfiling application: ./merging.out
==26601== Profiling result:
Type Time(%) Time Calls Avg Min Max Name
GPU activities: 67.36% 609.41us 2 304.71us 286.34us 323.08us [CUDA memcpy
HtoD]
27.63% 250.02us 1 250.02us 250.02us 250.02us [CUDA memcpy DtoH]
5.01% 45.344us 1 45.344us 45.344us 45.344us
merge_parallel_pragma_30_gpu(unsigned char*, unsigned char*, unsigned
```

```
char*, long, long)
...
```

As you can observe in the preceding profiling output, 94% of the time is spent on data transfers while only 5% of the time (45 microseconds) is spent on kernel execution. The query you might have is: How do I know which kernel this is? If you look closely at the name of the GPU kernel, `merge_parallel_pragma_30_gpu`, the PGI compiler generated a CUDA kernel in the `merge_parallel_pragma` function at line 30, and that is how we can relate it back to the pragmas that put in a function at that line number.

So we know the problem, but what about the solution? The optimization technique that we will use to hide this latency is blocking. We will cover more about the blocking technique, and using the asynchronous clause to overlap this transfer, in upcoming sections.

Asynchronous programming in OpenACC

In order to achieve better performance for merging parallel code, we will make use of a concept called blocking. Blocking basically means that, rather than transferring the whole input and output arrays in one shot, we can create blocks of the array which can be transferred and operated in parallel. The following diagram demonstrates creating blocks and overlapping data transfers with the kernel execution:

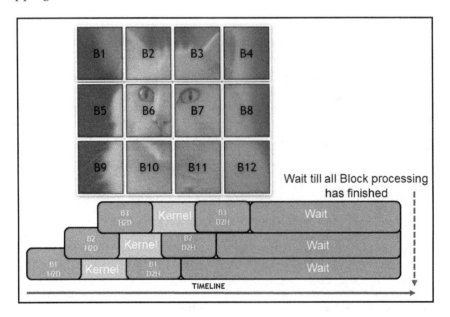

The preceding diagram shows that different blocks are transferred and the kernel execution of these blocks can be independent of each block. In order for this to happen, we need the data transfer commands and kernel calls to be fired and executed asynchronously. In order to achieve blocking, we will be introducing more directives/clauses in this section: the structured/unstructured data directive and `async` clause. We will showcase each of them and finally apply them to our basic OpenACC merge parallel code.

Structured data directive

The OpenACC data directives allow the programmer to explicitly manage the data on the device (in our case, the GPU). The following code snippet shows an example of marking a structured data region:

```
< Initialize data on host (CPU) >
#pragma acc data < data clauses >
{
    //< Code >
}
```

Device memory allocation happens at the beginning of the region, and device memory deallocation happens at the end of the region. Additionally, any data movement from the host to the device (CPU to GPU) happens at the beginning of the region, and any data movement from the device to the host (GPU to CPU) happens at the end of the region. Memory allocation/deallocation and data movement are defined by which clauses the programmer includes.

Encompassing multiple compute regions: A single data region can contain any number of parallel/kernels regions, as shown in the following example:

```
#pragma acc data copyin(A[0:N]) create(C[0:N])
{
    #pragma acc parallel loop
    for( int i = 0; i < N; i++ )
    {
        C[i] = A[i] + 10;
    }
    #pragma acc parallel loop
    for( int i = 0; i < N; i++ )
    {
        C[i] = C[i] / 10;
    }
}
```

Unstructured data directive

There are two unstructured data directives:

- **enter data**: Handles device memory allocation, and copies from the host to the device. The two clauses that you may use with enter data are:
    - `create`: This will only perform device memory allocation.
    - `copyin`: This will perform allocation along with a memory copy to the device.
- **exit data**: Handles device memory deallocation, and copies from the device to the host. The two clauses that you may use with exit data are:
    - `delete`: This will perform only device memory deallocation.
    - `copyout`: This will first do a memory copy from the device to the host, followed by device memory deallocation.

Unstructured data directives do not mark a data region as you are able to have multiple enter data and exit data directives in your code. It is better to think of them purely as memory allocation and deallocation. The largest advantage of using unstructured data directives is their ability to branch across multiple functions. You may allocate your data in one function, and deallocate it in another. We can look at a simple example of that:

```
#define N 1024
int* allocate(int size)
{
    int *ptr = (int*) malloc(size * sizeof(int));
    #pragma acc enter data create(ptr[0:size])
    return ptr;
}
void deallocate(int *ptr)
{
    #pragma acc exit data delete(ptr)
    free(ptr);
}
int main()
{
    int *ptr = allocate(N);
    #pragma acc parallel loop
    for( int i = 0; i < N; i++ )
    {
        ptr[i] = 0;
    }
    deallocate(ptr);
}
```

The preceding code snippet shows that allocation happens in the separate `allocate()` function, and deletion happens in `deallocate()`. You can link the same concept to `enter data create` as part of the constructor and `exit data delete` as part of the destructor in C++.

Asynchronous programming in OpenACC

By default, all OpenACC calls are synchronous in nature. Which means that, after every call to a data transfer or every kernel call to the GPU, a synchronization gets added implicitly. The CPU will wait till the OpenACC call has finished and then start executing the next instruction. To make the call asynchronous, we can make use of the `async` clause along with the data and parallel directive, as shown in the following code:

```
#pragma acc data copyin(a[:N]) async
// performing copyin asynchronously
#pragma acc parallel loop async
//performing parallel loop asynchronously.
```

The primary benefits of using `async` can be summarized as follows:

- If we want to execute host and device code simultaneously, we can launch our device code with `async`, and while that executes we can go back to the host to continue unrelated (non-device dependent) code.
- We can *queue up* multiple device kernel launches so that they execute back to back, which in some cases can reduce the overhead associated with launching device kernels.
- We can perform device computation at the same time as data movement between host and device. This is the optimization we will be applying to our code, and is the most general use case of `async`.

Under the hood, whenever we use the `async` clause, we are adding some *work* to a queue. Work that is submitted to different queues can execute *asynchronously*, and work that is in the same queue will execute *sequentially* (one after the other). When we use `async`, we are able to specify a queue number. If no queue number is specified, then a default will automatically be used.

Applying the unstructured data and async directives to merge image code

Let's now try to apply data directives along with the `async` clause to merge parallel code:

```
void merge_async_pipelined(unsigned char *in1, unsigned char*in2,unsigned
char *out, long w, long h)
{
    long x, y;
    #pragma acc enter data create(in1[:w*h], in2[:h*w], out[:w*h])
    const long numBlocks = 8;
    const long rowsPerBlock = (h+(numBlocks-1))/numBlocks;
    for(long block = 0; block < numBlocks; block++) {
        long lower = block*rowsPerBlock; // Compute Lower
        long upper = MIN(h, lower+rowsPerBlock); // Compute Upper
        #pragma acc update device(in1[lower*w:(upper-lower)*w],
                            in2[lower*w:(upper-lower)*w])
                            async(block%2)
        #pragma acc parallel loop present(in1,in2, out) async(block%2)
        for(y = lower; y < upper; y++) {
            #pragma acc loop
            for(x = 0; x < w; x++) {
                out[y * w + x] = (in1[y * w + x]+in2[y * w + x])/2;
            }
        }
        #pragma acc update self(out[lower*w:(upper-lower)*w])
                            async(block%2)
    }
    #pragma acc wait
    #pragma acc exit data delete(in1, in2, out)
}
```

We have made use of data directives and also an `async` clause to implement the blocking concept. Let's break down the overall implementation, which will make it simpler to understand:

1. **Enter data region**: The `enter data create` clause allocates memory for the `in1` and `in2` variables and `out` in the GPU.

2. **Creates blocks**: We decided that we will split the image into eight blocks. The blocks are split across rows. The outer `for` loop for the block gets added for this reason.

3. **Transfer data from host to device asynchronously**: `acc update device` basically copies data from the host to the device asynchronously as we have added an `async` clause to the same.

4. **Launch parallel loop asynchronously**: The `async` clause is added to the parallel clause to launch the GPU kernel asynchronously.

5. **Transfer data from device to host asynchronously**: `acc update self` basically copies the data from the device to the host asynchronously as we have added an `async` clause to the same.

6. **Wait**: `acc wait` will make sure the CPU waits till all the OpenACC launches have finished, prior to moving forward in all the queues.

7. **Exit data region**: `acc exit data delete` will delete the `in1` and `in2` vectors and `out`, which were allocated in the `enter data` clause.

Let's try to understand the compiler output of the `merge_async_pipelined` function:

```
merge_async_pipelined(unsigned char *, unsigned char *,
                      unsigned char *, long, long):
    67, Generating enter data create(out[:h*w],in2[:h*w],in1[:h*w])
    74, Generating update device(in1[w*lower:w*(upper-lower)],
                                 in2[w*lower:w*(upper-lower)])
        Generating present(in1[:],out[:],in2[:])
        Accelerator kernel generated
        Generating Tesla code
        74, #pragma acc loop gang /* blockIdx.x */
        76, #pragma acc loop vector(128) /* threadIdx.x */
    76, Loop is parallelizable
    81, Generating update self(out[w*lower:w*(upper-lower)])
    84, Generating exit data delete(out[:1],in2[:1],in1[:1])
```

The preceding compiler output shows that, for the `merge_async_pipelined` function, the following actions have been generated by the compiler:

- At line 67 , the `data create` region has been generated for the `in1`, `in2` and `out` variables.
- At line 74 , `update device` is called for `in1` and `in2`, and the transfer of data to the device is restricted to block the upper and lower bounds:
  `in1[w*lower:w*(upper-lower)],in2[w*lower:w*(upper-lower)]`.
- At lines 74 and 76 , the Tesla kernel code has been generated.

- At line 81, update self is called for the out variable, and the transfer of data from the device is restricted to block the upper and lower bounds:
out[w*lower:w*(upper-lower)].
- At line 84, the data region ends, and delete is called to free up the memory allocated on the GPU.

When the code is run on V100, the time taken by this whole kernel is 0.0008 seconds. To understand this in more detail, let's go back to the profiler. This time we will visualize the output by making use of the NVIDIA Visual Profiler:

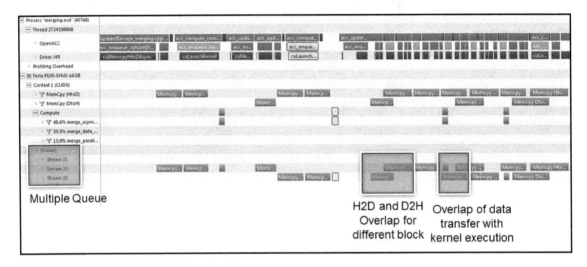

Output by using NVIDIA Visual Profiler

The preceding screenshot shows the Visual Profiler output after using async and blocking. The key message from the profiler window is as follows:

1. We see three streams being created and used. This is because our code uses async(block%2), which means that we have requested max 2 queues. The third queue is the default queue and is not used during the pipeline execution.
2. We see that the host-to-device and device-to-host transfer also overlaps as the GPU has two **Direct Memory Access (DMA)** engines, and hence the data transfer in the opposite direction can be overlapped.
3. We also see that our kernel execution overlaps with the data transfer.

So far we have seen key directives that helped us to make sequential code for image merging to run on a GPU. In the next section, we will introduce you to more clauses which will help you to optimize your OpenACC code further.

Additional important directives and clauses

In this section, we will cover other important, widely used directives that we can apply to our merge algorithm.

Gang/vector/worker

Gang/worker/vector defines the various levels of parallelism we can achieve with OpenACC. This parallelism is most useful when parallelizing multi-dimensional loop nests. OpenACC allows us to define a generic gang/worker/vector model that will be applicable to a variety of hardware, but we will focus more on a GPU-specific implementation. The following diagram shows an OpenACC parallel programming model:

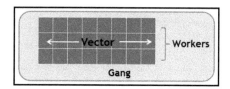

This preceding diagram represents a single gang. When parallelizing our `for` loops, the loop iterations will be broken up evenly among a number of gangs. Each gang will contain a number of threads. These threads are organized into blocks. A worker is a row of threads.

In the preceding figure, there are three workers, which means that there are three rows of threads. The vector refers to how long each row is. So in the preceding graphic, the vector is eight, because each row is eight threads long. By default, when programming for a GPU, gang and vector parallelism is automatically applied.

As OpenACC is an open standard and targets multiple hardware; it provides generic constructs. But how does this construct get mapped to a particular target device? The answer is simple; it depends on the architecture and compiler, and hence providing performance portability. If we were to map how the current PGI compiler maps this concept to CUDA (NVIDIA GPU), it would be as follows:

- The OpenACC gang maps to a CUDA block.
- The worker essentially maps to a CUDA warp.
- The OpenACC vector maps to `threadIdx.x` and (X dimension).
- The OpenACC worker maps to `threadIdx.y` (Y dimension).

Again it is important to reiterate that this is how the PGI compiler maps the OpenACC constructs. Other compilers might map this differently. Specifically for NVIDIA GPUs, the gang worker vector will define the organization of our GPU threads. By adding the following clauses, the developer can tell the compiler which levels of parallelism to use on given loops:

- `gang`: Marks the loop for gang parallelism.
- `worker`: Marks the loop for worker parallelism.
- `vector`: Marks the loop for vector parallelism.

The following code snippet has three loops, and each loop parallelism has been explicitly defined: the outer loop as `gang`, the middle loop as the `worker` loop, and the innermost loop as the `vector` loop:

```
#pragma acc parallel loop gang
for( i = 0; i < size; i++ )
    #pragma acc loop worker
    for( j = 0; j < size; j++ )
        #pragma acc loop vector
        for( k = 0; k < size; k++ )
            c[i][j] += a[i][k] * b[k][j];
```

Adjusting gangs, workers, and vectors: The compiler will choose a number of gangs and workers and a vector length for you, but you can change it with the following clauses:

- `num_gangs(N)`: Generates the N gangs for the parallel region
- `num_workers(M)`: Generates M workers for the parallel region.
- `vector_length(Q)`: Uses a vector length of Q for the parallel region

For an example in the following code snippet we have set the number of gangs to 2, the number of workers to 2 and the vector length to 32:

```
#pragma acc parallel num_gangs(2) \
  num_workers(2) vector_length(32)
{
    #pragma acc loop gang worker
    for(int x = 0; x < 4; x++){
        #pragma acc loop vector
        for(int y = 0; y < 32; y++){
            array[x][y]++;
        }
    }
}
```

It is rarely a good idea to set the number of gangs in your code—let the compiler decide. Most of the time you can effectively tune a loop nest by adjusting only the vector length. Also, it is rare to use a worker loop for the GPU.

Managed memory

OpenACC provides an option to allow the compiler to handle memory management. We will be able to achieve better performance by managing memory ourselves; however, allowing the compiler to use the managed memory is very simple. We do not need to make any changes to our code to get the managed memory working.

In order to make use of the managed memory, we can pass the managed flag to the `pgc++` compiler like this:

```
$ pgc++ -c -acc -ta=tesla:managed scrImagePgmPpmPackage.cpp
$ pgc++ -c -acc -ta=tesla:managed -Minfo=accel image_merging.cpp
$ pgc++ -o merging.out -acc -ta=tesla:managed -Minfo=accel
scrImagePgmPpmPackage.o image_merging.o
$ ./blurring.out
```

After adding the managed clause, the compiler will basically ignore the data clauses, and the managed memory is used to transfer data between the CPU and GPU. Note that the managed memory is only for heap data and not stack/static data. The unified memory concept that we covered in the previous chapter will remain the same.

Kernel directive

The kernel directive allows the programmer to step back and rely solely on the compiler. Some sample code using a kernel directive is as follows:

```
#pragma acc kernels
for (int i = 0; i < N; i++ )
{
    //< loop code >
}
```

Just like in the parallel directive example, we are parallelizing a single loop. Recall that, when using the parallel directive, it must always be paired with the loop directive; otherwise, the code will be improperly parallelized. The kernel directive does not follow the same rule; in some compilers, adding the loop directive may limit the compiler's ability to optimize the code.

The kernel directive is the exact opposite of the parallel directive. This means that the compiler is making a lot of assumptions, and may even override the programmer's decision to parallelize the code. Also, by default, the compiler will attempt to optimize the loop. The compiler is generally pretty good at optimizing loops, and sometimes may be able to optimize the loop in a way that the programmer cannot describe. However, usually programmers will be able to achieve better performance by optimizing the loop themselves.

If you run into a situation where the compiler refuses to parallelize a loop, you may override the compiler's decision. (However, keep in mind that by overriding the compiler's decision, you are taking responsibility for any mistakes that occur from parallelizing the code!) In this code segment, we are using the independent clause to assure the compiler that we think the loop is parallelizable:

```
#pragma acc kernels loop independent
for (int i = 0; i < N; i++ )
{
    //< loop code >
}
```

One of the most telling advantages of the kernel directive is its ability to parallelize many loops at once. For example, in the following code segment, we are able to effectively parallelize two loops at once by utilizing a kernel region:

```
#pragma acc kernels
{
    for (int i = 0; i < N; i++ )
    {
        //< loop code >
    }
... some other sequential code
    for (int j = 0; j < M; j++ )
    {
        //< loop code >
    }
}
```

Collapse clause

The **collapse clause** allows us to transform multi-dimensional loop nests into a single-dimensional loop. This process is helpful for increasing the overall length (which usually increases parallelism) of our loops, and will often help with memory locality. Let's look at the syntax:

```
#pragma acc parallel loop collapse( 3 )
for(int i = 0; i < N; i++)
{
    for(int j = 0; j < M; j++)
    {
        for(int k = 0; k < Q; k++)
        {
            < loop code >
        }
    }
}
```

The code will combine the three-dimensional loop nest into a single one-dimensional loop.

Tile clause

The **tile clause** allows us to break up a multi-dimensional loop into *tiles*, or *blocks*. This is often useful for increasing memory locality in some code. Let's look at the syntax:

```
#pragma acc parallel loop tile( 32, 32 )
for(int i = 0; i < N; i++)
{
    for(int j = 0; j < M; j++)
    {
        < loop code >
    }
}
```

The preceding code will break our loop iterations up into 32 x 32 tiles (or blocks), and then execute those blocks in parallel.

CUDA interoperability

As mentioned earlier in the chapter, OpenACC is not an alternative to CUDA languages; in fact, developers can start making use of OpenACC to port hotspots to a GPU. They can start integrating CUDA kernels for the most critical function only. There are several ways to turn an OpenACC/CUDA into interoperable code. We will look at some of them in this section.

DevicePtr clause

This clause can be used to map the CUDA device pointer allocated using `cudaMalloc` and pass it to OpenACC. The following code snippet shows the use of the `deviceptr` clause:

```
double *cuda_allocate(int size) {
    double *ptr;
    cudaMalloc((void**) &ptr, size * sizeof(double));
    return ptr;
}
int main() {
    double *cuda_ptr = cuda_allocate(100);
    // Allocated on the device, but not the host!

    #pragma acc parallel loop deviceptr(cuda_ptr)
    for(int i = 0; i < 100; i++) {
        cuda_ptr[i] = 0.0;
    }
}
```

Normally, the OpenACC runtime expects to be given a host pointer, which will then be translated to some associated device pointer. The `deviceptr` clause is a way to tell the OpenACC runtime that a given pointer should not be translated since it is already a device pointer.

Routine directive

The last topic to discuss is using CUDA device functions within OpenACC parallel and kernel regions. These are functions that are compiled to be called by the accelerator within a GPU kernel or OpenACC region. To use CUDA `__device__` functions within our OpenACC loops, we can also use the routine directive:

```
//In CUDA code
extern "C" __device__
int cuda_func(int x) {
        return x*x;
```

```
}

//In OpenACC Code
#pragma acc routine seq
extern int cuda_func(int);

...

int main() {
    A = (int*) malloc(100 * sizeof(int));
    #pragma acc parallel loop copyout(A[:100])
    for(int i = 0; i < 100; i++) {
        A[i] = cuda_func(i);
    }
}
```

 Please note that this chapter provides a practical approach to making use of OpenACC and does not cover the whole standard API. For extensive API information, see https://www.openacc.org/.

Summary

In this chapter, we provided you with an alternative approach to making use of a GPU. This directive-based programming approach using OpenACC is really popular for legacy applications, and also for new applications it provides a very easy and portable approach. Using this approach, you can see how compilers have become more advanced. User feedback on directives has been used by making use of directives can generate optimal parallel code for different architectures.

We covered parallel directives that provide an instruction/hint to the compiler about which part in the code to make parallel. We also made use of data directives to take control of the data transfer instead of relying on managed memory. With the use of an asynchronous clause, we also tried optimizing our application by overlapping kernels and data transfers. We explored mapping OpenACC constructs to the CUDA hierarchy, and also how OpenACC and CUDA C/C++ code can interoperate.

In the next chapter, we will start applying our knowledge of CUDA to deep learning.

10
Deep Learning Acceleration with CUDA

Deep learning is a machine learning method that can interpret data based on artificial neural networks. Specifically, we provide data that a machine can understand and build neural network models that learn representations from data. We can use this technique to build models that recognize speech, classify objects from images, understand text, translate languages, transform data domains, and so on. Basic neural networks include the **fully connected layer** (**FCL**), the **convolutional neural network** (**CNN**), and the **recurrent neural network** (**RNN**). These architectures show strong accuracy in data classification, regional understandings, and sequential relationships.

Deep learning requires large computations so that it can be widely used. However, this issue was resolved because we can reduce the training time significantly by using GPU computing power. This is because the basic architecture of neural networks is based on matrix operations and GPU is a hardware platform that's been optimized for this. Specifically, the innovations of deep learning were tackled with NVIDIA CUDA accelerations as many algorithms in deep learning can be accelerated.

In this chapter, we will review the neural network operations briefly and discuss how these can be accelerated on GPUs. As practice, we will implement a convolutional network using the cuDNN and cuBLAS CUDA libraries. The cuDNN library is NVIDIA's CUDA library that optimizes deep learning operations specifically. We will cover its implementation across three sections. We will also cover how GPUs can optimize the required operations. Then, we will cover how using the cuDNN library is effective by comparing the performance of the **long short-term memory** (**LSTM**) network. Then, we will cover profiling methods in deep learning using the **NVIDIA Tools Extension** (**NVTX**). This measures network operations on the GPUs so that we can analyze the operations in the timeline and understand their performance.

In this chapter, we will cover the following topics:

- Fully connected layer acceleration with CUBLAS
- Element-wise layers with cuDNN
- Softmax and loss functions in cuDNN/CUDA
- Convolutional neural networks with cuDNN
- Recurrent neural networks with CUDA
- Profiling deep learning frameworks

Technical requirements

This chapter requires the cuDNN library and CUDA Toolkit to be installed. We also need CUDA-enabled GPUs. This chapter will cover the fundamentals of deep learning and its performance, and so will not require new GPU features. In other words, if you covered most of the content in the previous chapters, you will have a proper GPU to work with.

To install the cuDNN library, you need to download the package from `https://developer.nvidia.com/cudnn`. You need to log in to the NVIDIA developer site to access the download page. You will need to register for an NVIDIA developer account if you don't have an account already. Make sure that cuDNN is compiled with the CUDA version you have installed.

Fully connected layer acceleration with cuBLAS

The fully connected layer is the basic architecture of deep learning. Let's review its operations and see how CUDA accelerates neural networks in terms of the forward and back-propagation procedures. Then, we will apply them to the GPU.

Neural network operations

A neural network's basic operation is to perform dot operation between the input data and parameters. We call this perception. In deep learning, the neural network connects multiple perceptions in a layered manner. We call these feed-forward neural networks. The following diagram shows a perceptron and the basic neural network:

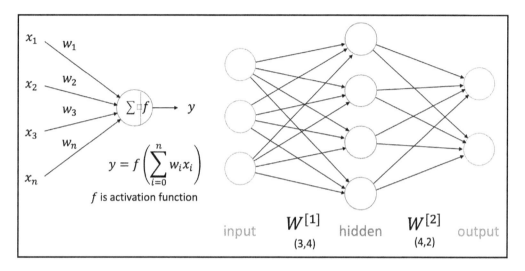

The perceptron's basic operation is to create a dot product with the input data and appropriate weights. Then, it performs a non-linear operation with an activation function such as a sigmoid or **rectifier linear unit** (**ReLU**). In feed-forward neural networks, the operation is just an affine transformation followed by the application of an activation function. A vector will be fed to the neural network as input and multiplies it with weight parameters between each node in the two layers.

To train the neural networks, we perform forward propagation, loss calculation, and gradient back-propagation, and then use the update parameter. Let's cover them briefly. Then, we will match each step using cuBLAS and other CUDA operations.

The forward operation can be denoted by the following equation:

$$h = \sigma(z) = \sigma(W^{T[1]}x + b^{[1]}),$$
$$\hat{y} = softmax(o) = softmax(W^{T[2]}h + b^{[2]})$$

Here, $\hat{y}$ is a prediction result from the given input vector, x, W is the weight parameter matrix, and σ is the activation function. As we can see, the basic operations in the fully connected layer are matrix operations. Therefore, we need to implement the matrix multiplication operation to the inputs and activation function. Because we take the classification task, we use a softmax function to normalize the output and obtain a probabilistic distributed result in the next layer.

To obtain the loss between the true value, we apply one-hot encodings on the label and get cross-entropy loss by obtaining the entropies from each element, like so:

$$Loss = J_{CE}(\hat{y}, y) = -\sum_{i=0}^{m} y^{(i)} log\hat{y}^{(i)}$$

We can obtain the total loss value by means of the sum of each cross-entropy loss. Then, we can obtain the gradient from the preceding equation. This looks like a complicated operation, but it can be simplified, as follows:

$$\frac{\partial L}{\partial o^{(i)}} = \hat{y}^{(i)} - y^{(i)} = \delta_1$$

Now, we will propagate the gradients to the previous layer, which is called back-propagation. In this task, we use the chain rule to obtain the gradients for each weight and bias parameter. Then, we can update the weight parameter's set and bias. For example, we can obtain the gradients of the weights and biases with the following equation:

$$\frac{\partial L}{\partial W^{[2]}} = \frac{\partial L}{\partial o} \frac{\partial o}{\partial W^{[2]}} = \delta_1 h^T,$$
$$\frac{\partial L}{\partial b^{[2]}} = \frac{\partial L}{\partial o} \frac{\partial o}{\partial b^{[2]}} = \delta_1$$

We can obtain the gradients to propagate to the previous layer with the following equation:

$$\frac{\partial L}{\partial z} = \frac{\partial L}{\partial o} \frac{\partial o}{\partial h} \frac{\partial h}{\partial z} = \delta_1 W^{T[2]} \frac{\partial h}{\partial z} = \delta_1 W^{T[2]} \sigma'(z)$$

Here, $\sigma'(z)$ is the gradient of the activation function. Therefore, we need to obtain $\delta_2 = \delta_1 W^{T[2]}$ from the second layer for the first layer. Then, the first layer's gradients of weight and biases can be obtained with the following equations:

$$\frac{\partial L}{\partial b^{[1]}} = \frac{\partial L}{\partial z}\frac{\partial z}{\partial b^{[1]}} = \delta_2^T,$$

$$\frac{\partial L}{\partial x} = \frac{\partial L}{\partial z}\frac{\partial z}{\partial x} = \delta_2 W^{[1]}$$

Now, we can update the weights and biases based on the gradient descendant rule, as follows:

$$W^{[l+1]} = W^{[l]} - \mu \nabla W^{[l]}, b^{[l+1]} = b^l - \mu \nabla b^l$$

Here, n is the iteration step.

The gradient of the activation function σ' can be different, as well as its type. The implementation of this activation layer will be covered in the next section. The derivation of the activation functions can be denoted by the following equation:

$$relu'(o) = \begin{cases} 1 \text{ if } o > 0 \\ 0 \text{ if } otherwise \end{cases}, \quad sigmoid'(o) = \delta(o)(a - \delta(o))$$

As a result, the neural network operations are a set of linear algebra operations and can be covered with the cuBLAS library. The implemented code can be found in `01_ann`. We will cover these implementation details in *Implementing a fully connected layer*, *Implementing layer operation*, and *Implementing the softmax layer* sections.

Design of a neural network layer

Before we write our code, let's cover how we can package the operations into a layer configuration:

1. First, we perform forward operation.
2. Then, we perform backward operation.
3. Then we get a weight update from the gradient.
4. Finally, the output layer will obtain the loss.

In this manner, the layer can be configured as follows:

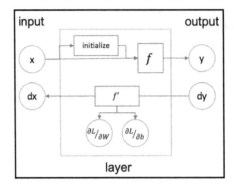

It has standardized inputs and outputs and two types of input, depending on the workflow. The left-hand data path will be named with the input while the right-hand side will be named with the output. The data is fed in two phases (forward and backward). We will use blobs to manage the parameters and input/output data. The blob is a wrapper of data that's processed across layers and helps manage memory space. We will use this design every layer to simplify the network's configuration. Every layer will have each blob's descriptors and forward/backward processing operations.

Now, let's create a layer class that will be the base class of all the layers. The following code shows how the `class` public function stacks. And, you can find its implementation in `layer.h` and `layer.cu` in `01_ann/src/` directory. This has not only forward and backward operations but also weight update controls and loss calculations:

```
class Layer
{
public:
    Layer();
    ~Layer();

    std::string get_name() { return name_; }

    virtual Blob<float> *forward(Blob<float> *input) = 0;
    virtual Blob<float> *backward(Blob<float> *grad_input) = 0;

    virtual float get_loss(Blob<float> *target);
    virtual int   get_accuracy(Blob<float> *target);

    void set_cuda_context(CudaContext *context) { cuda_ = context; }

    /* weights update control */
    void freeze() { freeze_ = true; }
```

```
    void unfreeze() { freeze_ = false;}
    void set_load_pretrain() { load_pretrain_ = true; }
    void set_gradient_stop() { gradient_stop_ = true; }
```

To support these operations, the layer class maintains several cuDNN descriptors, blob pointers, and weight update controllers. The detail implementations will be covered when we cover the network implementations:

```
protected:
    std::string name_;

    // Tensor descriptor for the input/output tensor
    cudnnTensorDescriptor_t input_desc_;
    cudnnTensorDescriptor_t output_desc_;
    // filter and bias descriptor for weights and biases
    cudnnFilterDescriptor_t filter_desc_;
    cudnnTensorDescriptor_t bias_desc_;
    // output memory
    Blob<float> *input_ = nullptr;        /* x */
    Blob<float> *output_ = nullptr;       /* y */
    Blob<float> *grad_input_ = nullptr;   /* dx */
    Blob<float> *grad_output_ = nullptr;  /* dy */

    // master weights & bias
    bool freeze_ = false;                 /* control parameter updates */
    Blob<float> *weights_ = nullptr;      /* w */
    Blob<float> *biases_  = nullptr;      /* b */
    Blob<float> *grad_weights_ = nullptr; /* dw */
    Blob<float> *grad_biases_  = nullptr; /* db */

    int batch_size_ = 0; // mini-batch size
    // cuda handle container
    CudaContext *cuda_ = nullptr;

    // initialize weights along with the input size
    void init_weight_bias(unsigned int seed = 0);
    void update_weights_biases(float learning_rate);

    // pretrain parameters
    bool load_pretrain_ = false;
    int load_parameter();
    int save_parameter();

    // gradient stop tagging
    bool gradient_stop_ = false;

    friend class Network;
}
```

This layer class will be used across deep learning network implementation in other sections. For this reason, it has `cudnnTensorDescriptor_t` variables for cuDNN operations, as well as the `get_loss()` and `get_accuracy()` functions.

Tensor and parameter containers

In our implementation, we will use a data container named `Blob`. Its name was borrowed from Caffe. This allows us to store tensors or network parameters with its dimensional size information and memory points. We will connect each layer using this. This helps each layer initialize its weights based on the input tensor's size information. Also, each layer can validate its result based on the information of the `Blob`.

This blob will require the dimensional size information in the neural network, as shown in the following line of code. Then, its constructor will create a host-side buffer following the size information:

```
Blob<T>(int n, int c, int h, int w)
```

`Blob` can also handle memories in the host and device and can help us access those memories. `Blob` has the following memory access helper functions:

```
// get specified memory pointer
ftype *ptr() { return h_ptr_; }

// get cuda memory
ftype *cuda()
{
    if (d_ptr_ == nullptr)
        cudaMalloc((void**)&d_ptr_, sizeof(ftype) * len());
    return d_ptr_;
}

// transfer data between memory
ftype *to(DeviceType target) {
    ftype *ptr = nullptr;
    if (target == host)
    {
        cudaMemcpy(h_ptr_, cuda(), sizeof(ftype) * len(),
                cudaMemcpyDeviceToHost);
        ptr = h_ptr_;
    }
    else // DeviceType::cuda
    {
        cudaMemcpy(cuda(), h_ptr_, sizeof(ftype) * len(),
                cudaMemcpyHostToDevice);
```

```
        ptr = d_ptr_;
    }
    return ptr;
}
```

As we discussed earlier, `Blob` can store tensors, we also need to provide tensor shape information as a descriptors required by cuDNN APIs. Therefore, `Blob` can create and set the tensor descriptor using the following code:

```
/* Tensor Control */
bool is_tensor_ = false;
cudnnTensorDescriptor_t tensor_desc_;
cudnnTensorDescriptor_t tensor()
{
    if (is_tensor_)
        return tensor_desc_;
    cudnnCreateTensorDescriptor(&tensor_desc_);
    cudnnSetTensor4dDescriptor(tensor_desc_,
                               CUDNN_TENSOR_NCHW, CUDNN_DATA_FLOAT,
                               n_, c_, h_, w_);
    is_tensor_ = true;
    return tensor_desc_;
}
```

Now, let's implement a fully connected layer using `Blob`.

Implementing a fully connected layer

In this section, we will write a fully connected network using cuBLAS. For this layer, we will create a `Dense` class derived from the `Layer` class. The class constructor will receive the default layer configuration information, as follows:

```
Dense::Dense(std::string name, int output_size)
{
    name_ = name;
    output_size_ = output_size;
}
```

But this is not enough to configure the whole layer. The missing information will be provided from the input because the input size will be determined by the previous layer. Now, let's cover forward propagation.

Implementing forward propagation

In forward propagation, we can break the forward process into two steps, as follows:

$$h = W^{T[1]}x$$
$$h = h + b^{[1]}$$

Since the weight size does not have to be affected by the batch size, we only consider the number of input weights and output weights. On the other hand, data feeding blobs, such as input and output, are affected by the batch size. So, our GEMM operation with the filter and input data can be designed as follows:

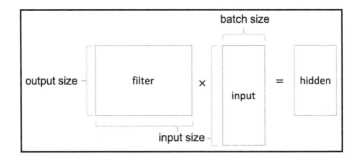

The hidden output will be added with the bias values. The input data is not limited to the data from the data loader. As we stack the layers, the output of the previous layer will be the current layer's input data. The forward operation can be implemented as follows:

```
Blob<float> *Dense::forward(Blob<float> *input) {
    .. { blob initialization } ..

    // output = weights^T * input (without biases)
    cublasSgemm(cuda_->cublas(),
          CUBLAS_OP_T, CUBLAS_OP_N, output_size_,
          batch_size_, input_size_,
          &cuda_->one, weights_->cuda(), input_size_,
          input_->cuda(), input_size_,
          &cuda_->zero, output_->cuda(), output_size_);

    // output += biases * one_vec^T
    cublasSgemm(cuda_->cublas(),
          CUBLAS_OP_N, CUBLAS_OP_N, output_size_, batch_size_, 1,
          &cuda_->one, biases_->cuda(), output_size_, one_vec, 1,
          &cuda_->one, output_->cuda(), output_size_);
    return output_;
}
```

At the first iteration, each layer needs to initialize its weight and bias. For example, this `Dense` layer can initialize its weights, biases, and output tensor elements. We can separate this initialization task into two phases. The first is for the weights and biases, as follows:

```
// initialize weights and biases
if (weights_ == nullptr)
{
    // setup parameter size information
    input_size_ = input->c() * input->h() * input->w();
    // initialize weight, bias, and output
    weights_ = new Blob<float>(1, 1, input_size_, output_size_);
    biases_ = new Blob<float>(1, 1, output_size_);
}
```

The next phases is about updating the input information and initializing the output blob. When it's new or needs to be reconfigured, we need to do the following. In this task, we also need to create a vector filled with our batch size. This will be used in biases addition:

```
// initilaize input and output
if (input_ == nullptr || batch_size_ != input->n())
{
  input_ = input;
  batch_size_ = input->n();

  if (output_ == nullptr)
    output_ = new Blob<float>(batch_size_, output_size_);
  else
    output_->reset(batch_size_, output_size_);
  output_->tensor();

  if (d_one_vec != nullptr)
    cudaFree(d_one_vec);
  checkCudaErrors(cudaMalloc((void**)&d_one_vec, sizeof(float) *
batch_size_));
  init_one_vec<<< (batch_size_+BLOCK_DIM_1D-1)/BLOCK_DIM_1D, BLOCK_DIM_1D
>>>(d_one_vec, batch_size_);

  if (!freeze_)
    init_weight_bias();
}
```

This initialization task triggered not only the first iteration but also batch size changes. Checking the batch size is not required in the training phase, but it will be useful in the testing phase. This is because the batch sizes in training and inference are different. In this case, we need to create an output blob following the new batch size. The output tensor's size is determined as the channel size. The output blob's creation code, as follows, creates a blob of size (`batch_size_`, `output_size_`, 1, 1):

```
output_ = new Blob<float>(batch_size_, output_size_);
```

This creates flattened tensors. Then, we feed these tensors, which requires them to be aligned in channels. This alignment is specifically required in the softmax layer. We will cover this in the softmax layer's implementation.

Another important task in this phase is to initialize weights and biases. In our implementation, we will use the ReLU as an activator. We will use the normal initializer (https://arxiv.org/abs/1502.01852) technique to make the network trainable. Following the guidelines in the preceding paper, the required weight values can be generated with the following equation:

$$W_{ij} \sim U\left(-\sqrt{\frac{6}{n_{in}}}, \sqrt{\frac{6}{n_{in}}}\right)$$

n_{in} is the number of inputs from the previous layer. For this reason, we can initialize the parameters after we update the input tensor information. Also, the bias values will be initialized as 0. The following code shows the implementation of this:

```
void Layer::init_weight_bias(unsigned int seed)
{
    // Create random network
    std::random_device rd;
    std::mt19937 gen(seed == 0 ? rd() : static_cast<unsigned int>
                                          (seed));

    // He normal distribution
    float range = sqrt(6.f / input_->size());
    std::uniform_real_distribution<> dis(-range, range);

    for (int i = 0; i < weights_->len(); i++)
        weights_->ptr()[i] = static_cast<float>(dis(gen));
    for (int i = 0; i < biases_->len(); i++)
        biases_->ptr()[i] = 0.f;

    // copy initialized value to the device
    weights_->to(DeviceType::cuda);
```

```
    biases_->to(DeviceType::cuda);
}
```

Now, let's cover backward propagation.

Implementing backward propagation

As we discussed earlier, the gradient from the next layer is propagated to this layer. Based on propagated gradients, we need to obtain three gradients for the weights, biases, and data (gradient of input). We need to create the blobs that can store them. Their size does not depend on the batch size, so we just need to make sure that we create them. The following code shows how we can create blobs for this purpose:

```
if (grad_weights_ == nullptr) {
  grad_output_ = grad_output;
  grad_weights_ = new Blob<float>(weights_->shape());
  grad_biases_ = new Blob<float>(biases_->shape());
  grad_input_ = new Blob<float>(input_->shape());
}
```

In the preceding code, `grad_output_` means the gradients of the output data that is propagated from the next layer, and `grad_input_` means the gradients of the input data that will be propagated to the previous layer. Therefore, we don't need to create a `grad_output_` blob. If you find these naming conventions confusing, it may be easier if you regard `grad_input_` as dx and `grad_input_` as dy.

The following code shows how we can implement this:

```
Blob<float> *Dense::backward(Blob<float> *grad_output) {
  .. { blob initialization } ..

  // db = (dy) * one_vec
  cublasSgemv(cuda_->cublas(),
    CUBLAS_OP_N,
    output_size_, batch_size_,
    &cuda_->one,
    grad_output_->cuda(), output_size_,
    one_vec, 1,
    &cuda_->zero,
    grad_biases_->cuda(), 1);
  // dw = x * (dy)^T
  cublasSgemm(cuda_->cublas(),
    CUBLAS_OP_N, CUBLAS_OP_T,
    input_size_, output_size_, batch_size_,
```

```
      &cuda_->one,
      input_->cuda(), input_size_,
      grad_output_->cuda(), output_size_,
      &cuda_->zero,
      grad_weights_->cuda(), input_size_);
    // dx = W * dy
    if (!gradients_stop_)
      cublasSgemm(cuda_->cublas(),
        CUBLAS_OP_N, CUBLAS_OP_N,
        input_size_, batch_size_, output_size_,
        &cuda_->one,
        weights_->cuda(), input_size_,
        grad_output_->cuda(), output_size_,
        &cuda_->zero,
        grad_input_->cuda(), input_size_);

    return grad_input_;
}
```

We can also skip computing the gradients of the input data if this layer is the first layer in the model since we don't have to do anything with it.

The weight and bias updates will be done when we want to update the weights. In this section, we will use **Stochastic Gradient Descent (SGD)** for this. This operation can be used in other layers as well. Here, we will place this function in the `Layer` class. The weight updates can also be done with `cublas` functions, as follows:

```
void Layer::update_weights_biases(float learning_rate)
{
  float eps = -1.f * learning_rate;
  if (weights_ != nullptr && grad_weights_ != nullptr) {
    // w = w + eps * dw
    cublasSaxpy(cuda_->cublas(),
      weights_->len(),
      &eps,
      grad_weights_->cuda(), 1,
      weights_->cuda(), 1);
  }

  if (biases_ != nullptr && grad_biases_ != nullptr)
  {
    // b = b + eps * db
    cublasSaxpy(cuda_->cublas(),
      biases_->b(),
      &eps,
      grad_biases_->cuda(), 1,
      biases_->cuda(), 1);
```

```
    }
  }
```

As you can see, we can update the weights and bias with the learning rate. Of course, you can change the `eps` operation to apply other optimization algorithms as well.

Layer termination

In C/C++ programming, the programmers should cover how to return the used resource when it terminates class instances. Following our design, the layer will create six blobs at most if they have weights parameters and can update them from the gradients. The following code shows the layer termination code, which terminates blobs that are created internally:

```
Layer::~Layer()
{
  if (output_ != nullptr) delete output_;
  if (grad_input_ != nullptr) delete grad_input_;

  if (weights_ != nullptr) delete weights_;
  if (biases_ != nullptr) delete biases_;
  if (grad_weights_ != nullptr) delete grad_weights_;
  if (grad_biases_ != nullptr) delete grad_biases_;
}
```

The input blob or tensor descriptors will be handled by other layers or blob terminations. The layer class is a base class to the other layers. Therefore, we can focus on terminating custom-created resources, because this termination code will be called together when we terminate any derived layers.

Even though we have architected the network and the layers, we should develop some additional layers to complete the network. For example, we didn't implement the activation, softmax, and loss calculation layers. We will cover these layers in the upcoming sections.

Activation layer with cuDNN

There are many element-wise operations in neural network layers. The activation function is one of these operations. The cuDNN library provides six activation functions: sigmoid, ReLU, tanh, clipped ReLU, ELU, and identity. In the cuDNN library, cudnnActivationForward() does forward operation and cudnnActivationBackward() does backward operation.

Let's look at the cuddnnActivationForward() function's interface, as follows:

```
cudnnStatus_t cudnnActivationForward( cudnnHandle_t handle,
    cudnnActivationDescriptor_t activationDesc,
    const void *alpha, const cudnnTensorDescriptor_t xDesc,
    const void *x, const void *beta,
    const cudnnTensorDescriptor_t yDesc, void *y)
```

Using cudnnActivationDescriptor_t, we can determine the types of the activation function. Alpha and beta are scalar values that determine the rate of input to be added. xDesc and yDesc hold the tensor's shape information. They can be created using cudnnCreateTensorDescriptor().

When you look at the cudnnActivationBackward() function, dy is the gradient input from the next layer and dx is the gradient output to the previous layer. In this case, y becomes the input. In this manner, dyDesc provides the gradient input shape information while dxDesc provides the gradient output shape information:

```
cudnnStatus_t cudnnActivationBackward( cudnnHandle_t handle,
    cudnnActivationDescriptor_t activationDesc,
    const void *alpha, const cudnnTensorDescriptor_t yDesc,
    const void *y,
    const cudnnTensorDescriptor_t dyDesc, const void *dy,
    const cudnnTensorDescriptor_t xDesc,  const void *x,
    const void *beta,  const cudnnTensorDescriptor_t dxDesc, void *dx)
```

In general, we can expect the tensor shape between layers to not change. Due to this, we can use the same tensor descriptor for x and dx. It is the same as using y and dy.

Now, let's implement the cuDNN-enabled activation function using the cuDNN API. To use the cuDNN API, we need to provide a tensor descriptor to specify the input and an output tensor dimension to the cuDNN functions. We also need to specify the activation operation.

Layer configuration and initialization

While our example implementation does not use the layer interface, we need to integrate our example into the layer interface. In our layer design, the activation layer can be implemented like this:

```
class Activation: public Layer
{
public:
  Activation(std::string name, cudnnActivationMode_t mode,
             float coef = 0.f);
  ~Activation();

  Blob<float> *forward(Blob<float> *input);
  Blob<float> *backward(Blob<float> *grad_input);

private:
  cudnnActivationDescriptor_t act_desc_;
  cudnnActivationMode_t mode_;
  float coef_;
};
```

At the initialization step, we need to create several tensor descriptors and an activation descriptor. The cuDNN library requires the developers to provide a tensor size or any other operational handles corresponding to the API:

```
Activation::Activation(std::string name, cudnnActivationMode_t mode, float
coef)
{
  name_ = name;
  mode_ = mode;
  coef_ = coef;

  cudnnCreateActivationDescriptor(&act_desc_);
  cudnnSetActivationDescriptor(act_desc_, mode, CUDNN_PROPAGATE_NAN, coef);
}
```

In cuDNN, we specify the activation function operation using an activation descriptor. We do this with the cudnnSetActivationDescriptor() function. Then, it can determine the cudnnActivationForward/Backward() function's operation. We will cover this in the next section. Before we do that, however, we need to implement the class destructor so that it destroys the activation descriptor, like so:

```
cudnnDestroyActivationDescriptor(activation_desc);
```

Now, let's cover the activation layer's forward and backward operations.

Implementing layer operation

This is also known as the caution operation. This layer does not require that we handle weights and biases, and so it is simpler to implement than the dense layer.

Implementing forward propagation

At the first iteration, we need to initialize the input descriptors, output descriptors, and output blob. We will update the output blob when the batch size is changed. However, we don't have to initialize the weights and bias because it doesn't have those. The following code shows its implementation:

```
if (input_ == nullptr || batch_size_ != input->n())
{
  input_ = input;
  input_desc_ = input->tensor();
  batch_size_ = input->n();

  if (output_ == nullptr)
    output_ = new Blob<float>(input->shape());
  else
    output_->reset(input->shape());

  output_desc_ = output_->tensor();
}
```

After initialization, we use the `cudnnActivationForward()` function in cuDNN for the activation process, as follows:

```
cudnnActivationForward(cudnnHandle, act_desc_,
    &one, input_desc_, d_input, &zero, output_desc_, d_output);
```

This activation function's operation is determined when we initialize this layer, as we discussed earlier.

Implementing backward propagation

The next step is to implement backward propagation. We will reuse the input/output tensor descriptors we already have. Now, we have to initialize the gradients we wish to back-propagate:

```
if (grad_input_ != grad_output_)
{
  grad_output_ = grad_output;
```

```
    grad_input_ = new Blob<float>(input_->shape());
    grad_input_->reset(input_->shape());
}
```

After the initialization, we can call the `cudnnActivationBackward()` function, as follows:

```
cudnnActivationBackward(cudnnHandle, activation_desc,
    &one, output_desc_, output_->cuda(), output_desc_,
    d_grad_output, input_desc_, input_->cuda(),
    &zero, input_desc_, grad_input_->cuda());
```

Note that we reuse the input tensor descriptor and output tensor descriptor that we created in the forward pass. We can do this because the activation operation does not change the tensor's size. We could simplify our implementation by using the cuDNN API in activating backward propagation.

The output of the `cudnnActivationBackward()` function is `d_grad_input`. As we described in the previous section, this gradient will be passed to the lower layer.

Now, we will implement the softmax layer and integrate our layer implementations as a network. Then, we will discuss the fully connected layer's accuracy in the image classification task.

Softmax and loss functions in cuDNN/CUDA

For the MNIST dataset classification, we will use the softmax classifier. The softmax function normalizes the inputs and generates the probability distribution of K probabilities. The softmax operation can be denoted as follows:

$$softmax(o^{(i)}) = \frac{exp(o^{(i)})}{\sum_{j=0}^{m} exp(o^{(j)})}$$

cuDNN's softmax forward function supports this operation, along with the channels and all the instances. Previously, we aligned the dense layer's output with the channels. Therefore, we will apply the softmax operation along with the channels.

To confirm that our training is done effectively, we need to calculate the loss function. The softmax loss function is called cross-entropy loss since its loss function is used to obtain loss across K probabilities. The loss function is as follows:

$$L = J_{CE}(\hat{y}, y) = -\sum_{i=0}^{m} y^{(i)} log\hat{y}^{(i)} = -\sum_{i=0}^{m} y^{(i)} log(softmax(o^{(i)}))$$

We need to obtain the gradient of this softmax loss to update the neural networks. Fortunately, the gradient of softmax loss is simple after the derivation, as follows:

$$\frac{\partial L}{\partial o} = \hat{y} - y$$

For the forward operation, we will use the cuDNN function to get the softmax's output. To obtain gradients, having a custom operation is more intuitive and simple.

Implementing the softmax layer

Now, let's see how the softmax layer can be implemented using cuDNN and CUDA code.

Implementing forward propagation

We can obtain the softmax cost function's outputs using `cudnnSoftmaxForward()` from the cuDNN library:

```
cudnnSoftmaxForward(cudnnHandle, CUDNN_SOFTMAX_ACCURATE,
        CUDNN_SOFTMAX_MODE_CHANNEL,
        &one, input_desc, d_input, &zero, output_desc, d_output);
```

One of the most important parameter settings to use in this situation is `CUDNN_SOFTMAX_MODE_CHANNEL`. This option enables channel-level softmax operations following the input tensor descriptor information. By doing this, we can provide tensors that have been aligned by channels from mini-batch inputs from the dense layer.

Implementing backward propagation

The backward pass in the softmax layer is different from other layer implementation. This operation takes the labels of the input data as input and obtains the appropriate gradients. As we discussed earlier, the gradients of the softmax loss can be obtained using the following equation:

$$\nabla J_{CE}(\hat{y}, y) = \hat{y} - y$$

We can implement this operation using `cublasSaxpy()`, as follows:

```
// set grad_input_ as predict
cudaMemcpyAsync(grad_input_->cuda(), output_->cuda(),
                output_->buf_size(), cudaMemcpyDeviceToDevice));
// set grad_input_ = predict - target
cublasSaxpy(cuda_->cublas(), target->len(), &cuda_->minus_one,
            target->cuda(), 1, grad_input_->cuda(), 1));
```

In the preceding code, the target blob contains one-hot-encoded target vectors, so adding negative target vectors to the predicted values produces the appropriate gradients. After that, we need to normalize batch gradients ahead of propagation to the previous layer, as follows:

```
int grad_output_size = target->n() * target->c() * target->h() *
target->w();
float scale = 1.0f / static_cast<float>(target->n());
cublasSscal(cuda_->cublas(), grad_output_size, &scale, grad_input_->cuda(),
1);
```

Since this introduces the mean of the weighted sum, we can expect that the gradients of each batch are normalized.

Implementing the loss function

Calculating the loss value of softmax is optional. This means its value is not accounted for in training and inference. However, we can use this as an indicator of the training.

The softmax loss function should implement the following equation, as we discussed earlier:

$$Loss = J_{CE}(\hat{y}, y) = -\sum_{j=0}^{m} y_j log \hat{y}_j$$

We can obtain the loss from each sample's output and cumulate them using a kernel function, as follows:

```
__global__ void
softmax_loss_kernel(float *reduced_loss, float *predict,
                    float *target, int size)
{
  int batch_idx = blockDim.x * blockIdx.x + threadIdx.x;

  extern __shared__ float s_data[];
  float loss = 0.f;

  // each thread calculate entropy for each data
  // and accumulate to shared memory
  if (batch_idx > 0)
    return;

  for (int c = 0; c < num_outputs; c++)
    loss += target[batch_idx * num_outputs + c] * \
              logf(predict[batch_idx * num_outputs + c]);
              workspace[batch_idx] = -loss;

  // Then, we do reduction the result to calculate loss
  // Using 1 thread block
  if (blockIdx.x > 0) return;

  // Cumulate workspace data
  s_data[threadIdx.x] = 0.f;
  for (int i = 0; i < batch_size; i += blockDim.x)
    s_data[threadIdx.x] += workspace[threadIdx.x + i];

  __syncthreads();

  // Reduction
  for (unsigned int stride = blockDim.x / 2; stride > 0; stride >>= 1)
  {
    if (threadIdx.x + stride < batch_size)
      s_data[threadIdx.x] += s_data[threadIdx.x + stride];
    __syncthreads();
  }

  if (threadIdx.x == 0)
    reduced_loss[blockIdx.x] = s_data[0];
}
```

This operation uses parallel reduction, which we covered in Chapter 3, *CUDA Thread Programming*, to obtain the cumulated loss value in a batch. Since we will just use this reduced loss value to confirm the training, we will simply monitor its output rather than taking its average.

Now, let's integrate all the layers we have implemented with an MNIST dataset loader.

MNIST dataloader

One of the important parts of this entire process is having a dataloader for a specific dataset. In this lab, we will use the MNIST dataset, which contains 60,000 samples. When it comes to initialization, we tell the data loader whether it should load either the train or test set. After that, the data loader will load some magic numbers in the dataset, along with all the samples and their labels. The loaded data will be stored in vectors and shuffled with the same random seed. Since the data loader builds and shuffles the sample vector, the training loop or test loop may get randomized input data for each iteration. The fully implemented code can be found in the src/mnist.cpp file in this book's GitHub repository.

Managing and creating a model

When we have multiple layers, we need an object that can manage those layers with neural network operations, that is, forward/backward propagation and weight updates. In this lab, we will have an array of layers and iterate the array for forward processing. For example, the forward operation can be performed with the following code:

```
Blob<float> *Network::forward(Blob<float> *input) {
  output_ = input;
  for (auto layer : layers_)
    output_ = layer->forward(output_);

  return output_;
}
```

Backward propagation can also be done by iterating over the array in reverse order:

```
void Network::backward(Blob<float> *target) {
  Blob<float> *gradient = target;
  // back propagation.. update weights internally.....
  for (auto layer = layers_.rbegin(); layer != layers_.rend(); layer++) {
    // getting back propagation status with gradient size
    gradient = (*layer)->backward(gradient);
  }
}
```

As you can see, we manage the layers in the vector and have each layer's operations. Adding a new layer into the network is even simpler, as shown in the following code:

```
void Network::add_layer(Layer *layer) {
  layers_.push_back(layer);
}
```

By using the Network class, we can use various model management functions, such as parameter updates, layer registration, layers initialization, and so on. Also, we can build a neural network like a modern deep learning framework. For example, we can create a model as follows:

```
// step 1. loading dataset
MNIST data_loader = MNIST("./dataset");
// create training dataset loader and shuffling the data
data_loader.train(batch_size, true);

// step 2. model initialization
Network model;
model.add_layer(new Dense("dense1", 500));  // 1st layer
model.add_layer(new Dense("dense2", 10));   // 2nd layer
model.cuda();       // set cuda context for each layer
```

We can also have the following training loop:

```
// get data sample's shared buffer
Blob<float> *train_data   = data_loader.get_data();
// get target's shared buffer
Blob<float> *train_target = data_loader.get_target();
// load data and targets with the batch size
data_loader.get_batch();
tp_count = 0;   step = 0;
while (step < num_steps)
{
  // transfer loaded data to the GPU
  train_data->to(cuda);
  train_target->to(cuda);
```

```
    model.forward(train_data);      // forward
    model.backward(train_target);   // backward
    learning_rate *= 1.f / (1.f + lr_decay * step);
    model.update(learning_rate);    // update

    step = data_loader.next(true);  // load next data

    ... monitoring logic ...
}
```

For the testing phase, we create another dataset loader for the test dataset and only iterate with the forward pass. The following code shows its implementation:

```
test_data_loader.test(batch_size_test);                    // create test
dataset loader
Blob<float> *test_data = test_data_loader.get_data();      // get sample
data shared buffer
Blob<float> *test_target = test_data_loader.get_target();  // get target
shared buffer
test_data_loader.get_batch();      // load samples and targets with the batch
size
tp_count = 0; step = 0;
while (step < num_steps_test) {
  // transfer loaded data to the GPU
  test_data->to(cuda);
  test_target->to(cuda);

  model.forward(test_data);   // forward
  tp_count += model.get_accuracy(test_target);

  step = test_data_loader.next(); // load next data
}
float accuracy = 100.f * tp_count / num_steps_test / batch_size_test;
```

In the testing phase, we will obtain the accuracy after we finish testing all the samples in the testing dataset. Now, we need to obtain the accuracy after the testing loop.

Network training with the MNIST dataset

Now, let's run our implemented code and see its result. For the training phase, we will iterate 2,400 steps with a batch size of 256. The MNIST dataset has 60,000 samples in the training set. 2,400 steps means that we will take the iteration of about 10 epochs. The sample code can be compiled with the following command:

```
$ nvcc -run -m64 -std=c++11 -I/usr/local/cuda/samples/common/inc -gencode
arch=compute_70,code=sm_70 -lcublas -lcudnn -lnvToolsExt -o train
./train.cpp ./src/layer.cu ./src/loss.cu ./src/mnist.cpp ./src/network.cpp
```

The following screenshot shows the training and test output of our implementation:

```
$ ./train
== MNIST training with CUDNN ==
[TRAIN]
loading ./dataset/train-images-idx3-ubyte
loaded 60000 items..
.. model Configuration ..
CUDA: dense1
CUDA: relu
CUDA: dense2
CUDA: softmax
.. initialized dense1 layer ..
.. initialized dense2 layer ..
step:  200, loss: 7.567, accuracy: 77.715%
step:  400, loss: 7.239, accuracy: 92.031%
step:  600, loss: 8.048, accuracy: 92.596%
step:  800, loss: 9.668, accuracy: 92.586%
step: 1000, loss: 7.468, accuracy: 92.609%
step: 1200, loss: 7.278, accuracy: 92.594%
step: 1400, loss: 7.147, accuracy: 92.588%
step: 1600, loss: 7.472, accuracy: 92.600%
step: 1800, loss: 7.080, accuracy: 92.588%
step: 2000, loss: 7.123, accuracy: 92.604%
step: 2200, loss: 8.899, accuracy: 92.596%
step: 2400, loss: 7.757, accuracy: 92.586%
[INFERENCE]
loading ./dataset/t10k-images-idx3-ubyte
loaded 10000 items..
loss: 3.487, accuracy: 77.400%
Done.
```

In the training iteration, the network achieved 92 percent accuracy from the training dataset. However, the testing accuracy is only 77 percent, which is a relatively low score against the training result. There can be many reasons why inferencing shows a large gap in accuracy between training and inference. One possible reason is that the fully connected layer does not consider the regional information that's shown in the preceding screenshot. In deep learning, we use a convolutional layer to make the network learn about the spacial information.

Now, let's implement the convolutional layer with cuDNN, add this to the network, and compare the model's performance.

Convolutional neural networks with cuDNN

The cuDNN library provides optimized performance for convolutional operations. By creating a convolutional layer, we will cover the API's configuration for the forward and backward operations.

The convolutional network layer performs convolution to the input data with its weights. This network architecture is useful when you want to build a neural network that's aware of regional information. Recall from the convolution implementation in Chapter 7, *Parallel Programming Patterns in CUDA*, that it needs considerable memory bandwidth and requires further optimization to get optimal performance. However, using the cuDNN library, we can obtain the best performance as well since we don't have to reinvent the wheel.

The implementation of a convolutional layer is similar to the fully connected layer implementation. There are two differences, however, thanks to the cuDNN library: we don't have to fully implement as much detail as we did previously and we need to allocate a workspace size for the operation. For each convolution operation – forward, backward for the filter, and backward for the input – extra memory space is needed, depending on their algorithm. The algorithm can vary following the given input/output/filter tensor dimensions. The detailed API call will be handled later.

Like other layers, it has three work phases. For the inference phases, we will call `cudnnConvolutionForward()` and `cudnnAddTensor()`. For the backward phase, we will call `cudnnConvolutionBackwardData()`, `cudnnConvolutionBackwardFilter()`, and `cudnnConvolutionBackwardBias()`. Finally, for the update phase we can reuse the code from the fully connected layers. An overview of the layer's configuration is as follows:

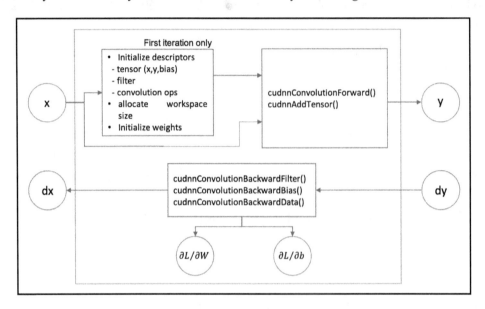

In deep learning neural networks, it is common to use a pooling layer along with the convolutional network. Pooling layers simply select input data to output following a simple rule. The following diagram shows examples of max-pooling:

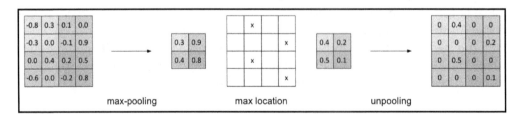

Using the cuDNN library, we will implement these two convolution operations.

The convolution layer

Like a fully connected layer, this convolution layer has weights and biases parameters. In the fully connected layer, we used cuBLAS and it does not require cuDNN-related descriptors. However, we will be using cuDNN convolution functions, and so we need to use a filter descriptor and convolution operation descriptor. The following code shows what resources we should initialize while the layer is being constructed:

```
Conv2D::Conv2D(std::string name,
        int out_channels, kernel_size, stride, padding, dilation):
        out_channels_(out_channels), kernel_size_(kernel_size),
        stride_(stride), padding_(padding), dilation_(dilation) {
  name_ = name;
  cudnnCreateFilterDescriptor(&filter_desc_);
  cudnnCreateConvolutionDescriptor(&conv_desc_);
  cudnnSetConvolution2dDescriptor(conv_desc_,
    padding_, padding_, stride_, stride_, dilation_,dilation_,
    CUDNN_CROSS_CORRELATION, CUDNN_DATA_FLOAT);
}
```

Since we provide convolution operation information when the model is constructed, we can specify the convolution descriptor. However, the filter's operation can be specified at inference time since we can learn the input tensor's size at that time. Now, let's implement the forward pass in the convolution layer.

Implementing forward propagation

As we discussed earlier, we can initialize the convolution layer with the input tensor size. This input tensor size makes an impact on the output tensor's size. The following code shows the parameter initialization step in the forward pass:

```
// initialize weights and bias
if (weights_ == nullptr) {
  // initialize containers handles
  cudnnSetFilter4dDescriptor(filter_desc_,
    CUDNN_DATA_FLOAT, CUDNN_TENSOR_NCHW,
    out_channels_, input->c(), kernel_size_, kernel_size_);

  weights_ = new Blob<float>(out_channels_, input->c(), kernel_size_,
kernel_size_);
  biases_ = new Blob<float>(1, out_channels_); // bias size
  bias_desc_ = biases_->tensor();
}
```

Then, we need to update the input resources, initialize the output blob, create a cuDNN workspace, and initialize the weights parameters, as follows:

```
// initilaize input and output
if (input_ == nullptr || batch_size_ != input->n()) {
  // initialize input
  input_ = input;
  input_desc_ = input->tensor();
  batch_size_ = input->n();

  // getting output tensor size
  cudnnGetConvolution2dForwardOutputDim(
    conv_desc_, input_desc_, filter_desc_,
    &output_size_[0], &output_size_[1],
    &output_size_[2], &output_size_[3]);

  // initialize output blob
  if (output_ == nullptr)
    output_ = new Blob<float>(output_size_);
  else
    output_->reset(output_size_);
  output_desc_ = output_->tensor();

  // initialize weights
  if (!freeze_)
    init_weight_bias();

  // initialize workspace for cudnn
  set_workspace();
}
```

To obtain the output tensor size, we use the `cudnnGetConvolution2dForwardOutputDim()` function. This function outputs dimensional size information based on the input tensor size, the convolution operation, and the filter size. Then, we reuse the same parameter initialization code that we used in the fully connected layer.

To call cuDNN's convolution APIs, we need to provide its working algorithm and workspace memory. We do this because cuDNN selects the optimal convolution algorithm based on the convolution size, and its measurement needs to be done immediately. When the algorithm is determined, cuDNN can determine the workspace size. The convolutional layer needs to have the convolution operation for the forward pass, gradients of input data, and gradients of weights. We need to handle each algorithm individually, but we can allocate just one workspace because the workspace is used for each convolution operation exclusively.

So, we create the workspace with the maximum size among each convolution algorithm workspace size that's required. The following code shows how we can use them and manage the workspace:

```
Conv2d::set_workspace() {
  size_t temp_size = 0;

  // fwd
  cudnnGetConvolutionForwardAlgorithm(cuda_->cudnn(),
    input_desc_, filter_desc_, conv_desc_, output_desc_,
    CUDNN_CONVOLUTION_FWD_PREFER_FASTEST, 0, &conv_fwd_algo_);
  cudnnGetConvolutionForwardWorkspaceSize(cuda_->cudnn(),
    input_desc_, filter_desc_, conv_desc_, output_desc_,
    conv_fwd_algo_, &temp_size);
  workspace_size = std::max(workspace_size, temp_size);

  // bwd - data
  cudnnGetConvolutionBackwardDataAlgorithm(cuda_->cudnn(),
    filter_desc_, output_desc_, conv_desc_, input_desc_,
    CUDNN_CONVOLUTION_BWD_DATA_PREFER_FASTEST, 0,
    &conv_bwd_data_algo_);
  cudnnGetConvolutionBackwardDataWorkspaceSize(cuda_->cudnn(),
    filter_desc_, output_desc_, conv_desc_, input_desc_,
    conv_bwd_data_algo_, &temp_size);
  workspace_size = std::max(workspace_size, temp_size);
  // bwd - filter
  cudnnGetConvolutionBackwardFilterAlgorithm(cuda_->cudnn(),
    input_desc_, output_desc_, conv_desc_, filter_desc_,
    CUDNN_CONVOLUTION_BWD_FILTER_PREFER_FASTEST, 0,
    &conv_bwd_filter_algo_);
  cudnnGetConvolutionBackwardFilterWorkspaceSize(cuda_->cudnn(),
    input_desc_, output_desc_, conv_desc_, filter_desc_,
    conv_bwd_filter_algo_, &temp_size);
  workspace_size = std::max(workspace_size, temp_size);

  if (workspace_size > 0) {
    if (d_workspace != nullptr)
      cudaFree(d_workspace);
    cudaMalloc((void**)&d_workspace, workspace_size);
  }
}
```

Each convolution algorithm is specified with individual types, that
is, `cudnnConvolutionFwdAlgo_t`, `cudnnConvolutionBwdDataAlgo_t`,
and `cudnnConvolutionBwdFilterAlgo_t`. We can use them by declaring them as class
member variables, that is, `conv_fwd_algo_`, `conv_bwd_data_algo_`,
and `conv_bwd_filter_algo_`.

Now, we write the forward processing code after initialization. We do convolution with the
filter and add a bias. The following code shows the cuDNN convolution forward
implementation:

```
cudnnConvolutionForward(cuda_->cudnn(), &cuda_->one, input_desc_,
input_->cuda(), \
    filter_desc_, weights_->cuda(), conv_desc_, conv_fwd_algo_,
d_workspace, workspace_size, \
    &cuda_->zero, output_desc_, output_->cuda());
cudnnAddTensor(cuda_->cudnn(), &cuda_->one, bias_desc_, biases_->cuda(), \
    &cuda_->one, output_desc_, output_->cuda());
```

The result of convolution will be passed to the next layer using the output blob.

Implementing backward propagation

In back-propagation, we should compute the gradients of the bias, the gradients of weights,
and the gradients of the input data. To do this, we need to create blobs at the first iteration
so that we can store them. Their size does not depend on the batch size, so we just need to
make sure they are created. The initialization step can be implemented as follows:

```
// initialize grad_output back-propagation space
if (grad_weights_ == nullptr) {
  grad_output_  = grad_output;
  grad_weights_ = new Blob<float>(weights_->shape());
  grad_biases_  = new Blob<float>(1, biases_->c());
  grad_input_   = new Blob<float>(input_->shape());
}
```

Then, we call the cuDNN backward convolution APIs, as follows:

```
Blob<float> *Conv2D::backward(Blob<float> *grad_output) {
  ... { initialization step } ...

  // gradients of biases
  cudnnConvolutionBackwardBias(cuda_->cudnn(),
    &cuda_->one,
    output_desc_, grad_output->cuda(),
    &cuda_->zero,
```

```
    bias_desc_, grad_biases_->cuda());
  // gradients of weights
  cudnnConvolutionBackwardFilter(cuda_->cudnn(),
    &cuda_->one,
    input_desc_, input_->cuda(),
    output_desc_, grad_output_->cuda(),
    conv_desc_, conv_bwd_filter_algo_, d_workspace, workspace_size,
    &cuda_->zero,
    filter_desc_, grad_weights_->cuda());

  // gradients of input data
  if (!gradient_stop_)
    cudnnConvolutionBackwardData(cuda_->cudnn(),
      &cuda_->one,
      filter_desc_, weights_->cuda(),
      output_desc_, grad_output->cuda(),
      conv_desc_, conv_bwd_data_algo_, d_workspace, workspace_size,
      &cuda_->zero,
      input_desc_, grad_input_->cuda());
```

Then, we pass the gradients of the input data to the previous layer to propagate the gradients. We will update the gradients of the weights and biases at the update step by using the base class' gradients update code. We covered this when we implemented backward propagation in the fully connected layer. We also can skip computing the gradients of the input data if this is the first layer.

Pooling layer with cuDNN

The pooling layer has two features. First, its output size is different compared to the convolution layer and cuDNN provides the corresponding API for this. Second, it does not have any internal weights.

To specify the pooling operation, we can use cuDNN's `cudnnPoolingDescriptor_t` function and create and specify the cuDNN's pooling descriptor in the class constructor, as follows:

```
cudnnCreatePoolingDescriptor(&pool_desc_);
cudnnSetPooling2dDescriptor(pool_desc_, mode_, CUDNN_PROPAGATE_NAN,
  kernel_size_, kernel_size_, padding_, padding_, stride_, stride_);
```

Now, let's implement the forward and backward operation of the pooling layer.

Implementing forward propagation

The pooling layer contributes to reducing the tensor's size. Due to this, we need to compute the output size. We can compute the size using the `cudnnGetPooling2dForwardOutputDim()` function, like we did in the convolution layer implementation. Also, the tensor size depends on the batch size. This means we need to update the tensor size if the batch size is changed. The following code shows how we can initialize the input and output blobs:

```
if (input_ == nullptr || batch_size_ != input->n()) {
  input_ = input;

  // resource initialize
  input_desc_ = input_->tensor();
  batch_size_ = input->n();
  // setting output
  cudnnGetPooling2dForwardOutputDim(pool_desc_, input_desc_,
    &output_size_[0], &output_size_[1], &output_size_[2],
    &output_size_[3]);
  if (output_ == nullptr)
    output_ = new Blob<float>(output_size_);
  else
    output_->reset(output_size_);
  output_desc_ = output_->tensor();
}
```

For the forward pass, we call the `cudnnPoolingForward()` function, as follows:

```
Blob<float> *Pooling::forward(Blob<float> *input) {
  ... { initialization step } ...

  cudnnPoolingForward(cudnnHandle, pool_desc_, &one,
    input_desc_, input_->cuda(),
    &zero, output_desc_, output_->cuda());
}
```

Implementing backward propagation

For the back-propagation step, we call the `cudnnPoolingBackward()` function, as follows:

```
Blob<float> *Pooling::backward(Blob<float> *grad_output) {
  if (grad_input_ == nullptr)
    grad_input_ = new Blob<float>(input_->shape());

  cudnnPoolingBackward(cudnnHandle, pool_desc_,
    &one, output_desc_, output_->cuda(),
    output_desc_, grad_output->cuda(),
    input_desc_, input_->cuda(),
    &zero, input_desc_, grad_input_->cuda());
}
```

The pooling layer's tensor shape of inputs and gradients of inputs are same and the shape of outputs and gradients of outputs are same. Therefore, we can reuse the tensor descriptors respectively of inputs and outputs.

Now, let's integrate these into a single convolutional layer implementation.

Network configuration

Now, we will update our previous network, LeNet. The network code can be written as follows:

```
Network model;
model.add_layer(new Conv2D("conv1", 20, 5));
model.add_layer(new Pooling("pool", 2, 0, 2, CUDNN_POOLING_MAX));
model.add_layer(new Conv2D("conv2", 50, 5));
model.add_layer(new Pooling("pool", 2, 0, 2, CUDNN_POOLING_MAX));
model.add_layer(new Dense("dense1", 500));
model.add_layer(new Activation("relu", CUDNN_ACTIVATION_RELU));
model.add_layer(new Dense("dense2", 10));
model.add_layer(new Softmax("softmax"));
model.cuda();
```

Now, we can start the training and inference stages since we have configured our layers so that they're connected to each other. Let's compile the code with the following command:

```
$ nvcc -run -m64 -std=c++11 -I/usr/local/cuda/samples/common/inc -gencode
arch=compute_70,code=sm_70 -lcublas -lcudnn -lnvToolsExt -o train
./train.cpp ./src/layer.cu ./src/loss.cu ./src/mnist.cpp ./src/network.cpp
```

Then, we can see the training and test result as follows:

```
$ ./train
== MNIST training with CUDNN ==
[TRAIN]
loading ./dataset/train-images-idx3-ubyte
loaded 60000 items..
.. model Configuration ..
CUDA: conv1
CUDA: pool
CUDA: conv2
CUDA: pool
CUDA: dense1
CUDA: relu
CUDA: dense2
CUDA: softmax
.. initialized conv1 layer ..
.. initialized conv2 layer ..
.. initialized dense1 layer ..
.. initialized dense2 layer ..
step:  200, loss: 0.025, accuracy: 72.592%
step:  400, loss: 0.001, accuracy: 94.182%
step:  600, loss: 1.382, accuracy: 94.469%
step:  800, loss: 1.143, accuracy: 94.498%
step: 1000, loss: 0.004, accuracy: 94.516%
step: 1200, loss: 0.292, accuracy: 94.512%
step: 1400, loss: 0.064, accuracy: 94.488%
step: 1600, loss: 0.051, accuracy: 94.482%
step: 1800, loss: 0.031, accuracy: 94.484%
step: 2000, loss: 0.095, accuracy: 94.518%
step: 2200, loss: 0.118, accuracy: 94.521%
step: 2400, loss: 0.481, accuracy: 94.492%
[INFERENCE]
loading ./dataset/t10k-images-idx3-ubyte
loaded 10000 items..
loss: 2.704, accuracy: 87.000%
Done.
```

As you can see, the network achieved higher training accuracy and inferencing than when it used the fully connected network only. We also can confirm its operation by looking at the NVIDIA profile, as follows:

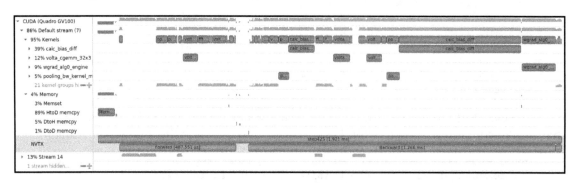

Mixed precision operations

The latest NVIDIA GPUs support mixed precision operation deep learning. We will not cover this in this book as it is outside of our scope. However, you can access the example that's provided by NVIDIA at `/usr/src/cudnn_samples_v7/conv_sample` if you wish to learn more. To access this example, you need to download the sample from the cuDNN web page. This example code shows how to use mixed precision operations using the cuDNN library.

To have the cuDNN APIs work with the tensor cores, we need to set the math type, as follows:

```
cudnnSetConvolutionMathType(cudnnConvDesc, CUDNN_TENSOR_OP_MATH);
```

Then, we need to initialize the tensor descriptors of the input and output tensors using `cudnnSetTensorNdDescriptor()`. This provides padding for the tensors so that we get optimized tensor core performance.

One good cuDNN-based implementation is `cudnn-training`: `https://github.com/tbennun/cudnn-training`. It implements LeNet as a sequence of cuDNN functions. You can follow each line to see how the CUDNN functions work.

If you are interested in deploying your network using cuDNN, please check out the following video about GTC-CNN inference with cuDNN (`https://developer.nvidia.com/gtc/2019/video/S9644/video`). This talk introduces useful performance optimization tricks on CNN inference using cuDNN.

Using half-precision in deep learning training requires more than FP16 operations utilization. We need to compute tensors in FP16 while we maintain the weights in FP32. Also, some operations require FP32. We call this the mixed precision. The cuDNN library provides a mixed precision inference example named mnistCUDNN. This example shows the conversion of input and layer data types. If you want to learn more about the mixed precision operation in deep learning and training, please read the following article: `https://devblogs.nvidia.com/video-mixed-precision-techniques-tensor-cores-deep-learning/`.

Now, we will cover other GPU use considerations in deep learning in terms of performance.

Recurrent neural network optimization

RRNs allow you to analyze sequential data in deep learning. Although this network has sequential dependencies, there's plenty of room for optimization. In this section, we will cover its algorithm and how cuDNN provides optimized performance.

There are many kinds of RNNs, but cuDNN only supports four, that is, RNN with ReLU, RNN with tanh, LSTM, and GRU. They have two inputs: the hidden parameters from the previous network and the input from the source. Depending on their types, they have different operations. In this lab, we will cover the LSTM operation. The following diagram shows the forward operation of the LSTM:

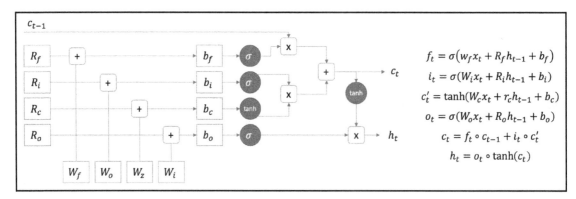

$$f_t = \sigma(w_f x_t + R_f h_{t-1} + b_f)$$
$$i_t = \sigma(W_i x_t + R_i h_{t-1} + b_i)$$
$$c'_t = \tanh(W_c x_t + r_c h_{t-1} + b_c)$$
$$o_t = \sigma(W_o x_t + R_o h_{t-1} + b_o)$$
$$c_t = f_t \circ c_{t-1} + i_t \circ c'_t$$
$$h_t = o_t \circ \tanh(c_t)$$

From a computing perspective, there are eight matrix-matrix multiplications and many element-wise operations. From this estimation, we can expect that LSTM could be memory-bounded since each operation is memory-bounded. On the other hand, CUDNN provides the `cudnnRNNForwardInference()` and `cudnnRNNFowardTraining()` RNN functions. We will cover the benefits of using this function by measuring the performance of this function and simulated LSTM. To do this, we will implement a virtual LSTM layer and compare its performance to the cuDNN LSTM function.

For test purposes, we will set the hyperparameter like so:

```
int mode = 2; // LSTM in CUDNN
int seq_length = 512;
int num_layers = 4;
int hidden_size = 512;
int input_size = hidden_size;
int batch_size = 32;
float dropout_rate = 0;
bool bidirectional = 0;
int persistent = 0;
```

The sequence length or hidden size can vary, depending on the problem. In this test, we will use 512 as the length, which is used a lot in sequence research. The CUDNN API requires more options to work, such as dropout rate, bidirectional or unidirectional, and persistent RNNs. We will only test the vanilla LSTM in this section.

Using the CUDNN LSTM operation

Let's write some code that executes the cudnnRNNForwardTraining() function as an LSTM layer:

1. We need to initialize the input and output memory space. To execute cuDNN's RNN API, we need to use the following variables:

```
// hx, cx, hy, cy, dhy, dcy, dhx, and dcs can be null.
void *x;             // input
void *hx = nullptr; // input of initial hidden state
void *cx = nullptr; // input of cell state (LSTM)

void *y;             // output
void *hy = nullptr; // output of final hidden state
void *cy = nullptr; // output of final cell state (LSTM)

void *dy;            // input of gradient
void *dhy = nullptr; // input of final hidden state
void *dcy = nullptr; // input of final cell state (LSTM)

void *dx;            // output of gradient at the input of rnn
void *dhx = nullptr; // output of gradient at the initial hidden
state
void *dcx = nullptr; // output of gradient at the initial cell
state
```

These variables are the inputs and outputs of LSTM. To provide the inputs and get the outputs, we need to allocate the appropriate memory space. Following the LSTM definition, we need to consider the length of the input, output, and hidden layers. These sizes can be determined as follows:

```
int input_length = seq_length * input_size * batch_size;
int output_length = seq_length * hidden_size * batch_size;
int hidden_length = hidden_size * batch_size * num_layers;
```

Then, we can allocate memory for each item.

2. Now, we need to set up the tensor descriptors for the cuDNN RNN API. The following code shows the required tensor descriptors that we should set up:

```
cudnnTensorDescriptor_t x_desc[seq_length], y_desc[seq_length], \
                        dx_desc[seq_length], dy_desc[seq_length];
cudnnTensorDescriptor_t hx_desc, cx_desc;
cudnnTensorDescriptor_t dhx_desc, dcx_desc;
cudnnTensorDescriptor_t hy_desc, cy_desc;
cudnnTensorDescriptor_t dhy_desc, dcy_desc;
```

For the input and output descriptors, we need to initialize each element, that is, the batch size and its input size. The other hidden tensor descriptors are initialized with the number of layers, the batch size, and the hidden size. This section will not cover how to write the initialization code. However, you can check out the code in the `10_deep_learning/03_rnn` file if you want to find out more.

3. We also have to provide a workspace for the RNN operation, just like we did for the convolution operation:

```
void *workspace;
cudnnFilterDescriptor_t w_desc, dw_desc;
cudnnSetRNNDescriptor_v6(cudnnHandle, rnn_desc,
                         hidden_size, num_layers, dropout_desc,
CUDNN_LINEAR_INPUT,
                         bidirectional ? CUDNN_BIDIRECTIONAL :
CUDNN_UNIDIRECTIONAL,
                         CUDNN_LSTM, CUDNN_RNN_ALGO_STANDARD,
CUDNN_DATA_FLOAT));
size_t weight_size;
cudnnGetRNNParamsSize(cudnnHandle, rnn_desc, x_desc[0],
&weight_size, CUDNN_DATA_FLOAT);
cudaMalloc((void**)&workspace, weight_size);
```

Then, we can set the filter descriptor based on the workspace's size, as follows:

```
dimW = {weight_size / sizeof(float), 1, 1}
cudnnCreateFilterDescriptor(&w_desc);
cudnnCreateFilterDescriptor(&dw_desc);
cudnnSetFilterNdDescriptor(w_desc, CUDNN_DATA_FLOAT,
CUDNN_TENSOR_NCHW, 3, dimW);
cudnnSetFilterNdDescriptor(dw_desc, CUDNN_DATA_FLOAT,
CUDNN_TENSOR_NCHW, 3, dimW);
cudnnRNNForwardTraining(cudnnHandle, rnn_desc, seq_length,
                        x_desc, x, hx_desc, hx, cx_desc, cx,
                        w_desc, w,
                        y_desc, y, hy_desc, hy, cy_desc, cy,
```

```
workspace, workspace_size, reserved_space,
reserved_size);
```

We can measure their performance using `cudaEvnetRecoard()` and flops computation. For example, the forward operation can be configured with the following equation:

FLOPS = (num of GEMM per layer) × FMA × (input size) × (hidden size) × (sequence length) × (batch size) × (number of × layers)

Then, we will test our implementation by changing the batch size from 32 to 256 by increasing the size with 32. The applicable test range can be different, as well as the GPU's memory size.

In this section, we implemented the LSTM-based simulation and `cudnnRNNForwardTraining()` call. Our partially simulated version only has GEMM operations, which are the most compute-intensive. Now, let's compare the performance of these implementations.

Implementing a virtual LSTM operation

In our implementation, we will focus on simulating LSTM's major operations rather than fully implementing it.

Let's determine the hyperparameters of the LSTM network. In general, the input sequence length ranges from 512 to 2,048. The number of layers varies. However, it cannot be large due to *tanh* operations. For the input size, we will use 512. Usually, the batch size is between 32 and 256 in terms of RNN usage. CUDNN requires more inputs about the dropout rate, bidirectional or unidirectional, and whether we're using a persistent RNN or not. We're just not using them right now. Our LSTM configuration information is as follows:

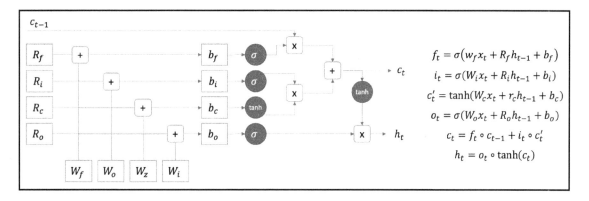

Now, we will have a partially implemented operation of LSTM to measure the compute intensity. As we discussed earlier, LSTM has two matrix-matrix multiplications that we need to compute. The LSTM operation will compute that for each element of the input sequence, as well as for each layer. Then, the operation can be configured as follows:

```
for (int layer = 0; layer < num_layers; layer++) {
    for (int linear_layer = 0; linear_layer < 4; linear_layer++) {
        for (int sequence = 0; sequence < seq_length; sequence++) {
            cublasSgemm(cublas_handle, CUBLAS_OP_T, CUBLAS_OP_N,
            hidden_size, input_size, batch_size,
            &alpha, input_weight, input_size, x, input_size,
            &beta, h, hidden_size);
            cublasSgemm(cublas_handle, CUBLAS_OP_T, CUBLAS_OP_N,
            hidden_size, hidden_size, batch_size,
            &alpha, recurrent_weight, hidden_size,
            h, hidden_size,
            &beta, y, hidden_size);
        }
    }
}
```

We can use more element-wise operations, but it will just approximate the compute intensity, so we will omit them for now.

Comparing the performance between CUDNN and SGEMM LSTM

Let's compare their there performance along with the different batch sizes as following codes implemented in `main()` function:

```
for (int step = 1; step <= 8; step++)
{
 batch_size = 32 * step;
 printf("Batch Size: %3d\n", batch_size);
 rnn_operation(seq_length, num_layers, hidden_size, input_size,
   batch_size, dropout_rate, bidirectional, mode, persistent);
 cublas_operation(mode, 2ull, input_size, hidden_size, seq_length,
batch_size, num_layers);
}
```

And, we can compile and execute the example source code with the following command:

```
$ nvcc -run -m64 -std=c++11 -I/usr/local/cuda/samples/common/inc -gencode
arch=compute_70,code=sm_70 -lcublas -lcudnn -lcurand -o rnn ./rnn.cpp
```

The following graph shows the measured performance of cuBLAS and cuDNN from a Tesla V100 card:

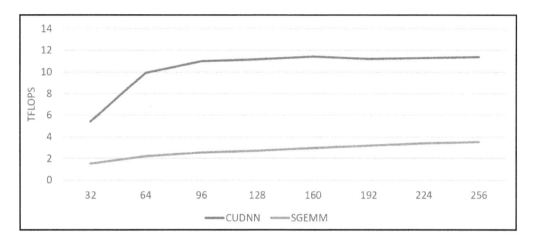

In the preceding graph, the two implementations show a huge difference in performance. The LSTM's performance of cuDNN is much better than the simulated LSTM using cuBLAS. Also, the LSTM operation's performance follows the roofline of the Tesla V100 GPU. On the other hand, the two SGEMM operations don't show this performance since the matrix size isn't large enough to get full performance. To obtain 10 TFlops from the Tesla V100, the matrix size should be similar to or larger than the square of 1,024. However, as we can see, our matrix size is around the square of 512.

LSTM optimization is explained in the following NVIDIA article: https://devblogs.nvidia.com/optimizing-recurrent-neural-networks-cudnn-5. It combines matrix-matrix multiplications, fusing element-wise operations, multiple streams, and multi-layer parallelization.

One of the optimization versions of the RNN is the persistent RNN (https://svail.github.io/persistent_rnns), which was introduced by Greg Diamos. Although his implementation does not include LSTM and GRU, you can learn how the RNN can be optimized.

Profiling deep learning frameworks

In general, we develop and research neural networks using deep learning frameworks such as TensorFlow, PyTorch, and MxNet. Thanks to these frameworks, we can develop sophisticated models effectively. However, when it comes to performance engineering, understanding the GPU operation underneath the framework is a steep learning curve because of the profiling tool's capabilities. For example, profiling with chrome tracing is useful when the model is simple, but isn't when the model is complicated.

In `Chapter 5`, *CUDA Application Profiling and Debugging*, we covered the **NVIDIA Tools Extension** (**NVTX**), which allows us to have custom annotations in the GPU applications and review the timeline using NVIDIA Nsight Systems. For complicated applications, it is useful for programmers to analyze their performance and find bottlenecks.

In this section, we will cover how to use NVTX in PyTorch and TensorFlow by modifying the ResNet-50 sample code. The example code can be found in the `10_deep_learining/05_framework_profile` folder in this book's GitHub repository. You can obtain the original source code from `https://github.com/nvidia/DeepLearningExamples`.

To make an easy working environment configuration, we will use **NVIDIA GPU Cloud** (**NGC**) deep learning containers for PyTorch and TensorFlow. If you need to learn about NGC or basic usage of the container, please visit the appendix for NGC in this book.

Now, let's begin with PyTorch first.

Profiling the PyTorch model

In PyTorch, we can place a custom tag using `torch.cuda.nvtx.range_push("foo")` and `torch.cuda.nvtx.range_pop()`. This maintains the original CUDA NVTX APIs, that is, `nvtxRangePush()` and `nvtxRangePop()`. Let's see how NVTX annotations can help us understand deep learning operations in the timeline. In the following steps, we will use the ResNet-50 example code in the `05_framework_profile/pytorch/RN50v1.5` file:

1. We will place NVTX annotations in the training loop in the `train()` function to annotate the `step` value. This function can be found in the `image_classificaiton/training.py` file. The following screenshot shows the training loop and the NVTX annotations at line **234** and line **260**, respectively:

```
231
232      for i, (input, target) in data_iter:
233          # NVTX: displaying step index
234          torch.cuda.nvtx.range_push("step:" + str(i))
235
236          bs = input.size(0)
237          lr_scheduler(optimizer, i, epoch)
238          data_time = time.time() - end
239
240          if prof > 0:
241              if i >= prof:
242                  break
243
244          optimizer_step = ((i + 1) % batch_size_multiplier) == 0
245          loss, prec1, prec5 = step(input, target, optimizer_step = optimizer_step)
246
247          it_time = time.time() - end
248
249          if logger is not None:
250              logger.log_metric('train.top1', to_python_float(prec1))
251              logger.log_metric('train.top5', to_python_float(prec5))
252              logger.log_metric('train.loss', to_python_float(loss))
253              logger.log_metric('train.compute_ips', calc_ips(bs, it_time - data_time))
254              logger.log_metric('train.total_ips', calc_ips(bs, it_time))
255              logger.log_metric('train.data_time', data_time)
256              logger.log_metric('train.compute_time', it_time - data_time)
257
258          end = time.time()
259
260          torch.cuda.nvtx.range_pop() # NVTX:step index
261
```

In the preceding code, the training operations are implemented in the step function, which is defined by the get_train_step() function. Therefore, we need to place NVTX annotations in that function to learn more about it.

2. Let's add some NVTX annotations to the `get_train_step()` function at line **164**. This function returns the `_step()` function, which includes the training operations. Therefore, we will place NVTX annotations in this function. The training procedures are forward and backward propagation, all-reduce, and optimization (update weights). The following screenshot shows the annotations of forward propagation at lines **166** and **171**:

```
163
164    def get_train_step(model_and_loss, optimizer, fp16, use_amp = False, batch_size_multiplier = 1):
165        def _step(input, target, optimizer_step = True):
166            torch.cuda.nvtx.range_push("forward")
167            input_var = Variable(input)
168            target_var = Variable(target)
169            loss, output = model_and_loss(input_var, target_var)
170            prec1, prec5 = torch.zeros(1), torch.zeros(1) #utils.accuracy(output.data, target, topk=(1, 5))
171            torch.cuda.nvtx.range_pop() # NVTX: forward
172
```

This way, we can place other annotations on the remaining operations.

3. We can also have NVTX annotations for the model layers. In this example, the ResNet-50 model is implemented in the `image_classification/resnet.py` file. The following screenshot shows the example annotations of the network:

```
187
188        def forward(self, x):
189            torch.cuda.nvtx.range_push("conv1")
190            x = self.conv1(x)
191            if self.bn1 is not None:
192                x = self.bn1(x)
193            x = self.relu(x)
194            torch.cuda.nvtx.range_pop() # NVTX: conv1
195
196            torch.cuda.nvtx.range_push("conv2")
197            x = self.maxpool(x)
198            x = self.layer1(x)
199            torch.cuda.nvtx.range_pop() # NVTX: conv2
200
201            torch.cuda.nvtx.range_push("conv3")
202            x = self.layer2(x)
203            torch.cuda.nvtx.range_pop() # NVTX: conv3
204
205            torch.cuda.nvtx.range_push("conv4")
206            x = self.layer3(x)
207            torch.cuda.nvtx.range_pop() # NVTX: conv4
208
209            torch.cuda.nvtx.range_push("conv5")
210            x = self.layer4(x)
211            torch.cuda.nvtx.range_pop() # NVTX: conv5
212
213            torch.cuda.nvtx.range_push("fc")
214            x = self.avgpool(x)
215            x = x.view(x.size(0), -1)
216            x = self.fc(x)
217            torch.cuda.nvtx.range_pop() # NVTX: fc
218
219            return x
```

As we can see, we can place NVTX annotations following the ResNet architecture. We can get more information if we place annotations in each building block.

4. Now, let's profile the model. As we discussed earlier, we will use the NGC deep learning container known as PyTorch. The `imagenet` dataset is located in the `/raid/datasets/imagenet/raw-data` folder. To limit the profiling time range, we will use the delay option (`-y`) and duration option (`-d`). The following code shows a bash shell script that executes the container and profiles the network:

```
#/bin/bash

CODE_PATH="RN50v1.5"
DATASET_PATH="/raid/datasets/imagenet/raw-data/"
OUTPUT_NAME="resnet50_pyt"

# default profile
docker run --rm -ti --runtime=nvidia \
    -v $(pwd)/${CODE_PATH}:/workspace \
    -v ${DATASET_PATH}:/imagenet \
    nvcr.io/nvidia/pytorch:19.08-py3 \
        nsys profile -t cuda,nvtx,cudnn,cublas -o ${OUTPUT_NAME}
          -f true -w true -y 60 -d 20 \
        python /workspace/main.py --arch resnet50 -b 64
          --fp16 /imagenet
```

After execution, the preceding code generates the profiled result in the RN50v1.5 directory, that is, `resnet50_pyt.qdrep`.

5. Finally, open the profiled output, `resnet50_pyt.qdrep`, using NVIDIA Nsight Systems and review the operations. The following screenshot shows a measured step with NVTX annotations:

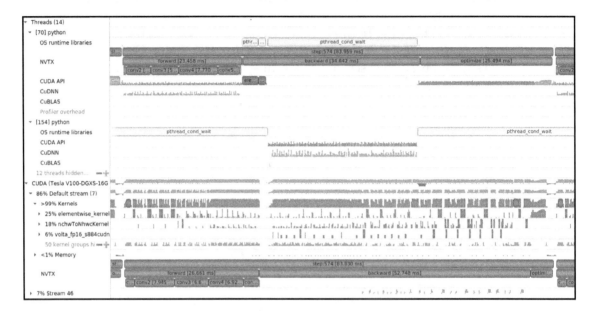

Here, we can see that the backward operations take twice as long as the forwarding operations. Also, PyTorch separates the host threads for the training loop and backward propagation. Looking at the kernel profiling, the most time-consuming points are element-wise kernel executions. Let's enlarge the forwarding pass to review the layers' execution time, as shown in the following screenshot:

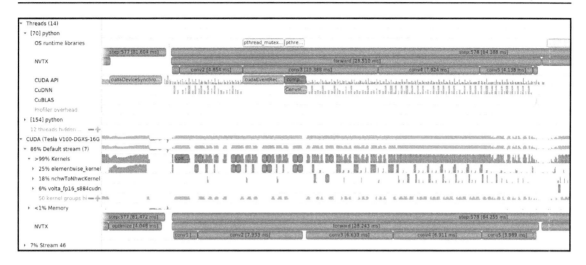

Here, we can see that the second convolution block takes the longest time to complete. If there are inefficient points in this layer, we can dig further. We can also analyze a specific kernel function using NVIDIA Nsight Compute if that operation is determined as a bottleneck and needs to be optimized. Comparing the host API tracing and the GPUs, we can see that the time durations are different. This is because the host and the GPU operations are asynchronous. So, we need to be cautious when we measure the GPU execution time from the host. Now, let's take a look at the optimization step, as shown in the following screenshot:

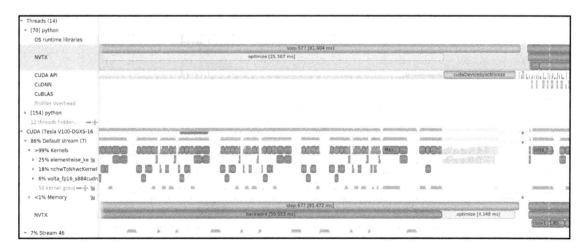

We can see that the huge difference was in the measured execution time from the host and the GPU. The host's measured execution time was 25.367 ms, whereas the GPU's time was 4.048 ms. Its operations are mainly element-wise operations and its execution is delayed until backward propagation has finished. We can find the asynchronous execution too. After that, we can see the `cudaDeviceSynchronize()` function, which prevents the current step from being updated by the next step.

We also can disable these asynchronous operations by setting an environment, that is, `CUDA_LAUNCH_BLOCKING=1`. We can pass this to the Nsight System's profile option using the environment option (`-e`). Then, we can analyze the application's `align` operation with the host and kernel functions.

PyTorch has several NVTX featured APIs in their CUDA objects. PyTorch documentation can be found at `https://pytorch.org/docs/stable/_modules/torch/cuda/nvtx.html`. By calling the NVTX APIs in PyTorch directly, the CUDA NVTX APIs are called. This means we could obtain custom-tagged NVTX marks in the profiled timeline.

Profiling a TensorFlow model

Profiling TensorFlow graphs requires that we have an NVTX plugin that enables NVTX annotations. To use NVTX annotations in TensorFlow, we need to install the `nvtx-plugins-tf` Python plugin using the following command:

```
$ pip install nvtx-plugins-tf
```

However, we don't have to do this if we use an NGC TensorFlow container later than version 19.o8.

TensorFlow graph APIs are symbolic APIs, so they require specific programming methods. The NVTX plugin provides two options for this: a decorator and a Python function.

Here is an example of an NVTX decorator:

```
import nvtx.plugins.tf as nvtx_tf
ENABLE_NVTX=true
@nvtx_tf.ops.trace(message='Dense Block', domain_name='Forward',
        grad_domain_name='Gradient', enabled=ENABLE_NVTX,
        trainable=True)
def dense_layer(x):
    x = tf.layers.dense(x, 1000, activation=tf.nn.relu, name='dense_1')
    x = tf.layers.dense(x, 1000, activation=tf.nn.relu, name='dense_2')
return x
```

The following is an example of an NVTX Python function:

```
import nvtx.plugins.tf as nvtx_tf
ENABLE_NVTX=true
x, nvtx_context = nvtx_tf.ops.start(x, message='Dense Block', \
        domain_name='Forward', grad_domain_name='Gradient',
        enabled=ENABLE_NVTX, trainable=True)
x = tf.layers.dense(x, 1000, activation=tf.nn.relu, name='dense_1')
x = tf.layers.dense(x, 1000, activation=tf.nn.relu, name='dense_2')
x = nvtx_tf.ops.end(x, nvtx_context)
```

The NVTX plugin provides NVTXHook, which allows us to profile the TF estimator and session. For example, we can use the hook as follows:

```
from nvtx.plugins.tf.estimator import NVTXHook

nvtx_callback = NVTXHook(skip_n_steps=1, name='Train')
training_hooks=[]
training_hooks.append(nvtx_callback)
```

Then, we can apply this to either option using the following code:

```
with tf.train.MonitoredSession(hooks=training_hooks) as sess:
```

Alternatively, we can use the following code:

```
tf.estimator.Estimator(hooks=training_hooks, ...)
```

Now, let's apply this to the sample ResNet-50 code and review the operation. The example code can be found in the `05_framework_profile/tensorflow/RN50v1.5` folder:

1. Let's begin by applying `NVTXHook` to the estimator. The training graph's definition can be found in the `runtime/runner.py` file on line 312. Ahead of building the graph, we will append `NVTXHook` to the list of hooks, as shown in the following block of code:

```
417
418    # NVTX
419    nvtx_callback = NVTXHook(skip_n_steps=1, name='Train')
420    training_hooks.append(nvtx_callback)
421
```

2. Then, we will apply the NVTX annotation to the model-building function. The `model_build()` function can be found in the `ResnetModel` class in the `model/resnet_v1_5.py` file. The following code shows an example of placing an NVTX annotation by using a Python function on the `conv1` layer in the `model_build()` function:

```
357
358    # NVTX annotation - conv1
359    inputs, nvtx_context = nvtx_tf.ops.start(inputs, message='conv1', \
360        domain_name='Forward', grad_domain_name='Gradient', enabled=True, trainable=True)
361    net = blocks.conv2d_block(
362        inputs,
363        n_channels=64,
364        kernel_size=(7, 7),
365        strides=(2, 2),
366        mode='SAME_RESNET',
367        use_batch_norm=True,
368        activation='relu',
369        is_training=training,
370        data_format=self.model_hparams.compute_format,
371        conv2d_hparams=self.conv2d_hparams,
372        batch_norm_hparams=self.batch_norm_hparams,
373        name='conv2d'
374    )
375    net = nvtx_tf.ops.end(net, nvtx_context) # NVTX: conv1
376
```

In the preceding code, we need to be cautious when to use proper inputs and outputs when using the `nvtx_tf.ops.start()` and `nvtx_tf.ops.end()` functions. Only place NVTX annotations in the other layers. Be sure that the final fully connected layer's output is the output of the network.

We also have to disable the code to check the number of trainable variables it has. If NVTX's `trainable` parameter's value is `True`, the size changes. At line 174 in the `resnet_v1_5.py` file, there's a block of assertion code that checks the number of that variable. Simply comment it out, as follows:

```
173
174     # if mode == tf.estimator.ModeKeys.TRAIN:
175     #     assert (len(tf.trainable_variables()) == 161)
176     # else:
177     #     assert (len(tf.trainable_variables()) == 0)
178
```

3. We also use NVTX decorators for the ResNet building blocks. In the `model/blocks` directory, we can find the `conv2d` and ResNet bottleneck block implementations in `conv2d_blocks.py` and `resnet_bottleneck_block.py`. In the `conv2d_blocks.py` file, we can decorate `conv2d_block()` function to annotate NVTX profiling, as follows:

```
23
24  import nvtx.plugins.tf as nvtx_tf
25
26  @nvtx_tf.ops.trace(message='conv2d', domain_name='Forward', grad_domain_name='Gradient', \
27      enabled=True, trainable=True)
28  def conv2d_block(
29      inputs,
30      n_channels,
31      kernel_size=(3, 3),
32      strides=(2, 2),
33      mode='SAME',
34      use_batch_norm=True,
```

In the same way, we can do the same to the `resnet_bottleneck_block.py` file:

```
26
27    import nvtx.plugins.tf as nvtx_tf
28
29    @nvtx_tf.ops.trace(message='bottleneck', domain_name='Forward', grad_domain_name='Gradient', \
30        enabled=True, trainable=True)
31    def bottleneck_block(
32        inputs,
33        depth,
34        depth_bottleneck,
35        stride,
36        training=True,
```

4. Now, let's profile the model. Like we did with the PyTorch container, we will use TensorFlow's NGC container. We will assume that the `imagenet` dataset's `tfrecord` files are located in the `/raid/datasets/imagenet/tfrecord` directory. The following code shows a bash shell script that executes the container and profiles the network:

```
#/bin/bash

CODE_PATH="RN50v1.5"
DATASET_PATH="/raid/datasets/imagenet/tfrecord"
OUTPUT_NAME="resnet50_tf"

# default profile
docker run --rm -ti --runtime=nvidia \
    -v $(pwd):/result \
    -v $(pwd)/${CODE_PATH}:/workspace \
    -v ${DATASET_PATH}:/imagenet \
    nvcr.io/nvidia/tensorflow:19.08-py3 \
        nsys profile -t cuda,nvtx,cudnn,cublas -o ${OUTPUT_NAME}
                    -f true -w true -y 40 -d 20 \
            python /workspace/main.py --mode=training_benchmark
                                    --warmup_steps 200 \
                --num_iter 500 --iter_unit batch
                --results_dir=results --batch_size 64
```

When we execute this function, we will get the `resnet50_tf.qdrep` file in the `RN50v1.5` directory.

5. Finally, let's review the profiled output using the NVIDIA Nsight System:

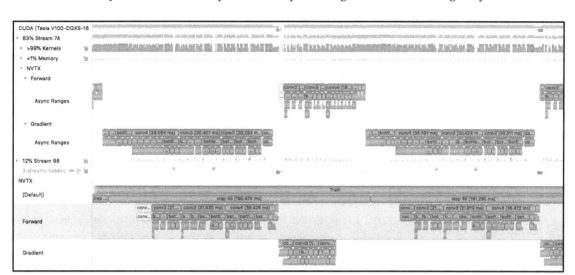

Here, we can confirm that backward propagation takes twice as long as the forward pass. This example code isn't synchronized with the CPU and the GPU. Due to this, we can see a larger time difference between the host and the GPU. As we place additional annotations in the building blocks, we will be able to see the sub-block annotations in the layers.

Profiling with NVIDIA Nsight Systems provides additional benefits when it comes to monitoring all-reduce's execution time in multi-GPU training. The following screenshot shows the profiling result of a GPU that was training with two GPUs:

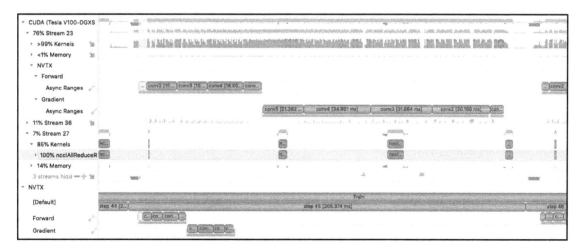

In the highlighted row, we can see the `ncclAllRecude()` function, which calls the backward propagation simultaneously. By doing this, we don't get the delay of all-reduce operation. This example code uses Horovod to train multiple GPUs. If you want to learn more about this, visit Horovod's GitHub page: `https://github.com/horovod/horovod`. You can get the document and example code from here.

Summary

In this chapter, we have learned how to use CUDA libraries for deep learning and performance benefits. While we reviewed their uses, we matched them with the deep learning mechanisms for each step. Thanks to the deep learning libraries that are available to us, we can implement a simple CNN without implementing the algorithms too. Then, we profiled the ResNet-50 model in PyTorch and TensorFlow using NVTX annotations.

Implementing the base algorithms may be impractical for some deep learning engineers and researchers. However, understanding the performance factors and the base operations can help you build efficient and effective deep learning-based products. Nowadays, we see many productized deep learning-based services. Engineers spend a lot of resources productizing their trained model, as well as training their model so that they get the lowest error rate possible. Hopefully, you managed to gain some insight into how you can use NVTX profiling on your deep learning applications. Using this knowledge, you can get more from your GPUs. Good luck!

Appendix

CUDA is a parallel programming platform. Learning CUDA means not only learning the language, but also having some engineering prowess with the GPU. That engineering area can be monitoring, environment settings, performance understanding, containerization, and so on. This chapter provides some tips to help engineers use GPUs. We could cover even more topics, but the following topics will be helpful for those of you who want to learn about CUDA and its GPU operations.

In this chapter, we will cover the following topics:

- Useful `nvidia-smi` commands
- WDDM/TCC mode in Windows
- Performance modeling
- Exploring container-based development

Useful nvidia-smi commands

In this section, we will cover the monitoring features and management operations of `nvidia-smi`. `nvidia-smi` is the **command-line interface (CLI)** of the **NVIDIA Management Library** (**NVML**). This library enables the management and monitoring of NVIDIA devices. `nvidia-smi` also provides direct queries and commands to the device through the library. The data is presented in either plain text or XML format via `stdout` or a file. It provides several management tools for changing device statistics.

`nvidia-smi` is a CLI application that wraps NVML C/C++ APIs. It obtains requested information from the `NVIDIA` driver via NVML. NVML also provides APIs to work with other languages, such as Python and Perl.

Basically, `nvidia-smi` reports the following installed GPU stats for the user:

- The first row reports the driver version, and the CUDA version supported
- The second row shows the GPU stats format
- Each consecutive row contains each GPU's stats, including the following:
  - GPU ID
  - Operation mode:
    - Persistence mode (ON/OFF)
    - **Tesla Compute Cluster (TCC)/Windows Display Driver Model (WDDM)** mode
  - Fan speed
  - GPU temperature
  - Performance mode
  - Power usage and capacity
  - Bus-ID
  - Memory usage and installed memory
  - Counted **error-correcting code (ECC)**
  - GPU utilization
  - Compute mode

Basically, `nvidia-smi` can handle all NVIDIA GPU cards, including Tesla, Quadro, and GeForce. Enabled features can vary in terms of the model and type. For example, the ECC error count is available in Tesla and Quadro cards, while it isn't in GeForce because it doesn't provide the ECC feature in its device memory.

The format of `nvidia-smi` reports is the same across operating systems. The following screenshot shows the output of Windows:

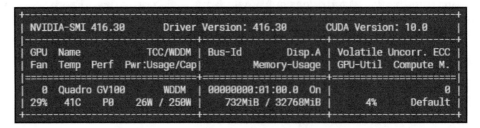

The following screenshot shows the output of Linux:

```
Mon Feb   4 11:14:15 2019
+-----------------------------------------------------------------------------+
| NVIDIA-SMI 410.57                 Driver Version: 410.57                    |
|-------------------------------+----------------------+----------------------+
| GPU  Name        Persistence-M| Bus-Id        Disp.A | Volatile Uncorr. ECC |
| Fan  Temp  Perf  Pwr:Usage/Cap|         Memory-Usage | GPU-Util  Compute M. |
|===============================+======================+======================|
|   0  Tesla V100-DGXS...  Off  | 00000000:07:00.0 Off |                    0 |
| N/A   38C    P0    38W / 300W |     12MiB / 16128MiB |      0%      Default |
+-------------------------------+----------------------+----------------------+
|   1  Tesla V100-DGXS...  Off  | 00000000:08:00.0 Off |                    0 |
| N/A   38C    P0    39W / 300W |     12MiB / 16128MiB |      0%      Default |
+-------------------------------+----------------------+----------------------+
|   2  Tesla V100-DGXS...  Off  | 00000000:0E:00.0 Off |                    0 |
| N/A   39C    P0    38W / 300W |     12MiB / 16128MiB |      0%      Default |
+-------------------------------+----------------------+----------------------+
|   3  Tesla V100-DGXS...  Off  | 00000000:0F:00.0 Off |                    0 |
| N/A   38C    P0    38W / 300W |     45MiB / 16128MiB |      0%      Default |
+-------------------------------+----------------------+----------------------+

+-----------------------------------------------------------------------------+
| Processes:                                                       GPU Memory |
|  GPU       PID   Type   Process name                             Usage      |
|=============================================================================|
|    3      6765      G   /usr/lib/xorg/Xorg                            16MiB |
|    3      6834      G   /usr/bin/gnome-shell                          15MiB |
+-----------------------------------------------------------------------------+
```

Therefore, we can read the reports and set GPU operations in the same format. Now, let's move on and look at the commands that are frequently used. The default `nvidia-smi` CLI's usage is as follows:

```
$ nvidia-smi [option1 [arg]] [option2 [arg]] ...
```

To begin with, the following options are frequently used depending on the monitoring purpose:

- `-i`, `--id=`: For selecting the targeting GPU
- `-l`, `--loop=`: Reports the GPU's status at a specified second interval
- `-f`, `--filename=`: For logging in to a specified file

This list covers `nvidia-smi` options that can help us to obtain detailed information from the GPUs.

Getting the GPU's information

`nvidia-smi` reports structured output when we use the `--query` (`-q`) option. Therefore, we can learn about which information is collected. We can obtain GPU information such as utilization, power, memory, and clock speed stats. On the other hand, this format is not helpful if we wish to monitor the GPU's status continuously.

Getting formatted information

The basic GPU stats that we need to monitor are power, temperature, core utilization, and memory usage. This can easily be done with the `--query-gpu` command:

```
$ nvidia-smi --query-
gpu=timestamp,name,pci.bus_id,driver_version,pstate,pcie.link.gen.max,pcie.
link.gen.current,temperature.gpu,utilization.gpu,utilization.memory,memory.
used,memory.free,memory.used --format=csv -l 1
```

The following command shows some options that we can use to detect performance draw reasons for clock throttling:

```
$ nvidia-smi --query-
gpu=index,clocks_throttle_reasons.active,clocks_throttle_reasons.gpu_idle,c
locks_throttle_reasons.applications_clocks_setting,clocks_throttle_reasons.
sw_power_cap,clocks_throttle_reasons.hw_slowdown,clocks_throttle_reasons.hw
_thermal_slowdown,clocks_throttle_reasons.hw_power_brake_slowdown,clocks_th
rottle_reasons.sync_boost --format=csv
```

The reasons for GPU clock throttling can be power brake, overheating, and sync boost. Power brake means that the GPU's power consumption is limited by the user's setting or the power supplier's performance in the system. Overheating is also a frequent throttling reason due to a poor cooling environment.

Power management mode settings

You can find out the maximum power consumption per GPU using the following command:

```
$ nvidia-smi -i <device id> -pl N
```

Setting the GPU's clock speed

By default, the GPU's clock speed changes based on demand and saves power consumption to maximize power efficiency. To maximize your GPU's performance and reduce latency, especially in a benchmark situation, we can ensure that the GPU has a maximum clock speed and disable the GPU driver.

First, we need to set the GPU in persistence mode. Doing this means that the GPU driver module is always loaded to the kernel and reduces the initial response time. This option is only available on Linux since Windows does not unload the GPU driver. The persistent mode setting command is as follows:

```
$ sudo nvidia-persistenced
```

Then, we can set the maximum supported clocks. This value will vary based on the GPU you are using:

```
$ nvidia-smi -q -d SUPPORTED_CLOCKS
$ sudo nvidia-smi -ac <Mem clock, Graphics clock>
```

For example, the Tesla V100 card can be set with the following commands:

```
$ sudo nvidia-smi -ac 877,1380 # V100 PCIe
$ sudo nvidia-smi -ac 877,1530  # V100 SMX
```

GPU device monitoring

This command probes the selected GPU's device status every second:

```
$ nvidia-smi dmon -s pucvmet -i -0
```

The following screenshot shows the result of the previous command. The device we are monitoring states that it has a GPU device status of 0:

```
$ nvidia-smi dmon -s pucvmet -i 0
# gpu   pwr gtemp mtemp   sm  mem  enc  dec mclk pclk pviol tviol   fb  bar1 sbecc dbecc   pci rxpci txpci
# Idx     W    C     C    %    %    %    %  MHz  MHz    %  bool   MB    MB  errs  errs  errs  MB/s  MB/s
    0    38   39    36    0    0    0    0  877  135    0    0   12     4    0     0     0     0     0
    0    38   39    36    0    0    0    0  877  135    0    0   12     4    0     0     0     0     0
    0    38   39    36    0    0    0    0  877  135    0    0   12     4    0     0     0     0     0
    0    38   39    36    0    0    0    0  877  135    0    0   12     4    0     0     0     0     0
    0    38   39    36    0    0    0    0  877  135    0    0   12     4    0     0     0     0     0
```

The collected information can be specified with the -s option, as follows:

- p: Power usage and temperature
- u: Utilization
- c: Proc and mem clocks
- v: Power and thermal violations
- m: FB and Bar1 memory
- e: ECC errors and PCIe replay errors
- t: PCIe Rx and Tx throughput

Monitoring GPU utilization along with multiple processes

If you're using multiple process operations on a single GPU, you may consider using this command. This command collects GPU stats, along with the process they are being used on. This means you can determine which process has been throttled by GPU sharing, the room for memory timings, and so on:

```
$ nvidia-smi pmon -i 0 -s u -o T
```

The following screenshot shows the output of nvidia-smi with **Process ID (PID)**, which helps in determining which process is using what GPU resources:

```
#Time       gpu    pid   type   sm   mem   enc   dec    fb   command
#HH:MM:SS   Idx      #   C/G    %     %     %     %     MB   name
 17:24:58     0   29919    C    19    13     0     0   2707   python
 17:24:58     0   30024    C    30    24     0     0   4081   python
 17:24:59     0   29919    C    18    12     0     0   2707   python
 17:24:59     0   30024    C    28    24     0     0   4081   python
 17:25:00     0   29919    C    19    13     0     0   2707   python
 17:25:00     0   30024    C    29    24     0     0   4081   python
```

Each column in the preceding screenshot shows each GPU's computing unit utilization or memory usage:

- sm%: CUDA core utilization
- mem%: Sampled time ratio for memory operations
- enc%/dec%: HW encoder's utilization
- fb: FB memory usage

Getting GPU topology information

In a multi-GPU system, it is useful to use `nvidia-smi` to obtain GPU topology information. The following command is an `nvidia-smi` command that shows the GPU topology of a multi-GPU system:

```
nvidia-smi topo -m
```

The following screenshot shows the output of `nvidia-smi` showing the system's topology. The result of DGX Station is that we have four NVLink-enabled V100 GPUs:

```
        GPU0    GPU1    GPU2    GPU3    CPU Affinity
GPU0    X       NV1     NV1     NV2     0-39
GPU1    NV1     X       NV2     NV1     0-39
GPU2    NV1     NV2     X       NV1     0-39
GPU3    NV2     NV1     NV1     X       0-39

Legend:

  X    = Self
  SYS  = Connection traversing PCIe as well as the SMP interconnect between NUMA nodes (e.g., QPI/UPI)
  NODE = Connection traversing PCIe as well as the interconnect between PCIe Host Bridges within a NUMA node
  PHB  = Connection traversing PCIe as well as a PCIe Host Bridge (typically the CPU)
  PXB  = Connection traversing multiple PCIe switches (without traversing the PCIe Host Bridge)
  PIX  = Connection traversing a single PCIe switch
  NV#  = Connection traversing a bonded set of # NVLinks
```

Following this result, we can confirm that the system's GPU topology is as follows:

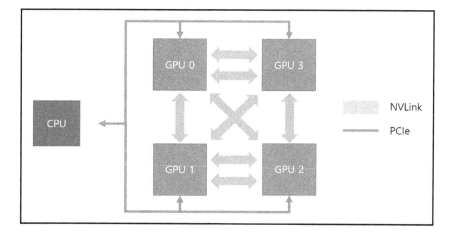

The following command identifies the peer-to-peer accessibility between GPUs. We used this command in `Chapter 6`, *Scalable Multi-GPU Programming*:

```
$ nvidia-smi topo -p2p rwnap
```

The following is the output of the `nvidia-smi` topology, which has four GPUs in a system:

```
        GPU0    GPU1    GPU2    GPU3
GPU0    X       OK      OK      OK
GPU1    OK      X       OK      OK
GPU2    OK      OK      X       OK
GPU3    OK      OK      OK      X

Legend:

  X     = Self
  OK    = Status Ok
  CNS   = Chipset not supported
  GNS   = GPU not supported
  TNS   = Topology not supported
  NS    = Not supported
  U     = Unknown
```

Peer-to-peer access is an important factor for scalability or operations. This command helps you confirm that the GPUs and your system can support peer-to-peer access between GPUs.

WDDM/TCC mode in Windows

On the Windows platform, the NVIDIA GPU has two modes: WDDM and TCC. WDDM is the graphics driver for video cards so that it can render desktops and applications. If the installed GPU is only used for computing, display rendering is useless overhead. In this situation, the NVIDIA GPU can switch to a mode that only focuses on computing. This mode is known as TCC mode.

WDDM allows the NVIDIA GPU to cooperate with Windows' WDDM driver, which serves displays. Supporting WDDM mode is a requirement for Windows graphics. On the other hand, TCC mode only works toward computing. Depending on your GPU products and configuration, the GPU's mode can be changed.

Operation mode follows four NVIDIA product classes, and its default mode can vary, as follows:

- **GeForce**: WDDM mode only.
- **Quadro/Titan**: WDDM mode by default, but can be used in TCC mode too.
- **Tesla**: Typically defaults to TCC mode.
- **Tegra**: Supports Linux only. No WDDM/TCC issues.

WDDM mode supports CUDA operations and debugging CUDA applications with Nsight, while also supporting the display. As a single host machine, you can do everything that the GPU can. However, TCC mode disables graphics on the graphics driver and enables GPU as a computing accelerator. In other words, this should be used when the graphics card does not have to serve displays.

TCC mode has some benefits over WDDM mode in CUDA processing, as follows:

- Serves large-scale computing
- Ignores Windows' display timeout interval (typically two seconds) to enable kernel operations that are longer than two seconds
- Reduces CUDA's kernel launch overhead on Windows
- Supports CUDA processing with Windows remote desktop service
- Enables the use of NVIDIA GPUs with non-NVIDIA integrated graphics so that you can save global memory

Therefore, TCC mode brings optimal configuration for GPUs as accelerators if they do not serve displays.

Setting TCC/WDDM mode

To change TCC or WDDM mode, use the `nvidia-smi` utility, as follows:

```
$ sudo nvidia-smi -dm {0|1}
```

0 means WDDM mode, and 1 means TCC mode.

If you want to set TCC mode for the selected GPUs, use the -g option to specify target GPUs:

```
$ nvidia-smi -g {GPU_ID} -dm {0|1}
```

This option is useful when you want to separate the purpose of GPU use for display and compute. After you've applied these settings, you may want to *reboot* your machine to apply these changes.

We can identify that TCC mode is enabled by using `nvidia-smi`. The following screenshot shows GPU operation mode in TCC:

By looking at the right-hand side of the GPU name in the first column, we can confirm that TCC mode is enabled.

Performance modeling

It is important to understand the characteristics of the application/algorithm and the GPU hardware to set realistic speedup targets. This can be achieved by adding parallelism. We also need to determine whether there's room to optimize the GPU when we optimize an application.

One simple approach is to apply Amdahl's law. We can predict that achievable performance gain in an application is limited by the sequential portion of the code. For example, only 50% of the code can be made parallel, while the rest is sequential in nature (such as reading from a file). If this is the case, the maximum speedup that can be achieved is 2x; that is, the program can only run twice as fast. However, this performance modeling only shows the maximum speedup. We can't help but assume that we can completely parallelize and eliminate the execution time in the parallel portion of the code.

Another performance modeling practice is to perform analysis based on the target architecture's performance bounding factors. In practice, we have hardware specifications, and its operations introduce inevitable performance limitations. By analyzing these limitations, we can establish whether there is room to perform optimization and look at the next set of optimization strategies.

The Roofline model

Every kernel function can be classified into one of the following categories:

- **Compute bound**: The kernel function does more arithmetic operations for every byte of data that is read or written. These applications demand more compute FLOPS from the hardware.
- **Memory bound**: The application spends most of its time reading and writing from memory and less computation. The application gets affected most by the memory bandwidth of the system rather than the FLOP rating of the hardware.
- **Latency bound**: The kernel function's CUDA threads spend most of their time in waiting rather than executing. There are many reasons for this scenario to occur. The primary reason is the sub-optimal level of parallelism or non-optimal usage of memory and computes resources.

Since all of these bindings are introduced by the hardware, we can graph the target hardware's peak performance and memory bandwidth along with their arithmetic intensity. The performance curve is bounded by the hardware's peak performance. We briefly touched on this in Chapter 3, *CUDA Thread Programming*, to determine the next optimization strategy. The following illustration was used in Chapter 3, *CUDA Thread Programming*, and shows an example of the Roofline model:

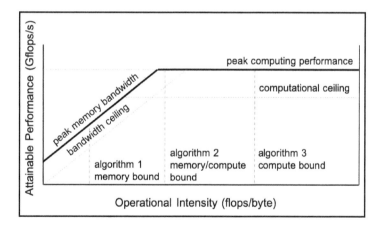

For any computation to happen, the data needs to be transported from memory to the arithmetic units. It traverses a different level of the memory hierarchy, and the peak memory bandwidth varies depending on the memory type. The algorithm's peak performance can be categorized following its arithmetic intensity. This intensity is determined by the amount of computing data versus loaded data. Also, there is a computational ceiling introduced by these latency-bound factors. By measuring the performance and analysis against the hardware specification, we can confirm that the target algorithm achieved peak performance or was bound by memory or latency. In either case, we can determine the next step. In `Chapter 3`, *CUDA Thread Programming*, we explored this in depth. In this section, we will focus on the Roofline model by looking at an example and seeing how useful it is.

The Roofline model takes into consideration the operational intensity of the application. In simple terms, this means that operations are done per byte from the main memory (DRAM). While there are more complicated models that also consider the cache to processor transfers, the Roofline model focuses more on the data transfer from DRAM to cache and, hence, focuses on the DRAM bandwidth that's needed by the CUDA kernel on a particular GPU architecture.

The Roofline model states the following:

> *"Attainable performance (GFLOP/s) = min (Peak Floating-Point Performance, Peak Memory Bandwidth * Operational Intensity)"*

Analyzing the Jacobi method

Let's try to understand this formula and get the Roofline model for the V100 GPU card. The V100 GPU has the following specifications:

- 80 SMs, each with 32 FP64 cores
- 900 GB/s aggregate bandwidth
- L2 cache: 6 MB
- L1 Cache: 10 MB
- Register: 62 KB/SM

Let's try to analyze a simple Jacobi method:

```
for (int iy = 1; iy < NoRows; iy++)
{
    for ( int ix = 1; ix < NoCols; ix++)
    {
        Anew[ix][iy] = rhs[iy*nx+ix]
```

```
              - 0.25f*(Aref[ix-1][iy] + Aref[ix+1][iy]
              + Aref[ix][iy-1] + Aref[ix][iy+1]);
       }
   }
```

Let's analyze the data transfer for the preceding code:

- Memory load of the vector (`Anew`, `rhs`, `Aref`): $I_{Load} = NoRow * NoCol * 3 * 8\ Bytes$ *(double precision)*
- Store for the vector (`Anew`): $I_{store} = NoRow * NoCol * 8\ Bytes$
- Floating-point operations: $I_{FP} = NoRow * NoCol * 6\ FLOP$

The following graph shows the Roofline analysis of the Tesla V100 card and the Jacobi method's arithmetic intensity:

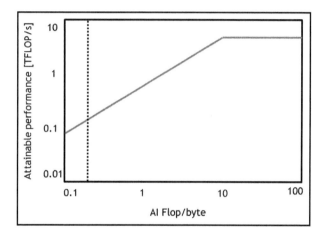

The arithmetic intensity of Jacobi on the V100 will be $I_{FP}/(I_{Load}+I_{Strore}) = 0.18\ FLOP/byte$.

The Roofline model clearly shows that the algorithm is memory bound and that the maximum attainable performance is 0.18 FLOP/byte only, and so will not be able to reach the peak FLOP rating of the V100, which is 7.8 TFLOPS. However, we can also predict the attainable performance after optimization by reusing the fetched data.

The Roofline model helps in defining the upper-performance limit for algorithms based on their hardware characteristics.

Jacobi method

This is an iterative algorithm for finding solutions for a system of linear equations. Its basic operations and GPU optimization are explained at `https://www.olcf.ornl.gov/wp-content/uploads/2016/01/Introduction-to-Accelerated-Computing-with-OpenACC-Jeff-Larkin.pdf`.

Exploring container-based development

One of the key challenges that developers and IT administrators who are maintaining the cluster face is the complexity of the software stack. Each and every application/framework has many dependencies. More complexity gets added when these dependencies are of different versions. For example, in DL, Caffe has different requirements of versions of cuDNN and Python than TensorFlow. In a particular organization/institute, there are many users, and each and every user may use different versions of the same framework. Installing all the right dependencies and setting up the right environment results in the loss of productivity. More time is spent on installation rather than doing the work. Another challenge that's faced is that it is almost impossible to reproduce the result/performance numbers by different individuals, even though they might run on the same system, due to dependency mismatch. For example, the GROMACS Molecular Dynamics framework has many settings, such as compile with multithreading or **Message Passing Interface** (**MPI**) support, the version on MPI, and the MPI type. Another challenge, especially in AI, is that every software framework that you can possibly think of is moving very fast, and new patches are added frequently.

Containers provide a solution to these problems. The key advantages of using containers are as follows:

- **Isolation**: Containers provide isolation of the environment for applications
- **Run anywhere**: Containers provide an easy way to share and test applications in different environments
- **Lightweight**: Containers are lightweight compared to using virtual machine-based solutions and provide almost negligible latency and overhead

Two of the most famous container environments are Docker and Singularity. Both have their advantages and disadvantages. Note, however, that this section is not an extensive guide to Docker or Singularity.

Developers usually create containers and publish them online for others to use. We will be explaining one such repository that's maintained by NVIDIA called **Nvidia GPU Cloud** (**NGC**) in detail. NGC is like a repository that hosts containers for popular **Deep Learning** (**DL**), **High-Performance Computing** (**HPC**), and **Virtual Reality** (**VR**) frameworks. NVIDIA tests these applications for different environments of GPU and goes through an extensive QA process before being made available to the public. This means that performance is guaranteed.

An analogy of NGC is the Android App Store, which provides a repository for different applications that can run on different mobiles running the Android OS. These applications get verified and go through a QA process. The NGC name sometimes confuses people and developers think that it is a cloud. It should be made clear that it is a repository of containers that can be pulled into a system with a GPU and run locally. The container can run on different systems with GPUs, just like it can run on the desktop with NVIDIA Titan cards, servers with Tesla V100 cards, or the NVIDIA AI supercomputer DGX. NGC containers can also be run on cloud platforms such as AWS and Azure.

NGC configuration for a host machine

The following steps cover how to configure an NGC working environment and find available images in NGC:

1. **Basic installation**: To make use of containers on a GPU system, you need to have installed the following:

   - Nvidia drivers
   - Docker
   - `nvidia-docker`

   `nvidia-docker` is an open source project that loads the NVIDIA components and modules into a container. It is basically a wrapper around Docker. You can download and see the installation instructions at `https://github.com/nvidia/nvidia-docker/wiki/Installation-(version-2.0)`.

2. **Visit the NGC website**: Now, you can go to the NGC website to choose a container (`nvidia.com/ngc`), as shown in the following screenshot:

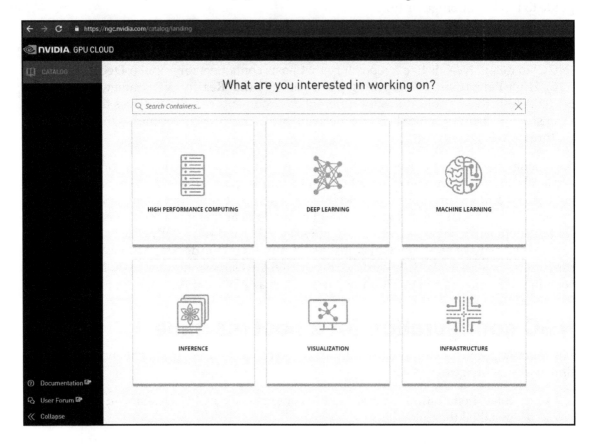

As you can see, there are six categories for containers. Choose the one that's relevant to you. The earlier version of NGC required users to register, but this requirement was removed recently.

Basic usage of the NGC container

In this section, we will cover how to pull containers from the NGC registry and how to customize our own. It's no different from using Docker, except we can access the NGC registry, nvcr.io. If you are already familiar with Docker commands, you can skip this section.

The following steps explain how to obtain and launch an NGC container on your local Linux machine in a Terminal session:

1. Find the software you want to use and copy the command from the NGC site.
2. Then, pull the container image by pasting the command into the Terminal. The following screenshot shows the pull commands and their Docker operation:

```
[bharatk@dgx07 ~]$ docker pull nvcr.io/nvidia/cuda:9.0-devel-ubuntu16.04
9.0-devel-ubuntu16.04: Pulling from nvidia/cuda
18d680d61657: Pull complete
0addb6fece63: Pull complete
78e58219b215: Pull complete
eb6959a66df2: Pull complete
6ef1ff668c93: Pull complete
f5f8f0544aa2: Pull complete
3d28d96eb352: Pull complete
1b48d63763c4: Pull complete
70fb71aabe87: Pull complete
Digest: sha256:7d95426c00962ef3352151ccf425eb0a446108589585995c2277e2201390918c
Status: Downloaded newer image for nvcr.io/nvidia/cuda:9.0-devel-ubuntu16.04
[bharatk@dgx07 ~]$ docker images
REPOSITORY            TAG                    IMAGE ID        CREATED        SIZE
nvcr.io/nvidia/cuda   9.0-devel-ubuntu16.04  07f3fc56927f    3 months ago   1.97GB
[bharatk@dgx07 ~]$ 
```

As you can see, Docker uses a layer-based approach. The CUDA container is built over the basic layer of Ubuntu. Also, the Docker images command showed us the locally pulled container on our machine.

3. Use the following command to launch the pulled container:

```
docker run --rm -it --runtime=nvidia nvcr.io/nvidia/cuda:9.0-devel-
ubuntu16.04
```

The GPUs are shown in the following screenshot:

```
[bharatk@dgx07 ~]$ docker run --rm -it 07f3fc56927f
root@a6997ed4faef:/# nvidia-smi
Thu Mar  7 15:34:23 2019
+-----------------------------------------------------------------------------+
| NVIDIA-SMI 418.25       Driver Version: 418.25       CUDA Version: 10.1      |
|-------------------------------+----------------------+----------------------+
| GPU  Name        Persistence-M| Bus-Id        Disp.A | Volatile Uncorr. ECC |
| Fan  Temp  Perf  Pwr:Usage/Cap|         Memory-Usage | GPU-Util  Compute M. |
|===============================+======================+======================|
|   0  Tesla V100-SXM2...  On   | 00000000:06:00.0 Off |                    0 |
| N/A   39C    P0    45W / 300W |      0MiB / 16130MiB |      0%      Default |
+-------------------------------+----------------------+----------------------+
|   1  Tesla V100-SXM2...  On   | 00000000:07:00.0 Off |                    0 |
| N/A   42C    P0    45W / 300W |      0MiB / 16130MiB |      0%      Default |
+-------------------------------+----------------------+----------------------+
|   2  Tesla V100-SXM2...  On   | 00000000:0A:00.0 Off |                    0 |
| N/A   43C    P0    43W / 300W |      0MiB / 16130MiB |      0%      Default |
+-------------------------------+----------------------+----------------------+
|   3  Tesla V100-SXM2...  On   | 00000000:0B:00.0 Off |                    0 |
| N/A   40C    P0    42W / 300W |      0MiB / 16130MiB |      0%      Default |
+-------------------------------+----------------------+----------------------+
|   4  Tesla V100-SXM2...  On   | 00000000:85:00.0 Off |                    0 |
| N/A   42C    P0    44W / 300W |      0MiB / 16130MiB |      0%      Default |
+-------------------------------+----------------------+----------------------+
|   5  Tesla V100-SXM2...  On   | 00000000:86:00.0 Off |                    0 |
| N/A   43C    P0    46W / 300W |      0MiB / 16130MiB |      0%      Default |
+-------------------------------+----------------------+----------------------+
|   6  Tesla V100-SXM2...  On   | 00000000:89:00.0 Off |                    0 |
| N/A   43C    P0    45W / 300W |      0MiB / 16130MiB |      0%      Default |
+-------------------------------+----------------------+----------------------+
|   7  Tesla V100-SXM2...  On   | 00000000:8A:00.0 Off |                    0 |
| N/A   39C    P0    44W / 300W |      0MiB / 16130MiB |      0%      Default |
+-------------------------------+----------------------+----------------------+

+-----------------------------------------------------------------------------+
| Processes:                                                       GPU Memory |
|  GPU       PID   Type   Process name                             Usage      |
|=============================================================================|
|  No running processes found                                                 |
+-----------------------------------------------------------------------------+
root@a6997ed4faef:/#
```

As soon as we run Docker, the shell login changes and we are logged into the container that's running as root. Due to this, we were able to run the `nvidia-smi` command inside the container.

4. We can also use the container to access the host resources by using its additional options. The most frequently used options are as follows:

- `-v`: For mounting the volume
- `-p`: For port forwarding
- `-u`: For user forwarding

The basic usage of `nvidia-docker` is similar to normal Docker usage, except we can use the GPUs. This means you can also get the added benefits of Docker.

Creating and saving a new container from the NGC container

You can also add layers to the existing container and save them for future use. Let's learn how to do this:

1. Create a `Dockerfile` and create some layers over the base image. For example, we can update APEX (`https://github.com/nvidia/apex`) in the NGC PyTorch container so that we can use its latest version:

```
FROM nvcr.io/nvidia/pytorch:19.03-py3
RUN git clone https://github.com/NVIDIA/apex /opt/apex && \
    cd /opt/apex && \
    pip install -v --no-cache-dir --global-option="--cpp_ext" --
global-option="--cuda_ext" .
```

   You can add your desired Ubuntu packages or Python package installation code to that file too.

2. Then, we can build a customized container with the `docker build` command. The following command shows the basic format of the Docker image `build` command:

```
docker build -t <image-name>:<tag> .
```

   This command will find the `Dockerfile` we created and launch each command line by line. Each line of the `Dockerfile` will create a Docker layer, so it is recommended to write a `RUN` command to cover a single objective.

3. Now, you need to back up your Docker images into your private registry or create a file. After you've finalized the container, you may want to propagate or reuse the container in other systems. In that case, you can push the Docker image into your registry. For instance, Docker provides a free registry if you have an account on `DockerHub`. You can push your container into the registry with the following command:

```
docker push <DockerHub-ID>/<image-name>:<tag>
```

   You can also create backup files and copy them over your local filesystem. The following command shows you how to create a container backup with compression:

```
docker save <image-name>:<tag> | gzip > container.tgz
```

Then, you can load that image using the following command:

```
gunzip -c container.tgz | docker load
```

You can create a local backup image without compression, but the output file is too large to deliver to the other systems in general.

In this section, we have covered some basic operations of Docker. However, Docker provides other plentiful functions and benefits too. Although Linux is only available for the use of CUDA in the Docker container, Docker will save you time when it comes to building the working environment and help you focus on your code development.

Setting the default runtime as NVIDIA Docker

With some modifications to the `nvidia-docker` configuration, we can launch GPU containers without notifying the GPU about this use. Because we can set the GPU runtime option to `nvidia-docker`, we can adopt Docker's runtime design. To do that, you need to insert `default-runtime": "nvidia",` as an option into `/etc/docker/daemon.json`. Then, the `daemon.json` file can be configured as follows if there is no other Docker configuration:

```
{
    "default-runtime": "nvidia",
    "runtimes": {
        "nvidia": {
            "path": "nvidia-container-runtime",
            "runtimeArgs": []
        }
    }
}
```

After doing this, reboot the system or restart the Docker daemon with the following command:

```
sudo systemctl restart docker
```

Now, we can enjoy GPU containers without the GPU command option in Docker commands.

An introduction to `nvidia-docker` is provided in the NVIDIA development blog, which can be found at `https://devblogs.nvidia.com/gpu-containers-runtime`. Here, you will learn not only about its configuration, but also how to integrate it with Docker compose or **Linux Containers** (**LXC**). It even allows GPU containers to work with Kubernetes via its GPU device plugin.

Another Book You May Enjoy

If you enjoyed this book, you may be interested in these other books by Packt:

Hands-On GPU-Accelerated Computer Vision with OpenCV and CUDA
Bhaumik Vaidya

ISBN: 978-1-78934-829-3

- Understand how to access GPU device properties and capabilities from CUDA programs
- Learn how to accelerate searching and sorting algorithms
- Detect shapes such as lines and circles in images
- Explore object tracking and detection with algorithms
- Process videos using different video analysis techniques in Jetson TX1
- Access GPU device properties from the PyCUDA program
- Understand how kernel execution works

Leave a review - let other readers know what you think

Please share your thoughts on this book with others by leaving a review on the site that you bought it from. If you purchased the book from Amazon, please leave us an honest review on this book's Amazon page. This is vital so that other potential readers can see and use your unbiased opinion to make purchasing decisions, we can understand what our customers think about our products, and our authors can see your feedback on the title that they have worked with Packt to create. It will only take a few minutes of your time, but is valuable to other potential customers, our authors, and Packt. Thank you!

Index

CPSIA information can be obtained
at www.ICGtesting.com
Printed in the USA
FSHW010648040920
73535FS

9 781788 996242